The book, *Critical Children's Rights Studies: A Research Companion*, thoughtfully brings together contemporary debates on critical approaches to children's rights, with the goal of deconstructing dominant discourses and offering alternative rights narratives. Whilst questioning binary approaches and discussing scholars' own positionality around the UN Convention on the Rights of the Child, this timely volume highlights the need to combine the theoretical focus of Critical Children's Rights Studies with substantial, practical contributions to children's lives.

Dr Patricio Cuevas-Parra, *University of Edinburgh, UK*

Critical Children's Rights Studies: A Research Companion is an essential work that challenges dominant discourses while advancing innovative paradigms. By bringing together leading scholars, it deepens our understanding of children's rights through critical, interdisciplinary perspectives. Indispensable for scholars and practitioners alike, this volume reshapes the field with rigour and insight.

Professor Shazly Savahl, *University of the Western Cape, University of Cape Town, South Africa, and Utrecht University, the Netherlands*

Critical Children's Rights Studies: A Research Companion rows through rivers less navigated to chart new waters in children's rights. A series of critical thinking seminars set the authors on their journey to uncover streams of research that flow towards a critical assessment of children. A must-read for those who take children's rights seriously.

Professor Ann Skelton, *Professor of Law, Leiden University, the Netherlands, and Chairperson, UN Committee on the Rights of the Child*

The contributors to the *Critical Children's Rights Studies: A Research Companion* engage in profound debates about the complexities of children's rights challenging dominant discourses as well as offering alternative paths to children's rights; the book is an outstanding contribution to current debates and to the emerging field of Critical Children's Rights Studies.

Professor Spyros Spyrou, *Professor in Sociocultural Anthropology, European University Cyprus*

Critical Children's Rights Studies: A Research Companion tackles global challenges facing children, offering profound insights into rights, power, and agency. This groundbreaking multidisciplinary volume reimagines debates on children's rights through diverse perspectives and methods, inspiring transformative thinking and action to advance their well-being in today's complex world.

Dr Jana Tabak, *Assistant Professor, State University of Rio de Janeiro (UERJ), Brazil*

Critical Children's Rights Studies

The field of children's rights studies is well established and largely dominated by a top-down approach that considers these rights as objective standards requiring implementation in practice or policy. This book argues for a critical perspective which views the area as contested terrain with conflicting normative foundations and traditions. The collection brings together established and rising scholars whose work has been central to not only challenging mainstream children's rights discourses but also provides alternative pathways to conceptualizing children's rights. It moves beyond critiques of these dominant discourses and sets out the emerging paradigm of Critical Children's Rights Studies drawing on contexts in both the Global North and Global South. It proposes new pathways and subjects these to scrutiny, illuminating the importance of contextual situatedness and acknowledging the need to consider researchers' own positionality when outlining their stance on children's rights.

Containing both empirical and theoretical scholarship, the book will be an essential resource for students, academics, researchers and policy-makers working in the multidisciplinary areas of childhood studies, children's rights studies and international human rights.

Valeria Llobet holds a PhD in social psychology from the University of Buenos Aires (Argentina). She is Professor in the School of Humanities, Universidad de San Martín (Argentina) and a researcher at CONICET (National Council of Research). Her work focuses on children's rights, gender and class inequalities.

Didier Reynaert is Lecturer in Social Work and Senior Researcher at the EQUALITY//ResearchCollective of HOGENT University of Applied Sciences and Arts, School of Social Welfare (Belgium). His expertise lies in the field of social work theory, social justice and human rights and Critical Children's Rights Studies.

Afua Twum-Danso Imoh is Associate Professor in Global Childhoods and Welfare at the University of Bristol (UK). Her work explores the intersections between children's rights and cultural norms in Ghana. She is an editor for the Palgrave Macmillan Study of Childhood and Youth Series and serves on the editorial boards of several journals.

Wouter Vandenhole is Full Professor of Human Rights and Children's Rights and directs the Law and Development Research Group of the University of Antwerp's (Belgium) law faculty. His research interests include children's rights, economic, social and cultural rights, the relationship between human rights law and sustainable development, and thicker human rights accountability.

Critical Children's Rights Studies

A Research Companion

Edited by
Valeria Llobet, Didier Reynaert, Afua Twum-Danso Imoh and Wouter Vandenhole

Routledge
Taylor & Francis Group
LONDON AND NEW YORK

First published 2025
by Routledge
4 Park Square, Milton Park, Abingdon, Oxon OX14 4RN

and by Routledge
605 Third Avenue, New York, NY 10158

Routledge is an imprint of the Taylor & Francis Group, an informa business

British Library Cataloguing-in-Publication Data
A catalogue record for this book is available from the British Library

ISBN: 978-1-032-82761-2 (hbk)
ISBN: 978-1-032-83623-2 (pbk)
ISBN: 978-1-003-51028-4 (ebk)

DOI: 10.4324/9781003510284

Typeset in Galliard
by Apex CoVantage, LLC

Contents

Contributors

Tatek Abebe is Professor of Childhood Studies at the Norwegian University of Science and Technology. His longitudinal ethnographic research in Ethiopia examines how young people are affected by, and shape, the sociocultural and political-economic environments they inhabit. He is a co-editor of *Childhood: A Journal of Global Child Research.*

Sarada Balagopalan is Associate Professor of Childhood Studies at Rutgers University-Camden (USA). Her research utilizes a postcolonial framework to engage marginal children's experiences with compulsory schooling, labour, gendered school spaces, children's rights discourses and pedagogies of 'citizenship'. She recently co-edited the *Bloomsbury Handbook of Theories in Childhood Studies* (2024).

Daniella Bendo is Associate Professor at King's University College at Western in the Department of Childhood and Youth Studies (London, Ontario, Canada). Her research focuses on children's rights, child and youth advocacy, participation, youth justice, community engagement, and child-centred research methodologies.

Nico Brando is Co-Director of the European Children's Rights Unit, and a Derby Fellow at the School of Law and Social Justice, University of Liverpool (UK). He does research in political and moral philosophy, working particularly on theories of justice, children's rights, vulnerability, and the capabilities approach.

Erica Burman is Professor of Education at the University of Manchester (UK) and Associate Fellow of the British Psychological Society. She is author of numerous books. Her research has focused on critical developmental and educational psychology, feminist and postcolonial theory, childhood studies, and critical mental health practice (particularly around gender and cultural issues).

Luan Carpes Barros Cassal is Honorary Research Fellow in Education at the University of Manchester (UK). In his PhD research, he used Child as method to analyze discourses and ideas of childhood in legal gender recognition rights in the UK. His research interests include childhood, gender, queer studies, decolonial studies, and public policies.

Dustin Ciufo is a faculty member in childhood and youth studies at King's University College at Western University, in London, Ontario, Canada. His teaching and research focus are on children's rights, participation, and activism in relation to peace and conflict, migration, and global development issues.

Anandini Dar is Associate Professor at the School of Liberal Studies, BML Munjal University (India). Her areas of research intersect childhood studies, development studies, sociology, education, and feminist studies. She has published on the topics of children's rights, political agency of youth, migration and development, de-colonialization of childhood and curricula.

Lucia Rabello de Castro is Professor of Childhood and Youth at the Federal University of Rio de Janeiro, Brazil. She is the current Chief Editor of the Latin American childhoods-focused journal, *DESIDADES*. Her research interests focus on childhood theories and methodologies, decolonial theories, and children's political participation.

Christine Goodwin-De Faria is an associate professor in child and youth studies at Trent University Durham (Canada). She holds a PhD in policy studies from Toronto Metropolitan University. Christine's research focuses on youth justice, participation, and child rights. Christine is a member of the Child Rights Academic Network.

Karl Hanson is Director of the Centre for Children's Rights Studies and Full Professor at the Law faculty of the University of Geneva, Switzerland. His publications and main research relate to interdisciplinary children's rights theories, working children and child labour norms and policies, international children's rights law, and juvenile justice.

Jonathan Josefsson is Associate Professor in the Department of Thematic Studies – Child Studies at Linköping University, Sweden. His research focuses on: child migration; young people's mobilization in migration, environmental politics, age, and democratization; and the political representation of children and youth in global politics.

Manfred Liebel is a sociologist and Professor Emeritus at Technological University of Berlin and Honorary Professor for Intercultural Childhood and Children's Rights Studies at Potsdam University of Applied Sciences, Germany. His main areas of research are children's rights, social movements, working and Indigenous children, adultism, racism, coloniality, and decolonization.

Valeria Llobet holds a PhD in social psychology from the University of Buenos Aires (Argentina). She is a professor in the School of Humanities, Universidad de San Martín (Argentina) and a researcher at CONICET (National Council of Research). Her work focuses on children's rights, gender, and class inequalities.

Therese Boje Mortensen is a postdoctoral researcher in the Department of Human Rights Studies, Lund University (Sweden). Her research interests include children's rights, ethnographic approaches to human rights studies, civil society, and young people's political activism including climate litigation. Her empirical focus has, throughout her career, been on contemporary India.

Didier Reynaert is Lecturer in Social Work and Senior Researcher at the EQUALITY//ResearchCollective of HOGENT University of Applied Sciences and Arts, School of Social Welfare (Belgium). His expertise lies in the field of social work theory, social justice and human rights, and Critical Children's Rights Studies.

Fernanda Bittencourt Ribeiro holds a PhD in social anthropology from the École des Hautes Études en Sciences Sociales (France). She is Professor at the Pontifícia Universidade Católica do Rio Grande do Sul (Porto Alegre, Brazil). Her research focuses on the anthropology of childhood and the governance of childhood and family life.

Bengt Sandin is Professor at the Department of Thematic Studies/Child Studies at the University of Linköping, Sweden. His research encompasses the social and cultural history of children and the construction of childhood. His publications include work on child labour, street children, children's rights, childhood and reparative justice, age, and voting rights.

Yitaktu Tibebu is a gender and social inclusion senior adviser and consultant. Her previous research focused on law, violence, changing gendered social norms (in the context of child marriage and domestic violence), child custody litigation, and group cognitive behavioural therapy. She holds a PhD in human rights.

Afua Twum-Danso Imoh is Associate Professor in Global Childhoods and Welfare at the University of Bristol (UK). Her work explores the intersections between children's rights and cultural norms in Ghana. She is an editor for the Palgrave Macmillan Study of Childhood and Youth Series and serves on the editorial boards of several journals.

Edward van Daalen is Postdoctoral Fellow of the Labour Law and Development Research Laboratory at McGill University (Canada). He works on the intersections of international labour law, children's rights, and development studies. He holds a PhD in law from the University of Geneva (Switzerland).

Wouter Vandenhole is Full Professor of Human Rights and Children's Rights and directs the Law and Development Research Group of the University of Antwerp's (Belgium) law faculty. His research interests include children's rights, economic, social and cultural rights, the relationship between human rights law and sustainable development, and thicker human rights accountability.

Carla Villalta holds a PhD in social anthropology. She is Adjunct Professor in the Faculty of Philosophy and Letters at the University of Buenos Aires (Argentina). She is a member of the Advisory Committee of the National Science and Justice Program at CONICET.

Basia Vucic is a visiting academic at the UNESCO Chair of Social Pedagogy in Poland, specializing in educational philosophy, history, and citizenship. She established the Children's Rights Centre in South Australia where she is imagining a new discipline, the Pedagogy of Law, and seeking radical democratization by placing legal instruments into the hands of children.

John Wall is Distinguished Professor of Philosophy, Religion, and Childhood Studies, as well as Founding Director of the Childism Institute, at Rutgers University Camden (USA). He is author or editor of nine books and dozens of articles/chapters. He is best known for developing the critical theory of childism as well as his advocacy for children's suffrage.

Acknowledgements

We are very grateful to the following institutions who provided funding to enable this volume to be published open access:

- The University of Antwerp (Faculty of Law) (Belgium)
- Université de Genève (Centre for Children's Rights Studies) (Switzerland)
- Linköping University (Sweden)
- Lund University (Sweden)
- The Norwegian University of Science and Technology (Department of Education and Lifelong Learning) (Norway)

Critical Children's Rights Studies

An introduction

Didier Reynaert, Wouter Vandenhole, Afua Twum-Danso Imoh and Valeria Llobet

Background

Children's rights have gained an important position in research in recent decades. Certainly, with the adoption of the United Nations Convention on the Rights of the Child (hereafter: UNCRC), a significant incentive was created 'to do' children's rights research (Bendo, 2020; Quennerstedt, 2013; Reynaert et al., 2009). It resulted in both a quantitative increase in the number of published research articles in scientific databases and a qualitative expansion of the object of study in terms of themes, approaches and disciplines (Quennerstedt, 2013). Today, children's rights research seems to be an '*established and legitimate field of study*' (Quennerstedt, 2013, p. 233), even to the extent that increasingly this field is referred to as 'Children's Rights Studies'. With this, it profiles itself in the academic landscape alongside other research fields such as childhood studies, human rights studies, welfare studies and development studies.

Notwithstanding (or partly due to?) this slow evolution of a research field's 'coming of age', more and more critical questions have been raised in recent years about the central object of study, being children's rights. These critical questions are significantly varied in nature and originate from different disciplines, but mostly have in common the premise that they do not seek to disqualify the concept of children's rights, but, rather, strive for a more profound and nuanced understanding of children's rights, *beyond* the UNCRC. Although these critical issues mostly start from a critique of mainstream children's rights discourses, the stakes are primarily a search for providing alternative pathways to understanding and enacting children's rights.

The present volume links up with the latter movement and aims to expand the 'critical turn' in Children's Rights Studies towards 'Critical Children's Rights Studies'. This builds on the predecessor to this volume, the *Routledge International Handbook of Children's Rights Studies* (Vandenhole et al., 2015), where the editors, two of whom are involved in this volume, outlined, in the introduction and conclusion, elements of an emerging field of Critical Children's Rights Studies. In doing so, they sought to set the preliminary scene of a scientific development that was already evident before the publication of the

DOI: 10.4324/9781003510284-1

handbook (see, for example, Abebe & Tefera, 2014; Hanson & Nieuwenhuys, 2013; Twum-Danso Imoh, 2013; Balagopalan, 2013; Liebel et al., 2012; Reynaert et al., 2012; Freeman, 1998). However, despite the progress made, it is fair to state that even today this 'critical turn' cannot be regarded as mature or unambiguous. On the contrary, critical perspectives in children's rights today operate at the margins of the children's rights field and go in very different directions. In order to obtain a better understanding of the different perspectives that are deployed in discussions framed under the umbrella of Critical Children's Rights Studies, the editors of the present volume took the initiative in the course of 2023 to bring together a group of approximately 20 critical scholars in the field of Children's Rights Studies to form a learning community. In a first phase, an online seminar series with this learning community was organized where the researchers involved could share with each other their topic area relating to children's rights, establish their main critique of mainstream children's rights and articulate their understanding of the meaning of a critical children's rights perspective. The discussions that took place during the seminar series shaped the development of our book proposal. Then, in a second phase, a new online seminar series was organized in 2024 in which draft papers were shared and discussed among the participants and written feedback was given. This eventually led to the present volume.

Closely linked to the process of creating this volume were a number of parallel initiatives that also revealed the need to further shape this critical turn in Children's Rights Studies. In 2022, alongside the final production of the book, *The Politics of Children's Rights and Representation* (Sandin et al., 2023), the Critical Children's Rights Research Network, an informal online network of approximately 25 researchers from different disciplines and countries all working within the fields of children's rights and childhood studies, came into being. This informal network meets regularly to enable members to share their ongoing research. The conversations within this network contributed to the organization of the international conference, *Critical Childhood(s): 100 Years of Children's Rights,* at the School of Law and Social Justice of the University of Liverpool in July 2024 and was instrumental in the organization of the Critical Children's Rights Network Online PhD Masterclass which was held in August 2024.

These various initiatives demonstrate the need to bring together critical perspectives related to children's rights, to engage in dialogue with each other to examine what this critical perspective means and, from there, explore alternative paths to children's rights. This is exactly what this Research Companion aims to do. Specifically, it seeks to bring together established and upcoming scholars whose work has been central to not only critiquing but also to moving beyond critiques of dominant children's rights discourses. This will enable us to start setting out the emerging paradigm of Critical Children's Rights Studies, drawing on contexts in both the Global North and Global South.

In this introduction, we outline more clearly the Critical Children's Rights Studies perspective in the broader context of children's rights research. To this end, we adopt a typology consisting of three 'streams' that together characterize the field of children's rights research. A first stream is that of research which is oriented towards 'implementing children's rights', a stream that took shape in the latter days of the adoption of the UNCRC. A second stream is what is emerging in recent years as 'Children's Rights Studies'. Finally, a third stream, the *Critical* Children's Rights Studies, is closely related to Children's Rights Studies but characterized by a clearer profile on its critical nature. This typology can be read and understood in different ways. The most apparent understanding is to see the three streams as chronologically successive approaches to children's rights research, with the next stream emerging from a critique of the shortcomings of the previous one. As we will see, this is true to a certain extent, but at the same time this understanding carries a naïve belief in progress that implies that children's rights research seems to be becoming more and more academic over time in order to eventually pass the test of what might be considered quality academic research today. This detracts from the existence of solid academic research in the early 'implementation years' after the UNCRC and the existence of a strong social commitment by various research teams to help shape the implementation of the UNCRC today. Thus, grasping the typology of children's rights research from a chronological lens is valuable but one-sided. In contrast, seeing these three streams as merely disconnected streams with their own distinguishable identities does not quite stand the test of reality either. A 'stream', defined as a coherent set of ideas and views shared by a group of people, acknowledges the existence of diverse, potentially conflicting views on children's rights research and provides a certain compass to better understand, analyze and further explore certain views on children's rights. But at the same time, the 'streams approach does not do justice to the interconnectedness that exists between streams, both in terms of their characteristics and the people who engage in them. No stream can claim complete uniqueness across a range of characteristics, just as most researchers do not have the complete 'purity' to commit entirely to a single stream. In other words, boundaries between streams have a distinctly porous nature that allows streams to blend into one another which, in turn, enables researchers to engage with various streams simultaneously. In short, this proposed typology that we will now outline does have analytical value on the one hand in the sense that it distinguishes various forms of research on children's rights, but at the same time it presents, to some extent, an ideal-typical model that cannot be found as such in reality since the distinct streams cannot be radically separated.

Children's rights research: realizing the implementation agenda

In his 1998 contribution on 'academic responsibility' as it relates to children's rights, Verhellen (1998, p. 97) stated that the UNCRC provided a 'timely impetus' for the interest in children's rights in the academic world. However, research on children's rights was already underway prior to the adoption of the UNCRC. This research focused mainly on the origins and early advocacy for children's rights as well as on philosophical debates about children's autonomy and self-determination and how to balance children's rights with parental authority (see, for example, Freeman, 1987; Takanishi, 1978; Gross & Gross, 1977). Particular attention was paid to the significance of the child liberation movement of the 1970s that advocated for expanded rights and freedoms for children (Farson, 1974; Holt, 1975; Veerman, 1992; see also van Daalen, this volume). Nonetheless, research attention was limited, and it was the UNCRC that pioneered a unified framework that realized significant growth in academic work in children's rights. It is therefore no coincidence that this stream of research is characterized by two interrelated features associated with the UNCRC: i) its instrumentalist character and ii) its legal character.

Research as an instrument to implement the UNCRC

Research on children's rights in the latter days of the adoption of the UNCRC is characterized by its implementation-driven nature: it is perceived as an instrument to implement the UNCRC. With children's rights clearly recognized and defined in the UNCRC, represented by a synthesis of 'earlier' protectionist approaches and 'later' liberal/libertarian lines, the question of what children's rights embrace faded into the background. In its place emerged a 'consensus-thinking' approach within the children's rights community, including academia, with a very technical-instrumental research approach (Quennerstedt, 2013; Reynaert et al., 2009) that was mainly concerned with providing answers to the 'how-question': how can children's rights best be implemented? Almost every scientific children's rights issue was reduced as a study of the 'gap problem': how to bridge the gap between the undesirable reality of children's daily lives on the one hand and the ideal of the UNCRC on the other (Vandenhole, 2015)? The provisions of the UNCRC were understood as new norms in children's lives with limited space or initiative to study, let alone criticize these new norms as such. Whether it was corporal punishment, child labour, or any other 'problematic' children's rights issue, research in each case was dominated by developing recommendations that did away with these practices – plain and simple. In this sense, research was highly ideologically driven, motivated by a strong belief that the UNCRC, with relevance to seemingly all areas of children's lives, could improve the living conditions of children around the world. In view of this, the implementation-driven nature of children's rights research was closely accompanied by a strong belief in change: the belief that the UNCRC is an instrument that also effectively contributes to changing the living conditions of children. The instrumental implementation agenda that came to underpin much research on children's rights thus had the merit of being distinctly practice- and policy-relevant, connecting to very concrete questions that emerged from practice and policy.

The orientation of research towards practice and policy at the same time caused a close intertwining of academia with activism. If research is indeed UNCRC implementation-driven, then the question arises about how the role of scholars in children's rights is distinct from that of practitioners in children's rights. In his 2014 article 'Killed by charity. Towards interdisciplinary children's rights studies', Hanson (2014, p. 443) criticizes the lack of distance that exists between activism and academia within the field: 'Children's rights research was, in particular, during the first decade after the adoption of the CRC, closely linked with the children's rights movement and was seen by both researchers and activists as two sides of the same coin'. Scholars in children's rights, in this sense, were very active in 'doing children's rights' rather than in 'doing research on children's rights', at least in the empirical sense. If any empirical evidence was needed at all for the realization of the ideologically driven implementation agenda, it had to come primarily from research into the views of children and young people themselves on numerous social issues. Hence, even research with children and young people served the implementation agenda.

The legal character of children's rights research

The implementation-driven research agenda that characterized children's rights research in the first years after the adoption of the UNCRC was also strongly coloured by its legal character. The adoption of the UNCRC has perpetuated and undoubtedly reinforced the dominance of the legal discipline in the field of children's rights, including in research (Bendo, 2020; Vandenhole, 2015; Hanson, 2014). The legal obligations associated with the ratification of the UNCRC (the 'pacta sunt servanda' principle) create the need to develop, adapt or renew numerous regulations and procedures at the national level. Researchers in the academic field of law addressed this and helped build the translation of the UNCRC at the domestic level. As explained by Verhellen (1998, p. 117):

> It's legally binding feature, especially at the formal level, needs more of a proactive and creative approach and research into all kinds of procedures such as amending new laws to transpose the Convention into national laws, its self-executing force, reporting mechanisms, monitoring systems and so on.

Legal scholars, as Vandenhole (2015) states, tend to see children's rights issues as implementation issues, focusing mainly on the realization of existing legal standards.

Although implementation-driven research and legal research were two distinguishable features of children's rights research in the early years, they were also closely related. Both started from an established normative frame of reference to be realized in which a technocratically coloured arsenal of means was deployed to achieve the predetermined goal of implementation. In this sense, the legal character of research is not simply legal but rather 'legal positivist': the law is deployed as a means to bridge the gap between reality and the ideal. Neither reality (the context in which children live) nor the ideal (the UNCRC) are the subject of research activities. It is a conception of law that is not only supposed to be neutral towards both reality and ideal, but equally unavoidable; it is the only conceivable way to implement the UNCRC (Tyesta et al., 2020). It, therefore, also carries within it a certain form of legal determinism: law unilaterally imposes the direction that reality must take. When we no longer have to ask questions about what children's rights are, since they are incorporated in the UNCRC, but only have to look for the best way to implement them, the legal discipline in its positivist understanding is a welcome ally.

This approach, in academia, practice and policy, has, hitherto, been very dominant. Nevertheless, it has also been questioned in recent years and does not remain free of critique. A compelling argument has been made regarding the explicitly decontextualized approach of the legal positivist perspective, which takes insufficient account of a plurality of living conditions of children and young people. By extension, the critique emphasizes that legal positivism pays little or no attention to the meaning of law in society, which in Western highly bureaucratized and juridified countries is different in nature from other countries where alternative legal systems exist. In short, the hegemony of positivist legal thinking in the field of children's rights research slowly became subject to numerous critical questions – critical questions that slowly but surely oriented the field towards 'Children's Rights Studies'.

'Children's Rights Studies'

The notion of 'children's rights studies' (hereafter: CRS) only emerged at the beginning of the 2010s, where it was initially used independently by various authors as a little-developed concept (see Vandenhole et al., 2010; Reynaert et al., 2010; Stalford, 2012; Hanson & Nieuwenhuys, 2013). However, no clear definition has ever been given for what this field of research exactly comprises. Nevertheless, a number of trends can be discerned that distinguish CRS from the early 'implementation years' of children's rights research.

The academic turn

The new field of Children's Rights Studies seeks to redefine the connections between scholarship and activism. With its focus on 'Studies', Children's Rights Studies strive to meet scholarly standards of, among other things, understanding and rigorously analyzing the social phenomenon of children's rights (Bendo, 2020; Hanson, 2014; Quennerstedt, 2013). In doing so, it focuses on the development of *scientific knowledge*, to be distinguished from *practical knowledge* and *experiential knowledge*. Whereas scientific knowledge is the result of systematic scientific research aimed primarily at understanding children's rights, practical knowledge is seen as implicit and embodied knowledge acquired through working in practice on the realization of children's rights, while experiential knowledge is a source of knowledge derived from children and young people's own personal experiences with their rights. However, the orientation of CRS towards scientific knowledge does not mean that children's rights research should henceforth be conducted from an ivory tower, detached from, and irrelevant to, concrete practice and policy (Hanson, 2019). However, it does mean seeking new relationships between academia and civil society, with the recognition of each having its own distinct and complementary role in relation to children's rights research and knowledge development.

The plea to more clearly distinguish academic research on children's rights from activist advocacy is accompanied by two related developments. A first development is a movement towards ***empiricism***. As argued, research on children's rights in the implementation stream is often ideology-driven, closely linked to the commitment of implementing the UNCRC and the abstract consensus of normatively accepted children's rights embodied in the UNCRC. The academic turn points to the importance, within Children's Rights Studies, of having research starting from the empiric where data are collected that provide insights into how children's rights are shaped in concrete contexts. Children's Rights Research thus started to become engaged in the analysis and understanding of this data to gain insight into the diversity of practices set up to realize children's rights (see also 3.3 The contextual turn).

A second development is one towards theory. The ostensible lack of solid theorization supportive of understanding children's rights has been repeatedly pointed out in the more recent literature on children's rights (see, among others, Arce, 2015; Quennerstedt, 2013; Reynaert et al., 2012). This lack of theorizing is also related to the hegemony of the UNCRC, as Quennerstedt (2013, p. 240) rightly asserts: 'My suggestion is that the analytic interest has been hindered by the hegemonic status of the Convention, thereby resulting in low levels of theorising and too little distinction between the proponent and analytic aspects of research'. A more theory-driven approach in children's rights could contribute to understanding and rigorously analyzing the social phenomenon of children's rights. However, Hanson and Peleg (2020, p. 17) offer some nuance to this stance by indicating that there is not so much a lack of theorization in the field of children's rights research as a lack of reflection 'about the normative relevance, the analytical qualities and explanatory powers of the mobilised theories'.

The (inter)disciplinary turn

The academic turn in the field of children's rights research has been accompanied by a double disciplinary movement towards the field of Children's Rights Studies. The first is a ***disciplinary expansion and strengthening*** on the topic of children's rights. When the focus is no longer on legal implementation but on the study of (this law in) empirical data, other tools than those in the legal toolbox are needed to understand and analyze children's rights. Consequently, disciplines such as anthropology, sociology, geography, social work, amongst others, gradually made their presence felt in the study of children's rights. Strengthening these individual disciplines in their study of children's rights is a plea strongly voiced by Quennerstedt (2013, p. 242):

> I believe that children's rights need to be examined more extensively within particular academic domains. . . . The matter of human rights for children accordingly needs to be incorporated into the core interests of a discipline or a perspective, and research problems about rights need to be formulated from such a merged position. This would mean that questions about children's rights in e.g. law studies are substantially different from those raised in e.g. educational studies, because these disciplines have very different knowledge interests.

At the same time, a second development is occurring that seeks a greater or lesser degree of ***dialogue between disciplines***. Indeed, the increasing presence of a diversity of disciplines in Children's Rights Studies demonstrates the complexity of the object of study – an object that cannot be fully understood by a single discipline. An interdisciplinary dialogue in the study of children's rights is, therefore, considered fundamental to fully understand the different aspects, ambiguities and dimensions of a children's rights issue (Bendo, 2020; Desmet et al., 2015; Hanson, 2014). Such an interdisciplinary approach brings multi-perceptiveness to the children's rights debate.

The extent to which different disciplines interact within the Children's Rights Studies varies from multi- over inter- to transdisciplinarity. In line with Mitchell (2015), Bendo (2020) argues for the expansion of Children's Rights Studies towards a 'problem-oriented approach' that transcends the discipline-centred approach. Such a transdisciplinary approach integrates not only disciplinary knowledge, but also nonacademic knowledge from practitioners, policy-makers as well as Indigenous partners, children and young people themselves and other stakeholders who can contribute to a better understanding of children's rights issues. This embraces the three previously mentioned sources of knowledge in children's rights research, i.e. academic, practical and experiential.

The contextual turn

The shift towards empiricism is essentially an orientation of children's rights research towards concrete contexts in which children's rights are realized. As such, a connection is made between the text of the UNCRC and the context of children's everyday lives. Critiques of the dominant top-down thinking of legal determinism led to the introduction of numerous contextual approaches to children's rights under various headings: 'children's rights from below'

(Liebel et al., 2012), 'contextualizing children's rights' (Fonseca, 2002, 2009; Llobet, 2011), 'living rights' (Hanson & Nieuwenhuys, 2013), 'localising children's rights' (see Vandenhole's chapter in Liebel et al., 2012), 'a lifeworld perspective' (Reynaert & Roose, 2015), 'historicizing rights-subjectivities' (Balagopalan, 2019), 'child rights governance' (Holzscheiter et al., 2019). These authors point to the importance of social, cultural, political, economic, geographical as well as historical differences that exist in a diversity of contexts, all of which have, to a greater or lesser extent, an influence on how children's rights are understood in a given context (see also Quennerstedt, 2013).

A first observation here is the great diversity of contexts in which children grow up and within which children's rights are to be realized. This puts an end to the consensus-thinking in children's rights research, predominantly expressing universal responses to children's rights issues from a top-down approach. A context-specific approach recognizes that a diversity of contexts also allows for a diversity of ways in which children's rights are translated into these contexts (Hanson & Nieuwenhuys, 2013) and may even be contradictory. This diversity of translations of children's rights should not be seen as a weakness where the notion of children's rights can seemingly go in any direction, but rather as a strength in that it engages with local needs, collectively shared values and traditions (see, for example, Twum-Danso, 2024; Vergara Del Solar et al., 2021; Corradi & Desmet, 2015; Abebe, 2013; Fonseca & Cardarello, 2005). All this does not mean that the 'universal' or the 'global' would no longer have a place in the field of Children's Rights Studies. To fully understand the local embedding of children's rights, the lens of the global is not only useful but even necessary. Indeed, both dimensions are in tension with each other as one helps to create the conditions for the other (see Conclusion, this volume). Just as a lack of attention to contextual translations of children's rights provoked critiques of its universalist nature, a lack of the global dimension of children's rights can be blamed for relativism. After all, just because children's rights take shape from a local dynamic does not mean that it is, therefore, a de facto legitimate form. Such an 'anything goes' approach risks creating the possibility of justifying every possible interpretation of children's rights. Brando (2019) argues that one way to deal with this universalist-relativist conflict is to involve children themselves in the decision-making process to ensure that their rights and interests are protected. We will return to this issue in detail in the conclusion of the volume.

Children's Rights Studies: an island in an academic archipelago

Whereas children's rights research in the period immediately following the adoption of the UNCRC was characterized by a strong activist appeal, driven by a solid implementation agenda and based on abstract legal principles, Children's Rights Studies as they have unfolded over the last decade can be seen as a field of study that is increasingly seeking nuance and depth and is, therefore, better able to grasp the complexity inherent in children's rights. Children's

Rights Studies have thus gradually begun to better prepare themselves to secure their place in the academic landscape and to take on a status where they can stand alongside other research fields. Children's Rights Studies today are slowly positioning themselves alongside related and less related fields of study such as childhood studies, human rights studies, women's studies, Black studies, queer studies, disability studies, amongst others, as an island in an academic archipelago with its own body of knowledge, scientific journals, educational programmes, conferences and academic networks.

Nevertheless, a number of issues remain understudied under the umbrella of Children's Rights Studies. Research in this field remains strongly linked to the UNCRC as the horizon along which normative foundations are sought to justify children's rights. However, the question is relevant whether there are other normative grounds on which children's rights can be thought of. Are there other normative schemes for justifying children's rights that go 'beyond the UNCRC'? This is a particularly significant question from the perspective of epistemic injustice, where the observation holds that knowledge production on children's rights is still strongly driven by an English-speaking research community. Are other knowledge schemes conceivable that could help shape the body of knowledge on children's rights? These are just some of the questions that form the foundation of a critical stream in Children's Rights Studies.

'Critical Children's Rights Studies'

Already from the very first echoes of Children's Rights Studies at the beginning of the 2010s, there were voices advocating for 'Critical Children's Rights Studies' (see, for example, Reynaert et al., 2012; Desmet et al., 2015). However, labelling one's own field with the concept 'critical' is not without commitment. This is to connect with a longer tradition in social science of critical thinking, which goes back to the critical theory of the 'Frankfurter Schule' and which has been developed in several variants up to the present day (see, for example, Celikates & Flynn, 2023; Rensmann, 2017). What these variants have in common is the understanding of their object of study (in our case children's rights) in critical relation with the existing social order – an order in which the researcher is engaged by questioning it for its role in serving particular interests. Social institutions and practices such as child-rearing and education, welfare and labour are seen, from the perspective of the critical approach, as initiating and socializing individuals into the existing social and political order, without questioning this order in itself. As a result, by definition, the interests of those in power are served. The fact that this social order can also foster exclusion, inequality, injustice or even oppression and exploitation is a central claim in the critical school of thinking. Critical approaches, however, strive not only to portray dynamics of exclusion and inequality through their research, but equally to bring about societal change towards greater equality and inclusion. Herein lies the emancipatory nature of the critical approach.

Therefore, the move towards a critical variant in Children's Rights Studies is not unique. The fields of study to which Children's Rights Studies is related – such as Childhood Studies, Human Rights Studies, Women's Studies, Race Studies, Queer Studies, Disability Studies – all witnessed a critical turn in recent decades. This was prompted by the observation that various categories and groups in society such as children, women, people from the LGBTQIA+ community, Black people, etc. persistently experience inequality due to exclusionary mechanisms whose root causes are inherently linked to the structures upon which society is organized. In the field of Critical Disability Studies, for example, the critical variant emerged from a critique of the normalization paradigm of persons with disabilities (Meekosha & Shuttleworth, 2009). Critical Race Studies focuses, among other things, on the structural mechanisms of discrimination embedded in social institutions (Teviño et al., 2008). And Critical Childhood Studies also explicitly focuses on real external environments within which children grow up. As Alanen (2011, p. 150) states:

> Critical Childhood Studies implies being critical not only of our own research practices but the very practices and social arrangements that we study in the 'real' world of children and childhood. Thus, making explicit the normative foundations of childhood research requires that we also address a number of normative issues concerning the practices and arrangements 'out there', and specify in what particular respects and for what specific reasons they are problematic. It also asks us to specify what constitutes a good, or at least a better life for children and for human beings in general.
>
> (see also Tisdall et al., 2023)

Building on Alanen's understanding of what 'critical' entails, we can essentially distinguish Critical Children's Rights Studies from Children's Rights Studies at the point at which they position children's rights in relation to the broader societal conditions. *Critical* CRS analyzes children's rights from the viewpoint of what these conditions consist of, whether these conditions contribute to a greater respect for children and on what normative grounds we can justify this respect. In other words, questioning the social conditions themselves is the fundamental stake in a critical approach. Here, unlike CRS, *Critical* CRS does not necessarily adhere to the normative horizon of the UNCRC. After all, the UNCRC too can be an instrument for the perpetuation of the existing order and thereby serves as a tool that reinforces inequality. In this sense, the normative scope of *Critical* CRS goes *beyond* the UNCRC and seeks grounds for justification of children's rights in alternative epistemic schemes.

These general, rather abstract, premises lead to three central focal points in our conceptualization of Critical Children's Rights Studies: i) the normative turn, ii) an orientation to equality and iii) a focus on epistemic injustice. In doing so, we join the rich tradition of critical theory but, at the same time,

Critical Children's Rights Studies seeks to deepen and complement the various strands of Children's Rights Studies outlined previously.

The normative turn

What is central to *Critical* CRS and where they clearly seek to distinguish themselves from previous streams is their explicit assignment to question underlying normative foundations that are constitutive of the shaping of society and, therefore, of children's rights. Any form of children's rights, whether in academia, practice or policy, is not a neutral concept with unambiguous meaning but a social construction shaped in a particular societal order from a diversity of normative understandings. *Critical* CRS aims to question and evaluate these underlying normative orders and foundations and to explore new grounds. This has far-reaching implications for doing research in the field of children's rights. Indeed, it means, among other things, that we need to reflect on our normative frames of reference that justify and give justification to the shaping of society and the embedded constructions of children's rights. In doing so, we go 'beyond the UNCRC', which as far as children's rights are concerned is mostly seen as the normative reference point for the construction of children's rights. We do not disqualify this normative point of reference, but we do note that in societies today that are often characterized by great diversity and where children's rights take shape at the intersection of numerous markers, ranging from race, culture, economic background, gender, sexual preference, amongst others, this Convention is insufficiently capable of operating as the only normative frame of reference to define children's rights. There is an increased sensitivity in both the Global North and the Global South to the importance of children's rights knowledge that critically approaches and even goes beyond the dominant UNCRC regime.

The normative turn in *Critical* CRS includes an orientation towards normative reference points that justify why we shape our current societies and children's rights in these societies as such. Several authors have incorporated this search in their research in an attempt to substantiate children's rights from a 'contextual normativity'. Examples are 'ethics of care' or an 'Ubuntu approach' as a counternarrative for often too individualized conceived notions of personhood, distinctive of Western societies (Twum-Danso, 2024; Songca, 2018; De Graeve, 2015). Taking such approaches in analyzing and shaping children's rights gives a more in-depth understanding of the underlying norms, values and logics that shape practices of children's rights in current societies and the way these norms, values and logics are understood.

An orientation to equality

Alongside the more process-oriented nature of the academic exercise of 'questioning normativity', the critical nature of *Critical* CRS is marked by their emancipatory struggle to transform societies by 'challenging inequality'. In recent years, the field of human rights studies has been critically examining the relationship between human rights and inequality. On the Northern forefront of this debate is Samuel Moyn (2018), who argues that human rights, which are powerless in the face of growing material inequality, share characteristics with neoliberalism and make only minimalist demands. He suggests that human rights focus on 'sufficiency' rather than 'equality', prioritizing minimum provisions over distributive justice. Moyn argues that human rights are often formulated in a way that emphasizes formal equality – legal and political rights – without adequately addressing substantive inequalities related to economic and social conditions. It can be assumed that this critique applies equally to the domain of children's rights as, similarly, children's rights seem to have little orientation towards equality and may even contribute to the reproduction of social inequality, as Vergara Del Solar et al. (2021) have shown in relation to the Latin America debate. While this is undoubtedly not the intention of children's rights measures, children's rights risk reproducing inequality if we do not sufficiently take into account a variety of markers important in the construction of children's rights. To date, this criticism has found little direct resonance in the field of Children's Rights Studies in the Global North (Daly et al., 2025), except indirectly, for example through the decolonial critique.

Whereas CRS explicitly situates children's rights in the connection between Global South and Global North, *Critical* CRS goes a step further and embraces the decolonial critique. Recent scholarship examines children's rights through a decolonial lens, challenging Eurocentric perspectives. They argue that the dominant children's rights regime demands a critical examination of how colonial legacies continue to influence the rights and experiences of children globally (de Castro, 2021; Balagopalan, 2019b). Decolonial theory underscores the need to deconstruct dominant narratives imposed by colonial powers, which often marginalize Indigenous and non-Western perspectives. Dominant frameworks of children's rights, such as those established by the UNCRC, are important, but they may also reflect particular Western-centric values and norms that do not always align with, or respect, diverse cultural practices and beliefs. Colonial histories have left lasting impacts on the ways societies view, and treat, children, often imposing foreign structures of governance and education that disrupt Indigenous ways of raising and caring for children. For instance, colonial systems frequently undermined traditional family structures and communal child-rearing practices, prioritizing instead Western models of individualism and formal education (Twum-Danso Imoh, 2020). This legacy can persist in modern children's rights discourses, where Western notions of autonomy, school-based education, and protection might overshadow or invalidate Indigenous practices and understandings of childhood.

Researchers in the field of *Critical* CRS argue for reimagining children's rights by deconstructing colonial influences and exploring alternative approaches. Rabello de Castro (2022), for instance, argues that decolonial critique can contribute to revisiting children's rights from a Global South perspective, addressing the particularities of childhoods shaped by colonial encounters. Others such as Cohen et al. (2023) advocate for a reimagining of children's rights that acknowledges and incorporates the voices and traditions of diverse cultural groups. Liebel (2020) highlights the need to address social inequalities exacerbated by capitalist globalization that disproportionately affect children in formerly colonized regions, such as poverty, lack of access to education and health disparities. By foregrounding the impact of colonialism on current inequalities, decolonial studies push for a rights framework that not only addresses immediate needs but also tackles the root causes of injustice and marginalization.

However, the decolonial critique might overlook the importance of the institutional histories of state-building in countries in the Global South. Vergara Del Solar et al. (2021, p. 15), amongst others, point out that South America was not 'virgin territory' when the UNCRC was adopted. On the contrary, many countries in South America already had their own debates about children's rights going back to the late 19th century. In fact, it is possible to go even further to argue that some South American countries contributed towards the development of the UNCRC, thereby disproving the myth that the creation of the UNCRC was a one-sided Western process. Vergara Del Solar et al. (2021, p. 15) put it well when they stated:

> Consequently, images that portray the children's rights discourse consolidated in the CRC as 'foreign' and imported omit the rich Latin American and South American history of debates around these rights (LLobet, 2020). Indeed, it was South American actors who formulated certain positions in the CRC drafting process based on their experiences of dictatorship.

Yet, many decolonial theorists tend to generalize such processes, often framing global frameworks like the UNCRC as merely imposed by the Global North without acknowledging the active contributions of Global South actors. This oversimplification overlooks the intercontinental exchanges and the historical agency of South American countries, for instance, thereby replicating the same homogenizing tendencies they critique in Eurocentric narratives. Moreover, the reliance on abstract theorization in decolonial critiques frequently comes at the expense of engaging with specific historical cases or institutional contexts. As Vergara Del Solar et al. (2021) highlight, South America's history reveals a rich tapestry of debates, practices and contributions to global discourses on children's rights. Ignoring these specificities risks reducing the diversity of these histories to a binary opposition between the Global North and South.

The fact that the UNCRC was implemented in a context of neoliberal reforms of welfare states in the region, which were modified in very specific ways by the social structure and children's welfare institutions, tends to be overlooked in favour of a North vs. South narrative. This underscores the need for historically informed debates that highlight structural inequalities and social oppression without resorting to reductive dichotomies. By engaging with these nuanced histories, scholars can better problematize the binary framing of some decolonial perspectives and illuminate the interconnected and multifaceted nature of these global exchanges.

Epistemic injustice

Following on from the two previous focal points, *Critical* CRS must engage with the issue of 'epistemic injustice' (Fricker, 2007). The recognition of children as distinct producers of knowledge was a claim already embedded in the children's rights movement of the 1970s. This remains a fundamental aspiration to this day, including in *Critical* CRS, especially with regard to 'marginalized groups' such as children with disabilities, children in poverty, children from migrant backgrounds, amongst others. Their knowledge is often still unrecognized or, at least, undervalued (Hanna, 2022). In developing their knowledge agenda, *Critical* CRS must continue to take to heart, in particular, the perspectives of these vulnerable groups of children themselves.

But what we especially want to point out in this introduction in putting epistemic injustice centre stage is the need to foreground knowledge on children's rights produced in the Global South – particularly, non-Anglophone – contexts. A form of discrimination exists in the global knowledge production ecosystem to this day, whereby non-English speaking knowledge is de facto excluded from the international body of knowledge on children's rights (see Twum-Danso Imoh et al., 2022). Children's rights conferences, scientific journals, research communities and the like share one common language through which knowledge is shared and reproduced, and that is English. The typology on children's rights research described previously does not escape from this injustice either. We do miss important voices in the scholarly debate on children's rights that reveal trends other than those described in the typology of this introduction. Research on children's rights in French-language literature, coming from countries on the African continent, for example, may not fit into the typology outlined previously. This applies equally to Spanish- or Portuguese-language literature on children's rights coming. The absence of this knowledge opens the door for the critique of Anglocentrism in the proposed typology – a critique we ironically wish to take to heart in the expansion of *Critical* CRS.

Critical CRS should engage with the issue of epistemic injustice when it further expands. To this end, it should actively seek out and connect with researchers in the Global South who are conducting research on children's rights from alternative perspectives or actively co-promote and facilitate such research itself. As a result, the *Critical* CRS research agenda should be developed more inclusively, which will not only provide a more layered and nuanced but also a more equitable picture of children's rights that counteracts inequalities in the global knowledge production system. Research into, for example, the social position of children and young people, which is currently commonly explored through the lens of concepts such as autonomy or citizenship, in line with views on liberal-democratic societies, can then be linked to understanding the social position of children and young people from the point of view of interdependence or valuing the community over the individual, as is more common in some communities in parts of the Global South, as reflected in concepts such as 'Ubuntu' and '*buen vivir*'. These concepts have not yet been sufficiently incorporated into the body of knowledge of Children's Rights Studies. Children's rights research is still too often a knowledge activity driven by insights, perspectives and ideas from the Global North than by views or notions and concepts from the Global South.

At the same time, we must also be alert not to fall into culturalisms with the glorification of so-called 'special' cultures that have a specific uniqueness or identity. Criticizing dominant conceptions of children's rights that circulate mainly in Anglo-Saxon spheres does not yet mean that they should be renounced in favour of so-called 'exotic' forms of children's rights. The reality in the way children's rights research has taken shape in recent years is not so much one of universal (Anglo-Saxon) views versus particular (majority world) views, but rather one of mixtures of diverse views that have already taken the first steps towards dialogue (see Vergara Del Solar et al., 2021). Under the motto 'walk the talk', in this book we have tried to strike a balance between authors coming from different parts of the world as well as chapters focusing on alternative views on children's rights coming from both the Global South and the Global North. We hope that this modest contribution will motivate and encourage other scholars in the field of Critical Children's Rights Studies to engage in additional analyses and interpretations which, in turn, can lead to treading new paths in Children's Rights Research.

An outline of Critical Children's Rights Studies

Based on the aforementioned, we define Critical Children's Rights Studies as follows:

1) **'Critical' as deconstructing 'obvious' beliefs**
   Critical Children's Rights Studies should engage in an ongoing exercise of questioning 'truths' and dominant assumptions, norms and values that shape the children's rights regimes. Particular assumptions of childhood or rights create specific understandings of children's rights. Revealing these assumptions, which often remain implicit, is the core of a deconstruction exercise.
2) **'Critical' as constructing alternative pathways**
   The awareness that children's rights are shaped in a particular way and governed by certain normative assumptions eliminates an objectifying understanding of children's rights. Deconstructing dominant understandings of children's rights, therefore, allows us to conceptualize alternative constructions. The constructing feature of a critical perspective is concerned with transforming children's rights along alternative normative lines. This

is where the emancipatory character of Critical Children's Rights Studies is situated: in constructing new normative discourses and regimes that overcome existing exclusions and inequalities of children.

3) **'Critical' as embracing situatedness**
The point of departure in a contextual approach is not so much the norm or rule of children's rights as they were written down in international conventions and other legal instruments, but rather the situatedness of experiences of children and their environment in their daily life. A situated approach of children's rights takes the variety of contexts in which children grow up into account. This means that constructive and deconstructive processes of children's rights might be very different, depending on very different situations. Consequently, children's rights can only be fully understood when interpreted in a situated way.

4) **'Critical' as examining our own positionality**
If contextuality matters in a critical perspective, it is also of crucial importance to take into account the context of the researcher when they move into the research field of children's rights. This is the issue of positionality. Also, in academia a certain tradition can be observed, to a greater or lesser degree, of activism arising from an ontological assumption that children's rights are, by definition, something good. In rather radical forms this can lead to a dogmatic, or even messianic, belief in children's rights where there is no space whatsoever to ask critical questions about the framework of children's rights, let alone to imagine alternative understandings of children's rights. How a researcher relates to the subject of children's rights must be subject to continuous reflection including on key variables such as geographical background, personal and professional histories, socio-economic and political environments and personal experiences with childhood, etc. It positions children's rights scholars in a constant field of tension between proximity and distance, as one needs to extensively engage with a particular children's rights issue in trying to understand it as fully as possible, but at the same time distance is needed to make sure that findings from research are subjected to scrutiny, especially in relation to how their own positionality may influence the questions they ask or the research they undertake.

5) **'Critical' as expressing critique to the critical perspective**
In line with the idea that every new construction of children's rights needs to subject itself to a deconstruction exercise, we ask that contributions continually reflect on the limitations of the critical perspective of children's rights. One key characteristic of the dominant children's rights approach is that often its language and principles are deployed unquestioningly/unproblematically, whether that be the definition of childhood, the universal premise of rights articulated in global norms etc. In adopting a critical perspective, we must not fall into the same trap and must, on an ongoing basis, engage in self-critique. In exploring this strand, papers can reflect on the silences, exclusions, marginalizations that are created by the adoption of a critical perspective.

These were the five themes that framed all the chapters in the volume. The chapters explore various dimensions of these five themes to varying degrees. The next section provides an overview of the chapters.

Overview of chapters

Nico Brando opens this volume with Chapter 1 which pursues a dual objective: to explore the conditions that make children's rights research 'critical', and to analyze the author's own work through this lens. In order to explore what critical children's rights research requires, a reflexive methodology is followed. The chapter emphasizes the need for self-awareness and vigilance against entrenched biases, and advocates for a dynamic and iterative approach to critical inquiry. Further, it underscores the imperative of contextualizing research within the evolving sociocultural milieu, accounting for power dynamics, and engaging meaningfully with the diverse voices and experiences of children. While acknowledging the inherent complexities and challenges, the chapter advocates for humility, introspection and a commitment to continuous improvement as foundational principles for fostering genuine critical scholarship in children's rights.

Edward van Daalen, in Chapter 2, seeks to expose how 'mainstream' children's rights scholarship has been eased into a false sense of 'liberal security' by relying on the works of John Holt and Richard Farson to define 'children's liberation' as meaning 'equal rights' for children and adults. In his chapter he argues that for this liberal iteration of children's liberation, Holt and Farson both heavily relied on Shulamith Firestone's call to abolish 'the family' and 'childhood' as part of her radical feminist manifesto, *The Dialectic of Sex*, but not before stripping it of its feminist and revolutionary intent. By uncritically latching onto the version presented by Holt and Farson, the bourgeoning scholarly field of children's rights allowed itself to adopt, critique and dismiss the notion of children's liberation within the familiar parameters of the UNCRC, while at the same time effectively shielding it from Firestone's radical pre-emptive and fundamental gender critique. The aim of this chapter is to lay the groundwork for critically addressing this bias, by reading and re-evaluating Firestone's manifesto against that of Holt and Farson with the help of John Irving's novel, *The Hotel New Hampshire.*

In Chapter 3 **Manfred Liebel** unpacks why children's rights must be reconceptualized to do justice to the interests and experiences of socially disadvantaged and marginalized children. It draws on the legal-philosophical and legal discussion on counter-rights and makes clear why this is also relevant for children. With reference to examples from the movements of working children in the Global South, the chapter illustrates possible alternative contours of children's rights that emerge from children's self-perception and actions. Counter-rights go beyond the bourgeois-liberal legal form and manifest themselves fluidly in a change of power relations, between adults and children as well as between different classes and genders and reject the characteristics of inferiority and imperfection ascribed to children. At the same time, counter-rights always remain precarious, as they are intended to change something that has not yet been changed. They are not only manifested in demands, but also in lived practice and the forms of counter-power that emerge in this practice.

In Chapter 4 **Lucia Rabello de Castro** problematizes children's emancipation processes simply through the re-creation of legal and political normativities of present liberal democratic societies. Her chapter focuses on the Brazilian context to discuss how its child rights' framework and its neocolonial political order encumber the attainment of a more egalitarian and fair society for children. It argues that it is only through the political action of the oppressed – a process of children's political subjectivization – that the status quo and its political gatekeepers can be challenged with the view to altering the pacts that produce and secure its present legal rights' order. To illustrate the argument, some research findings of children's demands for playtime in Brazilian state schools are analyzed as a process of children's political staging. However improbable children's politics seems to be, it can unveil the distinct and subtle features of processes of domination that naturalize situations of unfairness and inequality in present democracies.

In Chapter 5 **John Wall** starts from the observation that children's rights are commonly thought of as a subset of human rights limited by children's developing capacities. Critical children's rights theory has challenged this notion by arguing that children need to be understood as equal participants in the human rights community. This chapter advances the argument that children's equal human rights demand not just extending to children the rights of adults but revisioning human rights as such. Under a childist critique of human rights, similar to critiques from feminism and de-colonialism, it is not children's capacities that need to be put into question, but rather historical norms and structures built on adultistic and patriarchal assumptions. Such a critique deconstructs the conceptual, historical and political foundations of rights in order to reconstruct rights theories and practices in ways that are finally inclusive of children's particular lived experiences.

Karl Hanson engages, in Chapter 6, with the challenge to further develop conceptual clarifications of how children's rights relate to the future. The conceptual questions this chapter seeks to address are clarified by using the notion 'coevalness', that is, existing or originating at the same time. It pertains to synchronicity or simultaneity in time. The theoretical problem this chapter seeks to address is as follows: how to navigate modernity's emancipatory goal of making tomorrow better than today, which implies paying attention to children's future development, with its other normative ideal of granting equal value and respect to each person's worldview, which necessitates recognizing children's coevalness. Hanson argues that recognizing children as present future-makers with a past is crucial for advancing an emancipatory perspective on children's rights, as it creates conceptual space for children to critically engage with, and participate in, discussions, on equal footing with others, regarding their self-involved futures, future children and the future of humankind. The acknowledgment that children live, and are entitled to live, in the same 'time zone' as anyone else opens the door for a critical reappraisal of the three temporal dimensions 'been', 'being' and 'becoming' of the children's rights framework.

In Chapter 7 **Tatek Abebe** starts from the observation that the framework of children's rights inspired by the UNCRC not only ushered in hegemonic forms of social contracts that consolidate the sovereign, rights-claiming child subject of Western creation but also dislodged familial and community logics of childhood, detaching children from the complex webs of social and generational interdependencies. Drawing on research that situates children in broader contexts of development and social transformation in Ethiopia, this chapter draws attention to the notion of 'generationing rights' to critique the epistemic claim that views the human rights of children as different from the human rights of other generations, while simultaneously revealing how children's rights are fundamentally a relational product imbricated in multiple relations of power. Recasting children's rights as cyclical/reciprocal, relational and interdependent renders intelligible the modes of existence of children outside modernity's framework in ways that do not contradict their ethnocultural, 'unwritten' rights and responsibilities. This approach also makes it possible to reimagine the collective rights of children expansively and critically through the lenses of families and communities in which children are an integral part.

In Chapter 8 **Afua Twum-Danso Imoh** starts from the premise that the idea that the status of childhood is vastly different from that of adulthood is now firmly embedded within societies in both the Global North and the Global South. Such a distinction associates adults with all the attributes that children are perceived to lack such as maturity and competence. However, not all societies make the same dramatic distinction between adults and children and, therefore, they do not necessarily view childhood as a phase of life centred around incompetence, incapability and immaturity. This results in a significant tension between principles underlying dominant children's rights discourses, and any attendant initiatives seeking to realize them on one hand, and communities in both the Global North and the Global South that understand the distinction between childhood and adulthood in substantially different ways on the other. This, therefore, requires a new approach to thinking about childhood and adulthood, and the assumptions made about the competence levels that are typically associated with both phases of life. Drawing on West African notions of personhood and social relations, this chapter explores different understandings of childhood and children's capabilities and examines their utility for an alternative children's rights discourse which does not take childhood incompetence as its departure point.

Luan Carpes Barros Cassal and Erica Burman analyze, in Chapter 9, the 2017 attack on Judith Butler by ultraconservative demonstrators during an academic visit to São Paulo, Brazil in *Those afraid of gender and childhood: anti-gender attacks against Judith Butler in Brazil.* These demonstrations were part of an anti-gender agenda and organized in the name of idealized ideas of (gendered and stable) childhood. In this chapter, Child as method is used as an analytical lens to understand how ideas of childhood are used to oppose gender recognition rights. It is shown that those ideas are weaponized against gender-nonconforming rights, promoting injury and misrecognition, and challenging the field of children's rights. However, Butler's theoretical framework on gender, recognition and democracy supports a claim for non-violent action and self-determination – individual and collective – including on gender and childhood.

Chapter 10 by **Wouter Vandenhole and Yitaktu Tibebu** critiques the mainstream approach to child, early and forced marriage (CEFM) which is geared towards abolition. The legal human rights framework focuses on prohibiting underage marriage, which is defined as marriage below the age of 18. This chapter presents five critiques: the neglect of the complex interaction of socio-economic structural factors and social norms as drivers of CEFM; the universalist assumption of the chronological age of 18 as the marker of adulthood; the neglect of a gender perspective; the theoretical grounding in the neocolonial savage-victim-saviour paradigm; and the naive belief in legal change as a driver of social change. The alternative decolonized approach that the chapter proposes leads to a shift in emphasis to consent, with due attention, though, for the ageist and sexist power. A gender perspective necessitates a shift from protection to agency, with due acknowledgement of the structural causes of CEFM.

Bengt Sandin discusses in Chapter 11 how the analyses of long- and medium-term structural changes can give us tools to better understand the role of children's rights in society. Negotiations of the fundamental conflict between long and short processes of change lead to the redefinition of rights, rights claims and childhoods. It is historically not a homogeneous process, and the interaction between national, regional and international transformations has been contradictory and conflict-ridden. Children's rights, in legal terms, are not the only structuring phenomena in the past. This chapter illuminates the importance of other concepts – governance, surveillance and the transformation of concepts – as well as mundane popular culture notions of children's needs and interests. The study of rights must be set in a historical context with a sensitivity to the construction of historically defined welfare and children's rights regimes. Social changes are timed differently and different in diverse geographical locations. Long processes of change of relevance for children/young people have different temporal logics. They may conflict with institutional changes that change in a more limited timeframe – and childhood culture and lived lives are also on other clocks.

In Chapter 12, **Basia Vucic** explores the intersection of children's rights and sociopolitical movements to suggest an alternative historical model for rights theory and practice. While the history of child rights often acknowledges the Declaration of the Rights of the Child adopted by the League of Nations in 1924 as the work of Eglantyne Jebb, founder of the Save the Children Fund (SCF) in London, recent research has revealed the perils of accepting this historical narrative uncritically. This chapter critiques the dominant narrative of children's rights history by adopting a periphery perspective to show how it marginalizes alternative contributions. Poland has been a catalyst for children's rights; however, no scholarship explores its proposal of the UNCRC as non-Western emerging from national struggles for independence. This study joins the emerging trend of applied history to position the UNCRC as a decolonizing strategy emerging out of Polish resistance to oppression by its neighbours. The classification of children's rights within broader human rights categories, distinct from contemporary paradigms, emanates from Poland's historical struggle for independence and liberty. Amidst Cold War tensions, Poland advocated for children's rights to assert its place in international human rights discourse, challenging Western dominance to foster solidarity among emerging democracies.

How might we interpret the continuing inability of most subaltern populations in the majority world to make claims based on the legal guarantees made available by the new regime of child rights governance? Through a focus on India, **Sarada Balagopalan** attempts to answer this question in Chapter 13. It combines postcolonial theory with an analysis of postindependence policy-making to critically unpack India's recent paradoxical move to deregulate child labour. The chapter explores how the contemporary logics of child rights governance reproduce existing hierarchies and legitimizes new exclusions. The chapter's central argument is that historicizing rights subjectivities can help us critically engage with how the differential working out of citizenship in post-colonial contexts informs the rights-based claims made by subaltern children and their communities. This historicizing would allow us to better attend to, politicize and thereby work to narrow the stark gap between more recent laws that appear to uphold children's rights and the realization of justice for marginalized communities.

In Chapter 14, **Didier Reynaert** analyzes children's rights through the lens of social constructivism. Drawing on social movement studies, a capita selecta of key events and activities that have played a significant role in the origins of, and developments in, the children's rights movement in Flanders are examined. By studying three distinct time periods in which the Flemish children's rights movement emerged and evolved, various dimensions of the social construction process of children's rights are highlighted. Based on this enquiry, a social constructivist ontology of children's rights is proposed, characterized by three main features: i) children's rights are contextually constructed; ii) the social construction process of children's rights is essentially political; and iii) the social construction process of children's rights is deeply discursive. Through this framework, a contribution is made to the ongoing development of Critical Children's Rights Studies.

Valeria LLobet, Fernanda Bittencourt Ribeiro and Carla Villalta explore, in Chapter 15, the contested nature of children's rights within the sociopolitical contexts of Argentina and Brazil, focusing on their strategic uses by various actors to advance distinct agendas. The chapter critically examines how children's rights, rather than being a straightforward imposition of Western ideals, are dynamically reinterpreted and mobilized in local contexts. The study begins by tracing the historical evolution of children's rights in Latin America, highlighting their role in political struggles against authoritarian regimes and in advocating for marginalized groups. By examining the cases from Brazil and Argentina, the chapter argues for a nuanced understanding of children's rights that acknowledges their strategic deployment in local contexts. It critiques both hegemonic and critical perspectives for failing to fully capture the complex, contested nature of children's rights and calls for an analysis that considers their situated uses in challenging inequalities and injustices.

In Chapter 16 **Daniella Bendo, Dustin Ciufo and Christine Goodwin-De Faria** offer a critical children's rights response that seeks to move beyond the legal focus on implementation and, instead, arrive at a thorough problematization for the field. Specifically, they apply both critical disability theory and a feminist ethics of care to theoretically deconstruct the predominant legal focus, reconstruct alternative pathways and critique the critical approach itself so as to advance practical understanding for the state of neurodiverse justice-involved youth rights in Ontario, Canada.

Chapter 17 by **Anandini Dar** explores the relationship between play, childhood and children's daily life, and offers a critical perspective to children's right to play that moves beyond an individual understanding of rights, as enshrined in the universal UNCRC. By adopting a 'critical as situatedness approach', wherein examining children's right to play is possible through an analysis of the situated experiences of children and their environments in their daily life, this chapter argues that children's right to play manifests in the everyday socio-political and economic contexts in which they grow up and emphasizes the role of political economy and co-generationality in understanding children's right to play.

Therese Boje Mortensen, in Chapter 18, goes beyond critiquing the 'implementation gap' between law and practice that has long been noticed by scholars and practitioners of children's rights, by unpacking and deconstructing the very notion of 'implementation'. In her chapter she empirically studies how India's national child helpline, and thereby children's protection rights, are implemented in the state of Madhya Pradesh in North India. Instead of assuming that 'rights implementation' simply equals a technical application of law by the state, the chapter conceptualizes implementation as a 'lived practice' consisting of the interactive social meeting between children's rights law, its official and unofficial implementers, its beneficiaries (children) and their immediate relations (most often families). By showcasing how such a conceptualization came to be through ethnographic fieldwork, the chapter demonstrates how other critical children's rights researchers methodologically can use ethnography for critical theoretical development.

Finally, in Chapter 19 **Jonathan Josefsson** suggests that the field of Children's Rights Studies is underpinned by the assumption that even more or better inclusion of children in social and political life can act as a source of critique that will lead to societal transformations, children's emancipation and access to justice. However, if the calls for children's inclusion have constituted a continuum in societal and scholarly critique for decades, what is then left of its radical potential for societal transformation and what alternative pathways can we explore for a critical study of children's rights? In the first part, 'inclusion as critique', the chapter outlines some of the ideational roots to the current scholarly drive to include children as a critique of existing norms, practices and structures. In the second part, 'critique after inclusion', the chapter outlines a set of possible pathways forward to engage in critique in the study of children's rights that move beyond a focus on more and better inclusion of children.

Collectively, all those chapters offer an authoritative overview of the current critical perspectives in the field of Children's Rights Studies.

References

Abebe, T. (2013). Interdependent rights and agency: The role of children in collective livelihood strategies in rural Ethiopia. In K. Hanson & O. Nieuwenhuys (eds.) *Reconceptualizing children's rights in international development: Living rights, social justice, translations* (pp. 71–92). Cambridge University Press.

Abebe, T., & Tefera, T. (2014). Earning rights: Discourses on children's rights and proper childhood in Ethiopia. In A. Twum-Danso & N. Ansell (eds.) *Children's lives in an era of children's rights: The progress of the convention on the rights of the child in Africa* (pp. 53–71). Routledge.

Alanen, L. (2011). Critical childhood studies? *Childhood, 18*(2), 147–150.

Arce, M. C. (2015). Maturing children's rights theory: From children, with children, of children. *The International Journal of Children's Rights, 23*(2), 283–331.

Balagopalan, S. (2013). The politics of failure: Street children and the circulation of rights discourses in Kolkata. In K. Hanson & O. Nieuwenhuys (eds.) *Reconceptualizing children's rights in international development: Living rights, social justice, translations* (pp. 133–151). Cambridge University Press.

Balagopalan, S. (2019a). Why historicize rights-subjectivities? Children's rights, compulsory schooling, and the deregulation of child labor in India. *Childhood, 26*(3), 304–320.

Balagopalan, S. (2019b). Teaching "global childhoods": From a cultural mapping of "Them" to a diagnostic reading of "Us/US". In A. Twum-Danso, M. Bourdillon & S. Meichsner (eds.) *Global childhoods beyond the north-south divide* (pp. 13–34). Springer.

Bendo, D. (2020). Parallel lines? Childhood discourses emphasized by the children's rights movement and the emerging field of children's rights studies. *Childhood, 27*(2), 173–187.

Brando, N. (2019). Universalism, embeddedness and domination: An analysis of the Convention on the Rights of the Child. *Journal of Global Ethics, 15*(3), 270–286.

Celikates, R., & Flynn, J. (2023). Critical theory (Frankfurt School). In E. N. Zalta & U. Nodelman (eds.) *The Stanford encyclopedia of philosophy* (Winter 2023 Edition). Retrieved January 20, 2025, from https://plato.stanford.edu/archives/win2023/entries/critical-theory/

Cohen, N. B., Cooper, A., & Mackaway, H. D. (2023). (Re) Imagining children's participatory rights with decolonial learning. *O Social em Questão, 26*(56), 61–88.

Corradi, G., & Desmet, E. (2015). A review of literature on children's rights and legal pluralism. *The Journal of Legal Pluralism and Unofficial Law, 47*(2), 226–245.

Daly, A., Leviner, P., & Thorburn Stern, R. (eds.). (2025). *Treated like a child – non discrimination, children as a group, and international human rights law*, Stockholm Studies in Child Law and Children's Rights. Brill.

de Castro, L. R. (2021). Decolonising child studies: Development and globalism as orientalist perspectives. *Third World Quarterly, 42*(11), 2487–2504.

de Castro, L. R. (2022). Righting adults' wrongs: 'Generationing' on the battlefield: A decolonial approach. *Childhood, 29*(3), 355–370.

De Graeve, K. (2015). Children's rights from a gender studies perspective: Gender, intersectionality and ethics of care. In W. Vandenhole, E. Desmet, D. Reynaert & S. Lembrechts (eds.) *Routledge international handbook of children's rights studies* (pp. 147–163). Routledge.

Desmet, E., Lembrechts, S., Reynaert, D., & Vandenhole, W. (2015). Conclusions: Towards a field of critical children's rights studies. In W. Vandenhole, E. Desmet, D. Reynaert & S. Lembrechts (eds.) *Routledge international handbook of children's rights studies* (pp. 412–427). Routledge.

Farson, R. (1974). *Birthrights*. Collier Macmillan.

Fonseca, C. (2002). The politics of adoption: Child rights in the Brazilian setting. *Law & Policy, 24*(3), 199–227.

Fonseca, C. (2009). Transnational negotiations of the mechanisms of governance. Regularizing child adoption. *VIBRANT-Vibrant Virtual Brazilian Anthropology, 6*(1), 8–36.

Fonseca, C., & Cardarello, A. (2005). Derechos de los más y menos humanos. *Derechos humanos, tribunales y policías en Argentina y Brasil. Estudios de antropología jurídica*. Antropofagia.

Freeman, M. D. (1987). Taking children's rights seriously. *Children & Society, 1*(4), 299–319.

Freeman, M. D. (1998). The sociology of childhood and children's rights. *International Journal of Children's Rights, 6*, 433–444.

Fricker, M. (2007). *Epistemic injustice: Power and the ethics of knowing*. Oxford University Press.

Gross, B., & Gross, R. (eds.). (1977). *The children's rights movement: Overcoming the oppression of young people*. Anchor Press/Doubleday.

Hanna, A. (2022). Silent epistemologies: Theorising children's participation rights. *The International Journal of Children's Rights, 31*(1), 40–60.

Hanson, K. (2014). 'Killed by charity': Towards interdisciplinary children's rights studies. *Childhood, 21*(4), 44–446.

Hanson, K. (2019). Societal impact of academic childhood and children's rights research: Sooner or later? *Childhood, 26*(4), 409–413.

Hanson, K., & Nieuwenhuys, O. (2013). Reconceptualizing children's rights in international development: Living rights. In *Social Justice, Translations*. Cambridge University Press.

Hanson, K., & Peleg, N. (2020). Waiting for children's rights theory. *The International Journal of Children's Rights, 28*(1), 15–35.

Holt, J. C. (1975). *Escape from childhood: The needs and rights of children*. Penguin.

Holzscheiter, A., Josefsson, J., & Sandin, B. (2019). Child rights governance: An introduction. *Childhood, 26*(3), 271–288.

Liebel, M. (2020). *Decolonizing childhoods: From exclusion to dignity*. Policy Press.

Liebel, M., Hanson, K., Saadi, I., & Vandenhole, W. (2012). *Children's rights from below: Cross-cultural perspectives*. Palgrave Macmillan.

LLobet, V. (2011). Childhood policies and rights-based approach in Latin America: Some reflections on its theoretical approach. *Fractal: Revista de Psicologia, 23*, 447–460.

Meekosha, H., & Shuttleworth, R. (2009). What's so 'critical' about critical disability studies? *Australian Journal of Human Rights, 15*(1), 47–75.

Mitchell, R. (2015). Children's rights and citizenship studies: Re-theorising child citizenship through transdisciplinarity from the local to the global. In W. Vandenhole, E. Desmet, D. Reynaert & S. Lembrechts (eds.) *Routledge International Handbook of Children's Rights Studies* (pp. 164–182). Routledge.

Moyn, S. (2018). *Not enough: Human rights in an unequal world*. Harvard University Press.

Quennerstedt, A. (2013). Children's rights research moving into the future: Challenges on the way forward. *The International Journal of Children's Rights, 21*(2), 233–247.

Rensmann, L. (2017). Critical theory of human rights. In M. J. Thompson (ed.) *The Palgrave handbook of critical theory* (pp. 631–653). Springer.

Reynaert, D., Bouverne-de-Bie, M., & Vandevelde, S. (2009). A review of children's rights literature since the adoption of the United Nations Convention on the Rights of the Child. *Childhood, 16*(4), 518–534.

Reynaert, D., Bouverne-De Bie, M., & Vandevelde, S. (2010). *The children's rights movement: A social movement?* Paper presented at the 8th annual TiSSA Conference 'Social Work in Times of Crisis. What can Social Work deliver – And who benefits?' 25–27 August 2010 – Tallinn, Estonia.

Reynaert, D., Bouverne-De Bie, M., & Vandevelde, S. (2012). Between 'believers' and 'opponents': Critical discussions on children's rights. *The International Journal of Children's Rights, 20*(1), 155–168.

Reynaert, D., & Roose, R. (2015). Children's rights from a social work perspective: Towards a lifeworld orientation. In W. Vandenhole, E. Desmet, D. Reynaert & S. Lembrechts (eds.) *Routledge international handbook of children's rights studies* (pp. 94–111). Routledge.

Sandin, B., Josefsson, J., Hanson, K., & Balagopalan, S. (2023). *The politics of children's rights and representation*. Springer Nature.

Songca, R. (2018). The Africanisation of children's rights in South Africa: Quo Vadis? *International Journal of African Renaissance Studies-Multi-, Inter-and Transdisciplinarity, 13*(1), 77–95.

Stalford, H. (2012). *Children and the European Union: Rights, welfare and accountability*. Bloomsbury Publishing.

Takanishi, R. (1978). Childhood as a social issue: Historical roots of contemporary child advocacy movements. *Journal of Social Issues, 34*(2), 8–28.

Tisdall, K., Davis, J., Fry, D., Konstantoni, K., Kustatscher, M., Maternowska, C., & Weiner, L. (2023). *Critical childhood studies: Global perspectives*. Bloomsbury Publishing.

Treviño, A. J., Harris, M. A., & Wallace, D. (2008). What's so critical about critical race theory? *Contemporary Justice Review, 11*(1), 7–10.

Twum-Danso, A. (2024). *Turning global rights into local realities*. Bristol University Press.

Twum-Danso Imoh, A. (2013). Children's perceptions of physical punishment in Ghana and the implications for children's rights. *Childhood, 20*(4), 472–486.

Twum-Danso Imoh, A. (2020). Situating the rights vs. culture binary within the context of colonial history in sub–Saharan Africa. In J. Todres & S. King (eds.) *Oxford handbook on children's rights law* (pp. 427–449). Oxford University Press.

Twum-Danso Imoh, A., Rabello de Castro, L., & Naftali, O. (2022). Studies of childhoods in the Global South: Towards an epistemic turn in transnational childhood research? *Third World Thematics: A TWQ Journal, 7*(1–3), 1–16.

Tyesta, L. A., Saraswati, R., & Arif, F. (2020). Implications of legal positivism of the promotion of children's rights on national law. *Journal of Advanced Research in Law and Economics, 11*(2), 661–666.

Vandenhole, W. (2015). Children's rights from a legal perspective: Children's rights law. In W. Vandenhole, E. Desmet, D. Reynaert & S. Lembrechts (eds.) *Routledge international handbook of children's rights studies* (pp. 27–42). Routledge.

Vandenhole, W., Desmet, E., Reynaert, D., & Lembrechts, S. (eds.). (2015). *Routledge international handbook of children's rights studies*. Routledge.

Vandenhole, W., Vranken, J., & De Boyser, K. (2010). *Why care: Children's rights and child poverty*. Intersentia.

Veerman, P. E. (1992). *The Rights of the child and the changing image of childhood* (pp. 133–152). Brill Nijhoff.

Vergara Del Solar, A., Llobet, V., & Nascimento, M. L. (2021). South American childhoods since the 1990s: Between neoliberalisation and the expansion of rights: An introduction. In A. Vergara del Solar, V. Llobet & M. L. B. Nascimento (eds.) *South American childhoods: Neoliberalisation and children's rights since the 1990s* (pp. 1–43). Springer.

Verhellen, E. (1998). Children's rights: Education and academic responsibilities. In P. D. Jaffé (ed.) *Challenging mentalities: Implementing the United Nations Convention on the Rights of the Child/Défier les mentalités. La mise en oeuvre de la Convention des Nations Unies relative aux droits de l'enfant*, Ghent Papers on Children's Rights No. 4. Children's Rights Centre, University of Ghent.

1 Am I a critical children's rights researcher? A reflexive analysis of the adaptive model of childhood

Nico Brando

1.1 Introduction

Children's rights research has been dominated by doctrinal legal interpretation and analysis (Reynaert et al., 2009). With the UN Convention on the Rights of the Child (UNCRC) as a beacon, research has focused on interpreting UNCRC articles, implementing them, and monitoring compliance (Quennerstedt, 2013). While recognizing children as right-holders and protecting their interests, overreliance on the UNCRC limits the advancement of children's rights beyond current legal prescriptions. Several issues make the current standard for children's rights research problematic.

First, there is a problem with regressivity. Researchers have long shown concern with the 'aging' of the UNCRC (Veerman, 2010). It was drafted and written in a particular geopolitical context, with particular interests in mind, and particular scientific and moral perspectives on the status of children in society. Appealing to the UNCRC as the primary source of normativity on children's rights, slowly, but steadily, turns into a dogmatic relationship (Freeman, 2020). We read articles in the Convention as absolute mandates; if rights are enshrined in the UNCRC, they are the Law; if they are not included, they do not exist. Engagement with novel interpretations of what childhood is, the social and political realities and lived experience of children, and potential new rights and paths forward can be arrested by excessive reliance on the UNCRC as the primary source for research on children's rights (Hägglund & Thelander, 2011).

The second issue is the problem of 'wrongful universality'. Not only does the UNCRC appear as a timeless document, but it is also read as a spaceless document. Childhood has been interpreted as a singular, global phenomenon that affects, and relates to, children everywhere in the same manner (Rabello de Castro, 2020). All children around the globe have the same needs, interests, and rights. In an age sensitive to positionality and intersectionality, this is problematic (Alanen, 2016). It limits our capacity to understand plural forms, and manifestations, of childhood, the varied realities, needs, and interests of children based on their particular context, and the relationality and dynamic relationship between children and their rights (Hanson & Nieuwenhuys, 2013).

DOI: 10.4324/9781003510284-2

Finally, there is the problem of source (Cordero Arce, 2012). We tend to read the UNCRC as if it has come from a higher power, but understanding the power dynamics, political interests, and sources of its drafting and ratification can affect the way we perceive and read it. Mostly white adult men from the Global North (at the end of the Cold War period) drafted the UNCRC. This has a huge impact on what it says, what is included, and excluded. Do we need new sources of rights from different epistemic standpoints? What would it take to develop a truly 'critical' strand of scholarship on children's rights that avoids the issues of regressivity, wrongful universality, and lack of context present in children's rights research that relies too strongly on the UNCRC?

An important aspect of a critical approach to children's rights is its interest in overcoming the limitations of UNCRC-based research, by studying 'children's rights' free from the restrictions that dependence on legal doctrine imposes. Philosophical work on children's rights, in principle, takes this task head on. It does not take the law and doctrine at face value, rather attempting to explore what assumptions, inconsistencies, and biases might be hidden underneath standard understandings and definitions of childhood and children's rights.

As a philosopher, I have always considered myself to be a critical researcher. My work aspires to untangle questionable moral assumptions about issues of justice or equality in order to shed light on our biases, and wrongful constructions. However, despite seeing oneself as critical, we seldom reflect on what this means, and how we find ourselves positioned in relation to critical research. This chapter aims to act as a reflexive exercise on 'what it means to be critical', and to self-assess the standing of my own work within this approach to children's rights.

The five themes proposed in the Introduction to this volume (see Reynaert et al., 2025, Introduction to this volume) offer a valuable cue to embark on this road of self-analysis. Here, I aim to look reflexively at my Adaptive model of childhood and children's rights proposed in my book, *Childhood in Liberal Theory* (Brando, 2024), to evaluate its 'critical' credentials. I believe that this reflexive analysis is a first step when working in a burgeoning field. Merely showcasing our criticality without dissecting it can lead to biased reassurance. Establishing clear elements and guidelines to follow is an important contribution of this book, and this chapter furthers this goal by taking the five themes proposed in it, as elements that allow us to test and assess our critical credentials.

The chapter, first, introduces briefly the five themes proposed, and my Adaptive model of childhood and children's rights. The following sections engage with each one of the elements separately, exploring its features, its requirements, and evaluating my model based on them. I hope that the reflections in this chapter will aid others in the process of understanding what it means to be critical, and for it to provide good practice on how to reflect on one's own work.

1.2 The five elements

The introduction to this book proposes five elements for a critical approach to children's rights: deconstruction, alternative construction, situatedness, positionality, and ongoing critique. First, critical analysis asks us to deconstruct assumptions and 'truths' about childhood and children's rights, questioning the status quo. Researchers must dissect 'obvious beliefs' about children and their rights to reveal problems arising from stereotypes, social norms, and cultural values. It involves dissecting what 'children's rights' and 'childhood' are. Second, critical analysis requires developing new ways of conceiving children's rights. Beyond deconstruction, it necessitates constructing 'alternative normative lines' (see Introduction, this volume), learning from the deconstructive process to propose new approaches. The third element requires critical researchers to engage with childhood and children's rights from the lived experiences of actual children. Situatedness asks researchers to engage with the contextualized and lived reality of the plural ways in which childhood manifests itself. Childhood research cannot be done in a vacuum; it must be situated in the world and the subjective standpoint of children's actual lives and experiences, as well as contextualized in their social environment to meet its mark. Critical research needs to see the world from the eyes of the research subject.

The final two elements relate to the reflexive tasks of the researcher; they require thinking about one's positionality and ongoing re-evaluation of critical standards. Reflexivity involves examining our own positionality and epistemic standpoint as researchers. Doing research about 'the other' can be dangerous; regular checks on 'who we are?' and 'what are we doing?' are necessary to ensure a critical outlook (Jones, 2009). Failure to build this into our processes may lead to biases going unchecked. The final reflexive task involves reflecting on standards of critical research. It requires ongoing critique of what it means to be critical. Proposals of what being critical meant 50 years ago might not meet current 'critical' standards (Tisdall et al., 2023). Reflective research entails being open to shifting discourses, notions, and methodologies surpassing previous 'critical' accounts.

1.3 What is the adaptive model of childhood and children's rights?

Children hold a unique position within society, often perceived as different from adults and subjected to differential treatment in various spheres of life. But should this differential treatment be justified? Are children fundamentally different from adults in a way that justifies their distinct treatment under the law? These are the questions at the heart of *Childhood in Liberal Theory* (Brando, 2024), and the Adaptive model aims to provide an alternative understanding of both childhood and children's rights, which better accounts for the radically diverse realities of children's lives.

Central to my exploration is a critical analysis of liberal theories of childhood, refracted through the lens of what I label an Adaptive Model. Traditionally, liberal perspectives have grappled with how to reconcile the inherent differences between children and adults within the framework of equality and freedom. These perspectives often fall short of fully capturing the nuanced realities of childhood. The Standard Liberal approach typically justifies differential treatment of children by emphasizing their perceived vulnerability and developmental needs (see, for example, Archard, 2004; Brighouse, 2002; Gheaus, 2015). While acknowledging the importance of protecting children and fostering their autonomy, this perspective tends to essentialize childhood as a static stage of dependency (Brando, 2024, pp. 42–60). In contrast, the Liberationist perspective challenges the dichotomy between childhood and adulthood, advocating for equal treatment and recognition of children's agency (see Firestone, 1970; Farson, 1974; Holt, 1974). However, the Liberationist's emphasis on equality fails to account for the diverse needs and interests that stem from vulnerability, development, and children's embeddedness in specific cultural and social contexts (Brando, 2024, pp. 61–81).

An Adaptive model aims to provide an account of childhood and children's rights which accommodates the diversity of children's lives. It opposes accounts of childhood and children's rights which categorize childhood as systematically different from adulthood, thus requiring an all-encompassing differential (protective) treatment. To justify differential categorization of 'childhood', and treatment of children, a model must prove the justifiability of this differentiation based on the actual traits and characteristics of the individual, rather than through social categories. It argues that the traits, characteristics, and behaviours which may legitimize treating someone differently (say, by restricting their right to vote, to work, or to consent) exist throughout the whole life course, and vary substantially among human beings (Brando, 2024, pp. 82–101). Any reflection on justice, equality, and discrimination ought to take into account this variability in an individual's 'Constitutive Frameworks' (Brando, 2024, pp. 83–84), and how they affect their life, and freedoms.

An Adaptive theory argues that the assessment of justified differential treatment is conditioned by an individual's vulnerability (embodied framework), their developmental needs (temporal framework), and their embeddedness in their sociocultural environment (spatial framework), all this accounting for the individual's role as an active agent in their own life.

1.4 Deconstructing concepts and social categories

The Adaptive model starts with a rigorous process of deconstruction of the social category of 'childhood', and the core elements that are included in it. Social categories are among the most prevalent and deep-seated constructions in our social world. We classify, categorize, and assign behavioural traits and characteristics to individuals based on seemingly innocuous information such as gender, race, ethnicity, or age. Assuming who a person is based on social categorizations is, to some extent, inevitable due to our limited cognitive capacities (Schauer, 2003). To respond quickly and efficiently, our brains use information from previous encounters with similar others to engage with the person in front of us (Begby, 2021). Categorizing based on gender, race, or age (say, as 'woman', 'Black', 'child') is inescapable and sometimes necessary, but this does not mean we should take social categories at face value. When we categorize someone as a 'woman' or a 'child', we not only describe an individual; social categorizations come with hidden, sometimes pernicious, normative content (Ásta, 2018). Social constructions act in our brains as blueprints suggesting 'who we think a person is' and as maps guiding how we should treat these individuals, the rights they should have, and the restrictions imposed on them (Haslanger, 2012). If we label someone as a 'child', all assumptions, biases, and stereotypes associated with the label affect how they are treated.

The 'deconstructing' task demanded from the critical researcher requires uncovering these hidden assumptions, biases, and stereotypes to distinguish between meaningful and harmful features of a social category (Mallon, 2016). When using concepts referring to social categories, we must be cautious not to take our intuitive definitions for granted. Instead, we should flesh out the implications of using a particular concept to refer to a group or individual, how it frames and delimits our perceptions, and how it may affect or taint our study of them. My Adaptive model aims to flesh out what is inside a social construction and its implications for how individuals identified as 'children' are treated and perceived as right holders. If the societal construction of 'child' encompasses assumptions of heteronomy and incompetence, the resultant legal and social treatment inevitably reflects these biases (Brando, 2024, pp. 21–41). Consequently, children may find themselves subject to constant supervision, restricted freedoms, and unique protections not extended to other individuals. Take the example of how children are perceived in relation to their right to work (Satz, 2010); assumptions about children's vulnerabilities and lack of agency due to their age determine strict restrictions on their right to work. This does not account for context nor for children's variability in terms of competences and agency. The social category of 'childhood' assumes those categorized as children are put at risk or threatened or harmed by work.

Presumed constructions of 'childhood' are not the only concepts with potentially biased content affecting research. Many standard concepts in children's rights literature (for example, rights, development, vulnerability, freedom, autonomy, competence) may carry biased information. For instance, assuming 'development' as a scientific fact, assuming that individuals pass through strict stages of growth and maturity that lead to a 'normal' adulthood may bias our research on childhood (Goodey, 2021). We might categorize children into stages and periods of mental or moral growth that do not match their reality and lived experiences (Burman, 2008; Lancy, 2015). Awareness of the concepts that we use, awareness of their implications for our research, and a commitment to ensuring that we dissect and test their value and validity is a fundamental step in critical research.

Being critical requires children's rights researchers to exercise caution with the concepts they use, how they use them, and the resulting impact on how human beings are perceived and treated. This is the essence of deconstruction. It involves not only an awareness of hidden biases within our concepts, but also a deliberate acknowledgment of the constraints and potential implications that come with employing a concept. Additionally, it entails establishing clear definitions of key concepts (for example, childhood, rights, development, vulnerability, agency) to clarify which elements of socially constructed concepts are retained and which are rejected.

1.5 The conditions of critical reconstruction

Much critical theory, within the children's rights literature and beyond, has been criticized for stopping short of its full potential (Schaub, 2015). Many focus solely on deconstruction, analyzing and 'debunking' assumptions, biases, and myths within core concepts, without reconstruction. Is it the task of a critical researcher to 'construct alternative pathways' to define and utilize concepts in research? While deconstruction without reconstruction may seem incomplete, it could be seen as part of academic division of labour: some excel in analysis, others in synthesis, methodology, or implementation.

While there can be critical value in reconstructing concepts (Wall, 2019), reconstruction alone is not sufficient to consider an alternative pathway as 'critical'. The critical aspect lies in the content itself, and on how these 'alternative pathways' actually further critical analyses. One could deconstruct a concept and rebuild it in a way that still maintains assumptions, biases, and corrosive content within it. For example, in philosophical debates on the definition of the concept of 'childhood', an important strand of literature in the last couple of decades (see Macleod, 2010; Gheaus, 2015) has attempted to critically deconstruct 'becoming' (Sapling) conceptions of 'childhood', which perceived children as incomplete humans in the process of becoming adults. These approaches, termed as Caterpillar, or Intrinsic Value conceptions of 'childhood' (Tomlin, 2018), endorse that childhood should not be conceptualized as an incomplete stage leading towards 'normal' adulthood, but as having value and interest in itself (Uprichard, 2008; Gheaus, 2015). Children should be understood as beings, with interests and values intrinsic to this period of life, rather than solely dependent on their future value and interests as adults. While Intrinsic Value approaches critically deconstruct Sapling conceptions, they fail to offer a truly 'critical' understanding of 'childhood'. They view certain aspects of childhood (for example, dependence, innocence, freedom from responsibilities, play) as intrinsically valuable, shaping normative notions of justice for children and their rights. This leads to a new reconstruction of 'childhood' that boxes children within a predetermined notion of who they are, who they should be, and what they should value. It imposes a universal notion of 'the child' and expects diverse childhoods to be treated as this universal notion prescribes (Brando, 2024, pp. 52–54). This diverts from the critical agenda (particularly in relation to the themes of situatedness and reflexivity). While it offers tools to question previous understandings, it lacks an untainted 'alternative pathway' (Introduction, this volume) free from assumptions and biases about childhood's value and children's identities.

This example shows that reconstruction alone is not enough to assess critical credentials in children's rights research. We must consider content and procedure within reconstruction to evaluate its critical standards. I think we might need to appeal and test the critical credentials of a reconstructive process based on the other themes introduced in this volume. Does the alternative pathway address tainted concepts? Is it situated in the plural and diverse realities of children's lives? Does it show self-awareness of the researcher's positionality? These are the questions we should ask to assess whether our reconstructions might point in a critical direction.

My own reconstructive pathway, as outlined in my Adaptive model, aims, as a core commitment, to ensure that the normative outcome avoids the issues that affect previous conceptions. It sought to develop a reconstruction of what 'childhood' could be, through a cautious process of analyzing and dissecting some of the core traits which tend to structure our notions of 'childhood' (vulnerability, development, and dependence), and assess up to what point, and what aspects of it could be maintained in a novel reconstruction of the concept and which had to be left out (Brando, 2024, pp. 99–100). After thoroughly dissecting these core concepts, my task was to salvage their useful components for reconstructing an Adaptive 'childhood', while avoiding pitfalls. This involved: first, revising core concepts in a way that avoids binary oppositions between social categories (vulnerable/non-vulnerable; developing/developed; dependent/independent); second, proposing an alternative understanding of these concepts (as embodied, temporal, and spatial frameworks) in which they interact and condition each other; third, situating them within children's sociocultural environment, and showing sensitivity to variabilities in how these traits affect differently situated individuals; and finally, problematizing them through a commitment to understand that the particular impact on individuals is affected, and conditioned, by the individual's position as an agent who adapts and interacts actively with their frameworks.

However, there are limitations to the credentials of my Adaptive model as a critical reconstructive proposal. Instead of entirely discarding socially constructed concepts such as vulnerability, development, and dependence, my Adaptive model attempts to reinterpret these typically 'childish' traits as universal human traits. In other words, it suggests that it is not that children are not vulnerable, developing, or dependent, but rather that every human should be conceptualized as potentially vulnerable, developing, and dependent. While this diverges from standard notions of 'childhood' and standard interpretations of these concepts, their continued structural significance in the book's analysis raises questions about the critical depth of the task. While revising and deconstructing these concepts can help us utilize them without tainted assumptions or biases, alternative interpretations that question the use of these concepts altogether may suggest that the model is insufficiently critical.

My reconstructive endeavour consciously sought not only to provide a critical deconstruction of previous notions of childhood, vulnerability, or development but also to utilize meaningful and relevant content within these concepts without biases, assumptions, and corrosive material derived from top-down impositions through social categorization. It aspires to offer a conceptual framework that can be used to explore the study of children's rights critically. It might raise concerns, however, because it still makes use of certain concepts that can be considered as limiting from a critical standpoint.

1.6 Situating childhood and children's rights

As mentioned in the introduction, a significant issue raised with standard children's rights research is its 'spaceless' quality. Much work tends to treat the UNCRC and children's rights as timeless, spaceless, and source-less. Critical children's rights scholarship aims to address this omission by situating children's rights and lives in time, space, and context. The core critical standpoint is that contrary to standard assumptions about blanket categorizations of children and rights implementation, critical research requires engagement with subjects and topics within historical, cultural, and lived contexts. Childhood and children's rights cannot be studied in isolation; as Hanson and Nieuwenhuys (2013) argue, they should be understood as 'living rights', capable of evolving and adapting to children's circumstances and needs.

A core issue I identified in philosophical research on children's rights is the perception of 'childhood' and 'children's rights' as universal notions interpreted and applied uniformly across child populations (see Brando, 2019; Brando, 2024, pp. 121–145). The two main strands of literature I studied, Standard Liberal and Liberationist approaches, both take strict definitions of childhood and children's rights. Standard Liberals argue that childhood is a strictly different stage of life from adulthood, thus all children can be legitimately treated as different in many aspects of their lives (see Brighouse, 2002; Archard, 2004). On the other hand, Liberationists reject any distinction between childhood and adulthood as legitimate, advocating for strict equality between children and adults in terms of rights (Firestone, 1970; Farson, 1974).

A fundamental critique proposed by my Adaptive model to other philosophical accounts of children's rights is the necessity of considering the spatial framework and sociocultural context in which children and their rights are situated (Brando, 2024, pp. 180–184). Understanding the impact of global normative prescriptions, like international law on children's rights, on the diverse lives and interests of situated children is crucial for assessing their validity. Viewing children as embedded involves exploring how they adapt and accommodate to their environment and circumstances. Not all children are affected equally by similar circumstances, so studying how different forms of childhood engage with their social environment can inform the development of support mechanisms to protect their interests.

Studying the case of children in street situations (CISS) through my adaptive lens revealed numerous flaws and dangers in applying abstract philosophical notions of 'childhood' and children's rights to specific children entrenched in unique socioeconomic realities (Brando, 2024, pp. 240–249). The standard approach to addressing the interests and needs of CISS typically involves a 'rescue and restore' strategy (van Beers, 1996; Committee on the Rights of the Child, 2017). Children should not be on the streets, they should not be free from adult supervision and care, and they should be protected from the harms, threats, and vulnerabilities that life in the street creates for them. CISS should be rescued from the street and restored into a 'normal' childhood, with their guardians and going to school.

Assuming that a 'rescued' life will restore CISS's 'normal' childhood overlooks the complex realities many of these children face (Ennew, 2002). It disregards their past experiences and intricate relationships with family and care institutions. Additionally, it fails to consider the social bonds, relationships, and support networks developed on the streets, as well as their adaption to and navigation of street life. Most importantly, it neglects the need to listen to the demands and requests of CISS themselves regarding their situation from government and lawmakers. Many CISS have fled abusive home environments, rejected inadequate care institutions, and found meaning, freedom, and support in street life. However, this doesn't suggest that street life is beneficial for them, but rather underscores the importance of understanding their needs within their context. We must identify the resources, protections, and freedoms necessary to enhance their well-being and develop scaffolding to facilitate their transition to stable, healthy environments.

Situating childhood and children's rights involves examining how our concepts impact real-life populations. This entails contextualizing children's rights within their socioeconomic and cultural environments, and understanding how children interact with these contexts, adapt to them, and navigate them. This does not mean, however, that we must defer to and take social contexts at face value; situating research implies acknowledging that children's rights are embedded in particular contexts, and that in order to critically evaluate them, we must understand them from within these epistemic standpoints.

1.7 Positionality and reflexive analysis

Being critical involves self-assessment, recognizing one's position, biases, and limitations in conducting research. It requires examining one's privileges and intersectional epistemic standpoint to understand power dynamics and implications on research and outcomes. This entails acknowledging how one's identity as an adult researcher influences the research process and findings. Positionality requires considering how various factors influence our research (for example, age, gender, socioeconomic status), as well as how our ontological and ethical beliefs shape our methods (Darwin Holmes, 2020; Swaminathan & Mulvihill, 2018). Furthermore, it entails extensive self-reflection, not just on our epistemic standpoint's impact but also on the research itself. To truly be critical researchers, we must scrutinize our work, acknowledging where we succeed and where we fall short in meeting the critical standard.

It has been widely stated in recent decades that research in the social sciences cannot be fully 'objective' in its processes and results (Flyvbjerg, 2006). Our subject selection, methodologies, theories, ideologies, and ethical stances all influence both the research process and its outcomes, particularly in studies involving vulnerable populations like children (Moss, 2016; Patton & Winter, 2023). There is, in a sense, an inevitable power dynamic that develops between the privileged position of the (usually, adult) researcher, and the child subjects (Gallagher, 2008). In an attempt to understand how a critical researcher can counter these dynamics, Cuevas-Parra (2023, pp. 299–300) encourages the researcher to make themselves self-aware and reflect on the narratives upon which they are grounding their research, on the social constructions that guide (and may taint) their understanding of their research subjects and topic, and on whether the researcher's methods, approaches, and aims work as 'mirrors' that reflect back on themselves, or whether they work as 'windows' that guide towards other standpoints, views, and stories.

The methodology that grounds my Adaptive model is structured on two sources: reflective equilibrium, and social constructivism. The first is a method in philosophical analysis which aims at developing normative content by testing and reflecting between general moral principles and commitments a research project is based on, and the particular ways in which these principles and commitments are put into practice in specific circumstances and cases (Rawls, 2001). The aim of this Reflective method is for it to ensure, first, clarity on what are the core moral commitments and principles upon which one's research is based on, and second, to make the researcher constantly aware of the fact that these epistemic and moral starting points structure and delimit the type of outcomes that can come out of an evaluation. In my theory, social constructivism (Haslanger, 2012; Ásta, 2018) complements the Reflective method, further testing the consistency, transparency, and potential biases affecting research, through a thorough process of deconstruction of all relevant aspects in the research process. While the Reflective method secures transparency regarding one's moral and ethical starting points and consistency among these starting points and outcomes, social constructivism counters potential biases that affect the circularity of a Reflective method. It requires researchers to test and dissect the concepts used and the principles established based on their interaction and impact on sources, potential power dynamics, and ideological biases.

I must admit, however, that I do not believe my methodology, which demands a constant reflexive attitude and a recurrent dissection of potential biases and assumptions, is sufficient to fully satisfy a critical researcher's commitment to positionality and reflexivity. It merely achieves a part of the job.

It ensures that the research being carried out is sincere and transparent about its moral commitments, limitations, and the ways in which they affect the outcome's normative content. The research takes seriously the ethical claim that children are active agents, with voices, opinions, and unique perspectives, and its normative proposal aims to reflect this. However, it falls short in countering traditional power dynamics and hierarchies between the researcher and subjects and in acknowledging my positionality as an adult conducting research about children. Transparency about one's limitations, however, is not sufficient to pass the critical test. A commitment to positionality and reflexivity demands mechanisms to counter positional biases and limitations, ensuring the full inclusivity of the subjects' viewpoints.

1.8 Ongoing critique: critical when? critical to whom?

A crucial aspect of critical research is its adaptability to changing circumstances and the ability to re-evaluate whether, and to what extent, critical approaches remain relevant. Theories and proposals that once challenged existing assumptions and offered alternative reconstructions may no longer meet the criteria for being considered 'critical' in evolving environments and situations. The reflective element of our standpoint as critical researchers involves an iterative approach to our work. If discourses on a particular topic evolve, if conventional notions and expectations shift, if disciplinary standards are updated, critical research should be prepared to reconsider perspectives, concepts, and methodologies to maintain a critical mindset open to new possibilities and alternatives.

I believe this requires imposing temporal and disciplinary parameters on our role as critical researchers. Critical research should be viewed not only as grounded in specific contexts and linked to our positionality (as discussed in sections 6 and 7 previously) but also in terms of its relevance and critical significance in evolving times and disciplines. In essence, it is crucial to discern 'when' we are critical and 'for whom' we are critical. Regarding my Adaptive model, it is challenging to reassess the critical validity of research still in its infancy. This evaluation is better suited for a later time. However, certain questions should persistently guide this assessment process. Will the normative propositions of my Adaptive model still be pertinent after 20 or 30 years? Will they continue to challenge the established norms? Will my analysis of children's rights to vote, work, or participate in public spaces still interrogate prevailing assumptions about childhood and children's freedoms? How will evolving policies, laws, and political landscapes impact the reception of my proposals? These ongoing inquiries will help gauge the enduring relevance of research over time.

The second aspect of reassessing critical credentials pertains to the impact, influence, and evolution of one's work within the scholarly landscape. This temporal dimension extends beyond changes in laws, policies, and realities to encompass evolving expectations, standards, methodologies, and approaches within our respective disciplines (Dar, 2024). The question arises: Who determines the 'critical' nature of my research? Childhood studies span a spectrum of disciplines, including sociology, geography, law, anthropology, philosophy, psychology, history, and more, each contributing to the field and shaping its discourse (Alanen, 2012). However, what is considered 'critical' within one discipline may not necessarily be viewed the same across others. Despite interdisciplinary exchanges, the perceived criticality of our contributions may vary depending on the disciplinary lens through which they are evaluated (Punch, 2016).

I am acutely aware of the restricted critical scope of my Adaptive model in this regard. The conventional political philosophy of childhood and children's rights appears quite conservative and, in many aspects, outdated when compared to other branches of childhood studies (Archard & Wall, 2022). It predominantly employs a limited set of analytical tools and tends to be insular, often failing to engage deeply with childhood and children's rights research beyond its disciplinary confines. Moreover, it hinges on numerous conceptual assumptions about childhood and children's rights that may not withstand scrutiny beyond abstract philosophical inquiries. The primary aim of my Adaptive model was to highlight the limitations, biases, and issues within the discipline while endeavouring to invigorate philosophical discussions about childhood and children's rights by incorporating and engaging with advancements made in childhood studies across various disciplines. Consequently, much of the work proposed by the Adaptive model does not represent a radical advancement in critical children's rights research beyond philosophical literature. Instead, the Adaptive model draws insights from critical sociological, psychological, anthropological, and legal literature to advance and enrich philosophical discourse.

It is crucial to comprehend our position within the broader landscape of childhood studies beyond our disciplinary boundaries. This understanding fosters humility and awareness regarding our contributions, shortcomings, and the potential beneficiaries of our work. While critical researchers outside the philosophical tradition may indeed benefit from the Adaptive model, it's essential to recognize the specific audience and context for which our critical insights are most relevant. This reflection on our work and limitations as critical researchers necessitates a clear understanding of our intended audience and the communities we aim to impact.

1.9 Conclusion

Moving beyond legal and doctrinal studies on children's rights requires new ideas, novel methodologies and ways of thinking. This chapter aimed to contribute to this endeavour by both explaining what critical research in children's rights requires and carrying out a reflexive analysis of my own work in relation to those critical standards. Labelling ourselves as either critical or uncritical falls short of elucidating the complexity of research in the field and our position within it. The same study can be radically critical in some respects, and incredibly conservative or regressive in others. This is not necessarily a bad thing. We must start by understanding where we stand, who we are, and what our work does. By carrying out this reflexive analysis we can locate ourselves better within our discipline, learn from our mistakes, and work towards research methods and practices that better reflect the goals that we aspire to reach.

References

Alanen, L. (2012). Disciplinarity, interdisciplinarity and childhood studies. *Childhood, 19*(4), 419–422.

Alanen, L. (2016). "Intersectionality" and other challenges to theorizing childhood. *Childhood, 23*(2), 157–161.

Archard, D. (2004). *Children: Rights and childhood* (2nd ed.). Routledge.

Archard, D., & Wall, J. (2022). The value of theory for child-related research. In N. Brando, D. Lawson & H. Stalford (eds.) *Children in theory: Theoretical methods and approaches to the study of childhood.* Online Masterclass Series. University of Liverpool. Retrieved January 15, 2025, from www.liverpool.ac.uk/humanities-and-social sciences/research/researchthemes/children-childhood/children-in-theory/introduction/

Ásta. (2018). *Categories we live by. The construction of sex, gender, race, and other social categories.* Oxford University Press.

Begby, E. (2021). *Prejudice: A study in non-ideal epistemology.* Oxford University Press.

Brando, N. (2019). Universalism, embeddedness and domination: An analysis of the convention on the rights of the child. *Journal of Global Ethics, 15*(3), 270–286.

Brando, N. (2024). *Childhood in liberal theory: Equality, difference and children's rights.* Oxford University Press.

Brighouse, H. (2002). What rights if any do children have? In D. Archard & C. M. Macleod (eds.) *The moral and political status of children* (pp. 31–52). Oxford University Press.

Burman, E. (2008). *Deconstructing developmental psychology* (2nd edition). Routledge.

Committee on the Rights of the Child. (2017). *General comment No. 21 on children in street situations.* Adopted 21 June 2017 [CRC/C/GC/21].

Cordero Arce, M. (2012). Maturing children's rights theory. *The International Journal of Children's Rights, 23*(2), 283–331.

Cuevas-Parra, P. (2023). Positionality and reflexivity: Recognising and dismantling our privileges in childhood research through the use of windows and mirrors. *Global Studies of Childhood, 13*(4), 295–309.

Dar, A. (2024). A new "discipline" or a "conversational community". In B. P. Remesh & R. Kumar (eds.) *Practicing interdisciplinarity: Convergences and contestations* (pp. 210–222). Routledge.

Darwin Holmes, A. G. (2020). Researcher positionality – a consideration of its influence and place in qualitative research: A new researcher guide. *Shanlax – International Journal of Education, 8*(4), 1–10.

Ennew, J. (2002). Outside childhood: Street children's rights. In B. Franklin (ed.) *The new handbook of children's rights. Comparative policy and practice* (pp. 388–403). Routledge.

Farson, R. (1974). *Birthrights.* Macmillan Publishers.

Firestone, S. (1970). *The dialectics of sex.* Bantam Books.

Flyvbjerg, B. (2006). Social science that matters. *Foresight Europe, 2*, 38–42.

Freeman, M. (2020). *A Magna Carta for children? Rethinking children's rights.* Cambridge University Press.

Gallagher, M. (2008). Foucault, power and participation. *The International Journal of Children's Rights, 16*(3), 395–406.
Gheaus, A. (2015). Unfinished adults and defective children: On the nature and value of childhood. *Journal of Ethics and Social Philosophy, 9*(1), 1–21.
Goodey, C. (2021). *Development: The history of a psychological concept.* Cambridge University Press.
Hägglund, S., & Thelander, N. (2011). Children's rights at 21: Policy, theory, practice introductory remarks. *Education Inquiry, 23*, 365–372.
Hanson, K., & Nieuwenhuys, O. (2013). Living rights, social justice, translations. In K. Hanson & O. Nieuwenhuys (eds.) *Reconceptualizing children's rights in international development* (pp. 3–26). Cambridge University Press.
Haslanger, S. (2012). *Resisting reality: Social construction and social critique.* Oxford University Press.
Holt, J. (1974). *Escape from childhood.* John Holt GWS Press.
Jones, O. (2009). Approaching the otherness of childhood: Methodological considerations. In L. van Blerk & M. Kesby (eds.) *Doing children's geographies* (pp. 195–212). Routledge.
Lancy, D. F. (2015). *The anthropology of childhood: Cherubs, chattel, changelings* (2nd edition). Cambridge University Press.
Macleod, C. (2010). Primary goods, capabilities, and children. In H. Brighouse & L. Robeyns (eds.) *Measuring justice: Primary goods and capabilities* (pp. 174–192). Cambridge University Press.
Mallon, R. (2016). *The construction of human kinds.* Oxford University Press.
Moss, P. (2016). Where am I? Position and perspective in researching early childhood education. In A. Farrell, S. L. Kagan & E. K. M. Tisdall (eds.) *The SAGE handbook of early childhood research* (pp. 89–102). Sage Publications.
Patton, K., & Winter, K. (2023). Researcher positionality in eliciting young children's perspectives. *Journal of Early Childhood Research, 21*(3), 303–313.
Punch, S. (2016). Cross-world and cross-disciplinary dialogue: A more integrated, global approach to childhood studies. *Global Studies of Childhood, 6*(3), 352–364.
Quennerstedt, A. (2013). children's rights research moving into the future – challenges on the way forward. *The International Journal of Children's Rights, 21*(2), 233–247.
Rabello de Castro, L. (2020). Why global? Children and childhood from a decolonial perspective. *Childhood, 27*(1), 48–62.
Rawls, J. (2001). *Justice as fairness: A restatement.* The Belknap Press of Harvard University Press.
Reynaert, D., Bouverne-de-Bie, M., & Vandevelde, S. (2009). A review of children's rights literature since the adoption of the United Nations Convention on the Rights of the Child. *Childhood, 16*(4), 518–534.
Reynaert, D., Vandenhole, W., Twum-Danso Imoh, A., & Llobet, V. (2025). Critical Children's Rights Studies: Introduction. In V. Llobet, D. Reynaert, A. Twum-Danso Imoh & W. Vandenhole (eds.) *Critical Children's Rights Studies: A research companion.* Routledge.
Satz, D. (2010). *Why some things should not be for sale.* Oxford University Press.
Schaub, J. (2015). Misdevelopments, pathologies, and normative revolutions: Normative reconstruction as method of critical theory. *Critical Horizons, 16*(2), 107–130.
Schauer, F. (2003). *Profiles, probabilities and stereotypes.* The Belknap Press of Harvard University Press.
Swaminathan, R., & Mulvihill, T. M. (2018). *Teaching qualitative research: Strategies for engaging emerging scholars.* The Guilford Press.
Tisdall, K., Davis, J., Fry, D., Konstantoni, K., Kustatscher, M., Maternowska, C., & Weiner, L. (eds.). (2023). *Critical childhood studies: Global perspectives.* Bloomberg.
Tomlin, P. (2018). Saplings or caterpillars? Trying to understand children's wellbeing. *Journal of Applied Philosophy, 35*(S1), 29–46.

Uprichard, E. (2008). Children as "being and becomings": Children, childhood and temporality. *Children & Society*, *22*, 303–313.
van Beers, H. (1996). A plea for a child- centred approach in research with street children. *Childhood*, *3*, 195–201.
Veerman, P. (2010). The ageing of the UN convention on the rights of the child. *International Journal of Children's Rights*, *18*, 585–618.
Wall, J. (2019). From childhood studies to childism: Reconstructing the scholarly and social imaginations. *Children's Geographies*, *20*(3), 257–270.

2 Children's liberation

A critical return to the radical work of Shulamith Firestone

Edward van Daalen

2.1 Introduction

In 1970, Shulamith Firestone (1945–2012) published her groundbreaking work, *The Dialectic of Sex: The Case for Feminist Revolution* (Firestone, 1970). The book is first and foremost a utopian manifesto for a world in which women and children (as well as men, eventually) are liberated from the oppression of capitalist patriarchy. Based on a feminist reading of Marxist and Freudian theory, she observed that biological reproduction, the nuclear heterosexual family and 'childhood' have sealed the economic dependency of women and children on men. In Firestone's (1970, p. 206) vision, once women are freed from the 'tyranny of their productive biology by every means available', and once the 'family' and 'childhood' as central units of society have been abolished, our social and economic structures can be transformed to accommodate women's and children's self-determination, including political, economic and sexual autonomy. Because of its radical ideas and revolutionary intent, *The Dialectic of Sex* found a wide readership at the time,[1] including two men whose names will sound familiar to most who studied children's rights: John Holt and Richard Farson.

We know this, because a few years later both Holt and Farson cited Firestone in their own books on children's liberation, respectively *Escape from Childhood: The Needs and Rights of Children* (Holt, 1974) and *Birthrights: A Bill of Rights for Children* (Farson, 1974). Besides being published at the same time, the books are, to use the words of the reviewer for the New York Times, 'remarkably similar in rhetoric and substance' (Levine, 1974, Section 7, p. 4). In this essay, I argue that the reason for this is that they are each but a deradicalized, liberal iteration of Firestone's critique of 'childhood' as described in *The Dialectic of Sex*. After stripping it from its feminist and revolutionary intent, what was left by Holt and Farson was a call to recognize children's self-determination by providing children with equal legal rights as

1 For a discussion of the support and critique *The Dialectic of Sex* received at the time, see Margree (2018, Chapter 1).

DOI: 10.4324/9781003510284-3

adults, such as the right to vote, to work, to own property and to choose one's own place to live.

Whereas the 'equal rights' thesis is, in its own right, an interesting debate,[2] the problem lies with the fact that is has come to define the term 'children's liberation' in mainstream children's rights scholarship. As such, children's liberation has been generally dismissed as a 'silly' theoretical precursor of what would become a 'serious' scholarly field preoccupied with the praxis of the 1989 United Nations Convention on the Rights of the Child (UNCRC), a growing pain worth mentioning to show 'our' strength in overcoming it. This form of semantic bleaching, I argue, has created a liberal 'liberation bias' in the field, effectively shielding it from Firestone's radical theory and her implicit, yet fundamental gender critique of the family-centred UNCRC project, and its role in sustaining a form of global capitalist patriarchy.

The aim of this chapter is to lay the groundwork for addressing this bias, by making the case for why Firestone should not be considered as part of the 'liberation through equal rights movement', as some children's rights historiographies make it out to be, but rather as its first, pre-emptive critic. This is important because while Firestone's manifesto is not without serious flaws, her arguments for the abolition of 'the family' and of 'childhood' remain a powerful alternative to 'mainstream' children's rights praxis. Furthermore, a new generation of radical scholars such as Sophie Lewis (2021a, 2021b, 2022) and M.E. O'Brien (2023) is addressing similar questions that Firestone raised back then. This growing body of work constitutes a valuable source of critical theory to question the centrality of 'the family' and 'childhood' in the UNCRC project, and what doing away with these institutions would mean for 'children's rights'. In what follows, I read the works of Holt and Farson against that of Firestone to elaborate, and substantiate, my claims and arguments, and I will do so with the help of John Irving's (1981) novel *The Hotel New Hampshire*. The novel has been rightly lauded as a 'modern fable' (Leonard, 1981), and like all good fables it is full of existential themes and moral dilemmas that resonate and illustrate well beyond the plot.

2.2 Dark Inge and *The Hotel New Hampshire*

The story of *The Hotel New Hampshire* (Irving, 1981) is set in the decades following World War II and revolves around the Berry family that manages a series of hotels. One of the hotels is located in Vienna, Austria, where the Berrys find themselves living in between a collective of sex workers, who lodge on the ground floor below them, and a group of political radicals who have taken over the upper floor. Loud screams are commonplace indications of the sex workers trying to make ends meet, while the relentless sound of typewriters

2 See for instance Hafen (1976), Archard (1993, Chapter 5, 6), Purdy (1994), McGillivray (1994), Byrne (2016).

is the audible evidence that the radicals are working on the means to their revolutionary ends.

The four Berry children are raised by all those who inhabit the hotel, and quickly befriend 'Dark Inge', the 11-year-old daughter of one of the sex workers. What makes the subplot of Dark Inge disturbing is that she is herself involved in Hotel's sex trade, even if 'she worked as a tease; [and] she was not a real whore' (Irving, 1981, p. 224). Men can only look at her, she is not allowed to take her clothes off, and she is never to be alone. In fact, Susie, the hotel's bear (it is a rather long story), guards over her at all times. Despite this 'security system' designed to keep her as 'safe' as possible, Dark Inge 'had a most unhappy life' (Irving, 1981, p. 224). Yet the Berrys accept the situation, in all its complexity, as it is situated within the particular space of the Hotel New Hampshire.

But when more conventional morality penetrates the walls of the hotel, in the form of a Rockwellian American nuclear family that rents a room for a few nights, the Berrys are forced to face their norm myopia. One evening, the guests are drawn out of their room by loud screams coming from the ground floor. Assuming that someone is being murdered, the husband, wife and their young daughter make a scene in which the four Berry children, their father and Dark Inge all become involved. Once the notion that the hotel is populated by sex workers dawns on the American husband, Dark Inge ups the ante by identifying herself as one of them: 'We're all whores. . . . What's wrong with that?' (Irving, 1981, p. 269). Now understanding that the screams are a result of sex instead of a murder, the husband grabs his daughter and covers her ears. 'You should be ashamed,' her mother snaps, 'Exposing children to this sordid life' (Irving, 1981, p. 269). Even though one of the Berry children recognizes the entrenched hypocrisy in the parents' behaviour when she remarks that 'They would bring their daughter to see a murder, but they wouldn't even let her hear about an orgasm' (Irving, 1981, p. 268), the Berry father is clearly taken aback when confronted with the hegemonic conception of children as innocent, apolitical and asexual beings, that are best raised within a conventional heterosexual nuclear family and are to spend their days learning at school.

There is little debate over whether this particular conception of childhood was on the mind of most of those involved in drafting the UNCRC (Holzscheiter, 2010). Whereas the UNCRC is generally lauded for recognizing children as 'subjects' rather than 'objects' of rights, its provisions are first and foremost aimed at protection, which subjects children to a regime governed by what adults believe is their 'best interest' (Pupavac, 2001). This paternalistic approach, as embodied and articulated by the American family, prescribes that the children of the Hotel New Hampshire are best placed in a 'real', conventional family so they can get their childhood 'back'.

But just after the accusatory dust of the scene has settled and all children are sent back to their rooms, a sudden loud noise is produced by the revolutionaries residing on the upper floor. The noise, the story will later reveal, came from the making of a large bomb devised to blow up the Vienna Opera House, which, if it were to be successful, would announce the beginning of their revolution to liberate society. From what exactly remains unclear, but in the words of one of the characters, they sought to 'change fucking everything . . . to start again . . . to wipe the slate clean . . . a whole new ball game' (Irving, 1981, p. 220). When taken as an invitation to explore what 'liberation' would mean for the children in the hotel, almost all roads in 'mainstream' children's rights scholarship lead to John Holt and Richard Farson.

2.3 Holt and Farson: 'Radical' Reformers

Holt (1923–1985) was trained as an educator and worked as a schoolteacher in Boston for many years. Before he wrote *Escape from Childhood* (Holt, 1974), he had already published several books on the failing public education system and would become a fierce proponent of a form of homeschooling known as 'unschooling', and continues to be well-regarded as one of the more important early figures of this movement.[3] Farson (1926–2017) was the more conventionally 'academic' of the two, having received his PhD in psychology. *Birthrights* (Farson, 1974) was his first work directly addressing children. The main problem, both authors agree (as they agree on pretty much everything else), is that what we think is good for children, i.e. subjecting them to our current conception of childhood, is mostly bad for them. By thinking that we are keeping children safe by segregating them from (most other) adults within the confines of the nuclear family and school, we are actually oppressing them into a private life of obedience, servitude and 'cuteness', in which they can do very little against the many harms and dangers that they experience in these so-called 'safe spaces'. For both Holt and Farson, the key to liberating children lies in recognizing that children too have a right to self-determination and that, subsequently, they should be granted equal, or at least similar, civil, social, economic and political rights as adults.[4]

However, they argued that this does not mean that we should just leave children to fend for themselves. Nor do they suggest that we should accept situations which are rightfully criminalized, such as the sexual exploitation of children. Instead, under a system of children's rights as conceived by Holt and Farson, children who, like Dark Inge, find themselves in severely detrimental situations would be able to call on all the rights that adults have in trying to change their situation. Dark Inge would have the right to leave and live somewhere else if that is what she wanted. She, of course, has the right to go to school, but she would equally have the right to not go to school and to, instead, earn money by doing appropriate, preferably meaningful, work

3 See, for instance, Dickerson (2019).

4 Holt, for instance, argues for a system in which children can opt in and out of 'self-determination', and that adults are to respect both choices, autonomy or dependency, as well as the rights attached to the respective statuses.

through which she is positively socialized. She would also have the right to political participation to try to change the broader socio-economic structures around her. Whereas her role in the sex trade is immoral and illegal, she should, Holt and Farson would both argue, be free to explore her own sexuality with other children, and even with adults, as long as all parties involved consent.

The two books were widely sold, publicized, discussed and reviewed, including pieces in *Newsweek* and *The New York Times*. Children's rights scholar Philip Veerman wrote in his influential early work that Holt and Farson are 'unquestionably the two most important exponents of the Children's Liberation Movement' (1992, p. 133). Yet, in children's rights scholarship, little intellectual value is attributed to this equal rights 'movement' itself. In defence of separated rights regimes, Michael Freeman (1979) provided the first substantial 'mainstream' children's rights critique of Holt and Farson.[5] His main problem with their accounts was that he believed them to be willfully ignorant of the fact that children have different vulnerabilities, needs, claims and interests. Freeman takes issue with the centrality of a child's right to self-determinism, especially since children cannot be expected to produce the duties and responsibilities that come with having most 'adult' rights, nor the capability to give well-considered consent to something as precarious as sexual relations. Freeman, thus, came to the often-cited conclusion that what Holt and Farson were arguing for was 'politically naive, philosophically faulty and psychologically wrong' (1979, p. 13).[6] A few years later, another major figure in children's rights studies, philosopher David Archard, dedicated two chapters of his influential book *Children: Rights and Childhood* (1993) to Holt and Farson, in which he exposes the flaws in the internal 'logic' of their propositions, taking particular aim at their rather flimsy conceptions of age, capacity and consent. But perhaps the fiercest critique of the equal rights thesis was given by Laura Purdy (1994) who, crudely put, argued that the millions of children who are suffering from violence and hunger need to be 'practically' protected, not 'legally' liberated. Her second, consequentialist critique is that 'giving' children equal rights will result in a society that is even worse off, because children 'have relatively undeveloped capacities to function prudentially and morally' (Purdy, 1994, p. 229). Despite some academic following,[7] and some later attempts to more favourably engage with Holt and Farson,[8] these early critiques by Freeman, Archard and Purdy sealed the fate of what many consider to be a radical challenge to mainstream children's rights praxis.

5 For a more critical discussion of the separate childhood laws and rights, see Hanson (2016).

6 In his later work, Freeman's view of Holt and Farson became less harsh. Referring to himself perhaps, Freeman wrote that 'the children's liberation movement was ridiculed at the time', and suggests that it is possible that the movement had some influence on the development of the UNCRC, and that it deserved a reassessment (2014, p. 4).

7 In particular with the work of Howard Cohen (1980) and later that of Manfred Liebel (2004, 2013).

8 See, for instance, Byrne (2016) and Peleg (2019).

But how radical is the equal rights thesis really? 'Not very', the revolutionaries on the upper floor of the Hotel New Hampshire would instantly, and unanimously, conclude. 'This is no liberation, no revolution', they would shout from above, 'but mere reform'. And as with all reformist projects, 'children's liberation through equal rights' was subject to a critique that sought to understand it within the status quo, within the rules of the game. A 'truly' revolutionary plan for children's liberation can be found in Firestone's work *The Dialectic of Sex*, which, as I mentioned earlier on, is one of the few works cited by both Holt and Farson. In a short paragraph, Holt discusses *The Dialectic of Sex*, but only to directly quote from Firestone's elaborate discussion of the work of historian Philippe Ariès, which, as we will see, she took as material evidence for the notion that modern childhood is but a social construct. In the few sentences that Farson dedicates to Firestone, he, at least, recognizes, albeit in passing, her foundational understanding that children's liberation is a feminist concern, but then emphasizes a peripheral point about children not being able to write their own manifestos, seemingly to justify why a middle-aged man is calling for the liberation and self-determination of children. But a careful reading of *Escape from Childhood* and *Birthrights* against *The Dialectic of Sex* makes it abundantly clear that both Holt and Farson rely much more heavily on Firestone's work than they make it out to be, which goes towards explaining the curious similarity between *Escape from Childhood* and *Birthrights*. Besides Firestone's reading of Ariès, Holt and Farson both also reproduce her critical analysis of the production and reproduction of the oppressive power dynamics within the nuclear family, her critique of compulsory schooling as an oppressive institution, her critical account of children's 'cuteness', as well as her call for children's liberation through self-determination and economic, political and sexual autonomy. However, they entirely leave out the radical feminist theory and revolutionary intent which, as I will show in what follows, lies at the heart of Firestone's project.

2.4 Shulamith Firestone: down with childhood

Firestone was born in Canada, and grew up in the American Midwest where, during the 1960s, she became heavily involved in the women's liberation movement, fighting for a feminist revolution (Margree, 2018). She founded several radical feminist groups and was, much like the revolutionaries of the upper floor of the Hotel New Hampshire, dedicated to nothing less than a radical overhaul of everything or, in her own words, 'a matter-antimatter explosion, ending with a poof! culture itself' (Firestone, 1970, p. 190). The *Dialectic of Sex* was her magnum opus, in which she presented her view of radical feminism which, she emphasized, cannot be contained by the words 'political' or 'revolution', 'because they are not big enough: radical feminism bursts through them' (Firestone, 1970, p. 1). In her postrevolutionary feminist utopia, women and children have been liberated from patriarchy, as the social institutions that sustain it (in particular biological reproduction, the nuclear family and childhood) have been abolished.

As the title of her book suggests, for the theoretical foundation of her feminist revolution Firestone built on Marx and Engels and their theory of historical materialism. In her opening chapter she observes that socialist theorists who proceeded them, the likes of Charles Fourier and Robert Owen, who had their work published in the early 19th century, had been merely moralizing about inequalities, projecting an ideal world in which privilege and exploitation 'should' not exist. The first wave of feminists should be understood in a similar vein, she argues, since they merely conceived of a world without male privilege and exploitation, to be established by the virtue of good will. Similar to how Marx and Engels dared to expose how the unequal social and cultural development of society is driven by a class struggle over the means of production, Firestone pushed feminist theory further to identify not the dialectic of class, but that of sex as the principal driver of the social oppression and economic inequality under a capitalist patriarchy. What she sought to develop was 'a materialist view of history based on sex itself', by which she meant to draw a circle around Marxist historical materialism, so that it is included within a larger critical analysis of sex as class (Firestone, 1970, p. 5). In her view, for all that they got right, Marx and Engels failed to (sufficiently) recognize that the original division of labour between man and woman, for the purpose of child breeding, is not distinct from the means of production, but lies at its core. Firestone does not contest that difference in sex comes from biological reality, but argues that this fact does not necessitate the development of a class system since there is nothing 'natural' about it. The goal of her feminist revolution was thus not just the elimination of male privilege, but of sex distinction itself. She was out to create a world in which biological sex no longer matters 'culturally'. Otherwise, she was convinced, those who yield power (i.e. upper-class men) will surely find a way to keep women and children in a system of exploitation.[9]

In what follows I will focus on the children's liberation dimension of her feminist revolution, most of which is presented in the chapter 'Down with Childhood'. But a few words on some of the highly problematic aspects of Firestone's manifesto are warranted. To start with the most glaring one: her

9 The other major influential theory on which she built her blueprint for a feminist revolution is the Freudian belief that much of our psychology can be boiled down to the tension between 'sex' dynamics within the nuclear family and the reality of what lies outside of it. While Firestone considers this to be a foundational understanding in support of her arguments, she takes aim at Freud's theory, and even more with the supposed solution, i.e. psychoanalytic therapy, for accepting the status quo, for not questioning the oppressive patriarchal family and society at large, and for thinking that 'we' need to be adjusted to function within the system, instead of the other way around. Only through a radical feminist lens, Firestone posits, does Freudianism help us understand what to undo in revolution. For a more in-depth, critical discussion of Firestone's engagement with Freudian theory, see Margree (2018, Chapter 6).

chapter on race in America is deeply problematic and is in itself racist. Instead of grounding her analysis in a critical race theory that recognizes the wake of colonialism and slavery, she uses Freudian theory to explain why the race 'question' should be understood as a sex 'question' in an attempt to show that her sex class analysis lies at the root of all social problems; a proposition that has been rightly judged as 'old racist sophistry' and a 'theoretical clusterfuck' (Lewis, 2021a, p. 209). Firestone also presents a rather ambiguous account of homosexuality, again steeped in Freudian theory, which can be interpreted as sketchy at best and downright homophobic at worst. Sophie Lewis, who says she both admires and loathes *The Dialectic of Sex*, contends that these flaws are big enough to be fatal, but I agree with her that Firestone, nevertheless, deserves our critical attention for 'charting the way to a place where it would be possible to be a heterosexual feminist, a femme intellectual, and a comrade child' (Lewis, 2021a, p. 215).

One of Firestone's basic tenets is that yes, mothers and children are tied by a special bond, but that it is one of shared oppression. The core of women's oppression is her childbearing and rearing. Children are necessarily defined (socially, culturally, psychologically) in relation to this role, and will reproduce it, either as man or a woman. We, therefore, cannot speak about women's liberation without children's liberation and vice versa. Yet, she recognizes the danger of lumping women and children together, and, thus, stresses that one of the revolutionary demands should be that children are no more women's charge than anyone else's. But until the revolution, radical feminists need to include the oppression of children in any attempt at a feminist revolution, to avoid making the same mistake as Marx and Engels who did not go deep enough in their analysis.[10]

Firestone's view of 'modern' childhood is, to put it gently, less than favourable. In no uncertain terms she posits that 'childhood is hell' and that it is, therefore, no wonder it brings forth 'the insecure, and therefore aggressive/defensive, often obnoxious little person we call a child' (Firestone, 1970, p. 103). To explain how this 'childhood hell' is equally rooted in sex class, and how it is something of our own making that we can remake if we want to, she heavily draws on Philippe Ariès' now famous book, *Centuries of Childhood: A Social History of Family Life* (Ariès, 1962). In it, he makes the case that our current conception of childhood 'did not exist' until the Middle Ages, and that there is nothing 'natural' about keeping children segregated from most of the adult world.[11] There were no family 'homes' as we know them now, only

10 For various critical discussions of the debate over the relation between feminism and critical childhood studies, many of which engage with this dimension of Firestone's book, see Rosen and Twamley (2018).

11 While contested ever since it appeared (in particular its scope, methods and blind spots), the idea that the nuclear family and childhood are not 'natural' but social constructs, or 'invented institutions', is one that has shaped the new sociology of childhood studies. For an insightful analysis of *Centuries of Childhood*, its praise and critique, see Retford (2016).

large, collective 'households' in which people lived. There was a sex difference between men and women, but not an adult–child one.

With Ariès' theory on dress codes, Firestone believed she had found concrete historical and material evidence for her theory of sex class reproduction through the nuclear family, and, thus, for the further shared oppression of women and children. According to Ariès, only upper-class boys would, at one point, be given special clothing to mark their transition into adulthood. Girls and working-class boys did not 'need' special clothes, as they did not need to be 'freed' from childhood, because they would come to serve upper-class men and forever remain 'children' of the reigning classes. The accompanying system of education further exposed the sex class basis of childhood, since it was initially not for girls and working-class boys. From this, Firestone understood children of every class to be lower class, just like women, with only upper-class boys being freed from it to become oppressing heads of nuclear households themselves.

Having established this, Firestone then rebukes the idea that things got better since. She argues that the increasing privatization of family life brings ever more oppression to children. Instead of emancipating, we have merely expanded children's oppression through schooling during the 20th century, which has only brought about the pseudo-emancipation of children. If she would have continued her critical writing,[12] she would have likely ripped into the children's rights movement revolving around the UNCRC for being instrumental in the further institutionalization of this pseudo-emancipation throughout the 21st century. She, furthermore, recognizes that the historical myth of childhood, which was only really intended for upper-class children anyway, continues today through the commodification of childhood, i.e. buying and organizing things to make sure childhood is a happy and segregated place until the moment we have no choice but to confront young people with the perils of adulthood, and until it is time for them to start planning their role in their own oppressive family. This has created a system in which adults are merely projecting on the child what they wished they still had, namely a sense of 'duty-free' freedom.

Going back to the Hotel New Hampshire, Firestone would admire, and encourage, the kind of collective childcare that is practiced. It provides a glimpse into the type of alternative living arrangement that in her feminist utopia would be widely available to all. Firestone would also applaud the fact that the children are actively involved in the politics and economics of the hotel. She sees this as a precondition for more 'open' child–adult relationships, which are to be determined by both sides, as 'some adults might prefer certain children over others, just as some children might prefer certain adults over others' (Firestone, 1970, p. 233). This would, controversially and

12 As recounted by Margree (2018), Firestone retracted herself from the public and political sphere not long after the publication of *The Dialectic of Sex*.

problematically, include sexual relationships between children, and between children and adults. As with all components of their respective liberation projects, Firestone's thinking goes much deeper than Holt's and Farson's, who merely see sexual freedom as part of the child's right to self-determination. Firestone reasons, through a feminist reading of Freud, that once the 'incest taboo' attached to the nuclear family is lifted by the abolition of the latter, there is no reason to continue to suppress the sexuality of women and children. However, shifting between Freud and Marx, as she does throughout her book, she would read the situation of Dark Inge through a feminist-Marxist lens, i.e. an extreme and perverse outcome of the inherently oppressive and exploitative nature of capitalist patriarchy.

Firestone would not have spent too much time arguing with the sex workers, the Berrys and the American nuclear family on the ground floor about what is right or wrong, appropriate or inappropriate. And for her, the 'equal rights' debate over whether to recognize and institutionalize 'special' children's rights to protect them or to extend to them the full package of rights so they can protect themselves is for now irrelevant. Because arguing that children should have the right to vote, or to drive or to own property remains an aesthetic project that will not contribute to children's liberation, and will ultimately only benefit upper-class men (current or becoming), as long as it is not also part of a feminist revolution to dismantle capitalist patriarchy by abolishing the family and childhood altogether. She, instead, would run up the stairs to make sure the radicals on the upper floor went deep enough in their thinking about 'sex as class' for their postrevolutionary world.

2.5 Concluding remarks

I hope to have made clear that the project shared by Holt and Farson relates to that of Firestone in the same way that, in Firestone's view, the work of Fourier and Owen relates to that of Marx and Engels. Namely, as a naïve and reformist endeavour which never got much further than moralizing about inequalities and projecting an ideal world into a political vacuum, vis-à-vis a radical, revolutionary social theory which dares to fundamentally challenge the institutions and gender dynamics that are generally considered to be 'natural'. The main difference being that the work of Marx and Engels succeeded that of Fourier and Owen, which Firestone considered to be theoretical progress, whereas Holt and Farson took Firestone's revolutionary manifesto, isolated her call for children's liberation and removed it of its radical feminist intent to serve their liberal project of liberation through equal rights. It is hardly surprising that the bourgeoning scholarly field of children's rights studies latched onto this latter iteration of 'children's liberation', which could be understood, critiqued and dismissed within the familiar parameters of the UNCRC. Moreover, by defining 'children's liberation' as such, the field effectively shielded itself from the fundamental gender critique that Firestone's account poses for the UNCRC project and its fetishization of 'childhood' within the nuclear family.

Firestone herself noted that

> The classic trap for any revolutionary is always, 'What's your alternative?' But even if you could provide the interrogator with a blueprint, this does not mean he would use it: in most cases he is not sincere in wanting to know.
>
> (Firestone, 1970, p. 226)

At the time of writing this, thousands of Palestinian children have been ruthlessly killed or injured by Israeli bombs within the span of a year, with many more facing all but certain death. The leading cause of death of children in the US is gun violence, and all over the Global North and Global South, hundreds of millions of children are growing up under the poverty line, their livelihood ever more threatened by the damning and worsening effects of the climate crisis. In light of this, I hope that I made a convincing case for why sincerely wanting to know about Firestone's alternative will be a fruitful endeavour for any critical children's rights scholar interested in questioning whether our liberal children's rights framework can offer any relief to the many children who find themselves struggling to grow up, or whether the project perhaps is, as Firestone would argue, instrumental in upholding a global form of capitalist patriarchy which lies at the heart of all these problems, and should thus also be abolished.

However, a 'return' to Firestone should always be a critical one since, as we have seen, part of her account is deeply flawed and deeply problematic, such as her takes on Black and queer issues and children's sexual 'freedom'.[13] Fortunately there is a new generation of radical scholars who have recognized and reassessed Firestone's ideas for all their flaws as well as their potential. These include Victoria Margree (2018), Sophie Lewis (2021a, 2021b, 2022) and M.E. O'Brien (2023) whose works constitute an important contemporary contribution to that of critical childhood and children's rights scholars who have long questioned the gender- and adult-biased conceptions of 'child', 'childhood' and 'children's rights'.[14] Finally, engaging with Firestone as an author and activist will also open the doors to a 'practical' history of children's liberation during 1970s, as part of women's liberation movements (Barrett Meyering, 2022) and gay liberation movements (Bronski, 2018), which has remained grossly overlooked or ignored in mainstream children's rights scholarship, but which holds important insights into the synergies between theory and activism and lessons for future action.

13 See Margree (2018, Chapter 6) for a more detailed discussion of these dimensions of her work, and the critique it garnered.

14 See for instance, Nieuwenhuys (1994, 2007), Burman (2020), Burman & Stacey (2010), Rosen & Twamley (2018), Wall (2023).

Acknowledgements

I would like to sincerely thank Basia Vucic, Hoko Horii, Olga Nieuwenhuys, Maartje Smits, Aurélie Lanctôt and Wouter Vandenhole for taking the time to read and comment on previous versions of this chapter. All errors, flaws and shortcomings are my own.

References

Archard, D. (1993). *Children: Rights and childhood*. Routledge.
Ariès, P. (1962). *Centuries of childhood: A social history of family life*. Vintage Books.
Barrett Meyering, I. (2022). *Feminism and the making of a child rights revolution 1969–1979*. Melbourne University Press.
Bronski, M. (2018). When gays wanted to liberate children. *Boston Review*. Retrieved January 21, 2025, from www.bostonreview.net/articles/michael-bronski-gay-family/
Burman, E. (2020). *Developments: Child, image, nation*. Routledge.
Burman, E., & Stacey, J. (2010). The child and childhood in feminist theory. *Feminist Theory*, *11*(3), 227–240.
Byrne, B. (2016). Do children still need to escape childhood? A reassessment of John Holt and his vision for children's rights. *The International Journal of Children's Rights*, *24*(1), 113–134.
Cohen, H. (1980). *Equal rights for children*. Rowman & Littlefield.
Dickerson, A. (2019). *John Holt: The philosophy of unschooling*. Springer.
Farson, R. E. (1974). *Birthrights*. Macmillan.
Firestone, S. (1970). *The dialectic of sex: The case for feminist revolution*. Morrow.
Freeman, M. (1979). Children's right: Some unanswered questions and some unquestioned answers. *Poly Law Review*, *5*, 9–15.
Freeman, M. (2014). *The future of children's rights*. Brill Nijhoff.
Hafen, B. C. (1976). Children's liberation and the new egalitarianism: Some reservations about abandoning youth to their rights. *Brigham Young University Law Review*, *1976*(3), 605–658.
Hanson, K. (2016). Separate childhood laws and the future of society. *Law, Culture and the Humanities*, *12*(2), 195–205.
Holt, J. (1974). *Escape from childhood: The needs and rights of children*. Penguin Books.
Holzscheiter, A. (2010). *Children's rights in international politics: The transformative power of discourse*. Springer.
Irving, J. (1981). *The hotel New Hampshire*. E.P. Dutton.
Leonard, J. (1981, August 31). The hotel New Hampshire. *New York Times*.
Levine, G. (1974, May 19). Should children decide what is best for them? *New York Times*.
Lewis, S. (2021a). Disloyal children of Shulamith Firestone: Updating gestational utopianism for the twenty-first century. *Interfere*, *2*, 201–217.
Lewis, S. (2021b). *Full surrogacy now: Feminism against family*. Verso Books.
Lewis, S. (2022). *Abolish the family: A manifesto for care and liberation*. Verso Books.
Liebel, M. (2004). *A will of their own: Cross-cultural perspectives on working children*. Zed Books.
Liebel, M. (2013). Do children have a right to work? Working children's movements in the struggle for social justice. In K. Hanson & O. Nieuwenhuys (eds.) *Reconceptualizing children's rights in international development: Living rights, social justice, translations* (pp. 225–249). Cambridge University Press.
Margree, V. (2018). *Neglected or misunderstood: The radical feminism of Shulamith Firestone*. John Hunt Publishing.
McGillivray, A. (1994). Why children do have equal rights: In reply to Laura Purdy. *International Journal of Children's Rights*, *2*, 243.

Nieuwenhuys, O. (1994). *Children's lifeworlds: Gender, welfare and labour in the developing world*. Routledge.
Nieuwenhuys, O. (2007). Embedding the global womb: Global child labour and the new policy agenda. *Children's Geographies*, *5*(1–2), 49–163.
O'Brien, M. E. (2023). *Family abolition: Capitalism and the communizing of care*. Verso Books.
Peleg, N. (2019). *The child's right to development*. Cambridge University Press.
Pupavac, V. (2001). Misanthropy without borders: The international children's rights regime. *Disasters*, *25*(2), 95–112.
Purdy, L. M. (1994). Why children shouldn't have equal rights. *International Journal of Children's Rights*, *2*, 223–241
Retford, K. (2016). Philippe Ariès's "discovery of childhood": Imagery and historical evidence. *Continuity and Change*, *31*(3), 391–418.
Rosen, R., & Twamley, K. (eds.) (2018). *Feminism and the politics of childhood–friends or foes?* UCL Press.
Veerman, P. E. (1992). *The rights of the child and the changing image of childhood* (Vol. 18). Martinus Nijhoff Publishers.
Wall, J. (2023). Childism: Transforming critical theory in response to children. In S. Balagopalan, J. Wall & W. Karen (eds.) *The Bloomsbury handbook of theories in childhood studies* (pp. 208–222). Bloomsbury Publishing.

3 Children's rights as counter-rights

How the paternalism of the UN Convention on the Rights of the Child can be countered

Manfred Liebel

3.1 Introduction

Around 20 years ago, children's rights researcher and activist Judith Ennew called for the rights codified in the UN Convention on the Rights of the Child (UNCRC, 1989) to be expanded to include 'unwritten rights.' She considered this necessary to do justice to children who are particularly socially disadvantaged, marginalized and discriminated against and whom she called 'children outside childhood'. Included in the list of unwritten rights that Ennew produced were, for example, 'the right not to be labelled', 'the right to work, and to do so in fair conditions and for fair wages' or 'the right to have their own support systems respected' (Ennew, 2002, pp. 399–401). Ennew, thus, wanted to address the specific living conditions and experiences of these children in more detail than is the case in the abstract language of the UNCRC. In doing so, she also wanted to make the rights more attractive to the children by strengthening them as subjects of their own rights and make them more capable of acting.

In this chapter, I want to take Judith Ennew's idea further, concretize it and explain it in more theoretical detail, similar to the concept I introduced in the past under the term 'children's rights from below' (Liebel, 2012a). To this end, I will draw on the legal-philosophical and legal discussion on *counter-rights* or *counter-hegemonic rights* and make it clear why this is also relevant for children. I will show why the concepts of childhood and children's rights on which the UNCRC is based are not sufficient to do justice to the interests of children. This applies principally to those children whose lives do not correspond to the dominant bourgeois-Western pattern of childhood and whom I refer to as 'children of the Global South' (Liebel, 2023). Using examples from the Global South, I will show that these children provide inspirations that can provide important clues for the conceptualization of counter-rights.

After an overview of the discussion on counter-rights to date, I will explain why the legal subjectivity of children established in the UNCRC follows a paternalistic pattern that makes it difficult for children to claim the rights granted to them in their own collective interest. I will then take up examples from the movements of working children in Latin America and Africa to

DOI: 10.4324/9781003510284-4

illustrate possible alternative contours of children's rights. Having set out the basic outlines of the concept of counter-rights contained therein, I will conclude by discussing some of the challenges associated with counter-rights and how they could be addressed.

3.2 On the concept of counter-rights

The idea of counter-rights is justified in various ways in legal and legal-philosophical discussions. Two main strands of discussion can be distinguished. The first strand understands counter-rights as a means of decolonization. Accordingly, they are primarily intended to enable people in former colonial territories to free themselves from postcolonial dependencies and subjugation. They are equally directed against the legal system adopted by the colonial powers after independence and the selective instrumentalization of human rights in favour of former colonial powers (Wallerstein, 2006). This concept calls into question the (national) state as the guarantor of rights and emphasizes the need for a collective countervailing power of subjugated and exploited peoples. In this sense, the African legal scholar, Issa Shivji (1989, 1995), speaks of 'counter-hegemonic rights.' The concept has also been taken up in debates and social movements pushing for a 'counter-hegemonic international law' (Rajagopal, 2006) and a 'counter-hegemonic globalisation' (De Sousa Santos & Rodriguez-Garavito, 2005; Carroll, 2007), which oppose the supremacy of multinational corporations, financial institutions and trade organizations and their arbitration tribunals as part of investment protection agreements.

The second strand understands counter-rights as a kind of a 'new right' concept that leaves behind the paradoxes of bourgeois-liberal 'civil law' and counteracts the individualization and depoliticization of legal subjects. It is intended to resolve the paradox of granting equal rights to all people on the one hand, but denying most people access to these rights due to their disadvantaged social situation on the other, thus perpetuating social inequality. This concept of counter-rights goes back primarily to the legal philosopher Christoph Menke (2018, 2020), which in turn ties in with Marx's critique of bourgeois law (Marx, 2009 [1843–44]). It has been differentiated and critically analyzed by other legal and social philosophers in recent years (see, for example, Fischer-Lezcano et al., 2018; Teubner, 2020; Kutting, 2023).

Menke develops his concept of counter-rights from the critique of subjective rights in bourgeois-capitalist society. He sees the legal subjects created by civil law as alienated beings who are enclosed in the private sphere and thus depoliticized. In the discussion, it is repeatedly pointed out that there are some problems associated with the historically developed figure of subjective rights. One of these problems is that the idea of human relationships as legal relationships alienates people from one another, as they are dominated by individual interests that are claimed over others. In bourgeois-capitalist society, this applies above all to the right to private property, namely in relation to the means of production and real estate for profitable utilization.

Understanding a person as a legal subject means reducing their characteristics as a human being to legal aspects. Under these aspects, the human being is seen, on the one hand, as a person who is obliged, or even subject, to certain set rules (laws, norms codified by the state), and, on the other hand, as a person who has claims against other persons or institutions. In any case, the relationship between the individual and other persons or state institutions means a reduction of human life and coexistence to questions of obeying or demanding. It makes it difficult to imagine relationships of love, friendship or solidarity and can, thus, contribute to an impoverishment of human relationships. In the attempt to claim their own rights, it is precisely those who are marginalized and whose rights are massively violated who are forced to abstract from their concrete everyday experiences and enter a terrain in which they were already disadvantaged. Legal philosopher Daniel Loick (2017, p. 22) refers to such legal thinking as 'juridism' and argues in favour of arriving at a 'post-juridical law.' To achieve emancipatory significance, 'the atomizing and disciplinary aspects of law' would have to be pushed back or neutralized (Loick, 2017, p. 181; own translation).

By establishing counter-rights, Menke hopes to liberate the subject and counteract the depoliticization of isolated and opposing individuals. However, it remains uncertain 'how exactly counter-rights should work towards the dialectical mediation process as a countermeasure to depoliticization' (Kutting, 2023, p. 378; own translation). The underlying logic of counter-rights is to ensure the success of social practices. 'The contrast is that subjective rights are based on the individual's own rights, while the other right is based on the success of social practice' (Menke, 2018, p. 25; own translation). However, a focus solely on the *form* of the right is not suitable for 'making a representative statement about subjective rights' (Kutting, 2023, p. 281; own translation). Analyzing the form of subjective rights 'cannot capture the complexity of the essence of subjective rights' (Kutting, 2023, p. 281; own translation).

Legal scholar Sonja Buckel, therefore, emphasizes the need to move from a legal-philosophical to a social-theoretical perspective. To this end, 'procedures must be developed with which the subjects not only become authors of their laws, but also authors of the network of political conditions surrounding them' (Buckel, 2018, p. 138; own translation). This understanding refers to theories of radical popular sovereignty, 'which define subjective rights as an immanent moment of democratic self-legislation that must never become independent through the interpretative sovereignty of state apparatuses' (Buckel, 2018, p. 139; own translation). Beyond 'defensive struggles, an offensive hegemonic project is required' (Buckel, 2018, p. 140; own translation). The counter-rights conceived as part of such a project are occasionally also referred to as 'trans-subjective rights, which neither end with an object nor exhaust themselves in a subject' (Femina, 2018, p. 381; own translation).

In these debates, children have not yet emerged as legal subjects or actors of possible countervailing power. Before I turn to the question of the extent to which, and the way in which children can also be understood as subjects of these counter-rights and, in some cases, bring them into being themselves, I will explain why it is necessary to go beyond the UNCRC.

3.3 The paternalism of the UNCRC

The need for counter-rights of children arises from the fact that the existing international system of children's rights remains largely ineffective. Although the UNCRC has helped to raise awareness about the injustices inflicted on children, it has done little for the children who continue to live in precarious conditions. The states and governments that have been entrusted and given responsibility for children have largely failed and proved unsuitable as guarantors of justice. For the children themselves, the rights assigned to them by the UNCRC were an unsuitable, abstract instrument. The main reasons for this lie in its paternalistic conception and in the fact that it is based on a pattern of childhood that essentially conceptualizes children as legal subjects in need of protection and dependent on adults.

The paternalism of the UNCRC is evident in several respects. It was drafted by adults without any involvement of children. Only after it was adopted were occasional attempts made to involve children in its interpretation, for example, at so-called children's summits at United Nations headquarters or through initiatives by the UN Committee on the Rights of the Child to involve children in the deliberation of General Comments. The overriding principle of the UNCRC is the need to protect children, which is understood as a natural characteristic of childhood. It is based on a concept of childhood that follows Western bourgeois ideas and, thus, negates differently conceived and experienced childhoods, despite the recognition of different cultures emphasized in the preamble (Pupavac, 1998; Valentin & Meinert, 2009; Vandenhole, 2020). This applies above all to many childhoods in the Global South.

The 'best interest' of children, which is a central principle of the UNCRC, is left to the interpretation of adults, nation-states or governments appointed as guarantors. The participation rights enshrined for the first time in the UNCRC are designed to ensure that adults or states listen to children. This exposes participation rights to the danger of being reduced to an integration medium at the mercy of those who have power over children. As the rights in the UNCRC are conceived of as individual rights, they reproduce the paradoxes of civil law. Like the human rights inscribed in international law, the UNCRC rights have the problem that, although they are supposed to apply equally to all people, they can only be utilized by them to varying degrees or not at all. This has to do with the fact that people's living conditions and political status are extremely unequal. The assumed equality of rights or equality 'before the law' can, therefore, have the effect of reinforcing inequality 'after the law' (from a feminist perspective, see Brown, 2002).

The UNCRC is based on the idea that children need specific rights because they are particularly vulnerable, still immature and, therefore, dependent on adults. These characteristics of being a child are considered anthropological universals in the dominant understanding of children's rights. In the UNCRC, they mean that the focus is on protection and provision rights and that the fulfilment of participation rights is linked to certain conditions such as age, maturity and capacity for judgement. They also mean that not only are special rights created for children, they are also denied rights, in particular certain political rights (for example, universal suffrage) or economic and labour rights (for example, rights in the workplace).

Using the example of Article 12 of the UNCRC, sociologist Teresa Behrends investigated the question of whether recognizing children as legal subjects means that they have the same legal status as adults. She concludes that this is not the case, and in this sense speaks of a specific 'child legal subjectivity' (Behrends, 2017, p. 28; own translation). According to Article 12, children have the right to express their views and to be heard in administrative and court proceedings. However, while adults can decide whether they express their views at all, whether they do so for their benefit or to their detriment, children can only do this *as children* and only insofar as the child 'is capable of forming his or her own views' (UNCRC, 1989). Whether, and when, this ability is given cannot be decided by the children themselves, but

> is determined by the courts themselves or by expert practices associated with them. . . . In this case, the law is therefore not bound by the will of the individual holder of the right but decides according to its rules whether and when this will be mature enough to be heard.
>
> (Behrends, 2017, p. 28; own translation)

Furthermore, the nature and extent of the power conferred is always limited to matters 'affecting the child' (UNCRC, 1989). Which matters these are 'is not determined by the child's legal subject itself. In this case, the child does have an (individual) right, which semantically shows great similarities with the form of subjective right' (Behrends, 2017, p. 28; own translation), but a central and decisive difference is marked. According to Behrends, this consists in the fact that 'the subject of this right is entirely a child and cannot step out of being a child even with this right. The power conferred by Art. 12 is entirely a child-like power pre-formed by adults or institutions' (Behrends, 2017, p. 28; own translation). Accordingly, she poses the question of

> what consequences it has that, on the one hand, childhood is produced in and by modern civil law and, at the same time, represents an additional break in its premise of equality, which once again runs through the paradoxical form of subjective rights.
>
> (Behrends, 2017, p. 34; own translation)

The codification of special children's rights contains the inherent contradiction of naming specific vulnerabilities to which children are exposed, but thereby losing sight of the fundamental disadvantages of being socially constructed *as a child*. This applies, for example, to the right to nondiscrimination, as enshrined in Article 2. It can itself result in discrimination, as it ignores the (lower) age as a possible reason for discrimination, as if the mere existence of the UNCRC already guarantees that the special characteristics of children are considered. Legal scholars Daly et al. (2022) refer to this as the 'CRC paradox.'

Another example is the protection against economic exploitation granted in Article 32 and the requirement to set minimum age limits for work. Here, children are excluded from economic activity solely because of their young age, without considering the specific circumstances of the children's lives, the conditions of the work and, above all, the children's own will. This exclusion- – and prohibition- – focused thinking excludes children from being agents who want to take on responsibility for their families or communities, for example, and for whom work experience *can* contribute to the development of vital skills. Such guidelines also accept that children are incapacitated solely by reference to their young age and prevented from defending themselves against life circumstances that are harmful to them and that they do not want to accept (Liebel, 2013, 2021).

A central question is how the differences between children and adults and the special characteristics of children can be understood and legally defined without violating the principle of equality. When defining children's rights as specific rights, there is the alternative of understanding the disadvantage and vulnerability attributed to children as an inherent characteristic of childhood or as a condition to be overcome. If the special nature of childhood is understood as an anthropological universal, then it tends to make conditions of disadvantage and vulnerability permanent. If, on the other hand, these are understood as the socially generated result of unequal power relations, the perspective arises of conceptualizing rights as a possible means of overcoming disadvantage and vulnerability (for a discussion of the paternalism of the UNCRC, see also Peleg, 2023).

Due to the basic paternalistic tendency of the UNCRC, children remain dependent on the benevolence of those people and institutions who have power over them. Many children in the Global South, at least, have no reason to trust them. They have no choice but to fight for their rights themselves, and this requires new instruments. These can also include rights that children consider appropriate and necessary for themselves.

3.4 How children's counter-rights arise

To get a better idea of how children's counter-rights are brought about, I will refer to the movements of working children that have emerged in Latin America since the 1970s and in Africa and parts of Asia since the 1990s (Liebel, 2004, 2012c; Nieuwenhuys, 2009). I base this partly on my own experiences in Latin America since the 1990s and partly on available documents and self-portrayals by actors in these movements. It will become clear that the children in these movements generally do not express their ideas of their own rights in the language of law and that they repeatedly must deal with conflicting interests of adults and institutions dominated by these.

As a first example, I will refer to a three-day meeting I attended in Nicaragua in the early 1990s, which was largely self-organized by children between 10 and 16 years of age. When they elected their representatives, they had a heated discussion about the criteria that these should fulfil. Among other things, they had to be active, articulate, take initiative, be honourable, responsible, serious, respectful and not boasters. Some of the girls present insisted that they should be equally represented and that the younger children also be considered. The rule of gender parity created by the children in this way did not exist in any other organization in the country at the time.

At the same time, efforts were made to enshrine the basic principles of the UNCRC in national laws and the constitution. In Nicaragua, the then government invited children to make suggestions for this. In a workshop that I helped to organize, the children were initially enthusiastic that their voices were being sought. However, as the workshop progressed, some children grew dissatisfied with the fact that although they were able to make suggestions, they had no influence on whether, and how, these would be implemented in the law. They felt exploited and demanded to have a say in decision-making in parliament. Although they were met with rejection, they had concretized the idea of children's political participation as a counter-right.

After the children organized in the movement began to draw public attention to their situation and protest the violation of their rights, they did receive some friendly comments, but they were rarely taken seriously. It was only when they started unannounced 'visits' to the offices of journalists and politicians that they began to receive serious attention. For example, some media agencies soon stopped calling them 'street children' or 'vagabonds' and started referring to them as 'working children,' or there were more calls for the children to be heard and their rights to be respected.

With the growth of the children's movement, the children's self-confidence and collective claim to autonomy grew. When a government decree banned them from continuing to work on the streets, they blocked traffic and, instead, demanded that the police protect them from aggressive drivers. They demanded that the city council widen the lines between the lanes at the traffic lights to reduce the risk of accidents. They also demanded that the city council build small shelters at the side of the road where children can rest and protect themselves from the burning sun.

After meeting similar movements in other countries, the children explicitly centred their demands on the *right to work with dignity*. This right, which is found neither in the UNCRC nor in national laws, is directed against the blanket ban on child labour and is intended to enable children to have rights in their workplaces and to be able to claim them. By emphasizing their own dignity, working children underline that they not only want to be protected from harmful working conditions, as provided for in the UNCRC, but also that economic exploitation itself must be ended.

Occasionally, children's organizations also try to influence the legislative process in their country. In 2014, for example, the Bolivian Union of Working Children fought for a law through months of public campaigns and persistent negotiations that took their living conditions into account and at least partially took their rights seriously (for details, see Liebel, 2015). The children's movement did not achieve its goal of granting children the right to work regardless of their age, but it had succeeded in pushing through a law that recognized children's work as legitimate under certain circumstances from 12 years of age for dependent work and from 10 years of age for self-employed work. Although the relevant provisions of the law have since been repealed under pressure from the International Labour Organization (ILO) and the US government (see Liebel, 2019), the children are sticking to their collective demand to be able to work in dignity. In doing so, they are reminiscent of communal forms of work that have been practised in Indigenous communities for centuries.

Twenty years earlier, in 1994, the founding document of the African Movement of Working Children and Youth had explicitly formulated '12 rights' (AMWCY, 2001, pp. 19–90), which continue to guide this movement today (Benedix & ENDA Jeunesse Action, 2025). These rights are partly based on rights codified in the UNCRC, but they are tailored to the situation and specific experiences of working children and concretized accordingly. They also contain rights that are not included in any official legal document, such as 'the right to remain in the village.' What makes them counter-rights is not only the specifics of the rights, but also the fact that they were formulated by the children themselves, and their implementation is monitored by them. It is intended that the extent to which the rights have been realized and how this can be achieved in the future will be assessed in the grassroots groups and at the movement's international meetings, which are usually held every two years. The implementation of the rights is, therefore, not only the responsibility of states, but the children organized in the movement ensure this themselves. The right 'to self-expression and to form organisations' is not limited to the right to be heard granted to children by state authorities but empowers children to stand up for their rights in the way they find adequate (for details, see Liebel, 2012b).

3.5 Basic principles of children's counter-rights

Counter-rights are characterized by the fact that they arise from the joint actions of children. They aim at improving their situation and take account of the different realities and experiences of the children involved. They are formulated in such a way that other children in similar circumstances can identify with them and adopt them as their own.

Children's counter-rights often refer to codified rights (the UNCRC or regional children's rights treaties) but reinterpret and reformulate them to improve a situation they have experienced themselves. Usually, they are not elaborated in the language of law but can be inferred from the children's actions. Sometimes, but not always, they aim to reformulate official legal norms. The counter-rights emanating from children gain their strength from their experiences in their own living environment and the self-organization that arises here. The subjects of counter-rights do not see themselves as (mutually isolated) legal subjects, but as *social* subjects with common interests and are focused on achieving a society that is just for children and future generations. In this sense, counter-rights conceived by children can be understood as transsubjective rights.

As subjects of counter-rights, children do not see themselves as 'inherently' inferior and subordinate to adults. If we relate this self-image to the usual distinction between children's rights in terms of protection, provision and participation rights, the following consequences emerge: *Protection rights* are understood to enable and facilitate children to protect themselves and to have a decisive say in measures taken for their protection. *Provision rights* are understood in such a way that their realization is not primarily achieved through measures taken by state or adult authorities, but that the entire society is restructured in such a way that all people of different ages become active subjects of these rights, considering their respective starting conditions. *Participation rights* are understood in such a way that they eliminate the unequal distribution of power between adults and children, i.e. they become political rights that children can utilize in their own individual and collective interests, just like adults, but considering their starting position.

This understanding of children's rights turns them into *counter-hegemonic* rights that can be utilized by children both individually and collectively. They are aimed at strengthening the social position of children and counteracting all forms of social and generational disadvantage, subordination and discrimination. In this way, they can also help to make social relations more egalitarian and democratic and to challenge any kind of unequal power. As counter-hegemonic rights, children's rights are particularly important for those children who are especially socially disadvantaged, marginalized and oppressed. These children can be found in all parts of the world, but especially in those regions that are affected by the inequality of the postcolonial world order (Liebel, 2020). Counter-rights, in the sense I understand them, are similar to what anthropologist Olga Nieuwenhuys and legal scholar Karl Hanson call 'living rights' (Nieuwenhuys & Hanson, 2023), but the concept of counter-rights emphasizes more strongly the agency, activism and protagonism of these children (Taft, 2023; Liebel, 2023).

The counter-rights are based on an understanding of childhood that goes beyond the bourgeois Western pattern of childhood as a preliminary stage of adulthood and are directed against its dominance in the world. They focus on children, who are often referred to as 'children without childhood' and are thus additionally discriminated against and marginalized, and whose experiences, knowledge and skills are disregarded. They express the specific interests and experiences of these children and demand that they be recognized. In this sense, they aim to liberate children from the stage of subalternity, to realize a society in which children are seen as subjects with equal value and dignity. They are not directed against adults as persons, but against their hegemony.

3.6 Challenges for children's counter-rights

Children's rights as counter-hegemonic rights face the problem that the realities and interests of children can only be reflected in abstract form as rights that apply equally to all children. The challenge arises as to how rights can do justice particularly to socially disadvantaged and marginalized children and their experiences and expectations, especially as these children have so far had little reason to trust the form of rights and the existing legal system. To this end, it is necessary to go beyond the abstract legal form of liberal law and the rights must be concretized in such a way that they apply to the experiences of the children. This includes the right to oppose all forms of discrimination and violence resulting from unequal power relations, including those between adults and children, which is commonly referred to as *adultism* (Alderson, 2020; Liebel & Meade, forthcoming; Taboo, 2024). However, counter-rights cannot be based solely on the common interests of all children as a social group, but must also consider other specific forms of oppression and marginalization experienced by children (such as classism, sexism, racism, ableism), i.e. an intersectional perspective is indispensable (Liebel & Meade, 2024).

For the question of how unequal power can be overcome in its structural forms and in personal relationships, it is essential to question the temporal developmental pattern of childhood, which defines it as an imperfect preliminary stage of supposedly perfect adulthood. This developmental pattern has so far contributed to the permanent reproduction of adultism through processes of internalization. It is equally important that children succeed in changing their living environment to some extent through their own actions in the sense of recognizing their moral equality. The invoked self-efficacy should not only be considered from the psychological aspect of gaining the self-confidence necessary for action but also in the sense that reality itself is transformed by children's own actions. Counter-rights can have a supporting function in that they additionally justify, and legitimize, the actions. They take the law out of the 'legal sky' and become an integral part of everyday life. The 'power' of counter-rights and their counter-hegemonic effect result from the specific experiences of children in their living environment and the forms of organization and resistance that arise here. They are subjective in the sense of a rebellious *political subjectivity* that involves the whole body and emotions, and thus become the driving motive for targeted action.

One open question is how children can free themselves from their seemingly natural dependence on adults and not only formulate their rights but also claim and enforce them. This includes the question of how counter-rights that do not have an external guarantor (the state) or cannot rely on it can become effective. It seems essential to me that children in similar life situations succeed in developing elements of countervailing power in their own specific places, which those who previously had power over the children can no longer ignore. To this end, it may be useful to distinguish between micro- and macro-political levels of action and to identify the interfaces and transitions at which one level merges into the other and intervenes in it.

The concept of counter-rights does not preclude the invocation of codified 'official' rights, but rather their subjects seize them and attempt to utilize and reconceptualize them according to their specific interests wherever possible, hence, in a counter-hegemonic sense. Independent human and children's rights institutions and complaints centres, which are also easily accessible to socially disadvantaged children and can effectively intervene in political decision-making processes at all levels, can be of particular importance in this regard. Counter-hegemonic children's rights do not become effective simply by taking children into consideration, and it is not only the personal relationships between children and adults that need to change, but societies need to be changed in terms of social and generational justice. This is the responsibility of adults and children alike.

3.7 Conclusion

Children's rights must be transformed into counter-rights, since the current system of state-guaranteed codified rights is designed in a paternalistic manner. The latter has failed because it is based on the premise of a pattern of childhood that devalues the great majority of children in the world and disregards their knowledge and agency. Counter-rights point beyond the bourgeois-liberal legal form and manifest themselves fluidly in a change of power relations, between adults and children as well as between different classes, genders and denying the characteristics of inferiority and imperfection ascribed to children. At the same time, counter-rights always remain precarious, as they are intended to change something that has not yet been changed. They are not only manifested in demands but also in lived practice and the forms of counter-power that emerge in this practice. As children alone cannot generate the necessary counter-power, adults who think, and act, in solidarity are challenged to facilitate and enable such practice.

References

Alderson, P. (2020). Adultism. In D. T. Cook (ed.), *The SAGE encyclopaedia of children and childhood studies* (pp. 538–542). SAGE.

AMWCY. (2001). *Voice of African children: Work, strength and organisation of working children and youth*. Occasional papers no. 217. ENDA Tiers-Monde.

Behrends, T. (2017). Das Kind als (Menschen-)Rechtssubjekt: zur Form der Kinderrechte. In A. Fangmeyer & J. Mierendorff (eds.) *Kindheit und Erwachsenheit in sozialwissenschaftlicher Forschung und Theoriebildung* (pp. 27–36). Beltz-Juventa.

Benedix, N., & ENDA Jeunesse Action (2025). *Enquête sur la perception du Mouvement Africain des Enfants et Jeunes Travailleurs (MAEJT)*. A l'occasion du 30e anniversaire du MAEJT en 2024. ENDA Tiers-Monde.

Brown, W. (2002). Suffering the paradoxes of rights. In W. Brown & J. Halley (eds.) *Left legalism/left critique* (pp. 420–434). Duke University Press.

Buckel, S. (2018). Die Bürde der subjektiven Rechte: eine Auseinandersetzung mit der Rechtsphilosophie Christoph Menkes. In A Fischer-Lescano, H. Franzki & J. Horst (eds.) *Gegenrechte* (pp. 125–140). Mohr Siebeck.

Carroll, W. K. (2007). Hegemony and counter-hegemony in a global field. *Studies in Social Justice*, *1*(1), 36–66.

Daly, A., Thorburn Stern, R., & Leviner, P. (2022). UN convention on the rights of the child, article 2 and discrimination on the basis of childhood: The CRC paradox? *Nordic Journal of International Law*, *91*(3), 419–452.

De Sousa Santos, B., & Rodriguez-Garavito, C. A. (eds.). (2005). *Law and globalization from below: Towards a cosmopolitan legality.* Cambridge University Press.

Ennew, J. (2002). Outside childhood: Street children's rights. In B. Franklin (ed.) *The new handbook of children's rights: Comparative policy and practice* (pp. 201–215). Routledge.

Femina, P. (2018). Transsubjektive (Gegen)Rechte, oder die Notwendigkeit, die Wolken in einem Sack zu fangen. In A. Fischer-Lescano, H. Franzki & J. Horst (eds.) *Gegenrechte* (pp. 343–356). Mohr Siebeck.

Fischer-Lescano, A., Franzki, H., & Horst. J. (eds.). (2018). *Gegenrechte: Recht jenseits des Subjekts.* Mohr Siebeck.

Kutting, I. M. (2023). *Die Normativitätsstruktur subjektiver Rechte. eine rechtsdogmatische Untersuchung ausgehend von Menkes "Kritik der Rechte".* Duncker & Humblot.

Liebel, M. (2004). *A will of their own: Cross-cultural perspectives on working children.* Zed Books.

Liebel, M. (2012a). with contributions by K. Hanson, I. Saadi, & W. Vandenhole. *Children's rights from below: Cross-cultural perspectives.* Palgrave Macmillan.

Liebel, M. (2012b). Children's work, education and agency: The African Movement of Working Children and Youth (AMWCY). In G. Spittler & M. Bourdillon (eds.) *African children at work: Working and learning in growing up for life* (pp. 303–332). LIT Verlag.

Liebel, M. (2012c). Child-led organizations and the advocacy of adults: Experiences from Bangladesh and Nicaragua. In M. Freeman (ed.) *Law and childhood studies: Current legal issues* (Vol. 14, pp. 92–103). Oxford University Press.

Liebel, M. (2013). Do children have the right to work? Working children's movements in the struggle for social justice. In K. Hanson & O. Nieuwenhuys (eds.) *Reconceptualizing children's rights in international development: Living rights, social justice, translations* (pp. 225–249). Cambridge University Press.

Liebel, M. (2015). Protecting the rights of working children instead of banning child labour: Bolivia tries a new legislative approach. *The International Journal of Children's Rights*, *23*(3), 491–509.

Liebel, M. (2019). Children's rights: Bolivia bows to international pressure. *D+C – Development and Cooperation* (May), 14–15.

Liebel, M. (2020). *Decolonizing childhoods: From exclusion to dignity.* Policy Press.

Liebel, M. (2021). Economic and labour rights: A blind spot in the discourse on children's rights. *Nordic Journal of Human Rights*, *39*(2), 163–179.

Liebel, M. (2023). In collaboration with R. Budde, U. Markowska-Manista & P. Meade. *Childhoods of the Global South: Children's rights and resistance.* Policy Press.

Liebel, M., & Meade, P. (forthcoming). *Adultism: A critical introduction to discrimination against children.* Policy Press.

Liebel, M., & Meade, P. (2024). Intersectional tensions in theorizing adultism. *Taboo – The Journal of Culture and Education*, *22*(1), 96–123.

Loick, D. (2017). *Juridismus: Konturen einer kritischen Theorie des Rechts.* Suhrkamp.

Marx, K. (2009 [1843–44]). *Critique of Hegel's 'Philosophy of right'.* Cambridge University Press.

Menke, C. (2018). Genealogie, Paradoxie, Transformation: Grundelemente einer Kritik der Rechte. In A. Fischer-Lescano, H. Franzki & J. Horst (eds.) *Gegenrechte* (pp. 13–31). Mohr Siebeck.
Menke, C. (2020). *Critique of rights*. Polity.
Nieuwenhuys, O. (2009). From child labour to working children's movements. In J. Qvortrup, W. A. Corsaro & M.-S. Honig (eds.) *The Palgrave handbook of childhood studies* (pp. 289–300). Palgrave Macmillan.
Nieuwenhuys, O., & Hanson, K. (2023). Living rights theory. In S. Balagopalan, J. Wall & K. Wells (eds.) *The Bloomsbury handbook of theories in childhood studies* (pp. 167–179). Bloomsbury Academic.
Peleg, N. (2023). A children's rights dilemma – paternalism versus autonomy. In R. Adami, A. Kaldal & M. Aspán (eds.) *The rights of the child: Legal, political and ethical challenges* (pp. 7–12). Brill/Nijhoff.
Pupavac, V. (1998). The infantilisation of the south and the UN convention on the rights of the child. *Human Rights Law Review*, *3*(2), 3–8.
Rajagopal, B. (2006). Counter-hegemonic international law: Rethinking human rights and development as a third world strategy. *Third World Quarterly*, *27*(5), 767–783.
Shivji, I. G. (1989). *The concept of human rights in Africa*. CODESRIA.
Shivji, I. G. (1995). The rule of law and Ujamaa in the ideological formation of Tanzania. *Social & Legal Studies*, *4*, 147–174.
Taboo. (2024). Special issue on adultism. *Taboo – The Journal of Culture and Education*, *22*(1).
Taft, J. K. (2023). Protagonismo and power: Building political theory with young activists. In S. Balagopalan, J. Wall & K. Wells (eds.) *The Bloomsbury handbook of theories in childhood studies* (pp. 180–193). Bloomsbury Academic.
Teubner, G. (2020). Counter-rights: On the trans-subjective potential of subjective rights. In *The law of political economy: Transformation in the function of law* (pp. 372–393). Cambridge University Press.
UNCRC. (1989). *Convention on the rights of the child*. Adopted 20 November 1989 by General Assembly resolution 44/25.
Valentin, K., & Meinert, L. (2009). The adult North and the young South: Reflections on the civilizing mission on children's rights. *Anthropology Today*, *25*(3), 23–28.
Vandenhole, W. (2020). Decolonising children's rights: Of vernacularisation and interdisciplinarity. In R. Budde & U. Markowska-Manista (eds.) *Childhood and children's rights between research and activism* (pp. 187–206). Springer VS.
Wallerstein, I. (2006). *European universalism: The rhetoric of power*. The New Press.

4 Children's search for equality

Between the legal and the political

Lucia Rabello de Castro

4.1 Introduction

What are the ways of children's emancipation? How can children unsettle the present social order so that situations of domination and unfairness can be mitigated or eradicated? These questions problematize children's condition today and their position in a generational order that brought about the most stringent regulation and government of childhood (Rose, 1999). An age-based episteme (Castro, 2020) has underpinned children's subordinate position within this order stipulating what children are allowed or not allowed to do. It consists of an entrenched knowledge that essentializes what children are, or can be, in the sense of defining their limited abilities in relation to adults and, accordingly, their differential positions of capacity and power. Such an adultist standpoint in construing children and legitimating their inferior status vis-à-vis adults has been criticized on account of being based on prejudice (Alderson, 2020) and/or just reproducing and maintaining power position privileges (Bell, 1995). Arguably, the present generational order can be accounted for as embedding practices of the domination of children (Smith, 2024). More often than not, children's rebelliousness, negativity and insurgence against domination have been regarded as no more than recalcitrant behaviours needing discipline and correction. Being regarded as not yet political subjects, or not yet full citizens (Hobson & Lister, 2002) in the present liberal democracies, their antagonism to the status quo has not been straightforwardly signified as a committed engagement to change their life for the better.

Nevertheless, adults' concerns about an undue provision of care towards children have, in the late 20th century, brought about specific rights' legislation, international and national, to secure children a formal position of dignity and social visibility before adults. Children's rights legislation have, to say the least, foregrounded the legitimacy of granting children fairer conditions of existence and more equal relationships with adults themselves. However, differently from other social categories, like women, for instance, children were not major protagonists in presenting and discussing their demands in the process of drafting what would eventually constitute the international charters and national laws of children's positive rights (Josefsson et al., 2023). Therefore,

DOI: 10.4324/9781003510284-5

even if one could rejoice about the civilizational advancements concerning the recognition of children's full humanity and dignity, this legal advance was not paired with a significant recognition of children's *political* stance and their capacity to know about, and advance, their interests. In fact, the sidelining of children in the long process of making children's rights lawful actually hindered opportunities for them to learn about, and take part in, public dialogue.

This chapter discusses, and critiques, how both formal liberal politics and the legal order that underpins it, despite clear advances in promoting more fairness to children, have been insufficient in transforming an entrenched adult-dominated system to allow for children's emancipation. It is argued that the legal rights' framework has indeed empowered children making them cognizant of the legitimacy of their claims for dignity and justice and of the fact that some of these are now lawful. This has certainly enhanced their self-esteem and self-conception as well as adults' responsibilities towards them. Furthermore, in countries such as Brazil, for instance, children's legal rights' framework (*Estatuto da Criança e do Adolescente,* Brazil 1990) has introduced, in the social imaginary, a novel conceptual key whereby the ever racialized and disadvantaged children shall be included in the social category of children, and hence, perceived as equally worthy of respect, care and dignity as all other children (Pinheiro, 2006). However, as it is argued here, the legal framework, by itself, does not conform social practices accordingly, especially in circumstances where it disallows engrained social practices. Using a decolonial analytical lens, I discuss how, in countries such as Brazil, where colonization and slavery have moulded our very deep and unconscious dispositions as a collectivity, children's legal rights framework must be critically evaluated in view of its historical, political and cultural context. Furthermore, I argue that legal children's rights, *policy,* as Rancière (1996) would put it, have not called for children's participation to a large extent. Rather, they expressed the compromise solution found among differently positioned sectors of adult society – politicians, child advocates, practitioners, professionals, corporations, child scholars and so on – towards the 'best interests of the child'. As a domain of positivized social values, children's rights have hegemonized what is good and desirable for children from adults' point of view, shutting down claims for other desirable social realities put forward by children themselves. Arguably, different children's codes could be written, were it possible to include children in the process of public discussion and drafting.

On the other hand, the critique targeted at legal rights' framework must also critically evaluate its imbrication with formal politics. It is argued how political action in liberal democracies has been regarded as a prerogative of citizen subjects in the public sphere (Saward, 2008). A disembodied notion of citizenship modelled on the idealized vision of the White adult male individual in Western societies (Pateman, 1992) has thus downgraded the formal political status of children to that of a pre-political subject, circumscribing children's actions to the private sphere. Hence, children lack the means and resources to articulate their claims as recognizable speech, to 'stage the political' (Oswell,

2019, p. 200), their demands for equality and justice being permanently looked down on as strident noise or babbling. Cordero Arce (2019), based on his research on child labour movements in Bolivia, argues that citizen subjects, or *subjects-as-citizens,* are all those who have a right to count and a duty to be held accountable – conditions which are necessary to their present communities. For him, children are active subjects in the construction of their society, what justifies the representation of their legal and political subjecthood in the present – the here and now. Liberal constitutionalism has also been critiqued by feminist (Young, 2000; Lister, 1997) and post-structuralist scholars (Mouffe, 1993). For the latter citizenship is more made than given, meaning that abstract and normative notions of how and why to belong and be a member of a social group are actually worked out in real life practices. Lister's (2007) and Moosa-Mitha's (2005) critiques go in the direction of questioning the normativity of the political in liberal societies. Lister indicates the need to enlarge the notion of citizenship, beyond a male adult-centred normativity, so as to acknowledge the specific ways in which children are members of, and responsible for, their environment and communities. In the same vein, Moosa-Mitha argues for a difference-centred model of citizenship to allow for the specificity of children's social position. She points out how social practices and institutional cultures reflect, despite their norms, racialized, gendered and adultist assumptions about children which exclude them from being seen as equals, within and outside the family.

In the present discussion, it is problematized whether children's emancipation can be secured by just re-creating the normativities of the legal and the political via, at best, the enlightened initiative of adults. In what follows I focus on how the legal and the political domains intertwine in liberal democracies leading to a conundrum of possibilities for children's emancipation since normative assumptions stipulate, and limit, not only who children are, their identity and capacities, but also to what participation in the public culture they are entitled. Following Rancière's (1992, p. 59) inspiration that 'policy wrongs equality', I explore how children can possibly question an unfair social order, even if situations of injustice are normalized and appear as the way 'reality' is and should be. I focus on the Brazilian context to discuss how its child rights' legal framework and its neocolonial political order encumber the attainment of a more egalitarian society for children. To illustrate my argument, I discuss some research results carried out in state schools in Rio de Janeiro (Brazil) showing children's tortuous process of political subjectivization (Castro, 2022) when they were able to construct their demands and claims for equality despite adults' complacent paternalism and/or sheer disregard.

In this research, conducted during 2019 and then resumed in 2022–2023, I investigated how children at the fundamental level of Brazilian state schools in Rio de Janeiro constructed collective meanings about their school experience: what was important to them, what they found missing, what changes they would consider desirable and how they regarded their relationships with adults. About 2,000, aged from 10 to 13, from 35 different schools took part in this research. They were asked to look at an imaginary school situation shown in a booklet and, in groups of five or six, provide an answer that reflected the small group's point of view. What was deemed striking in the results was the consistency of children's collective views and demands across so many different schools. It was impressive how some problems were regarded as urgent and how children's demands emerged in a convincing, convergent and organic way.

Based on these data I argue that the peculiarity of children's social position can deepen our understanding of the tensions that articulate the domains of what is positively right, the legal, that should be followed and corroborated, and that of *politics* in Rancière's terms (2006) – that which makes visible another not yet existing reality and turns not yet political subjects into political ones.

4.2 Empowering through rights? Navigating neocolonial pacts in Brazil

In Brazil, as in many Global South countries, the legal framework of positive rights, including children's rights, has not evolved as part of the processes of construction of modern institutions grounded on the principles of political and economic liberalism, like in the European context. Elsewhere (Castro, 2022; Castro & Tavares, 2021), I have discussed how children's educational rights in Brazil, for instance, were shaped by the neocolonial pacts of élites aimed at reinforcing historical and long-standing social and racial hierarchies and privileges with a semblance of modernity and its universal value of equality. Modern forms of intergenerational solidarity, like adults' duties concerning the *universal* care, provision and protection of the new generation, were, here, reworked to maintain the discriminatory Creole élites' positions of privilege, and of their descendancy, in what Mignolo (2011) has coined 'the creole white consciousness'. Practically, in Brazil, rights have remained a bestowment of the powerful used to show their magnanimity to the powerless, as various Brazilian scholars have shown (Santos, 1979; Gomes, 2006). As a gift (Telles, 1998) bestowed under the discretion and the convenience of the powerful, it reinforces hierarchies of power and prestige, keeping under control subalterns' dissatisfaction.

In relation to postcolonial India, Balagopalan (2019) has noted the peculiarities of the emergence of forms of governance and citizenship. Differently from the metropolis, the hegemony of liberal norms and values was not present in the colonial context which calls for the need to historicize the assumption of a universal rights' subjectivity which, being conversant with liberal modes of being and understanding the world, adequately performs the claiming of one's entitled rights. Thus, the claim that rights stand as an idiomatic resource to plead for, and gain access to, what is legally secured is often disconfirmed by too frequent situations of subjective 'bafflement' as indicative of a subjective inadequacy to change an unfair state of affairs specially by those marginalized populations.

The different histories of colonization, oppression and silencing in many countries of the Global South have been interwoven with the introduction of the modern European legacy of legal rights' framework which certainly produced some familiarity of the marginalized with these new entitlements. However, as Nyamu and Wamahiu (2022, p. 424) argue, within the context of Kenya, 'coloniality produced an ***ambivalent*** and inadequate juvenile justice and child welfare system' (my italics) since it was built upon the enforcement of violence to maintain order and the normativity of standards of children's rights and formal schooling. Thus, by and large, different histories of modernization in parts of the Global South put into question the general assumption that the modern institution of legal rights has equally provided, to individuals and collectivities, these specific subjective dispositions and social knowledge of self-determination and self-interest characteristic of European modernization.

The Brazilian Statute of Children's and Adolescents' Rights (Brazil/Cedca, 1990) was praised as a laudable construction in the advent of re-democratization processes after over 20 years of military dictatorship. And indeed, it has been, since it was consecrated, in the social imaginary, the doctrine of the 'integral protection' of all children under 18 years of age. Nevertheless, the formality of the legal apparatus, as a top-down mechanism to face inequalities and injustices, has had to gain 'flesh and blood' in the midst of the manifold existing structures of oppression re-edited through the neocolonial pacts of domination in most Global South countries (Pavón-Cuellar, 2021). As an aspect of social transformation, albeit seemingly non-enforceable, children's rights had to be navigated in the context of the entrenched racism, paternalism and authoritarianism of Brazilian society.

The impasse of the non-enforceability of children's rights reiterates stigmatization and criminalization processes of a specific population of children and youth. This can be illustrated by the poignant situation of children in conflict with the law which shows how child and adolescent justice is based on a punitive mentality of control, discipline and punishment of the lower classes which is reminiscent of past legacies of oppression of Brazilian society (Castro & Kosminsky, 2010; Fávero, 2020; Siqueira, 2014). Leal and Macedo (2017) refer to a process of 'penalization of misery' in the judicial system, or in Wacquant's (2015) terms, the establishment of a Brazilian Penal State, which operates a selective process of criminalization and incarceration of children and adolescents of the disadvantaged classes. Although the Brazilian Statute of the Child and the Adolescent (Brazil/Cedca, 1990) guarantees that all efforts should be undertaken to avoid incarceration in cases of children in conflict with the law, it is mostly lower-class, Black, peripheric and unschooled adolescents who receive these socio-educational measures (Sinase/Brazil, 2023), an often traumatic 'early experience of punition' (Alvarez et al., 2017, p. 1). Thus, judicial practices concur to silence and humiliate these children and their families (Scisleski et al., 2017; Sartorio & Rosa, 2010), as they are looked down and prevented from having a say in the judicial process (Menezes & Castro, 2013; Segalin & Trzcinski, 2006). In fact, what underpins the application of rights consists of more of a perspective of disciplining and vengeance towards such potentially dangerous subjects rather than one of securing prerogatives for children and youth who have been social outcasts from birth. At its different levels, the judicial system is operated by magistrates and lawyers whose expertise is hardly informed by knowledge of the 'social question' (Netto, 2013), that is, a progressive political view that can interrogate how social inequalities come to be established and how they can be eradicated.

By and large, what can be highlighted in the situation of the poor, Black, peripheric, often out of school adolescents in conflict with the law is that the emancipatory potential of positive rights has been curbed by the virulent *force* of political conservatism, authoritarian and racist values of the élite, when, at stake, is the maintenance of neocolonial positions of social privilege and economic power.

4.3 Between the legal and the political: children's search for fairness and equality

In 1998, during a terrific rebellion followed by an extensive fire in one of the institutions for adolescent incarceration in the state of São Paulo, Brazil, an adolescent died in bizarre circumstances. Vicentin (2011) recalls this event drawing on reports gathered from other adolescents who survived. According to these reports when the fire started a boy aged about 17 whom has been referred to as M. scarred his own face with a shard of glass and insisted 'let's all stay here and die'. The reports all agree that M. could have run to save his life but, instead, carried on in the same mood until finally, he threw a mattress on the fire and launched his body on it which resulted in his death. Vicentin analyzes this and other terrifying events relating to insurgence and rebellion by incarcerated adolescents in conflict with the law and highlights the inexorability of rebellion in face of the visceral institutionalized annihilation of life in these institutions where isolation, corporal punishments, permanent fear of death and injury, psychological humiliation, violence and terror are rife. M.'s sacrificial death evokes the tragic aspect of worthless lives that are cast out and forgotten. On this account, adolescents' suffering can trigger a different analytical key – one that, rather than stigmatizing, pathologizing or blaming them for their lawlessness and moral transgression, stands as emblematic of the ferocity of power relationships imposed on them.

The vignette of (extreme) suffering presented previously imparts adolescent resistance to, and denunciation of, oppression constituting a *political* endeavour to make known the brutality of force inflicted on those dispossessed of rights to counter tyranny and sovereign power. In this sense, the bursting out of violence on the side of the adolescents signals a decisive moment of refusal to be vilified and objectified by eloquently – through fire, chaos, disorder, self-injury – affirming another subjective position of the oppressed. Thus, the emergence of political subjectivities entails the process of contesting, symbolically and materially, the evil of oppression (Castro, 2018) and envisaging realities not yet achieved.

In Brazil, as in other countries of the Global South, positive rights stand as double-bind mechanisms in their contradictory capacity for both failing their own stated normativity and representing a relevant regulative instance evocative of the ideal norms that we should live for. The search for justice aims, then, at not only claiming back those rights that haven't been enforced, or the 'lawful', but, most importantly, envisages an altogether different social order which can possibly legislate about rights *as well as* practise them. After all, shouldn't a social order – where rights are permanently wronged – be distrusted for the sheer fact that it betrays its own ideals and values? Doesn't the all too often instance of the non-enforceability of rights tell us about the pact of ferocious power relationships[1] that not only stand over and above the legal régimes but also secure them, demanding thus that such a pact become the target of one's struggle?

It can be argued, then, that emancipatory actions of the oppressed gain momentum as they challenge the status quo and its political gatekeepers with the view of dismantling the veiled pacts that have produced and secured the present legal rights' framework. In contrast, as Gordon (2021) discusses, the liberal political subjectivity remains captive of normative models when morality and law supervene over politics indulging in the complacency of the present, and its present order. For Gordon (2021, pp. 61–62), 'the past and the present . . . are both imperfect and, thus, required and still require work', which entails a necessary view of the future as neither foreclosed nor overdetermined but 'paradoxically through and beyond one's immediate reach'. Therefore, the struggle against oppression becomes imperative to unsettle our imperfect present as well as the imperfect legal positivism whose non-enforceability denounces the ill disposition of the powerful which cannot be curbed by rights' legislation.

Legal equality, thus, cannot secure effective equality unless *political action* alters the structure of power relationships that underpin this legal order embedded in racial, class and gender biases. At the same time, Brown and Halley (2002) have cautioned, one cannot live outside of the law, and secondly, in a liberal society, one cannot not want rights as they stand as the sole promise of equality. The evocation of rights are imbricated in the tacit normativity and language of daily life, so that even when collectivities strive for changes and struggle for them, the political debate is summarily converted into legal claims, often sapping further analysis about alternative projects. In this vein,

1 Drawing upon psychoanalytical inspiration (Moreira & Rosa, 2021), here the notion of 'ferocious social relationships' denotes a social pact where, owing to the vicissitudes of a specific historical trajectory of instinctual and cultural convergences, social violence is 'owned' by one (or ones) whose omnipotent will to dominate is not curbed by the expression of the will of many – the power of the law.

it seems that the incommensurability of the 'imperfection of the present' cannot, so far, do without rights even if their effects are contradictory. As Brown (2002, p. 432) puts, 'rights are politically essential and politically regressive'.

4.4 Children's search for equality: reconfiguring the political

The way towards freedom and equality through politics poses shortcomings and impasses. The subalternate position of children – with respect to not being recognized as legitimate claimers of their own perspectives – posits that 'politics' remains a colonized domain officially reserved for adults only whereby they can uphold their generational privileges (Wall, 2011). This does not mean that, despite nonrecognition as equal political partners, children cannot, and do not, act politically. As Nandy (2010), Scott (1990) and many others have shown the oppressed have their own means to resist and contest an unfair status quo even if their opposition is often camouflaged to prevent retaliation. Specially with children and youth, such disguised resistance and opposition are often read as recalcitrant or barbaric behaviours *depoliticized* and turned into sheer noise, not utterances. As children's actions against domination spring from marginal interlocutory positions devoid of political value the superior interlocutory position of the centre (the master, the oppressor, the adult) is naturalized. Hence, children's politics demands a repositioning and a redistribution of resources, relationalities and materialities – 'infrastructure' as Oswell (2016) has put it – in order that new political positions can be staged and assembled. In this vein, liberal democratic politics must be decolonized as different sensible re-orderings of the social (Rancière, 1992, 1996) are foregrounded by the force of children's acts of contestation. In this vein, the research assemblage itself can be a site of building up the infrastructure necessary for children to stage the political and address their political demands.

In what follows, by way of illustrating my argument, I discuss some of the results of my recent research which shows children's search for equality and justice, instigated both by the effect of rage and indignation that a wrong is being done to them and by the claim that they too should be listened to in their demands (or, in Arendtian terms, that they should be part of the political community and have the right to have rights). One of the most outstanding demands put forward by child participants in the research I undertook in a school in Rio de Janeiro was that they should have playtime (a daily break during classes to play) during their school day. Their claim was based on the fact that there was no provision for playtime in the school syllabus, which provided only – in most schools – a discretionary 15 minutes' break for lunch which, if eaten quickly, could allow children some free time. Despite the scientifically celebrated importance of play in childhood (Maturana & Verden-Zöller, 2004; Evans et al., 2016; Lester & Maudsley, 2007; Huizinga, 2008), the banning of playtime from the daily schedule of the school seemed to raise no concerns or uneasiness in anyone, except for the children. In this vein, the demand for playtime (and a space where it can take place in schools) seemed to represent students' own *perspectives* about what was good for them which was condescendingly discredited and devalued by educational staff.

Children's claims for a proper playtime and place at school were coded in varied expressions – grumbles, insignificant gestures, punctual and coded ironies, straightforward demonstrations of anger – requiring from us, researchers, a collaborative reflection to talk back to them so that these different messages could be cohered around a central claim. More to the point was their diffidence about not being in the position of rights-claimers and as being seen as incapable (in the staff's eyes) of proper interlocutory dialogue. Listening to children's variegated complaints about playtime unveiled children's *alternative* narratives about what school life, relationships with elders and educational transmission should be. In the utmost precarity of state schools in Rio de Janeiro, to dream *of another school* contradicted the fact that these poor Black children could only have what was offered to them. Their dream conveyed the possibility of *another place*, of freedom and respect (Gilmore et al., 2024). Their playtime claims contradicted an expected elocution based on rationality, rather mobilizing the possibility of an ethically oriented communication with adults (Critchley, 2007) whose compassion and identification could be demanded and reciprocity enhanced. After all, as children in this research put it, 'weren't adults once children and, as such, couldn't they remember their need to play?', or, 'why can't adults understand that after two or three hours listening to them in the classroom we need to refresh our minds?' Like the adolescent M. in the vignette outlined in Section 3, their claim was about the affirmation of another subject position – of being listened to – in relation to teachers, to us and to society at large, as in the present school order its oppressive normativity provided rules and authority but did not offer justice. The research assemblage proved then to be the site of a subjective and epistemic reconstruction process (Castro, 2025) which allowed for the emergence of children as political subjects. As put by Rancière (1992), political subjetivization consists of articulating 'wrong' or impossible combinations, like that of *children-as-capable*, *children-as-claimers*.[2] It also consists of creating this polemical commonplace for addressing this wrong or making it visible. For Rancière (2006), there is no prior political subject before the act of enacting and verifying in practice the ever so incommensurate principle of equality which holds that everyone is equal. Thus, our research project's epistemic reconstruction implied a painstaking process of repositioning our relationalities with children and school staff imbued with the strength of children's truth

2 Above all, the affirmation of 'impossible' combinations such as Black, peripheric, poor children as capable and as claimers: those who are the least supposed to claim anything, as is the case here. In this vein, Ferguson (2017) points out how in present capitalist societies play, as a sensuous, imaginative and autotelic activity counteracts capitalist designs for some subjectivities who must channel their energies and motivations to instrumentalized labor that is required to produce value for capital.

claims. These allowed for co-generational efforts between researchers and children in securing their demands.

4.5 Epilogue: what chances are there for children's emancipation?

Children's legal rights and its politico-juridical underpinnings have reflected adults' concerns (and prejudices) with the best interests of children reinforcing a conservative vision that children should be kept away from public concerns, dialogue and participation. Moreover, as it has been argued, in countries like Brazil with a legacy of colonization and slavery, the legal framework is firmly entrenched in a public culture of authoritarianism and racialization which thwarts the empowering effects of legal rights. Hence, the legal order and its political gatekeepers do not plausibly offer children reliable ways of emancipation which must be searched for as children mobilize the tensions, gaps, contradictions and insufficiencies of the legal and its political order. In doing so, children's actions reconfigure the normative reach of human reality bringing forth a transformation of the norms that conform to our sense of justice (Gordon, 2021).

However, a critique should be levelled at what can be considered the promise of emancipation through the process of children's political subjectivization as discussed here. In the first place, children's staging of the political can be a haphazard and unfortunate process, especially if it is protagonized by the most destitute of them: the globally and locally peripheric and disposable, the poor and racialized. Fierce destitution works in direct opposition to possibilities of access to, and use of, whatever infrastructure is necessary to stage the political. Hence, for these children enormous difficulties will have to be faced to revert their insufficient status as political actors so that, as Oswell (2009) has observed, a novel political acoustic architecture is constructed to facilitate them being listened to. Secondly, the political subjectivization process entails a collectivization of experiences over and above personal grievances and humiliations. As Qvortrup (1995) once noted, children are not 'a category for themselves', hardly cognizant of what their interests and perspectives as a collectivity can be. As privatized subjects, they are isolated in their homes with infrequent opportunities to be positioned as a same category. Except in the school context, their rare interactions *as a group* make it improbable that they can overcome the individualistic encroachment of personal humiliations and oppressions in order to build up cohesion around the same causes and demands. Even in school, the *absence of playtime* consists itself of a strategically political measure to ban their opportunities to interact together and develop a sense of collectivity. These are immense difficulties that pave the ways for children's emancipation as a collective political subject.

However, politics is about what is least expected and probable, a reason why Arendt (1998) conceived natality as quintessential to it. Children's politics seems to navigate the odds of what is improbable, with flimsy chances to reinvent the legal and the political normativities in force. Nevertheless, children can be regarded as singular political subjects endowed with a distinct contribution to democratic politics in the same way that women, Indigenous people and racialized groups are, and have been. They are, according to Eagleton (1988, p. 620), '*a type of critic of all kinds* . . . because their social marginality is the source at once of their blindness and insight' (my italics). It is then from children's specific position of domination and social marginality that present liberal societies must be questioned, and hopefully changed. These are children's assets that can counterbalance a more pessimistic outlook of children's emancipation through their own political actions and movements.

References

Alderson, P. (2020). Adultism. In D. Cook (ed.), *The Sage encyclopedia of children and childhood studies* (no pagination). Sage.

Alvarez, M., Lourenço, L., & Tonche, J. (2017). A 'experiência precoce de punição': justiça juvenil, adolescentes em conflito com a lei e instituições de internamento. *Plural, 24*(1), 1–9.

Arendt, H. (1998). *The human condition*. University of Chicago Press.

Balagopalan, S. (2019). Why historicize rights-subjectivities? Children's rights, compulsory schooling and the deregulation of child labour in India. *Childhood, 26*(3), 204–320.

Bell, J. (1995). *Understanding adultism: A major obstacle to developing positive youth-adult relationships*. YouthBuild USA. Retrieved November 11, 2024, from https://actioncivics.scoe.net/pdf/Understanding_Adultism.pdf

Brazil/Cedca. (1990). *Federal Law 8069 of July 13th 1990*. www.planalto.gov.br/ccivil_03/leis/l8069.htm

Brown, W. (2002). Suffering the paradoxes of rights. In W. Brown & J. Halley (eds.) *Left legalism, left critique* (pp. 420–431). Duke University Press.

Brown, W., & Halley, J. (2002). Introduction. In W. Brown & J. Halley (eds.) *Left legalism, left critique* (pp. 1–37). Duke University Press.

Castro, L. R. de. (2022). Righting adults' wrongs: "Generationing" on the battlefield – a decolonial approach. *Childhood, 29*(3), 355–370.

Castro, L. R. de. (2025). Development research with children from a decolonial perspective: Experimentation with knowledge and learning to think otherwise. In T. Abebe, A. Dar & K. Wells (eds.) *Handbook on childhood and global development* (pp. 32–45). Routledge.

Castro, L. R., & Tavares, R. (2021). Participation rights in Brazilian schools: Towards the politicization of adult-child relationships? In A. V. Solar, M. L. Nascimento & V. Llobet (eds.) *South American childhoods since the 1990s: Neoliberalisation and the exercise of children's rights* (pp. 175–203). Palgrave Macmillan.

Castro, L. R. de. (2018). The self under domination: A dialogue between Nandy's *The intimate enemy* and Dangarembga's *Nervous Conditions. Postcolonial Studies, 21*(2), 192–209. https://doi.org/10.1080/13688790.2018.1470448

Castro, L. R. De. (2020). Age epistemology and the politics of age. In C. Baraldi & L. R. de Castro (eds.) *Global childhoods in international perspective: Universality, diversity and inequalities* (pp. 33–50). SSIS Series. Sage.

Castro, L. R. de, & Kosminsky, E. (2010). Childhood and its regimes of visibility in Brazil: An analysis of the contribution of the social sciences. *Current Sociology, 58*(2), 1–26.

Cordero Arce, M. (2019). Who is (to be) the subject of children's rights? In S. Spyrou, R. Rosen & D. T. Cook (eds.) *Reimagining childhood studies* (pp. 169–182). Bloomsbury.
Critchley, S. (2007). *Infinitely demanding: Ethics of commitment, politics of resistance.* Verso.
Eagleton, T. (1988). The critic as clown. In C. Nelson & L. Grossberg (eds.) *Marxism and the interpretation of culture* (pp. 619–632). University of Illinois Press.
Evans, B., Horton, J., & Skelton, T. (eds.). (2016). *Play and recreation, health and well-being.* Springer Nature.
Fávero, E. T. (ed.). (2020). *Famílias na cena contemporânea: (des)proteção, (des)igualdades e judicialização.* Navegando.
Ferguson, S. (2017). Children, childhood and capitalism: A social reproduction perspective. In T. Bhattacharya (ed.) *Social reproduction theory: Remapping class, recentering oppression* (pp. 112–130). Pluto.
Gilmore, R. W., Antipon, L. C., Alves, C. N., & Novo, M. F. (2024). Ruth Wilson Gilmore – Freedom is a place. Ruth Wilson Gilmore e a Geografia Abolicionista. *Geousp, 28*(1), e-222824. www.revistas.usp.br/geousp/article/view/222824. https://doi.org/10.11606/issn.2179-0892.geousp.2024.222824.pt
Gomes, F. (2006). Conflito social e welfare state: Estado e desenvolvimento social no Brasil. *Revista de Administracao Publica, 40*(2), 201–236.
Gordon, L. (2021). *Freedom, justice and decolonization.* Routledge.
Hobson, B., & Lister, R. (2002). Citizenship. In B. Hobson, J. Lewis & B. Siim (eds.) *Contested concepts in gender and social politics* (pp. 23–54). Edward Elgar Publishing.
Huizinga, J. (2008). *Homo ludens: o jogo como elemento da cultura.* Perspectiva.
Josefsson, J., Sandin, B., Hanson, K., & Balagopalan, S. (2023). Representing children. In B. Sandin, J. Josefsson, K. Hanson & S. Balagopalan (eds.) *The politics of children's rights and representation* (pp. 1–28). Palgrave Macmillan.
Leal, D., & Macedo, J. P. (2017). A penalização da miséria no Brasil: os adolescentes em conflito com a lei. *Textos & Contextos, 16*(1), 128–141.
Lester, S., & Maudsley, M. (2007). *Play, naturally.* NCB.
Lister, R. (1997). *Citizenship: Feminist perspectives.* Macmillan.
Lister, R. (2007). Why citizenship? Where, when and how children? *Theoretical Inquiries in Law, 8*(2), 693–718.
Maturana, H., & Verden-Zöller, G. (2004). *Amar e Brincar.* Pala Athena.
Menezes, T., & Castro, L. R. de. (2013). Redução da idade penal: um questionamento sobre seus fins. *Mnemosine, 9*(1), 149–168.
Mignolo, W. (2011). La colonialidad a lo largo y a lo ancho: el hemisferio occidental en el horizonte colonial de la modernidad. In E. Lander (ed.) *La colonialidad del saber: eurocentrismo y ciencias sociales* (pp. 73–104). CICCUS/CLACSO.
Moosa-Mitha, M. (2005). A difference-centred alternative to theorization of children's citizenship rights. *Citizenship Studies, 9*(4), 369–388.
Moreira, J., & Rosa, M. (eds.). (2021). *Violência e Psicanálise: atualizações intersaberes.* Inst. Psicologia, USP.
Mouffe, C. (1993). *The return of the political.* Verso.
Nandy, A. (2010). *The intimate enemy: Loss and recovery of self under domination.* Oxford University Press.
Netto, J. P. (2013). A questão social na América Latina. In M. L. Garcia & E. Raizer (eds.) *A questão social e as políticas sociais no contexto latino-americano* (pp. 83–111). Edit. UFES.
Nyamu, I., & Wamahiu, S. (2022). What might a decolonial perspective on child protection look like? Lessons from Kenya. *Childhood, 29*(3), 423–438.
Oswell, D. (2009). Yet to come? Globality and the sound of an infant politics. *Radical Politics Today, 1*(1), 1–18.

Oswell, D. (2016). *Infrastructure, infancy and children's rights on the border: Between Butler and Rancière.* Paper delivered to ESA Sociology of Children and Childhood Network RN4, University of Ghent, Brussels, May 2016.

Oswell, D. (2019). What space for a children's politics? Rethinking infancy in childhood studies. In S. Spyrou, R. Rosen & D. T. Cook (eds.) *Reimagining childhood studies* (pp. 199–211). Bloomsbury.

Pateman, C. (1992). *Participacão e teoria democrática.* Paz e Terra.

Pavón-Cuellar, D. (2021). The still wretched of the earth: A critique of imaginary decolonization. In N. Gibson (ed.) *Fanon today: Reason and revolt of the Wretched of the Earth* (pp. 207–221). Daraja Press.

Pinheiro, A. A. (2006). *Criança e adolescente no Brasil: porque o abismo entre a lei e a realidade.* Editora UFC.

Qvortrup, J (1995). From useful to useful: The historical continuity of children's constructive participation. In A. M. Ambert (ed.) *Sociological studies of children* (Vol. 7, pp. 49–76). Emerald.

Rancière, J. (1992). Politics, identification and subjectivization. In J. Rajchman (ed.) *The identity in question* (pp. 63–72). Routledge.

Rancière, J. (1996). *O desentendimento.* Ed. 34.

Rancière, J. (2006). *Hatred of democracy.* Verso.

Rose, N. (1999). *Governing the soul* (2nd ed.). Routledge.

Santos, W. G. (1979). *Cidadania e justiça: A política social na ordem brasileira.* Campus.

Sartorio, A., & Rosa, E. (2010). Novos paradigmas e velhos discursos: analisando processos de adolescentes em conflito com a lei. *Serviço Social & Sociedade, 103*, 554–575.

Saward, M. (2008). Democracy and citizenship: Expanding domains. In J. Dryzek, B. Honig & A. Phillips (eds.) *The Oxford handbook of political theory* (pp. 400–419). Oxford University Press.

Scisleski, A., Checa, M., Bruno, B., Galeano, G., Santos, S., & Vitta, A. (2017). A lei em conflito com os jovens: problematizando políticas públicas. *Revista Polis e Psyche, 7*(2), 4–27.

Scott, J. (1990). *Domination and the arts o/resistance: Hidden transcripts.* Yale University Press.

Segalin, A., & Trzcinski, C. (2006). Ato infracional na adolescência: problematização do acesso ao sistema de justiça. *Revista Virtual Textos e Contextos, 6*, 1–19.

Sinase/Brazil. (2023). *Levantamento Anual 2023.* Ministério dos Direitos Humanos e da Cidadania.

Siqueira, L. (2014). A pobreza como 'disfunção social': a culpabilização e a criminalização do individuo. *Argumentum, 6*(1), 240–252.

Smith, K. (2024). Using adultism in conceptualizing oppression of children and youth: More than a buzzword? *Taboo: The Journal of Culture and Education, 22*(1), 227–254.

Telles, V. S. (1998). Direitos sociais: afinal do que se trata? *Revista USP, 37*, 34–46.

Vicentin, M. C. (2011). Corpos em rebelião e o sofrimento-resistência. *Tempo Social, 23*(1), 97–113.

Wacquant, L. (2015). *Punir os pobres: a nova gestão da miséria nos Estados Unidos.* Revan.

Wall, J. (2011). Can democracy represent children? Towards a politics of difference. *Childhood, 19*(1), 86–100.

Young, I. M. (2000). *Inclusion and democracy.* Oxford University Press.

5 Children's rights from a childist perspective

Theorizing social empowerment

John Wall

5.1 Introduction

It is sometimes said that children's rights are human rights. The suggestion is that children ought to be considered full members of the larger human rights community. While entirely correct so far as it goes, this formulation leaves unexamined a prior question: What is meant by the 'human' in human rights in the first place? If the subject of human rights is assumed in theory and practice to be primarily adult, then non-adults will tend to be presumed somehow lacking in human rights by definition. Indeed, exactly this normative problem has bedeviled the rights of many groups over history – women, racialized minorities, the poor, and others – invisibly marginalizing their claims to full inclusion in human rights. An important question for *critical* children's rights, then, is not just how children's rights are human rights, but also, and perhaps more profoundly, how human rights may be understood to include children.

This chapter aims to advance critical children's rights scholarship along such lines by critiquing human rights assumptions through the lens of childism. Childism is a critical theory similar to feminism, critical race theory, decolonialism, and the like (Wall, 2010, 2019a). It challenges society's underlying normative assumptions from the perspective not of gender, race, or class but instead age. As Frantz Fanon (1963, p. 2) says of decolonialism, childism too 'sets out to change the order of the world.' Of course, a childist critique of human rights must be made intersectionally with other systemic critiques. But since it has so far lacked the same scholarly and public attention, it also needs to be formulated in its own right. Indeed, childism has much to offer other critical perspectives, insofar as women, the colonized, the poor, racial and ethnic minorities, and the disabled are often denied full human rights precisely on account of their intersectionally supposed childlikeness.

This proposed childist critique of human rights is advanced in two ways. First, this chapter deconstructs adultistic or patriarchal assumptions that, both historically and today, have animated concepts and practices of human rights. And second, it reconstructs a childist understanding of human rights that responds to this adultism by accounting for the lived experiences of children as children. The argument made here is primarily a theoretical one, but it

DOI: 10.4324/9781003510284-6

is further illustrated by concrete and practical examples. The result of these explorations is that human rights need, once again, to be understood in a radically different way. Overall, it is argued, they need to be theorized as a means of not just individual but social empowerment.

5.2 The adultism of human rights

Much understanding of contemporary human rights is built on European Enlightenment ideas. But such ideas, it is rarely noted, involve efforts to carve out a public realm that explicitly excludes children. Rights here were specifically designed as a sphere of not only male-only, wealthy-only, and European-only but also, and just as importantly, adult-only public life. To have 'rights,' according to the adult White male theorists who most influenced their formation, is to participate in a realm of independent rational freedom. It is well known that this view of rights underwrote a wide range of wrongs: the colonizing of supposedly uncivilized non-Europeans (Rollo, 2024); the second-class citizenship of purportedly less than fully rational women (Beauvoir, 1971); the subjugation of the inherently dependent poor (Rancière, 2010); and the violence of the transatlantic slave trade and racism (hooks, 1981). But less well understood is the impact of such notions on the rights of children: despite the fact that, in the eyes of Enlightenment philosophers of rights, what generally renders any group less deserving of rights is precisely that group's childlikeness.

This centering of adulthood was constructed in various still influential ways. One is to suggest that rights are a means of pursuing rational self-interest. Such a view was developed by John Locke, an English theorist whose ideas profoundly influenced the United States' Constitution. Locke (1823, pp. 159–161) argued, at length and in several treatises, that 'natural rights,' as he calls them, consist in each individual's – and no longer each king's – God-given entitlement to preserve their own 'property,' that is, their life, liberty, and possessions. Children, however, are not their own property but the 'temporary property' of their parents, since children are mere 'white pages' lacking the rational capacities to preserve their own interests for themselves (Locke, 1823, pp. 126–133, 1989, p. 105). In fact, were children under the age of 21 to exercise their own rights, Locke argues, they would only do themselves and others harm.

Another way that rights were defined in the Enlightenment around adulthood is in the idea that children need to be protected from the worldly concerns of public life in a private sphere of natural innocence. This idea is formulated by the philosopher of the French Revolution, Jean-Jacques Rousseau, who, like Locke, has much to say about children and why they are unfit subjects of rights. Rousseau (1947, I.6) conceptualizes rights differently as freedoms to participate in forming society's 'general will' or common life. However, he argues that children are like 'noble savages' who need to be secluded from this common life so that their innate capacities can be nurtured over time. Only in this way can their inner moral sense eventually stand up for itself in the public sphere's corrupt and competitive arena (Rousseau, 1947, I.2 and I.4, 1979). Indeed, a civilized society depends on protecting children from it for a time so that each new generation can infuse it with untainted natural values.

A third way that adultism is built into fundamental European conceptualizations of rights is that children can be denied rights because of their supposed lack of full autonomy or independence. This notion is articulated by the German philosopher Immanuel Kant (1974), who defines rights as societies' means for respecting and protecting each individual's basic human 'dignity.' For Kant, children are, once again, explicitly to be excluded from rights, this time because they lack the basis of social dignity in the capacity for independent self-rule (Kant, 1974, para. 29). Indeed, in Kant's view, children are not only pre-rational but actively ir-rational. Having not yet formed the 'discipline' or 'cultivation' (*Bildung*) of adult reason, they remain much like 'animals' controlled by need and passion (1960, 1974, para. 28). Human rights, then, are fully afforded only to those (White, male, European) adults who are civilized enough to use them rationally.

I have elsewhere examined how these foundational understandings of modern rights weave themselves into contemporary human rights theory (Wall, 2008, 2016). The chief difference in philosophies of rights today is that these forms of adultism are now implicit. While Enlightenment theorists thought they needed to argue for why rights are not for children, the most influential contemporary political philosophers such as John Rawls (1999), Jürgen Habermas (1990), and Seyla Benhabib (2004) simply do not consider the situation of children at all. Shortly, I will show that neither, for the most part, do more critical human rights philosophies in feminism, postcolonialism, and Marxism. While children have, of course, gained many rights over the past century, theorists of rights have more or less forgotten that they exist. As a result, the notion that rights may involve a child-adult binary remains largely unthought.

While an extensive critique of contemporary rights theory cannot be undertaken here, allow me to provide just one telling example: the discussion of rights by the influential postcolonial theorist Gayatri Chakravorty Spivak. Spivak is a useful touchpoint because her work is centrally concerned with overcoming normative marginalization. And it has proven immensely useful in children's rights studies (Balagopalan, 2019). However, adultism is so profoundly embedded in contemporary human rights work that even Spivak fails to notice it. To take just one example, Spivak's (2004) published Oxford Amnesty Lectures, titled 'Righting Wrongs,' applies the postmodern deconstructive ideas of Immanuel Levinas and Jacques Derrida to developing a postcolonial critique of human rights philosophies, and it draws extensively on her fieldwork with children in poor rural Indian schools. Postcolonial theory would seem an especially fruitful avenue for unpacking adultism, considering that, as others have argued, it can be used to uncover oppressive strategies of colonialized peoples' 'infantilization' (Rollo, 2024; Biswas, 2023; Bray & Nakata, 2019).

In fact, however, Spivak's critique is developed exclusively on the bases of class, gender, and race. It does not consider questions of age in any normative sense. Her main argument is for 'suturing rights thinking into the torn cultural fabric of responsibility' (Spivak, 2004, p. 544). What she means is that European rights language remains meaningless in postcolonial environments because it lacks a poststructuralist sense of 'responsiveness to the other that is outside the self' (Spivak, 2004, pp. 544–545). The chief problem is that international human rights ideas involve a colonial imagination of the 'domestic middle class,' so that 'the usually silent victims of pervasive rather than singular and spectacular human rights violations are generally the rural poor' (Spivak, 2004, pp. 527 & 529). But children remain, in her analysis, an object rather than a subject of rights. For example, poor rural teachers are said to be trapped in a system of rote colonialist memorization that fails to inculcate in lower-class children 'the habit of independence' (Spivak, 2004, p. 552). Spivak's theories of rights are not inapplicable to children, but neither can they be said to have been developed with the specific issues of children as children in mind.

5.3 The ontology of deep interdependence

Overcoming the adultism built into assumptions about human rights requires a level of critique that is profound, systemic, and normative. It requires, in other words, a childist reconstruction of human rights' very concepts and structures. It is not sufficient merely to critique existing framings of the rights of children. Nor will it work to stick to implementing children's rights practices. Rather, the critique of age needs to be added to existing intersectional critiques of gender, class, race, and coloniality when it comes to understanding human rights as such. There are many ways to undertake such a reconstruction, but in the following I explore three basic dimensions of ontology, epistemology, and politics. Together, these suggest that human rights at present remain overly individualistic and need to be reimagined as means of social empowerment.

If human rights are to become truly human, at a very basic level they need to ground themselves in new understandings of the human being – that is, new ontologies. For, as we have seen, the history of human rights has purported to describe a kind of universal humanity which, however, defines humanity in primarily adultistic terms. Critiques of ontological assumptions have been made in recent decades in terms of class, gender, race, coloniality, and other dimensions of human existence, but rarely in terms of age. For example, feminists have argued that human rights need to better attend to gendered insights into social relationality (Gilligan, 1982). Critical race theorists propose reconceptualizing human rights as responding to systemically excluded human multiplicities (Delgado, 1999). Counteracting age marginalization depends, I now argue, on a new ontology of human rights that is based on a conception of the human as not only interdependent but *deeply* interdependent.

As we have seen, the persistent binary opposition of children's – and human – rights rests significantly on the Enlightenment assumption that children are not fully independent. A normative line separates humans who are supposedly rational, self-directed, and responsible from humans who appear irrational, dependent, and lacking capacities for responsibility. This latter group is often coded as children and childlike. It defines the social being of not just children but also anyone constructed as less than fully autonomous. Rights can be denied to colonized groups, for example, on the grounds of 'the infantilization of all Indigenous people as children of the colonial state who can never grow up' (Bray & Nakata, 2019, p. 303). For children in particular, it justifies divisions between general 'human' rights on one hand (such as in the Universal Declaration of Human Rights (UDHR) and the International Covenant on Civil and Political Rights (ICCPR)) and separate 'children's' rights on the other (such as in the Convention on the Rights of the Child (UNCRC)), so that children are constructed separately from adults as primarily needing protection and provisions with only carefully curtailed freedoms (Daly, 2018).

Theories of human interdependence have already been developed in various ways in feminist and poststructuralist political theory. It is a complex concept with different possible meanings. Judith Butler (2015) defines interdependence as human beings' precarity, embodiment, and dependence on wider communities. As she puts it,

> If we are living organisms who speak and act, then we are clearly related to a vast continuum or network of living beings; we not only live among them, but our persistence as living organisms depends on that matrix of sustaining interdependent relations.
>
> (Butler, 2015, p. 86)

The postcolonial philosopher Néstor García Canclini claims that participatory citizenship involves both 'interruption' and 'intermediation': interruption of normative assumptions but also intermediation between oppressed groups who form coalitions together. In yet another way, Jacques Rancière (2010, p. 46) describes social interdependence as wider societies responding to the 'dissensus' of nonnormative and hence invisible lives. In these and many other cases, the subject of human rights is not a modern autonomous agent but a postmodern participant in social interdependency.

Does consideration of childhood fit here or demand further theoretical innovation? Some put the aforementioned postmodern theorists to effective use in understanding children's rights (Devine & Cockburn, 2018; Fitzgerald et al., 2010; Jans, 2004; Roche, 1999; Woodhouse, 2008). But a truly critical theorization of children's rights needs to go further and break down the historically profound binary opposition in rights assumptions between independent adulthood and dependent childhood. It takes a more structural critique to start including children fully and equally in new norms of shared humanity.

To learn from childhoods means to understand the human in human rights as *deeply* interdependent (Wall, 2019b). The 'human' in human rights is not only defined by its wider social relations but also fundamentally reliant upon them. Individuals and groups are not only related to their broader societies but also essentially dependent upon them for active support and nurturance. No one survives or thrives apart from larger dependencies on groups. We exist in networks of social relations that are both horizontal and vertical: constructed by both shared relations and mutual reliance.

The notion of human beings as deeply interdependent draws in part on African concepts of community (see Abebe and Twum-Danso Imoh, both in this volume). As Hilda Tafadzwa Mugadza and colleagues (2019, p. 6) argue, sub-Saharan communities are 'founded on the core values of *Ubuntu* . . . which means "I am, because we are," [and] is founded on human connectedness, solidarity, and survival practices.' *Ubuntu* suggests a decolonial view of society that does not prioritize independence over dependence but, instead, puts forward a common, reciprocal, and compassionate sense of responsibility of all toward all (Mtata, 2021; Ndofirepi, 2011). What is helpful here for a childist social ontology is that human interdependence involves what I am calling a *deep* or vertical dimension of mutual reliance and responsibility. It is adultistic to assume that there is something wrong with acknowledging human dependency. Both adults and children share a common human reality of simultaneous independence from and dependence upon one another.

Consider, for example, the claims of youth climate activists. From an adultist point of view, such activists are expressing adultlike capacities for independence, freedom of expression, and human rights agency. But in reality, what they are doing is demanding that their own particular concerns for the present and the future transform the assumptions of the wider human community on which everyone's well-being depends. Human interdependence is not superficial but deep, a defining element in our very survival as a species. The human rights community has largely failed to respond to the climate concerns of children and youth because it tends to construct rights as assertions of independent individuals. Claims of vulnerability or calls for shared responsibility are considered secondary and easily brushed aside. The claim for a right to a healthy environment must compete with much more powerful claims to the contrary for freedoms to make money from oil companies and global corporations. If, in contrast, the human rights community recognized humanity's deep interdependence, it would also recognize its obligation to account more fundamentally to those depending on its response – that is, not just children, but all of us. It would be willing to tackle the difficult task of actively reaching out beyond those who have the most power to also include those most affected by its decisions.

5.4 The epistemology of lived experience

A childist reconceptualization of human rights additionally calls for new epistemologies, that is, new understandings of what counts as legitimate and valuable social knowledge. As Amanda Fricker (2007) argues, a fundamental dimension of social exclusion is 'epistemic injustice.' In her feminist interpretation, epistemic injustice refers to systemic biases against women's capacities as knowers, their being constructed by historical patriarchal norms as less than fully rational and worthy of being heard. This epistemic problem has also been described as a 'double bind': not only do women's experiences already count for less in the public sphere, but their efforts to make these experiences known are also assumed to carry less weight (Anderson, 1993). The question, when it comes to critical children's rights, is whether this epistemic consideration is the same for children as for women and other groups, or are children's ways of knowing excluded from public life in different and, perhaps, more complex ways? If so, then the epistemic dimension of human rights needs to be challenged from not only a feminist but also, and intersectionally, a childist perspective.

Fricker's notion of epistemic injustice has been usefully applied to children's rights. As Amy Hanna (2023, p. 43) argues, Fricker's theory helps to show how children's own rights concerns are routinely rendered 'silent' by the fact that discourses about them 'obstruct their voices and expressions.' A chief complaint of young people fighting for their rights is that even when they are given a voice, this voice is rarely taken seriously in actual policymaking (Wyness, 2005). There is no doubt that contemporary policymaking and laws marginalize children's own capacities as knowers of their own rights.

But the epistemic problem for children raises new questions about what it means to understand 'lived experience,' in the sense of the knowledge a person gains from their own first-hand engagement with the particularities of life, in contrast with the knowledge they gain from normative assumptions about it (Dilthey, 1907/2020). Such knowledge is inherently incomplete and 'different' in the sense that it is irreducible to generalized social explanation. Mehmoona Moosa-Mitha (2005, p. 375) applies this notion to children's rights by arguing that children's 'lived experiences' should be understood as an 'interrogation of hegemony,' an exploration of children's (or anyone's) 'right to participate differently.' From this perspective, epistemic injustice involves any violation of a marginalized group's right to larger societal recognition for their own particular lived experiences of difference.

In children's rights studies, this epistemological problem has most effectively been addressed under the umbrella of theories of 'living rights.' As Edward van Daalen et al. (2016, p. 818) describe it, 'living rights are already there, in the daily lives and struggles of people confronting the challenges of everyday life.' They represent 'children's agency in living with and through their rights' (van Daalen et al., 2016, p. 817). To be viewed as subjects of living rights is to be viewed as making claims on societies that are based, in the first instance, not on general laws and treaties, but on concrete and particular lived experiences. It also means that knowledge of rights arises, not from abstract social interest, but from immediate grassroots demand. Because all people, including children, experience their worlds in their own different ways, living rights express persons' 'non-essentialist' claims as these are 'embedded . . . in real-life contexts traversed by struggles for social justice' (Nieuwenhuys & Hanson, 2024, pp. 171 & 176–177).

This concept of living rights helps to provide a critique of adultistic approaches to knowledge. As Afua Twum-Danso Imoh and Samuel Okyere (2020, p. 1) explain it, compared to top-down ideas of rights, living rights are 'more holistic, inclusive and aligned with the meaning that children themselves attach to their everyday lives as well as to the personal and social relationships that they value.' It can illuminate, for example, the rights that are concretely at play as 'very young children [1–3 years old] enact their human rights in the preschool setting' such as to 'ownership, influence, and equal value' (Quennerstedt, 2010, p. 5). It can also help mount critiques of larger human rights systems:

> Like in a mirror maze, which obfuscates rather than enlightens where a person stands and how to move ahead, you cannot simply take for granted whose interests are represented nor the aims and direction of interventions and discourses on behalf of children.
>
> (Hanson, 2023, p. 182)

However, living rights theory can be taken a step further by addressing the deeper epistemological problem of children's lack of social standing to make their lived experiences visible in the first place. It is true that children of all ages are agents just like adults who, both explicitly and implicitly, demand their living rights. But children are also distinctly marginalized as children from being able to claim authority in doing so. All marginalized groups face the epistemic injustice of having their voices delegitimized. Children, however, are denied their voice, not only because they are considered less than fully rational, but also because childhood is coded in modern societies as the very epitome of knowledgelessness. It remains socially acceptable to tell adults not to 'act like a child' in ways it is no longer socially acceptable to tell men not to 'act like a woman.' Children are still socially constructed as 'innocent,' a term which can be interpreted to mean 'not knowing.' Critical children's rights need not only to acknowledge children's grassroots lived experience but also to overcome childhood's epistemological illegitimacy to make this experience known in the first place.

A childist analysis suggests that the kind of knowledge needed for human rights is not just the knowledge that arises from exercising one's voice and agency, but in a more complex way the knowledge of normative difference that arises from lived experience. Lived experience is never reducible to social beliefs about it or even grassroots expressions of it. It is knowable, rather, only as an always particular, concrete, and transformative challenge to accepted understanding. Take, for example, the human rights of child labourers, many of whom are fighting to be able to work with dignity and without exploitation (Liebel, 2013). The international human rights community, through International Labor Organization (ILO) treaties, claims that, unlike adults, children under 14 are necessarily exploited when they work for a living. But this view rests on beliefs about age that children's own lived experiences call into question. Child labourers who insist on the right to work are demanding, in effect, not only a voice in their rights but also a normative transformation in adultistic understandings of children's lives. Such lived experiences can be understood only via a systemic shift in understandings about childhood itself: from one based on children's need for labour protection to one based on children's need to also sometimes participate in the labour economy.

5.5 The politics of empowered inclusion

These ontological and epistemological considerations suggest, finally, possible new ways of theorizing politics. By politics I mean the broad exercise of both formal and informal power. Children are, of course, marginalized from power in many ways. They also exercise power in many ways. The question is how human rights need to be reimagined so that children's exercise of power is equal to that of adults, that is, so that the capacity to influence social life is no longer bifurcated by age. What would it mean for politics to no longer treat children as mere objects of power, and, indeed, the property of adults, but instead as equal subjects of power in their position as children? Following upon the notions developed previously of deep interdependence and lived experience, childist politics calls for reconceptualizing human rights as practices of empowered inclusion, that is, as socially active extensions of power in response to lived experiences of difference.

Political inclusion is defined by the influential political philosopher Iris Marion Young (2000, p. 8) as 'encourag[ing] the particular perspectives of relatively marginalized social groups to receive specific representation.' The important point Young makes is that political inclusion is not just a matter of being given equal agency and voice. Rather, as women and others have found, it demands new ways of responding to particular groups' 'specific issues of subordination and vulnerability' (Young, 2000, p. 271). This notion can be applied to children by recognizing that young people's exclusion from political life has deep and systemic historical roots. For example, Nicola Ansell (2016, pp. 173–174) uses Young to show that understanding child poverty in Africa depends on 'adopt[ing] a social justice lens to examine the contextually situated processes through which poor southern African children are systematically oppressed.' Children's exclusion from power is not just about the denial of their social agency. It is more profoundly about the denial of their normative inclusion.

This interpretation of political inclusion involves an element of emancipation. If a group is historically oppressed, then it makes sense that they demand freedom. Matiás Cordero Arce (2015, p. 31) argues that 'children are a minority group subjected to the structural oppression of an adultist system' who call for societies to 'overcome the adult as the measure of all human beings' by children's 'emancipation . . . from below.' For example, children's sexual rights may be marginalized by being constructed as deviant or nonexistent, instead of being recognized as responding to children's own 'distinct' sexual 'subjectivity' or 'difference' (Egan & Hawkes, 2009).

Another way to put this is to say that children's political inclusion involves fighting against systemic discrimination. Inclusion requires the overcoming of deep historical bias. As Aoife Daly et al. (2022, p. 427) argue, 'childhood should be recognized as a protected characteristic, as is the case for other groups such as women, ethnic and racial minorities, and people with disabilities.' The UNCRC's nondiscrimination article, Article 2, could in principle, even if not yet in practice, protect not only children's gender, ethnic, racial, and other traditional categories of prejudice, but also 'protect children from discrimination on the basis of childhood' (Daly et al., 2022, p. 450). The historical marginalization of children makes it necessary to emancipate them, not only from injustice, but also from all the ways that injustice is codified within existing social and legal structures. There are international treaties against gender and race discrimination, but none targeting age discrimination.

But the inclusion in power of children as children needs a still more childist theorization, based on the aforementioned ontological and epistemological considerations, in which politics is understood as a means toward what can be called '*empowered* inclusion' (Josefsson & Wall, 2020). Politics comes to include human lived experience in all its diversity and difference, not just by emancipating it from historical oppressions, but also by societies actively responding to ingrained power differences. Politics is not just about opening up shared space to new perspectives but also about deliberately reconfiguring shared space so that new perspectives actually make a difference within it. Empowerment is not meant here in the traditional modernist sense of the liberation of independent individuals from social strictures. Rather, empowerment ought to be understood, from a childist point of view, as a society's deeply interdependent response to marginalized experiences.

One example can be found in the worldwide movement for children's rights to vote. For many years, starting in the 1970s with advocates like John Holt (1974) and Richard Farson (1974), as well as from the 1990s with child-led groups like KRÄTZÄ (2024) and the Foundation for the Rights of Future Generations (2024), the argument for children's suffrage was that children deserve equal voting rights because they deserve to have their independent voices heard. Children should be included in politics as individual agents with their own distinctive voices (Umbers, 2018). However, it can be argued that such an approach assumes a normatively adultist conception of voting itself (Goodin & Lau, 2011; López-Guerra, 2014; Wall, 2021). A childist conception of the human right to vote might reimagine voting as an exercise of empowered inclusion. My own argument has been for a new kind of 'proxy-claim' right to vote, one in which anyone with strong dependencies on others for political empowerment – such as infants, the very young, adults with severe cognitive disabilities, adults hospitalized, or adults with dementia – should have a proxy vote by a guardian, much as in medical decisions; anyone who wishes to do so, regardless of age or any other factor, could claim the exercise of their voting right on their own behalf whenever they so desire (Wall, 2021). The right to vote has, in fact, undergone equally radical shifts in understandings of politics as suffrage has been gained by the poor, minorities, women, the formerly colonized, and others (Runciman, 2022). To systematize the political inclusion of children, and thereby make democracies more truly democratic, the normative structures of voting itself would need to shift away from practices of independent inclusion to practices of interdependently empowered inclusion.

5.6 Conclusion: social empowerment

These three dimensions of a new way of thinking about human rights amount in the end to the notion that human rights exist to serve not just individual but social empowerment. The key to children's continued lack of centrality in rights has been a globally influential European notion of rights as protections of independent and supposedly rational and disembodied individuals. This notion has, of course, been critiqued already from many different angles, as suggested previously. But its arguably most thorough critique needs to come from a childist deconstruction of the modern imagination of the human as quintessentially the independent adult. The reality is that there are not some members of societies who are independently self-empowered and others who are dependently empowered by others. Rather, human beings survive and thrive by means of the social empowerment of one another. Such is the true purpose of a system of rights.

One cannot pretend in one place to formulate a new theory of human rights overall, only to explore new possibilities in the hopes of stimulating further thinking. It would be important to engage systematically with both mainstream and critical rights theories in political science and philosophy. There would need to be wider conversations with the many new voices emerging around political rights in the interdisciplinary field of childhood studies. It would be vital to learn more from grassroots children's rights movements and struggles. Most of all, it would be necessary to engage more with children's own ideas, expressions, and experiences. All of these are emerging concerns among scholars of critical children's rights. All are needed as well in advancing childist human rights theory.

But in the end, critical children's rights must include an element of theoretical innovation. The problem of children gaining their rights is in no small part a normative problem of how to understand human nature and power. Until the human includes the child, children will continue to be written out of human rights.

References

Anderson, P. S. (1993). *Ricœur and Kant: Philosophy of the will.* Scholars Press.

Ansell, N. (2016). "Once upon a time . . .": Orphanhood, childhood studies and the depoliticization of childhood poverty in southern Africa. *Childhood*, *23*(2), 162–177. https://psycnet.apa.org/doi/10.1177/0907568215589419

Arce, M. C. (2015). *Maturing* children's rights theory: *From* children, *with* children, *of* children. *International Journal of Children's Rights*, *23*(2), 283–331. https://doi.org/10.1163/15718182-02302006

Balagopalan, S. (2019). Why historicize rights-subjectivities? Children's rights, compulsory schooling, and the deregulation of child labor in India. *Childhood*, *26*(3), 304–320. https://doi.org/10.1177/0907568219856077

Beauvoir, S. (1971). *The second sex* (H. M. Parshley, Trans.). Alfred A. Knopf.

Benhabib, S. (2004). *The rights of others: Aliens, residents, and citizens.* Cambridge University Press.

Biswas, T. (2023). Becoming good ancestors: A decolonial, childist approach to global intergenerational sustainability. *Children & Society*, *37*, 1005–1020. https://doi.org/10.1111/chso.12722

Bray, D., & Nakata, S. (2019). The figure of the child in democratic politics. *Contemporary Political Theory*, *19*(1), 20–37. https://doi.org/10.1057/s41296%2D019%2D00319%2Dx

Butler, J. (2015). *Notes toward a performative theory of assembly.* Harvard University Press.

Daly, A. (2018). *Children, autonomy and the courts: Beyond the right to be heard.* Brill.

Daly, A., Stern, R. T., & Leviner, P. (2022). UN convention on the rights of the child, article 2 and discrimination on the basis of childhood. *Nordic Journal of International Law*, *91*, 419–452. https://doi.org/63/15718107-91030007

Delgado, R. (1999). *When equality ends: Stories about race and resistance.* Westview Press.

Devine, D., & Cockburn, T. (2018). Theorizing children's social citizenship: New welfare states and intergenerational justice. *Childhood*, *25*(2), 142–157. https://doi.org/10.1177/0907568218759787

Dilthey, W. (1907/2020). *The essence of philosophy* (S. A. Emery & W. T. Emery, Trans.). The University of North Carolina Press.

Egan, R. D., & Hawkes, G. (2009). The problem with protection: Or, why we need to move towards recognition and the sexual agency of children. *Continuum: Journal of Media & Cultural Studies*, *23*(3), 389–400. https://doi.org/10.1080/10304310902842975

Fanon, F. (1963). *The wretched of the earth* (C. Farrington, Trans.). Penguin.

Farson, R. (1974). *Birthrights: A bill of rights for children.* Macmillan.

Fitzgerald, R., Graham, A., Smith, A., & Taylor, N. (2010). Children's participation as a struggle over recognition: Exploring the promise of dialogue. In B. Percy-Smith & N. Thomas (eds.) *A handbook of children and young people's participation* (pp. 293–305). Routledge.

Foundation for the Rights of Future Generations. (2024). Retrieved August 5, 2024, from www.intergenerationaljustice.org/

Fricker, A (2007). *Epistemic injustice: Power and the ethics of knowing.* Oxford University Press.

Gilligan, C. (1982). *In a different voice: Psychological theory and women's development.* Harvard University Press.

Goodin, R. E., & Lau, J. C. (2011). Enfranchising incompetents: Suretyship and the joint authorship of laws. *Ratio*, *24*(2), 154–165. https://doi.org/10.1111/j.1467-9329.2011.00490.x

Habermas, J. (1990). *Moral consciousness and communicative action* (C. Lenhardt & S. W. Nicholsen, Trans.). The MIT Press.

Hanna, A. (2023). Silent epistemologies: Theorising children's participation rights. *The International Journal of Children's Rights*, *31*(1), 40–60. https://doi.org/10.1163/15718182-30040003

Hanson, K. (2023). Children's representation in the transnational mirror maze. In B. Sandin, J. Josefsson, K. Hanson & S. Balagopalan (eds.) *The politics of children's rights and representation* (pp. 181–201). Palgrave Macmillan. https://doi.org/10.1007/978-3-031-04480-9_8

Holt, J. (1974). *Escape from childhood.* Penguin.
hooks, B. (1981). *Ain't I a woman? Black women and feminism.* South End Press.
Jans, M. (2004). Children as citizens: Towards a contemporary notion of child participation. *Childhood, 11*(1), 27–44. https://doi.org/10.1177/0907568204040182
Josefsson, J., & Wall, J. (2020). Empowered inclusion: Theorizing global justice for children and youth. *Globalizations, 17*(6), 1043–1060. https://doi.org/10.1080/14747731.2020.1736853
Kant, I. (1960). *Education* (A. Churton, Trans.). University of Michigan Press.
Kant, I. (1974). *The science of right* (W. Hastie, Trans.). A. M. Kelley.
KRÄTZÄ (KinderRÄchTsZÄnker). Retrieved August 5, 2024, from https://kraetzae.de
Liebel, M. (2013). Do children have a right to work? Working children's movements in the struggle for social justice. In K. Hanson & O. Nieuwenhuys (eds.) *Reconceptualizing children's rights in international development: Living rights, social justice, translations* (pp. 225–249). Cambridge University Press.
Locke, J. (1823). Two treatises on government. In *The works of John Locke* (new ed.), corrected, T. Tegg (ed.), Vol. V. W. Sharpe and son.
Locke, J. (1989). *Some thoughts concerning education* (J. W. Yolton & J. S. Yolton, Eds.). Oxford University Press.
López-Guerra, C. (2014). *Democracy and disenfranchisement: The morality of electoral exclusions.* Oxford University Press.
Moosa-Mitha, M. (2005). A difference-centered alternative to the theorization of children's citizenship rights. *Citizenship Studies, 9*(4), 369–388. https://doi.org/10.1080/13621020500211354
Mtata, K. (2021). Children in African theologies of community and the human person. In M. Bunge (ed.), *Child theology: Diverse methods and global perspectives* (pp. 33–51). Orbis Books.
Mugadza, H. T., Stout, B., Akombi, B. J., Tetteh, V. W., & Renzaho, A. (2019). The concept of a child within sub-Saharan African migrant homes: Reconciling culture and child rights. *Child & Family Social Work, 24*(1), 1–10. https://doi.org/10.1111/cfs.12632
Ndofirepi, A. P. (2011). Philosophy for children: The quest for an African perspective. *South African Journal of Education, 31*(2), 246–256. https://doi.org/10.15700/saje.v31n2a278
Nieuwenhuys, O., & Hanson, K. (2024). Living rights theory. In S. Balagopalan, J. Wall & K. Wells (eds.) *Bloomsbury handbook of theories in childhood studies* (pp. 167–179). Bloomsbury.
Quennerstedt, A. (2010). Children, but not really humans? Critical reflections on the hampering effect of the '3 ps'. *International Journal of Children's Rights, 18*(4), 619–635. https://doi.org/10.1163/157181810X490384
Rancière, J. (2010). *Dissensus: On politics and aesthetics* (S. Corcoran, Trans.). Bloomsbury.
Rawls, J. (1999). *A theory of justice* (Revised ed.). Harvard University Press.
Roche, J. (1999). Children: Rights, participation, and citizenship. *Childhood, 6*(4), 475–493. https://doi.org/10.1177/0907568299006004006
Rollo, T. (2024). Democracy and developmentalism: The logics of child exclusion. In S. Balagopalan, J. Wall & K. Wells (eds.) *Bloomsbury handbook of theories in childhood studies* (pp. 30–43). Bloomsbury.
Rousseau, J. J. (1947). *The social contract* (C. Franel, Trans.). Hafner.
Rousseau, J. J. (1979). *Emile: Or on education* (A. Bloom, Trans.). Basic Books.
Runciman, D. (2022). The enfranchisement of women versus the enfranchisement of children. In J. Wall (ed.) *Exploring children's suffrage: Interdisciplinary perspectives on ageless voting* (pp. 91–109). Palgrave Macmillan.
Spivak, G. C. (2004). Righting wrongs. *The South Atlantic Quarterly, 103*(2), 523–581. https://doi.org/10.1215/00382876-103-2-3-523

Twum-Danso Imoh, A., & Okyere, S. (2020). Towards a more holistic understanding of child participation: Foregrounding the experiences of children in Ghana and Nigeria. *Children and Youth Services Review*, *112*, 1–7. https://doi.org/10.1016/j.childyouth.2020.104927

Umbers, L. M. (2018). Enfranchising the youth. *Critical Review of International Social and Political Philosophy*, *23*(6), 1–24.

van Daalen, E., Hanson, K., & Nieuwenhuys, O. (2016). Children's rights as living rights: The case of street children and a new law in Yogyakarta, Indonesia. *International Journal of Children's Rights*, *24*(4), 803–825. http://dx.doi.org/10.1163/15718182-02404006

Wall, J. (2008). Human rights in light of childhood. *International Journal of Children's Rights*, *16*(4), 523–543. https://doi.org/10.1163/157181808X312122

Wall, J. (2010). *Ethics in light of childhood*. Georgetown University Press.

Wall, J. (2016). *Children's rights: Today's global challenge*. Rowman & Littlefield.

Wall, J. (2019a). From childhood studies to childism: Reconstructing the scholarly and social imaginations. *Children's Geographies*, *20*(3), 257–270. https://doi.org/10.1080/14733285.2019.1668912

Wall, J. (2019b). Theorizing children's global citizenship: Reconstructionism and the politics of deep interdependence. *Global Studies of Childhood*, *9*(1), 5–17. https://doi.org/10.1177/2043610618815484

Wall, J. (2021). *Give children the vote: On democratizing democracy*. Bloomsbury.

Woodhouse, B. B. (2008). *Hidden in plain sight: The tragedy of children's rights from Ben Franklin to Lionel Tate*. Princeton University Press.

Wyness, M. (2005). Regulating participation: The possibilities and limits of children and young people's councils. *Journal of Social Sciences*, *16*(4), 7–18. https://doi.org/10.1177/0907568209344274

Young, I. M. (2000). *Inclusion and democracy*. Oxford University Press.

6 Children's rights and the future

Karl Hanson

6.1 Introduction

The involvement of children and young people in struggles to fight climate change builds on the idea that we should recognize children's political engagements, as it is an expression of their status as subjects and rights holders in the present. This view is also prevalent in the Committee on the Rights of the Child's General Comment no. 26 (2023) on children's rights and the environment. However, by concentrating their claims on children's future well-being, young environmental rights activists confuse the mantra of the children's rights movement relating to the 'being' versus the 'becoming' child. For over three decades, children's rights advocates have been arguing that children's rights are not merely about their development and future well-being, but are also concerned with recognizing children's fundamental rights in the present. And now the *Friday for Future* movement is making use of children's actual civil and political rights to make statements about children's future well-being. Children who feel that there is 'no future', given the disastrous state of the planet, confront us with an unexpected critique of the optimistic and future-oriented worldview underlying the children's rights framework.

The chapter takes up the challenge to further develop conceptual clarifications about how children's rights relate to the future. This was outlined by Spyros Spyrou (2020, p. 5) as follows:

> Some would argue that in fact much of the work produced by childhood studies scholars has an implicit future-oriented impulse. After all, most of us are motivated in contributing to knowledge that seeks to create a better world. But much of this work, I would argue, is still rooted in 'a diagnostics of what is wrong,' a critique of sorts, rather than on the imaginative potential of scholarship that seeks to problematize the future; as a result, a serious consideration about the future as both a theoretical and methodological question that would offer childhood studies new and creative avenues of exploration has yet to take place.

DOI: 10.4324/9781003510284-7

A first section briefly retraces how I came to consider the relationship between children's rights and the future as a central problem in children's rights studies. This provides insights into my own situatedness and positionality within the field. The next section will clarify the conceptual questions this chapter seeks to address by exploring the notion of 'coevalness'. Taking the Committee on the Right of the Child's General Comment no. 26 (2023) on children's rights and the environment as a starting point, the following section indicates four different types of futures through which children's rights can be considered. The conclusion advances that children and young people's involvement in struggles to fight climate change provides an insightful case study for exploring new ways to consider the entanglements between children's past, present, and future rights.

6.2 A brief genealogy

Combining the rights and needs of the present generation with those of the future is not always an easy match. In May 1994, after having obtained a law degree at Ghent University in Belgium, I was then working as a research assistant at this university's Centre for Children's Rights. While in that role I attended the national conference of the French association of children and youth councils (*Association Nationale des Conseils d'Enfants et de Jeunes* – ANACEJ) that aims to promote the participation of young people in public decision-making and supports local authorities in setting up youth participation initiatives (Hanson, 1996). ANACEJ's 1994 conference brought together 300 delegates from municipal children's and youth councils from France. The conference had the environment as its central theme, using as its slogan 'What I do here and now, will have consequences tomorrow and over there'. The main speaker at the conference was the French national minister for the environment, who, rather than engaging with the members of local participation councils as active citizens, talked to them in a paternalist manner, considering children merely as passive recipients of orders given by experts. The young people were seen as 'not-yet' capable of holding informed opinions about the risks caused by pollution or global warming who will have to wait, according to the Minister, until adulthood before they can have a say on environmental politics.

The way children were patronized during this event illustrates one of the central theses developed by Eugeen Verhellen, then Director of the Centre for Children's Rights, with whom I worked as a research assistant from 1992 to 2002, and who was also my PhD supervisor. Verhellen had been teaching and doing research, since the 1970s, on child and youth protection and children's rights both in Belgium and internationally. According to him, the dominant conception of children as incomplete human beings – who need to be educated and socialized rather than participate in social and political life in the present – emerged in Europe during the Enlightenment period in the 18th century (Verhellen, 2000). At the heart of Enlightenment thinking, and central to modernity, was the belief in progress. Humanity was believed to have the capacity to improve its condition through science, education, and social reform, thereby shaping the idea that history moves toward greater freedom and knowledge. Within this ideology of progress, children were increasingly viewed as the future bearers of a forthcoming 'enlightened' society. As a result, they gradually came to be seen as a distinct social category with specific characteristics, oriented toward the future. My own research on the origins and development of both separate juvenile justice systems in Belgium and international child labour abolition laws and policies in the early 20th century confirmed Verhellen's thesis that the projection of children into the future was a key factor in the creation of separate institutions and legislations for them (Hanson, 2016). Throughout the 20th century, children, now seen as representing the future, were identified in the industrialized countries in the West as a distinct social category, setting them apart from the rest of society. The establishment of separate legal regimes for children – believed to better address their unique needs and prepare them for the future – stems from a view that sees children as inherently different from adults. However, this perspective has led to children being excluded from existing social and legal frameworks, limiting their ability to exercise agency on the same terms as anyone else. Rather than improving their actual social and legal position, the establishment of separate childhood laws in Europe and North America resulted from concern about the adults that children would become in future.

Throughout my later writings in the broad field of children's rights studies, I continued to reflect on childhood's complex temporal relationships. To understand what children are, I feel we need to understand children's past, present, and future as well as the dynamic temporal relationship and shifting sequences between the 'becoming', the 'being', and the 'been' child. Taking inspiration from writings on childhood and postcolonial thinking (Nieuwenhuys, 2013), I have argued in an editorial for the journal *Childhood* that we must pay sufficient attention to the dynamic articulation of children's and childhood's individual and collective past and future to understand children's present-days engagements with their own lives and the social world around them (Hanson, 2017).

6.3 Coevalness

Modern childhood has long been defined as an anticipation stage for the future. As children grow older, they acquire the knowledge and skills necessary for responsible adulthood. Children are destined to be 'waiting' (Qvortrup, 2004), not only to become adults but also for economic progress, social justice, peace, and a healthy natural environment that allow for not only a cheerful childhood but also a thriving adulthood free from poverty, discrimination, violence, or pollution. The concept of children's futurity involves improving individual opportunities as well as the idea that the progress of children contributes to the overall future of the nation (King, 2016) and the sustainable development of humankind. However, the vision of a bright future can be misleading, as waiting children understand that tomorrow might never come, which is why they ask for consideration for their present situation. The emergence of the children's rights discourse has, to an important extent, been a response to criticisms of prevailing approaches to children as future citizens but without recognizing their rights in the present. Before the 1989 Convention on the Rights of the Child (UNCRC), the dominant available approaches towards children highlighted the future adults they would become, thereby overseeing children's significant contributions in the present (James, 2009). To take children's rights more seriously, Michael Freeman (1997) argues, children must be treated with equal concern and respect. This involves recognizing their present autonomy while also safeguarding their capacity for future autonomy, particularly for younger children who require nurture, care, and protection, which in turn implies placing limits on their present autonomy. Children's rights studies now problematize tensions between children's protection rights, which aim at safeguarding their future, with children's participation rights that are focusing on children's actual understandings and contributions to both their own lives and to society.

This mainstream children's rights framework offers an attractive vision of what a better future could look like, and many view the implementation of international norms and programmes as the ideal path to bringing that future closer to reality. Discussions surrounding children and their rights are often dominated by references to both their future and that of society (see, for example Save the Children, 2024; United Nations Children's Fund, 2024). This is particularly evident in the context of children's active participation in climate change activism and their role in promoting sustainable development, aiming to create a better world than the one we currently have. People, institutions, and organizations often disagree on priorities within children's rights (Poretti et al., 2014), the strategies and alliances to pursue, or even the kinds of better future longed for. However, all children's rights advocates share one common goal: that we can and must make tomorrow better than today. This claim has been summarized by Michael Freeman (2007, p. 20) who contends that we must believe that the case for children's rights will prevail 'because out of it will emerge a better world for children and this will redound to the benefit not only of children but of all of us'. The idea that a better future for all is possible, which is central to modernity, conveys a reflexive and often impatient drive to continuously reshape the world, nature, and ourselves (Hanson, 2022). Paul James (2015, p. 192) argues that in modernity 'we feel we have no choice but to act upon what we, and the world, should look like'. Children, regarded as the future, align perfectly with modernity's telos: human progress. When modernity is reduced to its core idea that 'we can make tomorrow better than today', plans and ambitions about children and childhood take the spotlight. Considering the prominent role of children in modernity's focus on the future, examining the children's rights project becomes a means to explore the current state of modernity itself, one of the most dominant social projects of our time.

The projection of children into the future reflects the reverse of how anthropology in its early years projected 'other' cultures to the past by using labels such as 'primitive', 'backwards', or 'pre-modern'. In his book *Time and the Others*, Johannes Fabian (1983/2014, p. 146) spells out that early anthropologists were sometimes viewed as 'time voyagers' who could expand our understanding of the past by studying the social structures of non-Western societies. However, the temporal distancing of 'other' cultures amounts to, as Fabian puts it, denying them *coevalness*. The term 'coevalness' (a translation of the German word '*Gleichzeitigkeit*') refers to the state or condition of being coeval, meaning to exist or originate at the same time. It pertains to synchronicity or simultaneity in time. For Fabian coevalness is a normative ideal that involves granting equal value and concern for different, even conflicting, worldviews held by different people at different places. The exclusion of 'other' cultures from the present, hence the denial of their coevalness, prevents them from being granted equal status and recognition. Children's coevalness is similarly denied, not because they are perceived as living in the past like non-Western 'others', but because they are thought to belong to the future. An analysis of their positioning on the axis of time shows that it is impossible for either category to be regarded as fundamentally equal.

A critical approach to children's rights must navigate two strands of critique that are in tension – one focused on aspirations to improve children's future, and the other on the recognition of children's present. The first strand of critique mobilizes the children's rights framework to critique the present status quo where children's rights are being violated or insufficiently respected. We should, hence, all work towards an emancipatory future where the rights of all are fully respected, which will be beneficial for present and future generations of children and adults alike. The second strand of critique focuses on children not being considered as equal subjects of rights in the present. Their main status as 'not-yets', ascribed to children in order to protect their development into future well-being adults, excludes them from receiving the same consideration as those living in the present. This critique can be reframed as a call for the recognition of children's coevalness, meaning that their worldviews deserve equal status alongside those of other individuals or groups. The principles of equality and nondiscrimination require humans to be considered equal not only before the law but also before time: we are all coeval and all have a past, a present, and a future.

The theoretical problem this chapter seeks to address can be reformulated as follows: how does one navigate modernity's emancipatory goal of making tomorrow better than today, which implies paying attention to children's future development, with its other normative ideal of granting equal value and respect to each person's worldview, which necessitates recognizing children's coevalness? (Hanson, 2022). Are both ambitions, one directed to the future and one grounded in the present, reconcilable?

6.4 Four futures

The events at the 1994 conference of municipal children's and youth councils in France described previously stand in sharp contrast with the large mobilizations of millions of children and young people, who, especially since 2019, participated under the banners *Youth Strike for Climate* and *Fridays for Future* in worldwide climate protests. Children's environmental activism, both in their local and global dimensions, offers an illustration of the idea central in children's rights discourse that they are subjects and rights holders capable of expressing their opinion and engaging in political matters. Given the disastrous state of the planet, young climate activists who put the future of the world at the core of their demands warn that there might not even be a meaningful future anymore. In so doing, they confront us with an unexpected critique of the optimistic, future-oriented worldview of children's rights. To further explore conceptual questions regarding the future of children's rights – and how projecting children into the future can be reconciled with the need to take them seriously on political matters in the present, thereby no longer denying their coevalness – we will examine what can be learned from children's involvement in social movements demanding immediate worldwide action to curb global warming, reduce CO^2 emissions, and mitigate the impact of climate change on both present and future generations.

This section takes as starting point for conceptualizing the relationship between children's rights and the future General Comment No. 26 on children's rights and the environment, adopted by the Committee on the Rights of the Child in 2023. This international document was developed in response to children's efforts highlighting the current environmental crises and benefited from input by a children's advisory team, child participation during the Committee on the Rights of the Child's 2016 day of general discussion, and contributions from children in 121 countries through multi-method consultations (Committee on the Rights of the Child, 2023, para. 2). This General Comment addresses the relationship between the environment, children, and the future in at least four different ways. These conceptions include children's self-involved futures, future children, the future of humankind, and children as present future-makers. Each emphasizes a different facet of the future, which we will explore further making use also of broader discussions in childhood studies.

A first conception concerns *children's self-involved futures*. On many occasions, General Comment 26 expresses concern about the impact of environmental degradation and pollution on children's future lives as adults. What can seem like reasonable environmental decisions 'on a shorter timescale can become unreasonable in aggregate and when considering the full harm that they will cause to children throughout their life courses' (Committee on the Rights of the Child, 2023, para. 19). In addition, due to their ongoing physical development, children are more vulnerable to environmental degradation and suffer to a greater extent from pollution and climate change compared to fully grown bodies. Drawing attention to younger children's unique activity patterns, behaviours, and physiology, the Committee cautions that they are therefore particularly susceptible to environmental hazards: 'Exposure to toxic pollutants, even at low levels, during developmental windows of increased vulnerability can easily disrupt the maturational processes of the brain, organs and the immune system and cause disease and impairments during and beyond childhood' (Committee on the Rights of the Child, 2023, para. 24). The sections on the right to education and on the right to rest, play, leisure, and recreation highlight the importance of pursuing goals relating to 'the development of the child's personality, talents and abilities' (para 53) and of the development of children's 'creativity, imagination, self-confidence, self-efficacy and physical, social, cognitive and emotional strength and skills' (para. 59). The future adult lives of children are addressed not only from a healthcare, development, or educational perspective but also by children themselves who want to be living a future adult life on a planet free from climate disaster and pollution. Children's self-concern for the future is connected to the present generation of children, for whom this is the only planet they have, both now and in their future lives. Compared to adults and (aging) political leaders, who may soon no longer require a healthy planet to live on, the General Comment highlights the worries of the children consulted during its drafting. These children reported the negative effects of environmental degradation and climate change on their own future lives as follows:

> Adults [should] stop making decisions for the future they won't experience. [We] are the key means [of] solving climate change, as it is [our] lives at stake. I would like to tell [adults] that we are the future generations and, if you destroy the planet, where will we live?!
>
> (Committee on the Rights of the Child, 2023, para. 3)

In these instances, the idea of children's self-involved futures primarily reflects the view of childhood as 'becoming'. It reaffirms existing interpretations of the child's right to development (Peleg, 2019), encompassing the fundamental human right to a clean, healthy, and sustainable environment needed for children to survive, develop, and thrive to their fullest potential.

A second conception that can be distilled from the General Comment is that of *future children*. There is only one explicit reference in the document to children who are not yet there but who will be arriving soon in a nearby, tangible future. Not only the rights of children who are present on Earth need immediate urgent attention but also 'the children constantly arriving' (para. 11) are entitled to the maximum possible realization of their human rights. The conception of 'future children' is relevant to matters addressed mainly outside environmental politics. It can be understood as a collective project, such as government family policies aimed at increasing birth rates and supporting population growth. Moreover, even if they are not yet physically present, future children can exist as a concrete project in the minds of those planning to have them. For instance, a couple may plan to have children in an unspecified near future ('one day') and, therefore, take steps such as furnishing a bedroom for their anticipated children. Couples experiencing infertility or same-sex couples may turn to reproductive health services to help fulfil their desire to ever 'have' a child. It is in this latter area that 'future children' can be linked to the children's rights framework. While no one can be legitimately deprived of the right to have a child, stating that 'children have rights' does not imply the existence of a positive 'right to have a child' (Sándor, 2022). Given the latest developments in reproductive technologies, questions about the importance of adopting a children's rights perspective in the development of legal and ethical frameworks surrounding 'future children' are becoming increasingly complex.

A third conception addresses children who are projected, in an abstract manner, into an unspecified future. *The future of humankind* transcends self-interest and becomes altruistic, emphasizing intergenerational solidarity that extends beyond one's own lifetime. The 1992 United Nations Conference on Environment and Development (UNCED), an important milestone for the development of international environmental policy, was based on the concept of 'sustainable development'. The core idea of sustainable development refers to intergenerational solidarity, as it fosters development that meets the needs of the present but without compromising the ability of future generations to also meet their own needs. The Committee on the Rights of the Child subscribes to the sustainable development paradigm by stating that it 'recognizes the principle of intergenerational equity and the interests of future generations' (Committee on the Rights of the Child, 2023, para. 11). In contrast to a deep ecology approach that posits intrinsic value in nature, nonhuman beings, and ecological systems, the sustainable development approach adopts an expanded anthropocentric perspective, asserting that value can only be attributed through human agency (Brennan & Norva, 2022). An anthropocentric position advocates for human interaction with nature in a manner that does not jeopardize the quality of human life. As the climate crisis demonstrates the clear limits of a purely instrumental use of nature and the environment, an extended anthropocentric perspective urges us to broaden our understanding of humanity to encompass future generations. For François Ost (2012) preserving the natural environment is a crucial condition for the survival of the current and future generations of humankind. Central is the extension of the concept of human rights to future generations and the idea of intergenerational equity (Weiss, 1994). The latter concept posits that each generation receives nature and culture as a trustee from its preceding generation, and that it must maintain them in a good condition for the subsequent generation to also benefit from it. Intergenerational equity imposes on each generation the obligation to preserve inherited natural and cultural resources, as well as the environment, not only for its own children but also for all future generations. Weiss puts forward three principles of intergenerational equity. These are (1) Conservation of options: future generations must continue to have a range of choices regarding natural resources, such as biodiversity; (2) Conservation of quality; and (3) Conservation of access: everyone, present and future generations, has the right to equal access to natural resources. The rights of future generations and the duties of current and previous generations form the core of the intergenerational equity doctrine. Ost (2012) emphasizes the collective responsibility that our generation holds towards the future, arguing that this responsibility is commensurate with our power. Given that our influence over the planet extends into the future, particularly in light of the long-term impact of climate change on the environment, we also bear responsibility for that future. This conceptualization is no longer grounded in the view of the 'becoming' child; it combines the past, present, and future of humanity itself. Children, who are no longer seen as a separate category, are considered symbols for the future of humankind.

A fourth conception sees *children as present future-makers.* The General Comment includes numerous references to children's active involvements in environmental activism. Child human rights defenders are referred to 'as agents of change' who 'have made historic contributions to human rights and environmental protection' (Committee on the Rights of the Child, 2023, para. 3). The sections that deal with the right to be heard and with freedom of expression, association, and peaceful assembly highlight the importance of children's contributions for developing environmental politics. For example, the General Comment states that 'Children's voices are a powerful global force for environmental protection, and their views add relevant perspectives and experience with respect to decision-making on environmental matters at all levels' (Committee on the Rights of the Child, 2023, para. 26). Furthermore, it emphasizes that

> Children across the world are taking action, individually and collectively, to protect the environment, including by highlighting the consequences of climate change. States shall respect and protect children's rights to freedom of expression, association and peaceful assembly in relation to the environment.
>
> (Committee on the Rights of the Child, 2023, para. 29)

Children's political engagement in the climate debate demonstrates the key arguments of children's rights and childhood studies, particularly that children are not merely passive or naïve but are informed social actors who can sometimes act as catalysts for change (Spyrou, 2020). Young climate activists want to be taken seriously as present future-makers, thereby questioning established adult authority and control, and advocating for significant changes. Children as present future-makers are grounded in the view of childhood as 'being' children, who strive for a sustainable future for the planet not only for themselves, but also for future children and for the future of humankind.

6.5 Conclusion

This chapter has critically engaged with what has been presented as a central question in the field of children's rights studies: how can children be recognized as equals living at the same time as anyone else (explored through the notion of 'coevalness') with the emancipatory goal that underlies much of the work in this field aimed at creating a better world for all? Global attention to the enormous challenges posed by environmental degradation and climate change, particularly the role played by children and young people in social environmental movements, provided a fruitful starting point for developing four distinct conceptions of children's rights and the future.

The theoretical problem addressed in this chapter can be answered affirmatively: the underlying, emancipatory goals of the children's rights project, which we have grounded in modernity's goal of making tomorrow better than today, are consistent with children's fundamental right to equality and nondiscrimination, including the recognition of their coevalness. It is the distinctive type of 'children as present future-makers' that makes such a reconciliation between both ambitions possible. Children's coevalness – the acknowledgment that they live and are entitled to live in the same 'time zone' as anyone else – opens the door for a critical reappraisal of the children's rights framework itself. The three temporal dimensions, 'been', 'being', and 'becoming', can be grasped through the notion that children are 'present future-makers with a past'.

The balancing exercise prevalent in mainstream conceptions of children's rights between children's actual and future well-being – often analyzed through the conflict between the child's right to be heard and the best interests of the child principle – make use of children's self-involved futures. Although important, this relatively simple representation of the future insufficiently takes into account children's own active engagement with the different types of futures that were presented in this chapter. By stating that four different types of futures are at stake, we have been able to highlight the importance of the conception of *'children as present future-makers'* as a crucial idea for advancing an emancipatory perspective on children's rights, aligning closely with the agency championed in Critical Children's Rights Studies. This conception also creates conceptual space for children to critically engage with, and participate in, discussions, on equal footing with others, regarding their self-involved futures, future children, and the future of humankind. Recognizing children as present future-makers respects children's fundamental 'coevalness' and acknowledges their potential to contribute to emancipatory goals aimed at creating a better future not just for children but for all.

Children's rights provide a compelling normative anchor for reaffirming the importance of rights for children's development. *'Children's self-involved futures'* encompasses a well-established developmental paradigm concerned with the adults children will become, focusing on their rights related to, inter alia, education, leisure, health care, and protection against violence.

In addition to concerns about children's personal developments, it includes matters pertaining to the natural environment in which they will live their own future lives. Given the rapid advancements in reproductive technologies, the children's rights framework will increasingly need to address *'future children'* in relation to the accompanying ethical and legal questions surrounding these developments. The conception of *'the future of humankind'* creates a clear link between the children's rights agenda and a global understanding of the sustainable development paradigm. It potentially makes the consequences of environmental challenges more comprehensible to adults by drawing a connection to one's own children and grandchildren, who symbolically represent that future. However, emphasizing the symbolic role of children for the future carries the risk of conflicting with the children's rights framework, which attaches great importance to considering children's rights in the present.

In the genealogy section, we explained the origins of our interest in children's futures and coevalness, which both have their roots in, and continue, therefore, to be situated within, the Western philosophical tradition of the Enlightenment. While it can account for understanding the importance attached to children's future within modernity, the four different types of futures as well as the normative ideal of coevalness itself might insufficiently take into account the 'multiple childhoods' (Balagopalan, 2018) underlying children's rights in a globalizing world. Given the attention for epistemological diversity within Critical Children's Rights Studies, it would be interesting to learn how the future is conceptualized from within different approaches compared to the modern one adopted here.

While making an analytical distinction between these conceptions might not offer a definitive solution for fully grasping the ambiguous relations between children's rights and the future, it offers original avenues of exploration to help clarify existing confusion. Further developments in children's rights studies, including exploring other epistemological frameworks beyond modernity, will need to determine the extent to which these four conceptualizations have a sustainable future.

References

Balagopalan, S. (2018). Childhood, culture, history: Redeploying "multiple childhoods". In S. Spyrou, R. Rosen & D. T. Cook (eds.) *Reimagining childhood studies* (pp. 23–41). Bloomsbury Academic.

Brennan, A., & Norva, Y. S. Lo. (2022). Environmental ethics. In E. N. Zalta (ed.) *The Stanford encyclopedia of philosophy* (Summer 2022 Edition). Retrieved November 20, 2024, from https://plato.stanford.edu/archives/sum2022/entries/ethics-environmental/

Committee on the Rights of the Child. (2023). *General Comment no. 26 on children's rights and the environment, with a special focus on climate change*. Adopted 22 August 2023 [CRC/GC/26].

Fabian, J. (2014). *Time and the other: How anthropology makes its object*. Columbia University Press.

Freeman, M. (1997). Taking children's rights more seriously. In M. Freeman (ed.) *The moral status of children: Essays on the rights of the child* (pp. 19–45). Martinus Nijhoff.

Freeman, M. (2007). Why it remains important to take children's rights seriously. *The International Journal of Children's Rights*, *15*(1), 5–23.

Hanson, K. (1996). Waarom je kamer opruimen als de wereld toch al zo'n rotzooi is? Over milieu en rechten van kinderen. In E. Verhellen (ed.) *Rechten van kinderen in de wereld: Verzamelde lezingen naar aanleiding van de postacademische vorming Rechten van het Kind academiejaar 1994–1995* (pp. 245–268). Universiteit Gent, Centrum voor de Rechten van het Kind. www.anacej.fr/

Hanson, K. (2016). Separate childhood laws and the future of society. *Law, Culture and the Humanities*, *12*(2), 195–205.

Hanson, K. (2017). Embracing the past: "been", "being" and "becoming" children. *Childhood*, *24*(3), 281–285.

Hanson, K. (2022). Reinventing children's rights. *Childhood*, *29*(2), 149–156.

James, A. (2009). Agency. In J. Qvortrup, W. A. Corsaro & M.-S. Honig (eds.) *The Palgrave handbook of childhood studies* (pp. 34–45). Palgrave Macmillan.

James, P. (2015). Despite the terrors of typologies: The importance of understanding categories of difference and identity. *Interventions*, *17*(2), 174–195.

King, L. (2016). Future citizens: Cultural and political conceptions of children in Britain, 1930s–1950s. *Twentieth Century British History*, *27*(3), 389–411.

Nieuwenhuys, O. (2013). Theorizing childhood(s): Why we need postcolonial perspectives. *Childhood*, *20*(1), 3–8.

Ost, F. (2012). *La nature hors-la-loi: L'écologie à l'épreuve du droit*. La Découverte.

Peleg, N. (2019). *The child's right to development*. Cambridge University Press.

Poretti, M., Hanson, K., Darbellay, F., & Berchtold, A. (2014). The rise and fall of icons of 'stolen childhood' since the adoption of the UN convention on the rights of the child. *Childhood*, *21*(1), 22–38.

Qvortrup, J. (2004). The waiting child. *Childhood*, *11*(3), 267–273.

Sándor, J. (2022). The right to have a child: Through the lens of the third phase reproductive technologies. In M. Ienca, O. Pollicino, L. Liguori, E. Stefanini & R. Andorno (eds.) *The Cambridge handbook of information technology, life sciences and human rights* (pp. 56–69). Cambridge University Press.

Save the Children. (2024). *"We must be the change". Children's pact for the future*. Save the Children London.

Spyrou, S. (2020). Children as future-makers. *Childhood*, *27*(1), 3–7.

United Nations Children's Fund (UNICEF). (2024). *The state of the world's children 2024 The future of childhood in a changing world*. UNICEF Innocenti – Global Office of Research and Foresight. Retrieved January 21, 2025, from https://uniceflink.org/sowc-2024

Verhellen, E. (2000). *The convention on the rights of the child: Background, motivation, strategies, main themes*. Garant.

Weiss, E. B. (1994). In fairness to our children: International law and intergenerational equity. *Childhood*, *2*(1–2), 22–27.

7 Recasting children's rights as relational, circular, and interdependent

Tatek Abebe

7.1 Introduction

This chapter examines how families and communities who navigate marginality engendered by development conceptualize rights and how those conceptualizations inform our understandings of children's rights. I will explore intergenerational interdependence, highlighting children's active involvement in life-making labour that sustains families and communities experiencing livelihood transition through historical and ongoing development projects. I do this to situate childhood within broader contexts of political economy and engage with what I consider a missing debate in children's rights studies, namely 'generationing rights' (cf. Huijsmans et al., 2014) – foregrounding the centrality of generational relationships in the reproduction of rights and how children's rights are fundamentally a relational product imbricated in multiple relations of power. I will further argue that our ideas of children's rights are impoverished because of the neglect of worldviews on collectivist existence and relationality that might offer analytical lenses through which the moral and existential tensions of being part of the world might be reconceptualized.

The chapter builds on my longitudinal, ethnographic research on children and youth found on the margins of culture and political economy in post-socialist Ethiopia. The political-economic transformations are characterized not only by the reorientation of the national economy towards a mix of market liberalization and the 'developmental state' model but also by forms of a social contract that seem to dislodge the cultural logic of childhood, what it means to be a child, and the parameters within which children's everyday lives unfold. The precarity of childhood and reconfiguration of children's role in social reproduction that I discuss elsewhere (Abebe, 2013, 2017) include a situation where children become 'shock absorbers', putting in more hours in unpaid or low-paid activities such as producing food or caring for their siblings when adult men and women take on more arduous and specialty chores. It involves the transference to children of the burden of daily and generational reproduction, characterized by a general increase in the range, depth, and scope of children's involvement in livelihood activities to buffer against household poverty. It also entails the expanded field of children's work (for example,

DOI: 10.4324/9781003510284-8

through daily mobility) as well as increases in the duration and intensity of these daily tasks. These contexts within which the labour of children unfold are not only historically specific but also relationally produced, due to the extractive logic of the global capitalist system that entangles ideas of local/ national economic development with that of modernity. They underscore that the material contexts that shape children's role in social reproduction and the political-economic processes that create material conditions of life and transform familial and community relations are inseparable.

The structural roots of childhood precarity also offer formidable backdrop to the contestation of discourses of children's rights that are driven by powerful international children's rights institutions, shaping policies and programmes, and transforming the lived realities of marginal children. Global discourses of children's rights are implicated in the normative moral framework of what is best for children and their development that replicates contemporary values of the United Nations Convention on the Rights of the Child (UNCRC). The UNCRC assumes that children are first of all individuals directly connected to the state and only secondarily members of families and communities. It also carries unquestioned conceptions that a child is 'a universal subject who should everywhere enabled to be a free, autonomous, choosing, and rational individual' (Wells, 2009, p. 166). I will tease out these discourses, arguing that the neoliberal and right-claiming child subject of Western creation conceals relational rights and the socio-generational interdependence of children, families, and communities. I close out by reflecting on the analytical gains of the examples I discuss on inscribing children's rights as *relational*, *cyclical/reciprocal*, and *interdependent* as well as recognizing children's already existing, albeit unwritten, collective rights within the broader socio-material context in which they find themselves.

7.2 Refusals of rights sensitization and responsibilization

The UNCRC is domesticated into national laws in Ethiopia through its 1995 Constitution. Policies for children increasingly privilege an imported model of childhood, associated with the children's rights agenda, and promoted by donors, rescripting models of the family that render other forms of childcare collectives as problematic or even deviant and inferior. Schools offer instruction about children's rights as part of their curriculum, in a subject called civic and ethical education, and organize extracurricular activities like children's rights clubs. Rights sensitization workshops, media campaigns, and other activities funded by NGOs aimed at bringing 'behavioural change' in line with rights guaranteed by the UNCRC are also common. Children's parliaments – a flagship of Save the Children – have been promoted first in southern Ethiopia and scaled up throughout the country and are considered a 'model project' for NGOs (Lemessa & Kjørholt, 2013).

Hegemonic interpretation of children's rights is pervasive in laws and legislation, too. Harmonization of local and customary laws to international treaties and human rights laws are reflected in, for example, Ethiopia's Revised Family Code of 2000, which, in its preamble, states that one of the reasons for revision is to 'amend the existing law in such a way that it gives priority to the well-being, upbringing, and protection of children in accordance with the Constitution and International Instruments which Ethiopia has ratified' (FDRE, 2000, p. 2). Yet, implementation of the CRC ignores some important provision rights that are pivotal for social reproduction of poor communities such as children's rights to food and access to quality education. Advocates of the UNCRC tend to flag the participation rights of children in making decisions on matters that affect them as if children's decisions lack systemic challenges or are devoid of sociocultural and political structures. Hunger, illness, and disease are not just basic human rights that often go unmet. Rather, they are the byproducts of politics, policies, and economic structures that engender unequal childhoods. Communities connected their reluctance to accept children's rights with their lack of 'economic rights', questioning not only NGO education and awareness creation programmes that 'responsibilize' them but also individualize actions for structural problems of inequality and precarity.

Whereas the Ethiopian state appears as unable to break the intergenerational cycle of poverty and overcome childhood marginalization, multinational agencies, and bilateral donor countries follow their own logics, promoting neoliberal ideas that privilege particular forms of children's entitlements and rights that communities must respect. They often operate on decontextualized and narrow interpretations of children's rights, funding projects that exclusively focus on groups of children that are seen as the epitome of destitution – such as 'AIDS orphans' or 'street children' – to the neglect of large swathes of marginal children who are affected by, and live in, similar circumstances of poverty. An Ethiopian journalist, when asked about the UNCRC, commented that he did not 'begrudge Western NGOs' influence because of the minimal resources available to Ethiopian authorities', but he objected to 'the centrality accorded to the notion of the individual child' which he found 'irrelevant to the Ethiopian context' (Howell, 2006, cited in Brittingham, 2010, p. 15). He further noted that: 'Western targets for development are very idealistic, especially the stress that is continually placed on the best interest of the child' (See Brittingham, 2010, p. 15). Relatedly, Spivak (2004) reminds us of the colonial genealogy of human rights, emphasizing how international development and implementation of human rights have often justified political, economic, and military interventions that perpetuate neocolonialism and capitalist expansion. She argues that human rights regimes, while ostensibly benevolent, in fact, perpetuate epistemological violence by masking power asymmetries across various contexts and safeguarding those who benefit from these imbalances.

The deep-seated skepticism around NGOs' 'sensitization' activities is borne out of the disregard towards the local sociocultural world and constructions of childhood on which ideas of children's rights are imposed. According to one parent, NGOs have a 'hidden agenda of raising funds in the name of children' but instead of investing resources to improve children's lives, or fulfill their rights to food, healthcare, or schooling, he said, 'they teach us what we must do to fulfil their rights' (Abebe & Tefera, 2014, p. 61). The tensions further manifest themselves in how parents and community members describe children's duties, emphasizing the mutually interdependent nature of life as opposed to the independent rights that children's rights discourses promote (Abebe & Tefera, 2014). Parents spoke of the idea of rights as contradictory to 'our way of life', highlighting not only the inseparability of children's rights from the rights of other community members but also how children should *earn* their rights. They emphasized that the rights children are entitled to, when they can claim them, and under what circumstances, are all contingent on their contributions to, and continued involvement in, reproducing the daily lives of households (Abebe, 2013).

The paradoxes that involve, on the one hand, discourses by the state and NGOs that children have unique rights that families must uphold and, on the other, their inability or lack of political will to build up livelihoods, especially for those who need it most, implies the tension between the politics of recognition and the politics of redistribution. They reveal that the language of children's rights is not only a deeply contested terrain but also a moralized space filled with multiple practices of responsibilization (Alber, 2023; Masquelier, 2022). Alber (2023) operationalizes the concept of responsibilization in the context of schooling and care in West Africa, describing it as a set of processes in which parents become deeply involved and perceive themselves as primarily responsible for their children's educational success and outcomes. This concept of responsibilization is often associated with neoliberal governmentality ideologies, which shift the burden of social reproduction from the state to individual agents (Pyysiainnen et al., 2017).

Individual and collective resistance to/refusal of children's rights demonstrate the problems of rights discourses that tend to depoliticize systemic poverty. The contestations invite us to ask questions about the limits of children's codified rights – and the normative vertical state–child social contract it seeks to sediment – to instead explore the interdependent functions of children inside society, recognizing the multiple responsibilities children bear and the rights afforded to them by their families and communities. This invokes alternative interpretation of children's rights from a relational, collectivistic perspective, by moving beyond a singular reading of rights as a standard global benchmark against which all children's lives should be measured.

7.3 Vernacular conceptualizations of rights

7.3.1 Relational rights

I want to situate children's role in social reproduction against the backdrop of relational notions of personhood, to challenge the universalized model of childhood with its normalized ideas of rights, agency, vulnerability, development, and care. The image of childhood as a playful, work-free, and right-receiving phase of the life course, devoid of duties, is often placed in opposition to competence in adulthood, when a person assumes caring responsibilities and achieves maturity and economic independence (Abebe & Bessell, 2011). However, this opposition is fundamentally misleading and clouds our ability to understand how people define and experience their life trajectories (Di Nunzio, 2019). Families and communities seldom arrange life through a linear and gradual succession of steps, and that transition from childhood to adulthood is perceived as a continuum of responsibilities and social experiences (Di Nunzio, 2019).

As someone who was born and raised in Ethiopia, I recognize that to identify in relation to ancestors – as the son or daughter of somebody, or the grandson or granddaughter of somebody – is a central component of being a child and a lens through which children understand their social position in society. I experienced childhood and children's status as concepts that were explained almost always in relation to 'others' in the child's social circle: siblings, parents, neighbours, relatives, and extended families. This *relational identification*, which is also reflected in patronymic naming of Ethiopian children, is pivotal to children's belonging and secures their well-being. Anthropologist Eva Poluha (2004, pp. 55–56) discusses the social fabric that constitutes the Ethiopian episteme *mahiberawi nuro* (literally meaning 'collective existence').

> Life in Ethiopia . . . is dependent on your neighbors and friends; you must live social life or *mahiberawi nuro* and do so through membership in various social associations [such as solidarity groups, redistributive groups, work groups, religious groups, and funeral associations]. When you yourself or a member of your family become sick or die, your associations will help you manage socially, emotionally, financially, and morally; they are your social security.

Mahiberawi nuro produces relations that exist outside of the state and, hence, does not preoccupy itself with questions of citizenship that hegemonic human/children's rights discourses persuade us to adopt. And, as collective care is integral to its social safety net functions, members are supported, especially in times of adversity and, not the least, because the role of the state in resource provision is minimal. In contrast to the Western world, where individual rights are secured through citizens' participation in the workings of the nation-state, Ethiopian children have a more limited connection with, and claims to rights from, the state. Instead, children in Ethiopia are deeply embedded within the support system created by *mahiberawi nuro*, where growing up is closely intertwined with their contributions to collective livelihoods. Yet, this reliance on collective care, ethnocultural citizenship, and 'wealth in people' – i.e., networks of mutual aid, communal nurturance, and practices of social and material interdependence – appear so obvious that they often go unrecognized.

The sociality and reciprocity of ***mahiberawi nuro*** does not just govern everyday life but is also an anathema to the idea that children have special rights different from the rest of society. In Ethiopia, constructions of childhood are predicated on relational selfhood and emphasizes the mutuality of a collective life. Children see themselves, and are seen by society, less as individuals and more as members of family collectives (Abebe, 2013), navigating relational existence through fulfilling multiple social, cultural, economic, and moral expectations. As filial obligations supersede individual actions or choices, children's perspectives on rights are also founded on interdependence, where they recognize they have responsibilities and duties as much as (if not more than) any rights they might claim. These forms of relationalities represent the antithesis of the universal model of children's rights that is predicated on notions of protection, vulnerability, independence, and innocence of childhood. I argue this is so not because of Ethiopian communities' lack of acknowledgement of children's individuality. Rather, it is because of their growing resistance to a model of children's rights in which selected ideals from a once localized Western construction of childhood are deployed as global standards (Stephens, 1995). By drawing attention to the individual rights of children, translations of the UNCRC into development policies and practices not only suggest the superiority of the children's rights model as it evolved in the West and the need to impose this model on a global scale (Nieuwenhuys, 2001), but they also consolidate the belief that the richer world has the right to remake non-Western childhoods in Western forms.

Communality is emphasized in childcare as well as fosterage, i.e., bringing up a child who is not one's own offspring based on the notion of social parenthood (Bodja & Gleason, 2020). The practices of social parenthood resonate with how children outside of natal families are looked after and socialized, especially in the face of crisis. Keeping and raising children within the community is also preferred over institutional arrangements or official adoption (Duressa, 2002). In his study of the local epistemologies of childhood and the values of children's rights they embed, Tadesse Jaleta Jirata (2022, p. 400) argues that the collective rights of rural Ethiopian children include 'the right to communal care' which is to mean 'the right to be cared for not only by their parents or immediate families but also by community members'. Children are perceived to be collective gifts or assets, and they 'belong' to a community. Kassa and Abebe (2016) further discuss the practice of *qenja* (meaning 'teaming' or 'forming a coalition') and how sharing the labour power of children – as much as sharing the responsibility of ensuring their well-being – reflects wider socio-cultural logics of child upbringing. The practice reflects distributive caregiving as well as a strategy of cultivating children's interpersonal relationships. *Qenja* is a culturally engrained coping strategy that co-exists alongside gendered and generational relations and that – in contexts of unequal distribution of rural labour – includes children's involvement in *qenja* labour outside their natal home as a fundamental feature of social reproduction (Kassa & Abebe, 2016). These children's modes of living might contradict the hegemonic model of childhood premised on the idea that children should have a safe and happy existence. Yet, the active involvement of children in labour from an early age is a key feature of collective livelihood strategies which – far from being neglectful or abusive (as has been portrayed by the ILO) – is informed by a deliberate strategy of priming them for future response-abilities of adulthood.

The ethos of caring and guiding which inform childcare and socialization draws our attention to not just what is valued but how a child exists in the world. Inclusiveness, community-mindedness, and collaboration as forms of relational personhood open the lens to reconceptualizing children's rights. They imply that rights are predicated on, and are, the outcome and the means to (re-)producing a relationship that is ultimately dynamic, situated, and contextual. Conceptualized as such – rights as relational – the consideration of the community's understandings is a starting point to identify what kind of rights children have, how they obtain and exercise it, how context shapes it, and how their rights relate them to others, and with what outcomes (see Durham, 2011). The conceptualization of rights as relational is also significant in the analysis of the role and place of the adult generation in shaping children's rights in a way that is aligned with or reflects intergenerational expectations (a point I will return to later).

The reference to relational rights and non-sovereign relationalities of children is not new (Balagopalan, 2021). Scholars remind us that 'rights' neither belong to individuals nor arise from a need for self-preservation; rather they are grounded in, and arise from, responsibilities in human relationships (Minow & Lyndon, 1996; Murove, 2014). Murove (2014, p. 39) further argues that 'a proper understanding of responsibility presumes that as individuals we always respond to what we find in relationships, and if there are no relationships there cannot be anything like personal responsibility'. It is worth noting that relationships are often fraught with domination and subjugation and that any discussion of relational rights must also account for pervasive forms of inequality and uneven relations of power.

Although marginal in global discussions around children's rights, the coexistence of rights and duties is also made explicit in the African Charter on the Rights and Welfare of the Child (OAU, 1990), especially in Article 31 which foregrounds the 'dutiful child' whereby children's responsibilities to work for the cohesion of the family and to respect, and assist, their parents and communities are pivotal. Studies further highlight the role of customary laws in legally pluralist societies and advocate for vernacularizing children's rights (Kaime, 2010) both to acknowledge the already existing social and cultural rights children have in their families and communities *and* to not render those rights meaningless (Abebe & Tefera, 2014; Jirata, 2022). What I add to this debate is how childhood as a sociocultural construction informs our understanding of rights. That is, to not only analyze the ways in which ideas around children's rights relate children to families and communities – reflecting the sociocultural values and generational positions they inhabit – but also to understand how rights are borne out of social, economic, cultural, and moral relationships that embed and produce childhoods in particular contexts.

As rights get meaning in the interstices of social interactions, rather than being a product or an object that is out there to be claimed, stating that children have unique rights that others do not have in a particular context is problematic, especially if that right is a function of, or predicated on, an autonomous selfhood opposed to others or a sociocultural system (Durham, 2011). As Durham (2011) notes, children do not become independent holders of rights – nor liberalized – and do not, as part of their 'plot' of growing up, make something new. Their ability to shape the culture, social relations, and world around them rests more on their ability to nest these things in relationalities, which they only begin to wield effectively in later years.

7.3.2 Circular and reciprocal rights

Conditions of childhood poverty are relative and children in my research speak of their well-being as particularly relational, and frequently refer to cooperation to make ends meet when asked about their well-being. However, they also note how their well-being and well-becoming depend not only on resource availability but on reciprocal relationships with family collectives who mediate their access to food, clothing, materials for schooling, or opportunities for improving future life chances. For example, the accumulation, distribution, exchange, and utilization of resources in the rural communities I studied play out in a circular interdependence between the adults/elderly and young members of the family/community. The elderly generation has wealth in the form of land, cattle, and cash that affords them authority, which is vested in their right to make policies, settle disputes, and impose sanctions. The possession of these attributes gives the elderly the means of obligating the young but, in turn, they must give up most, and ultimately all, of their wealth to their children in the form of bride wealth, land, and cattle. These cyclical relations of subordination are not necessarily about the subjugation of the young because the elderly's role as mentors and guides also offers an environment of protection to the young. Nor do they necessarily imply the violation of children's rights as often understood as the exercise of individual choice and personal freedom. Instead, they create the conditions for children to plan for their future livelihoods, enabling their capacity for action.

Yet, young people who depend on their parents who may not have enough land or wealth express fears concerning inheritance and anticipate conflicts among siblings. Tensions and conflicts emerge in familial and intergenerational relationships when young people achieve relative economic independence (Di Nunzio, 2019). Young people may come to claim and perform roles that directly question and erode the authority of their parents, potentially leading to conflict as the latter try to enforce their role while the former attempt their positions of independence and authority (Heinonen, 2011). Children working in the informal economy, for example, develop relative economic independence that increases their negotiating power with their elders. For some young people, persistent conflict and confrontations with their parents were an important part of their existence (Di Nunzio, 2019) but having support from family members was also seen as pivotal to some children's ambitions to learn to become independent. Yet, even in those situations where children and young people are involved in independent paid work, their ability to earn money should not be confused with possession of autonomy, as they are rarely free from dependence on others. Interdependence may also take a form where families in adverse situations are forced to send their children to work because of economic necessity.

In rural Ethiopia, where 80% of its 120 million inhabitants live, children are 'born into families'; it is often adult members of the family that mediate a child's access to, and full membership of, the community/clan. The latter, in turn, bestows the child his/her rights to physical, social, and cultural resources (for example, land, dowry, inheritance). Children are primarily members of family collectives to whom they owe duties and obligations for securing their rights, existence, and well-being. As opposed to the UNCRC which emphasizes children's entitlement to judicial and discursively constructed rights from the state; children in Ethiopia almost always get their needs fulfilled by families and wider kins. Interdependence to cope with daily hardships of life is the prime expression of conviviality and sharing that underpins intergenerational relationships. In this web of relations, a child's relationship with family collectives is crucial not just as a path to securing individual rights but instead to 'attain ultimate well-being' (Murove, 2014, p. 37).

The previous analysis of rights as circular position children in relation to families and communities (as well as the life course) through a cyclical exchange system of livelihoods, resonating with many Indigenous epistemes where reciprocity is a key principle and practice of everyday life (Kuokkanen, 2007; Twum-Danso Imoh, 2022). Kuokkanen (2007, p. 145) writes about how this reciprocity 'is not practiced or understood in constrained terms of give and take', nor as the 'accumulation of gifts [and] insurance of countergifts as in the modern economy', but rather in terms of 'giving back and circulation'. Circular reciprocity implies response-ability, i.e. the ability to respond and remain attuned to the world beyond oneself, and the possibility of kinship formation through mutual aid and interdependence (Kuokkanen, 2007). Reciprocal and subordinate modes of existence also render intelligible rights as being replete with a variety of attributes that are often in the continuum, including independence-dependence, incompetence-competence, inabilities-abilities, duties, and responsibilities. They imply redefining children's rights beyond the vertical (child-state) or horizontal axis (child-family/community/society) to instead view them as cyclical and multidirectional.

7.3.3 *Rights as generational interdependence*

As I have argued previously, interdependence is a key strategy for increasing collective well-being in Ethiopia and, when speaking about how they are faring in life, people seldom refer to themselves alone but include the well-being of those who are dependent on them. Articulations of (generational) interdependence become particularly salient when people get their first 'dependents' regardless of their age – the first child, for girls, the first wife or girlfriend, for boys (Hoechner, 2018). Yet, it also informs the roles that individuals assume over the life course. Relatedly, Durham (2011) describes how 'success' and 'good life' are assessed not by a person's ability to become independent or the accumulation of personal wealth for individual liberty but instead by the capacity to 'attract' and support dependents. This includes the ability to assist siblings, siblings of relatives, or neighbours. If a wealthy man or woman does not begin to hire people or attach dependents for domestic or agricultural work or have children – the kind of things that begin the recognition of adulthood – that person is not seen as having a life worth living (Durham, 2011). As a person's status is shored up by the capacity to fulfill a growing range of social/material obligations to others as the person moves through the life course, they can also become more interdependent, not more individually autonomous. When engaging in material support practices, children, like adults in my research, describe complex layers of responsibilities for themselves and their immediate and extended families (Durham, 2011). Families, too, often extend support to orphans based on a shared sense of coping with adversity, but also because they value the significance of fostering in cementing social bonds and facilitating the socialization and development of children. Living with dependents that commensurate with one's material means are, therefore, common forms of social existence and an antipode to the notion of autonomous selfhood that often characterizes the gathering of wealth for personal freedom (Durham, 2011; Hoechner, 2018). These experiences resonate widely with the lifeworld of African children where sharing, mutuality of dependence, and reciprocal obligations are social norms (Twum-Danso Imoh, 2022).

My conception of rights as interdependent, thus, draws on the idea that children are neither independent nor autonomous individuals with separate rights but interdependent beings whose daily lives are intricately entwined with, and inseparable from, those of 'other generations'. Interdependent rights are borne out of the moral and existential tension, as children struggle to overcome the constraints of childhood marginality not just as individuals but as social beings who are part of the world. This framing of rights acknowledges how children's lives are connected to the lives of those with whom they relate in ways that see rights as contextual, and contingent upon familial and intergenerational interactions and power relations.

Interdependent rights also encompass fulfilling duties whereby the young generation, for example, has the role of serving the community through their activities in daily and generational reproduction while the elderly generation has the knowledge and wisdom to lead it. Jirata (2022, p. 394) explains the sociopolitical organization that is based on age-grade sets called the Gada system in Guji communities of southern Ethiopia and their conception of rights:

> Children's rights have been embodiments of this Indigenous system that prescribe children's entitlement to learning from contexts such as

> intergenerational interactions, participation in social roles per their ages and sexes, and community-wide care. Based on the Gada system, children are recognized as 'significant members' having the right to learn through participation in social events and being cared for by and caring for their siblings, parents, grandparents, relatives, and community members.

The aforementioned forms of generational interdependencies invite deeper reflections on the sociocultural constructions and 'values' of childhood. As the social constructions of childhood in Ethiopia emphasize seniority, drawing individuals from the world of childhood to the central stage of adulthood and eventually to eldership in the community, generation is key in structuring access to, and distribution of, resources, rights, and roles. The social positions of generations are, however, not static but subject to what Huijsmans et al. (2014) call 'generationing', a term they borrow from Alanen (2001) to theorize the ways in which children's role in social reproduction is constantly repositioned because of the changing terms brought about by development. I, in turn, borrow the concept of 'generationing' here to suggest the dynamic ways in which children's rights is relationally constituted, as children navigate their rights with multiple generations, in time, space, and over the life course. The notion of 'generationing rights' encompasses all people across the generational spectrum: infants, children, youth, adults, and the very elderly are all embedded in generational relations (Ansell, 2014). The analytical gain is that, by generationing rights, we shift attention from children to social relationships, from studying children's agency to claiming rights to understanding wider processes of change that reconfigure their roles and positions in society (Ansell, 2014, p. 283). Another key implication is whether children's rights should be decentred in favor of an analysis of intergenerational rights and interdependence. As Ansell (2014) suggests, this might be necessary because children encounter and exercise rights relationally – in response to their contexts, to other generations, and their own future aspirations and capacities.

7.4 Recasting children's unwritten, collective rights

What can we learn from homegrown versions of children's rights? And what might vernacular conceptions of children's rights offer in expanding the vision of the international children's rights framework? My analysis of the struggle for social reproduction draws analytical attention to not only the 'unwritten', ethnocultural rights of children – such as the right to collective care or the right to learn through work as opposed to only via schooling – but also to the practical conflicts and problems that the codified, globalizing children's rights conceals and, in so doing, forfeits the very rights that children have in their society. The UNCRC reinforced international – often argued to be Western – narratives around childhood by employing the language of 'the rights of the child', rather than the 'collective rights of children' (Stephens, 1995, p. 36).

Through appropriating the UNCRC into local policies and programmes, children are not only individualized, but they are also placed within a naturalized nuclear family wherein parents are to provide or made responsible for their rights.

Although the monadic and right-claiming child of Western creation sounds clear within the international community, it neither resonates with children's everyday lives nor transfers directly into local contexts. It is also at odds with the functioning of family collectives, sidestepping broader sociocultural narratives around ideas of obligations and responsibilities in which children are not seen as mere recipients of adult nurturance and care. Arguably, the contestation and refusals of mainstream children's rights in Ethiopia are not because parents believe that children have no rights or disrespect children's individuality but because they view their rights as integral to the wider kin networks with whom mutual and long-term livelihood strategies are set (Abebe, 2013). Communities' insistence on children's collective rights further exemplifies local epistemologies of childhood that both subvert and simultaneously call for freedom from a teleology of neoliberal rights that seem to dictate that this is the only possible framework for children's empowerment.

Children do not become aware of their rights because the Ethiopian state has ratified the UNCRC but, as Hanson and Nieuwenhuys (2013) argue, as they make sense of their daily existence and, in so doing, craft and bring to life what rights are, and become, in the social world. A mere focus on the codified aspects of children's rights not only obscures the existing rights of children and negates their entitlements within society, but also overlooks how they navigate their 'unwritten rights' while attempting to overcome the social, material, and political constraints of childhood. An alternative, more expansive conceptualization of children's rights liberates rights from their predetermined, legal constrictions so that the everyday possibilities and non-sovereign, emergent relationalities of childhood and children's lives are recognized and appreciated (see Balagopalan, 2021). This approach not only calls into question the state, NGOs, and formal institutions as the sole creditors and guarantors of children's rights but locates children's rights within the immediate reciprocal relationship and forms of social accountability that values the politics of care founded on collective relationalities. It also requires us to move beyond mere critiquing of the discursive reproductions of children's rights – the kinds of languages, ideas, rationales, tactics, and justifications mobilized and enforced by the children's rights regime – to instead interrogating the ontological/philosophical grounds that separate the rights of children from the rights of other generations.

The vernacular conceptualizations of rights I discussed previously – rights as relational, circular, and interdependent – do not just embed social relations but also get expressions in sociocultural fields and political-economic contexts within which any form of relationship unfolds. Neither of them is a neatly separate conceptual framework but instead interlinked to one another, demonstrating the multiplicities of relationalities and power dynamics within which the life worlds of children are imbricated. They draw attention to the fact that whereas the constraints of poverty, abjection, and lack of access to resources or social support systems are themselves a political and relational product (Di Nunzio, 2019), having an abundance of relations is not a guarantee that all relations work or are even desirable. In contrast to the abstract international children's rights framework, local children's priorities, and the stories they tell of their lives, are inseparable from the needs and interests of their families/communities. They underscore how it is difficult to separate what is 'individual' from what is 'collective', not least because children see themselves, and are seen, by society less as individual holders of rights and more as members of collectives to whom they owe duties and obligations (Abebe, 2013). By recognizing children's 'living rights' as multiple, contradictory, and embedded in, and productive of, wider social relationships (Hanson & Nieuwenhuys, 2013), recasting children's rights as relational and interdependent opens up the space to acknowledge the mundane and often unrecognized forms of rights that operate within the realms of the everyday, resonating with their lived realities.

The moral and existential tensions between children's attempts to overcome the conditions of deprivation and the awareness of living an existence embedded in precarity and exclusion remain unresolved (Di Nunzio, 2019). To account for this tension is vital not only to recentre the rights of marginal children but also make a case for Critical Children's Rights Studies' engagement with the politics of knowledge production. To examine how marginal children's modes of existence such as generational interdependence and subordination unfold, for example, offers new insights into the field of children's rights on how generational positions co-determine each other, and that the human rights of children and the human rights of other generations are not just oppositional but productive of one another. This recognition neither negates that children be right bearers nor invisibilizes their capacities to claim rights, or the need to respect their rights. Rather, it invites us to turn towards an alternative reading of children's rights, engaging with how age and generation are constituted relationally (Huijsmans et al., 2014) and how specific relations of dependency can enable or create room for children's capacity for action. Children's rights studies need to continue rebuilding 'emic' understandings of rights from non-adult centric positions and other critical views (for example, indigeneity, intersectionality, childism) to render intelligible the modes of existence of children outside modernity's framework. These approaches have the potential to illuminate what the aspirations, imaginations, struggles, and refusals of rights might mean for the intellectual and political project of decolonizing and vernacularizing children's rights as well as recognize the local, cultural resources that could be leveraged in the interest of empowering children.

References

Abebe, T (2013). Interdependent agency and rights: The role of children in collective livelihood strategies in Ethiopia. In K. Hanson & O. Nieuwenhuys (eds.) *Reconceptualizing children's rights in international development: Living rights, social justice, and translations* (pp. 71–92). Cambridge University Press.

Abebe, T. (2017). Political economy of children's work: Economic restructuring, the coffee trade and social reproduction in post-socialist Ethiopia. In N. Ansell, N. Klocker & T. Skelton (eds.) *Geographies of global issues: Change and threat. geographies of children and young people* (pp. 21–42). Springer.
Abebe, T., & Bessell, S. (2011). Dominant discourses, debates and silences on child labour in Africa and Asia. *Third World Quarterly*, *32*(4), 765–786.
Abebe, T., & Tefera, T. (2014). Earning rights – discourses on children's rights and proper childhood in Ethiopia. In A. Twum-Danso Imoh & N. Ansell (eds.) *Children's lives in an era of children's rights: The progress of the convention on the rights of the child in Africa* (pp. 43–62). Routledge.
Alanen, L. (2001). Explorations in generational analysis. In L. Alanen & B. Mayall (eds.) *Conceptualizing child-adult relations* (pp. 11–22). Routledge Falmer.
Alber, E. (2023). Entangled navigations: Intergenerational care relations in neoliberal eduscapes in Benin. *Critique of Anthropology*, *43*(4), 365–384. https://doi.org/10.1177/0308275X231216260
Ansell, N. (2014). Generationing development: A commentary. *European Journal of Development Research*, *26*(2), 283–291.
Balagopalan, S. (2021). Precarity and the question of children's relationalities. *Childhood*, *28*(3), 327–332.
Bodja, S., & Gleason, K. (2020). Domestic adoption in Ethiopia. In G. M. Wrobel, Helder & E. Marr (eds.) *The Routledge handbook of adoption* (pp. 49–61). Routledge.
Brittingham, S. (2010). *Birth families and intercountry adoption in Addis Ababa, Ethiopia*. Unpublished Master's thesis, Institute of Social Studies.
Di Nunzio, M. (2019). *The act of living: Street life, marginality, and development in urban Ethiopia*. Cornell University Press.
Duressa, A. (2002). *Guddifachaa: Adoption practice in Oromo society with particular reference to the Borana Oromo*. PhD Thesis, Addis Ababa University, Ethiopia.
Durham, D. (2011). Apathy and agency: The romance of agency and youth in Botswana. In D. Durham & J. Cole (eds.) *Figuring the future: Globalization and the temporalities of children and youth* (pp. 151–158). School for Advanced Research Press.
FDRE. (2000). *The revised family code (213/2000)*. Retrieved June 12, 2021, from www. unhcr.org/refworld/docid/4c0ccc052.html
Hanson, K., & Nieuwenhuys, O. (2013). Introduction: Living rights, social justice and translations. In K. Hanson & O. Nieuwenhuys (eds.) *Reconceptualizing children's rights in international development: Living rights, social justice and translations* (pp. 3–25). Cambridge University Press.
Heinonen, P. (2011). *Youth gangs and street children: Culture, nurture and masculinity in Ethiopia*. Berghahn Books.
Hoechner, H. (2018). *Quranic schools in Northern Nigeria: Everyday experiences of youth, faith, and poverty*. Cambridge University Press.
Huijsmans, R., George, S., Gigengack, R., & Evers, S. (2014). Theorising age and generation in development: A relational approach. *European Journal of Development Research*, *26*, 163–174.
Jirata, T. J. (2022). Indigenous rights of children among agropastoral communities in southern Ethiopia. *Childhood*, *29*(3), 389–405.
Kaime, T. (2010). "Vernacularising" the convention on the rights of the child: Rights and culture as analytic tools. *The International Journal of Children's Rights*, *18*(4), 637–653.
Kassa, S., & Abebe, T. (2016). *Qenja*: Child fostering and relocation practices in the Amhara region, Ethiopia. *Children's Geographies*, *14*(1), 46–62.
Kuokkanen, R. (2007). The gift logic of indigenous philosophies in the academy. In G. Vaughan (ed.) *Women and the gift economy. A radically different worldview is possible* (pp. 71–83). Toronto: Indiana Publications and Education Inc.

Lemessa, A., & Kjørholt, A. T. (2013). Children's parliament: A case study in Konso. In T. Abebe & A. T. Kjørholt (eds.) *Childhood and local knowledge in Ethiopia: Livelihoods, rights and intergenerational relationships* (pp. 45–71). Akademika Press.

Masquelier, A. (2022). "Girling" the future and "futuring" girls in Niger. In C. Greiner, S. van Wolputte & M. Bolling (eds.) *African futures* (pp. 309–319). Brill. https://doi.org/10.1163/9789004471641_026

Minow, M., & Lyndon, M. (1996). Relational rights and responsibilities: Revisioning the family in liberal political theory and law. *Family and Feminist Theory*, *11*(1), 4–29.

Murove, M. F. (2014). Ubuntu. *Diogenes*, *59*(3–4), 36–47.

Nieuwenhuys, O. (2001). By the sweat of their brow? "street children", NGOs and children's rights in Addis Ababa. *Africa*, *71*, 539–557.

OAU. (1990). *African charter on the rights and welfare of the child*. 36804-treaty-african_charter_on_rights_welfare_of_the_child.pdf

Poluha, E. (2004). *The power of continuity: Ethiopia through the eyes of its children*. Nordic Africa Institute.

Pyysiainnen, J., Halpin, D., & Guilfoyle, A. (2017). Neoliberal governance and "responsibilisation" of agents: Reassessing the mechanisms of responsibility-shift in neoliberal discursive environments. *Distinction: Journal of Social Theory*, *18*(2), 215–235.

Spivak, G. C. (2004). Righting wrongs. *South Atlantic Quarterly*, *103*(2–3), 523–581.

Stephens, S. (1995). Children and the politics of culture in "late capitalism". In S. Stephens (ed.) *Children and the politics of culture* (pp. 3–48). Princeton University Press.

Twum-Danso Imoh, A. (2022). Framing reciprocal obligations within intergenerational relations in Ghana through the lens of the mutuality of duty and dependence. *Childhood*, *29*(3), 439–454.

Wells, K. (2009). *Childhood in a global perspective*. Polity Press.

8 Destabilizing images of the competent adult vs. the incompetent child in dominant children's rights discourses through the lens of Akan notions of personhood and social relations

Afua Twum-Danso Imoh

8.1 Introduction

Today, the idea that the status of childhood is vastly different from that of adulthood is now seemingly ubiquitous in its 'taken-for-grantedness', with childhood defined as a phase of life which lacks the key attributes that adulthood possesses – competence, capability, maturity, and knowledge of the world. These ideas have taken root amongst diverse populations in both the Global North and the Global South as a result of colonialism, school-based education historically centred around a Christian and Eurocentric ethos, and the intensification of global processes in more recent years. Despite these developments which have had enormous ramifications and, at times, feel all-encompassing, not all societies and not all social groups within a particular locale view the status of childhood as being so dramatically distinct from that of adulthood. What this means, in effect, is that such societies make different linkages between the status of childhood and concepts such as competence, capability, and maturity. This leads to significant tensions between such communities which can be found not only in the Global South but also within the Global North, and the principles underlying dominant children's discourses, which take, as their departure point, the premise that childhood is distinct from adulthood, and, as a result, requires special protections. These tensions cannot simply be done away with through sensitization programmes to correct 'ignorant' and 'backward' people of their erring or misinformed ways. This is due to the fact that understandings about both childhood and adulthood are fundamental to how these societies conceptualize, and make meaning of, both personhood and social relations between generations as well as within. This, therefore, requires a novel approach to thinking about childhood and adulthood and the assumptions made about the competence levels that are typically associated with both phases of life in dominant rights discourses. This is what I seek to achieve with this chapter – to explore the contributions of West African, specifically Akan, notions of personhood and social relations to alternative ways of conceptualizing children's rights which do not take childhood incompetence as their departure point.

DOI: 10.4324/9781003510284-9

8.2 The emergence of the incompetent child: from 19th century child-saving movements to a global discourse of children's rights

The idea that the status of childhood is vastly different from that of adulthood emerged as part of 19th century child-saving movements and is now firmly embedded within dominant children's rights discourses best represented by the Convention on the Rights of the Child (UNCRC). This distinction between the two status groups has not only come to be marked by chronological age (specifically the age of 18) but also by key characteristics that are recognized as being attributable to each status group. In particular, the state of adulthood is positioned as possessing all the qualities that those within the childhood phase of life lack – autonomy (in its full sense), maturity, sound judgement, experience, competence, and knowledge of the world (Verhellen, 1994). Alongside the development and promotion of the distinct nature of childhood was a recognition that this distinctiveness should be respected. However, at the same time, there emerged the perception that this phase of life was inferior to that of adulthood due to the deficit association that came to be made between childhood and the aforementioned attributes. Therefore, children were seen as lacking the capabilities that adults, who were used as the yardstick to measure maturity and competence, possessed (see Boyden, 1997).

These transformations bestowed on individuals under a certain age a 'weakness' and 'innocence' that were not previously so firmly linked to this phase of life. Further, it made them dependent on adults, especially professionals. These developments were so effective that by the early 20th century adults and children in large sections of populations in Europe and North America (and amongst European settler populations in other parts of the world such as South America) had come to accept these attributes as part of the experience of childhood. It is against this backdrop that Bob Corbett (1985) once asserted that while modern society assumes that children are children by nature, they are, in fact, children by choice as it is this very society that has nurtured young people into 'childhood'. This is not to say that prior to the 18th century there was no understanding of childhood; certainly, the historical record shows us that, indeed, there was, but how this phase of life was understood was quite distinct from later conceptualizations that started being fine-tuned during the 19th century in Europe and the Americas (see Plumb, 1972).

Having developed as part of child-saving movements, which were firmly consolidated during the course of the 19th century, this conception of childhood that emerged in Europe and North America became part and parcel of the concept of children's rights as it started to gain momentum. While this process was initially centred around national boundaries, it gradually took the form of a global discourse, with the passage, most notably, of the 1924 Declaration on the Rights of the Child by the League of Nations, which, arguably, marked the first systematic attempt to globalize this concept. This treaty was later succeeded by the 1959 Declaration on the Rights of the Child and then, importantly, the first binding treaty on children's rights, the UNCRC, in 1989.

In this way much of the passivity, dependency, vulnerability, and immaturity that had been central tenets of European and North American child-saving movements became intertwined with global discourses of children's rights, especially in their early articulations.

The concept of children's rights is perceived to have evolved between the 1924 Declaration and the 1989 UNCRC, with numerous publications highlighting the various ways the latter is a step change in the advancement of children's rights, especially in relation to civil and political rights (see Doek, 2011; Veerman, 1992). Nevertheless, the concept of children's rights as it is understood today remains one that largely perceives those inhabiting the status of childhood as immature, incompetent, and weak, and, therefore, dependent upon, and requiring, the guidance of more competent and knowledgeable adults in order to transition into successful adulthood themselves. For instance, despite articles in the UNCRC that are seen to stipulate that governments must take steps to ensure children's access to key civil and political rights, these are limited to children 'having a say', notably on issues affecting them – which is envisaged as a process that, ultimately, requires adult management and control (see Pupavac, 2001; Liebel, 2012). Thus, while civil and political rights are incorporated into the notion of children's rights that is articulated in the UNCRC, what these rights mean for children is different from what they have, hitherto, meant for those recognized as adults in broader human rights principles (Twum-Danso Imoh, 2024b).

While the concept of children's rights has evolved and there is, today, an understanding that children have some degree of autonomy and competence, the extent to which these concepts are attributed to children remain limited in dominant rights discourses. Hence, although the binary between adulthood and childhood is said to have led to more respect for children's status in society, it has also resulted in viewing the status of childhood in deficit terms, as less than. For instance, in relation to the notion of competence, these developments have led to a situation whereby we discuss childhood competence in quite restrictive ways which does not allow for a comprehensive discussion about children and their responsibilities or duties. This can be attributed to dominant perceptions of children as immature, incompetent, and in need of protection by more competent and responsible adults. This consequently creates somewhat of an imbalance between the notion of children having duties or responsibilities and children's entitlements in dominant rights discourses.

This restricted approach to understanding childhood competence subsequently results in a mismatch between children's rights principles and the realities of children's lives in cultures which have different ways of measuring maturity and attributing competence to individuals which are not based on biological age. This creates a significant tension between principles underlying dominant children's rights discourses and any attendant initiatives seeking to realize them on one hand, and the norms and realities of such cultures on the other. This mismatch is not simply attributable to a lack of awareness that can merely be corrected through education programmes aimed at 'ignorant' communities who will change their behaviours once they have come to realize the 'error' of their ways. Instead, what drives this persisting dissonance is an inherent rejection of a rigid binary between the status of adulthood and the status of childhood due to a fundamental difference in how they conceptualize both personhood and social relations. The endurance of ideas such as these that are antithetical to dominant children's rights discourses 100 years after this concept was first articulated on a global platform makes it imperative to problematize the extent to which dominant discourses of children's rights are not only applicable in the lives of children in certain contexts but also hold real meaning for children and their families in their everyday lives and can, therefore, effectively serve as a tool for transformative societal change.

8.3 Methodology

Over the last 20 years I have undertaken fieldwork in Ghana on constructions of childhood, child-rearing practices and the implementation of global children's rights norms. This chapter draws on three of my studies. The first study, my PhD project (Study 1), for which fieldwork was undertaken between 2005 and 2006, focused on the implementation of the UNCRC in two communities in central Accra, the capital city – Nima and Ga Mashie. The second study (Study 2), which was undertaken in 2009, centred around eliciting children's perceptions on physical punishment in four communities in the Greater Accra and Eastern regions of the country: Nima, Ga Mashie (specifically one neighbourhood, Bukom), Pokrom Nsabaa, and Dodowa. Study 3, which was undertaken more recently in 2022 and 2023, focused on the development of children's rights discourses in Ghana. In terms of the methods deployed for these studies, these consisted of: participant observation (Study 1 and 2); the collection of data through participatory workshops and focus group discussions (FGDs) with children and young people aged between 10 and 21 (Study 1); semi-structured interviews with children aged between 10 and 16 (Study 2); diaries completed by children aged 10 to 16 (Study 2); and the administration of surveys to children (Study 1). In relation to adults, methods centred around FGDs (Study 1 and Study 2) as well as expert interviews (Study 1, 2, and 3). Ethical approval for all studies was obtained from the institution to which I was affiliated at the time I conducted the respective studies.

8.4 Embedding dominant children's rights into Ghanaian contexts: a conducive environment facilitated by centuries of social transformation?

Ghana presents an interesting example of a context which illuminates the duality of intersections between dominant discourses of children's rights and the lived realities of different social groups. This is a result of the co-existence that can be identified between new ideas about social relations and personhood that have emerged over the last few hundred years on the one hand, and the persistence of values and ways of being that have been transmitted from one generation to the next for thousands of years on the other. In relation to the new ideas that have emerged these can be attributed to the rapid social changes that Ghana has experienced which can arguably be traced back to the arrival of the Portuguese who were the first Europeans to claim monopoly of the coastal area of the land they called *Costa da Mina* in 1482. This marked the beginning of intense competition by different European states (the Netherlands, Sweden, Denmark, and Britain), sometimes in parallel, other times successively, to exert, initially, trading monopoly and, eventually, political control, over this area, starting along the coast and gradually, under the British in particular, making further incursions inland.

Beyond the establishment of colonial rule and the changes it brought about, other factors that have further compounded the transformations that Ghanaian society has experienced are: Christianity, which has become widely prevalent in the country; school-based education which remains, in many ways, shaped by the priorities and dictates of a Eurocentric and an anglophile curriculum; rapid urbanization; and globalization of not only economies, but also of cultures. This latter point about globalization is noteworthy, as the intensification of global processes includes those relating to the global spread of ideas around childhood, which have not only been disseminated through international laws and policies but also through media, travel, and migration and have come to be reproduced in national and local discourses by sections of the Ghanaian population. A notable example relates to the definition of childhood. While Ghanaian laws and policies such as the 1998 Children's Act and the 2003 Juvenile Justice Act have all been amended to ensure that they are based on an understanding that children are those under the age of 18, which aligns with the standards of the UNCRC, such ideas are now also identifiable in local discourses reproduced by sections of the population in different communities (see Twum-Danso Imoh, 2019).

This notwithstanding, there remain social groups who reject the concept of children's rights as articulated in dominant discourses due to the fact that they see it as a threat to the principles upon which key cultural values such as respect, reciprocity, and responsibility are based. In my first study in Ghana 20 years ago (Study 1) it became quickly evident that most adult participants objected to the idea of anyone, not least children, possessing rights *a priori* (see Twum-Danso, 2008; Twum-Danso Imoh, 2024a). For them, the idea that an individual could have rights without doing anything in return was an imported 'Western' concept that they felt would result in the production of unwanted behaviours in children. This, they believed, would, in turn, tarnish the whole fabric of their communities and, ultimately, lead to society's failure to produce the kind of 'proper' person that socialization strategies in this context have been seeking to produce for generations (see Twum-Danso Imoh, 2024a). That these ideas endure 18 years after data were gathered was illuminated in interviews I conducted with government officials and civil society representatives in 2022 and early 2023 in their attempt to explain contemporary attitudes towards children's rights (Study 3):

> There is some level of aversion for the term 'rights' by a good percentage of the population. A good percentage of the Ghanaian population perceive child rights as alien to them and therefore, [it] is an imposition. Child rights, according to most Ghanaians make children stubborn and difficult to control because it gives too much power and freedom to the child. Some aspects of child rights are perceived [as] anti-cultural e.g., [provisions on] corporal punishment and therefore [they] are resentful to the average Ghanaian.
>
> (see Twum-Danso Imoh, 2024a, p. 124)

As a result of this tension that continues to exist between dominant understandings of children's rights, and cultural and social norms, a hesitance has emerged amongst professionals in this context to use the language of children's rights in framing social justice concerns relating to children in their interventions with communities, with many preferring to foreground the concepts of child protection and children's needs instead (see McCrystal & Manful, 2011; Twum-Danso Imoh, 2024a).

Focusing more centrally on this idea of developing a 'proper' person, which is a key objective of socialization strategies in this context, is the notion of competence within conceptualizations of childhood. This conceptualization of personhood, and the attendant social relations that underpin it, has resulted in an understanding that childhood is a phase of life in which children are recognized as competent and capable. Embedded within this framing of childhood is that children provide help to adults, even as children. This help children undertake takes the form of duties that they are expected to perform from a young age, and which are often allocated based on gendered norms. Therefore, all children in the multiple studies I have undertaken in this context were very conscious that as part of their role as 'children' in their families they were expected to support, and assist, adults and other children within their households and communities. Interestingly, in discussing the importance of education, many children who participated in my studies made clear that for them, the definition of education was not only about attending school but also about receiving training in household chores, such as cooking, cleaning, and yard work (see Twum-Danso, 2009; Twum-Danso Imoh, 2024a).

In articulating what they understood as the definition of childhood a number of children made a linkage between this phase of life and concepts such as 'work', 'duty', and 'responsibility'. As one child put it, 'children must work' (FGD with Nima School Children IV October-December 2005, Study 1). Another explained it thus: 'children have to help parents in everything they are doing' (FGD with School Children at Sempe II Primary, 1 February 2006, Study 1). Consequently, the specific work tasks children undertook featured heavily in all their accounts of their everyday life, as is evidenced by this diary entry completed by a 16-year-old girl in Study 2 who lived with her aunt and uncle whom she referred to as mother and father:

> Every day when I wake up, I sweep, go to the stream to fetch water and bath; in the evening I help my mother [aunt] to cook in the kitchen. When I get up, I sweep the room I sleep in, sweep my father's [uncle] room and the compound. On school days I only sweep the compound and bath and go to school. When I come back, I go to the stream whilst my mother is boiling the cassava on the fire. By the time I finish fetching the water, the cassava will be well cooked, and I come and punt it. After that we all eat, bath and I will learn and go to bed.
>
> (Pokrom Nsabaa, Diary Participant, Age 16, Female, October 2009, Study 2)

It is important to note that this work that children undertake within their household becomes recognized, especially as they become more and more competent at completing a particular task, as being of 'good quality' as it makes significant contributions to the maintenance of the household. This is noted by German anthropologist Enid Schildkrout (1978), who, in her work in urban Kano (northern Nigeria) in the 1970s, concluded that as children in her research site assumed responsibilities from an early age, many of which adults relied on so they could undertake other tasks or adhere to religious or cultural practices (especially in the case of women), growing up, then, was not a case of children transitioning from being *unproductive* members of society to becoming *productive* members because, as children, they were already productive members of society. Central to the understanding of being a productive member of the household as a child is not simply about the ability to undertake work, but to do it so well that it enables the individual to be an effective contributor to the household. Therefore, part and parcel of the notion of being productive is that the work that is completed is of good quality. Returning to Schildkrout's thesis, the fact that adults in her research site had come to be dependent on children was not simply due to the availability of children to undertake work tasks or the quantity of work undertaken by children; it was also because the outputs of the work that children did produce were of good quality – to the extent that it *effectively* relieved the workload of adults and *added value* to the maintenance of the household. This notion of the quality of children's contributions to the family emerges more recently in anthropologist Jean Hunleth's account of children's caregiving within contexts of illness, specifically HIV/AIDs and tuberculosis in Zambia. Referring to one of her research participants, 'Maureen', who had been left weakened by tuberculosis, Hunleth (2017, pp. 2–3) writes that:

> Maureen said: 'the children are taking good care of me. People would think it is the elders who are helping and cleaning the place, but it is the children.' Maureen drew attention to the quality of her children's care.

> The children were not just taking care, they were taking good care of her. Their care was so good that people would think it 'the elders.' The elders – her mother, brother, and other adult relatives – were not able to take such good care. They too had their own care needs and demands on their time.

Thus, for Maureen, the quality of the care her children provided during her illness could not have been provided by the other adults in the family. In her opinion her children's care was not just an option of last resort on which she had to rely in the absence of available adults who could more efficiently take on the role; in fact, it seems she may have preferred the care of her daughters because it was more effective and enabled her to recover sufficiently to be able to relay her experience to Hunleth on a later visit.

Crucially, what emerges from the literature as well as my own data is that children have a clear understanding that the caregiver–child relationship is one based on mutual support and help, and that this expectation was embedded not just in the understanding of parenthood but also in their conceptualization of childhood (see Twum-Danso Imoh, 2022). This mutuality of duty was captured briefly by a female child participant in Study 1 who explained it thus: 'your mother has to help you, and you must help your mother' (FGD with Ga Mashie out of School Children II, 10 February 2006, Study 1). This brief statement captures the essence of the reciprocal obligations or mutual duty that both parties have within an adult and child relationship in this context. Therefore, while childhood was acknowledged as a period of dependency by many participants in this study, this state of dependence did not signify an inability of children to provide support, care, and assistance to key adults in their lives.

The stress by all informants in my studies on the importance of children's duties can be attributed to the value of reciprocity, which continues to underline many social relationships in Ghana (see Twum-Danso, 2009). According to Pellow (1977), writing about Ghana in the 1970s, while the concept of reciprocity is applicable to all societies, its special significance in Ghana lies in its pervasiveness and its explicit character. She further argues that:

> In its most crass form, reciprocity imputes a concrete value to any transaction or interaction. If one party gives or does something to (for) another, there is an 'equivalent' return to be made, contingent upon the role relationship. One does not receive something for nothing. Everything is given a concrete worth. Inherent in reciprocity is the quality of trust-trust in a just return. In Ghana this is not left to chance; the demands individuals make on one another are explicit.
>
> (Pellow, 1977, p. 42)

As a result of the key role of reciprocity in this locale, children grow up very much aware of their obligations to their parents, not only later as adults, but also as children (Twum-Danso Imoh, 2022). Consequently, it plays a significant role in why children in all my studies emphasized values such as responsibility and duty. They accept their position in society partly because it enables them to receive what they need from their parents or key adults in their lives. In fact, I would like to go so far as to suggest that by accepting their position in society, children are acting strategically because they are aware of the benefits that come with playing the subordinate role expected of them in society (see Twum-Danso, 2008). This is because they understand that by behaving like a 'good' child through their behaviours and fulfilling their responsibilities, they can make a request for their own needs which a 'good' adult would struggle to refuse. This is supported by Hardgrove (2017, p. 44) who, in her study focusing on children's lives in post-conflict Liberia, made the following observation about the caregiver and child relationship: 'Children were at the beck and call of their elders, but by fulfilling their obligations the younger ones earned the right to make certain requests of them. If unmet, these requests would appear equally shameful for the older superiors'. While much of the discussion about the tension between dominant discourses of children's rights and children's local realities have mainly focused on contexts in the Global South, it is important to note that such tensions continue to exist within specific communities in countries in the Global North. A notable example is Gypsy, Roma, and Traveller communities whose socialization strategies, despite being affected by enormous processes of social change, continue to foreground the importance of early responsibility in childhood, leading to children undertaking work, often alongside adults of the same gender, from an early age (Levinson, 2008). This focus on early responsibility can also be found in other less marginalized communities within this world area.

8.5 The contributions of Akan notions of personhood and social relations to problematizing notions of childhood incompetence

To understand the emphasis placed on childhood competence and responsibility in Ghana, there is a need to situate this analysis within broader discussions of personhood and social relations within this context as well as in sub-Saharan Africa more generally. Within the region, the organizing principle underpinning many societies historically was centred around interdependence between individuals which was underpinned by the principles of collectivism upon which these societies were based (see Twum-Danso Imoh, 2022, 2024a, 2024b). The concept that has come to be most well known as representing this system of social organization is *Ubuntu*, a Bantu philosophical and religious concept that acknowledges that the humanity of individuals is achieved through their social interaction with others, including those of different generations. This system of social organization, in turn, resulted in foregrounding values such as solidarity, co-operation, reciprocal obligations, and mutuality of duty.

Similar principles are reflected amongst the Akan ethnic group whose roots can be traced back to countries now called Ghana and Côte d'Ivoire and whose beliefs were historically based upon an ontological position which took, as its departure point, the principle that human beings are communal and social by nature. This worldview subsequently informs their vision of a human being:

> It is only through cooperation with other human beings that the needs and goals of the individual can be fulfilled. With his self-sufficiency whittled away by man's natural condition, the individual requires the succor and relationships of others in order to satisfy his basic needs. A social ethic that recognises the importance of the values of mutual help, good will, and reciprocity is the kind of ethic that will counter the lack of human self-sufficiency in respect of talents and capacities and in many ways help realize his basic needs.
>
> (Gyekye, 2013, p. 231)

The limitations to the self-sufficiency evident in individuals result in what Gyekye (2013, p. 232) calls the 'morality of a shared life' which demands mutuality or reciprocity 'as a moral mandate in a world in which human beings, weak and limited in many ways, are subject to vulnerable situations'. The principles underpinning this worldview were expected to be evident in how individuals related to each other. Specifically, within this context there was an understanding that individuals not only had duties towards each other, especially to members of their clan or *abusua*,[1] but also possessed rights they were entitled to claim from one another (Cobbah, 1987; Gyekye, 1996, 2013).

What these principles mean for adult–child relationships is that adults and children depend on each other in order to achieve their well-being and personal objectives as well as broader household or family needs. In effect, the achievement of personhood for both children and indeed, adults, is reliant on the interactions and the support between the two status groups.

8.6 The contributions of West African notions of personhood and social relations to alternative conceptualizations of children's rights

The question now becomes: what can an alternative conceptualization of children's rights gain from West African ontological frameworks, notably those of the Akan, that foreground interdependency and mutuality? First, such a conceptualization highlights that children, like adults, have both capability and competence and are able to provide assistance to others. This is due to the recognition of the vulnerability and interdependency of the general human

1 The Akan follow a matrilineal system of kinship whereby descent and inheritance is traced through the matrilineal descent group of their mothers known as '*abusua*'.

condition which requires a response from all individuals, regardless of age or social status, to help, care, and support each other.

With regards to the implications for children's rights this requires the space for the construction of a notion of rights that articulates not only the entitlements of children, but also the responsibilities or duties that this group has to their family, communities, and nation. Hitherto, such an open conversation about the notion of children having responsibilities has encountered restrictions as it has caused concern amongst dominant children's rights circles, leading to discussions on this topic to quickly shift to exploitative work practices that are feared to result from an emphasis placed on children's responsibilities (see Van Bueren, 1995; Nsamenang, 2004). This has resulted in shutting down any conversation about children having duties altogether. Consequently, a serious/open discussion about the meaning of children's duties and how it links to the notion of entitlements for children is yet to take place within the broader children's rights sector.

In terms of how such an open conversation can be initiated, the African Charter on the Rights and Welfare of the Child, adopted by the Organization of African Unity (now known as the African Union) in 1990, with its articulation of children's responsibilities in Article 31, presents *a good starting point* for the expansion of such a conversation on children's rights beyond the continent of Africa. This is important as duty and responsibility in childhood are features of socialization strategies in other contexts, including those in the so-called Global North. However, given that, overall, the Charter tows the dominant children's rights line, any discussion which seeks to fully explore the concepts of responsibility and duty as they relate to childhood cannot become too focused on the Charter. Instead, such a conversation needs to acknowledge the contributions of the Charter in incorporating the notion of duty in the first regional treaty on children's rights, but then it should seek to move beyond it in order to allow for a deeper and more open conversation about the linkage between entitlements, rights, and duties.

It is important to note that having responsibility should not simply be equated with work tasks that children may undertake within their household, some of which may, indeed, encompass activities which generate income for the child specifically or the household more generally; instead, there is a need to broaden this conversation and acknowledge that having a responsibility or a duty is also about civic responsibilities to nation and community (however defined), which may include acts of service, volunteering, or informal or formal forms of political participation, which include participation in social movements and even the right to vote. However, work is, indeed, a key element of having responsibility and that also needs to be considered in these discussions. Such conversations must be accompanied by the recognition that in communities where early responsibility is foregrounded, systems are often put in place to ensure the gradual assumption of responsibilities by children taking into consideration their abilities (Nsamenang, 2004). Thus, acknowledging that children have responsibility does not automatically equate to an acceptance of exploitative behaviours and practices. While it is possible that there are elements within different societies who may seize the notion of children having a responsibility or duty for their own agenda, which may, ultimately, lead to detrimental outcomes for children in, for example, criminal justice proceedings, the key point I am trying to make here is that within the field of children's rights there is a need for an open and rigorous conversation about the notion of children's duties and responsibilities and how these intersect with the concept of rights. This foundational conversation needs to take place before the topic can be advanced and considered from different angles.

It is worth noting that underscoring responsibility and duty is not only beneficial to communities and households; these concepts are also seen as valuable by children themselves. In Ghana (and Nigeria) where I have undertaken much of my research, children often emphasized their responsibilities to family and community in discussions of their rights (Twum-Danso, 2008, 2009; Twum-Danso Imoh, & Okyere, 2020). This can be attributed to the sense of belonging this allows them to develop as well as the achievement of their personal objectives. This latter point about achieving personal objectives reinforces the extent to which the principle of reciprocity is at the basis of social relations within these contexts. This is important to consider in conversations seeking to incorporate the notion of responsibility within children's rights discourses because while global children's rights norms may emphasize that rights are entitlements, given *a priori*, social relations in large swathes of the world, not just in Africa, are framed by the notion of reciprocity and mutuality, including those between different generations. This, consequently, requires us to have a serious conversation about the notions of reciprocity, duty, and responsibility and their implications for how we think about children's rights.

8.7 Concluding remarks: the limits to alternative conceptualizations of children's rights in Ghana

The need for alternative conceptualizations of children's rights notwithstanding, a word of caution about applying such conceptions in the context of Ghana is required at this point. This caution centres around the co-existence that can now be identified between new understandings about social relations that have emerged because of the enormous social changes that Ghana has experienced over the last 500 years or so, and traditional ways of being and relating that have been passed down for generations as a result of Indigenous worldviews and their attendant social norms. This has resulted in the development of differential attitudes to children and their entitlements and roles within Ghanaian society. What this means is that while alternative conceptualizations of rights outlined in this chapter (as well as in others within this volume) would be relevant to many demographic groups in this context, for others this conceptualization may no longer reflect the values underpinning their everyday lives. This is due to the social and historical positioning of their family and the extent to which they have been caught up in the wide-ranging processes of social change that have been ongoing for generations, the legacy of which continue to have ramifications for many citizens. Thus, there may need to be recognition that within this context no single conceptualization of children's rights can be universally applied.

It is because of the variability in the intersections between dominant children's rights principles and children's everyday realities that exists that has led me to start using the concept of a continuum to frame my understanding of the realization of children's rights in Ghana. While at one end of the continuum are realities of children's lives that are in stark contrast to the global ideals embedded within dominant rights norms, at the other end can be identified lived experiences that correspond quite closely with such global conceptualizations of rights in numerous respects. In between these two polar opposites are points along the continuum which reflect realities of, and attitudes towards, childhoods that combine both global and local conceptualizations to varying degrees of intensity (Twum-Danso Imoh, 2019, 2024a). Simply put, in the context of Ghana, a country which has long been characterized by its plurality, most notably reflected in its political, religious, and legal structures, as well as in attitudes toward healthcare and marriage practices, no single conceptualization of rights can effectively be applied to all demographic groups. This realization that one size of rights conceptualization (be it in its dominant or alternative form) cannot fit all children requires the opening up of spaces for multiple conversations about children's rights to take place in tandem with each other in the same way that pluralities of childhood understandings and lived experiences also exist in parallel in this context.

References

Boyden, J. (1997). Childhood and the policy makers: A comparative perspective on the globalization of childhood. In A. James & A. Prout (eds.) *Constructing and reconstructing childhood: Contemporary issues in the sociological study of childhood.* (2nd edition). Routledge Falmer.

Cobbah, J. (1987). African values and the human rights debate: An African perspective. *Human Rights Quarterly*, *9*(3), 309–331.

Corbett, B. (1985). *Centuries of childhood by Philippe Aries.* Vintage Books, 1962. 447 Pages. Retrieved December 13, 2022, from Faculty.webster.edu/corbetre/philosophy/children/aries.html

Doek, J. (2011). The CRC: Dynamics and directions of monitoring its implementation. In A. Invernizzi & J. Williams (eds.) *The human rights of children: From visions to implementation* (1st ed.). Routledge.

Gyekye, K. (1996). *African cultural values: An introduction.* Sankofa Publishing Company.

Gyekye, K. (2013). *Philosophy, culture and vision: African perspectives.* Sub-Saharan Publishers.

Hardgrove, A. (2017). *Life after guns: Reciprocity and respect among young men in Liberia.* Rutgers University Press.

Hunleth, J. (2017). *Children as caregivers: The global fight against tuberculosis and HIV in Zambia.* Rutgers University Press.

Levinson, M. P. (2008). Not just content, but style: Gypsy children traversing boundaries. *Research in Comparative and International Education*, *3*(3), 235–249.

Liebel, M. (2012). *Children's rights from below: Cross-cultural perspectives.* Palgrave Macmillan.
McCrystal, P., & Manful, E. (2011). Ghana's children's act 560: A rethink of its implementation. *International Journal of Children's Rights, 19*(2011), 151–165.
Nsamenang, A. B. (2004). *Cultures of human development and education: Challenge to growing up African.* Nova Science Publishers Inc.
Pellow, D. (1977). *Women in Accra: Options for autonomy.* Reference Publications Inc.
Plumb, J. H. (1972). *In the light of history.* Allen Lane the Penguin Press.
Pupavac, V. (2001). Misanthropy without borders: The international children's rights regime. *Disasters, 25*(2), 95–112.
Schildkrout, E. (1978). Age and gender in Hausa society: Socio-economic roles of children in urban Kano. In J. S. La Fontaine (ed.) *Sex and age as principles of social differentiation* (pp. 109–137). Academic Press.
Twum-Danso, A. (2008). *Searching for the middle ground in children's rights: Implementing the Convention on the Rights of the Child in Ghana.* Unpublished PhD Thesis, University of Birmingham.
Twum-Danso, A. (2009). Reciprocity, respect, and responsibility: The 3rs underlying parent-child relationships in Ghana and the implications for children's rights. *The International Journal of Children's Rights, 17*(3), 415–432.
Twum-Danso Imoh, A. (2019). Terminating childhood: Dissonance and synergy between global children's rights norms and local discourses about the transition from childhood to adulthood in Ghana. *Human Rights Quarterly, 41*(1), 160–182.
Twum-Danso Imoh, A. (2022). Framing reciprocal obligations within intergenerational relations in Ghana through the lens of the mutuality of duty and dependence. *Childhood, 29*(3), 439–454.
Twum-Danso Imoh, A. (2024a). *Turning global rights into local realities: Realizing children's rights in Ghana's pluralistic society.* Bristol University Press.
Twum-Danso Imoh, A. (2024b). Troubling the understanding of childhood competence in research ethics governance and its implications for research with children and their families. *Research in Education Journal (Special Issue: Democratic Methodologies in Education Research)*, ONLINE FIRST. https://doi.org/10.1177/00345237241288961
Twum-Danso Imoh, A., & Okyere, S. (2020). Towards a more holistic understanding of child participation: Foregrounding the experiences of children in Ghana and Nigeria. *Child and Youth Services Review, 112*(2020), 104927.
Van Bueren, G. (1995). *The international law on the rights of the child.* Martinus Nijhoff Publishers.
Veerman, P. (1992). *The rights of the child and the changing image of childhood.* Martinus Nijhoff Publishers.
Verhellen, E. (1994). *The convention on the rights of the child: Background, motivation, strategies, main themes.* Garant Publishers.

9 Those afraid of gender and childhood

Anti-gender attacks against Judith Butler in Brazil

Luan Carpes Barros Cassal and Erica Burman

9.1 Introduction

Judith Butler is a renowned US-based political philosopher who has been publishing groundbreaking work on gender, performativity, recognition and violence, amongst other subjects (see, for instance, Butler, 2024), as well as being a key architect and author associated with queer theory (see Butler, 1990). They[1] are not particularly known for work on childhood, though. The reader may wonder what relevance Butler has for a book chapter on children's rights. Our response, as authors of this chapter, is that, through theory and activism, Butler has long been engaging with discourses and images relating to childhood. This is evident in the ways the figure of childhood and discourses on children's rights are mobilized as weapons to produce harm – against Butler, but also potentially against gender-nonconforming children's rights, as they have also argued more recently (Butler, 2024). Butler (2020) argues for nonviolent action, including a range of practices to resist destruction, while also envisaging an interdependent society based on freedom and equality (Butler, 2020). In this chapter, we use Butler's theoretical framework on gender to consider how ideas of childhood are used to oppose gender recognition rights, promoting injury and destruction, and explore the development of nonviolent alternatives to that.

Our take on Butler's work and politics draws on a methodological approach called Child as method (Burman, 2019, 2023, 2024), which interprets the positions, and roles, of notions, representations, images and discourses of childhood in sociopolitical and cultural debates and actions, even when children are absent from, or forbidden to, engage with, and on, the topic (Cassal et al., 2024). Taking inspiration from postcolonial studies and migration studies as well as feminism, intersectionality and queer theory, Child as method engages childhood studies (including children's rights debates) with political theory and practices bidirectionally, by interrogating the role of claims to,

1 Judith Butler has been using they/them pronouns since the early 2020s. See for instance: www.theguardian.com/lifeandstyle/2021/sep/07/judith-butler-interview-gender

DOI: 10.4324/9781003510284-10

and about, children and childhood within wider sociopolitical and geomaterial contexts. Child as method has been engaged in research in different postcolonial contexts, including in Brazil (see Cassal et al., 2023; Mattos & Moura e Silva, 2023). Of particular relevance to this chapter is the claim (elaborated in detail in Burman, 2019, Chapter 2) that foundational societal norms and assumptions (what social theorists typically call 'ideology') are built upon the practice of lying to children such that the social fabric of presumed and regulated norms are maintained in the name of protecting children at the same time as actually deceiving them (see Mannoni, 2003). Questions of gender, sexuality and nation are among the most potent of these fictions that are sustained or anchored by claims about children and childhood (see also, for example, Millei & Imre, 2016).

While there may be limits on how, and whether, some adults feel able to listen to, engage with, acknowledge and understand gender-nonconforming children's perspectives, as with children's advocacy work more generally, there are important efforts underway to promote children and young people's protagonism (Ammaturo & Moscati, 2021). Still, our focus in this chapter is not on the material experiences of children, but rather on the sociopolitical (and largely hostile) deployment of ideas and images of childhood in attempts to block public debate. Hence, in this chapter, we analyze one particular event in which claims about, or ideas of, childhood were used by ultraconservative activists to attack Judith Butler in Brazil – and how their framework can help us to understand and navigate this harmful situation.

The analysis was informed by our situated knowledge as academics and activists (Haraway, 1988). The first author is a Brazilian academic and activist now based in the UK, working on childhood, queer and trans studies (see Cassal, 2024) and with knowledge of anti-gender discourses and politics in Brazil. Meanwhile, the second author is a British feminist academic and activist who has been engaging with the sociopolitical uses of ideas of childhood and its connections with gender, race and nation and their deep roots in racism and colonialism (see Burman, 2017, 2019, 2020, 2023, 2024), which are discussed in the anti-gender attacks analyzed. Thus, this chapter combines those positions and experiences to review the anti-gender attacks against Judith Butler in Brazil, address current concerns regarding children's rights and further discuss the Child as method analytical approach.

Hence, we suggest that this chapter contribute to children's rights debates in attending to how the construction and use of representations of childhood may impact the materialization and enforcement of children's rights. In doing so, we acknowledge the relevance of Butler's (1990, 1993, 2024) own ideas around performativity and reversing the sex/gender dichotomy that has underpinned dominant discussions of gender since second-wave feminism. From this, we connect with the child as method analysis we provide shortly to offer an alternative pathway to rights.

The debate around the status of children and childhood is particularly important considering that gender nonconformity in childhood might generate hostile reactions from other children (Riggs et al., 2023), especially in relation to gender-nonconforming boys (Braun & Davidson, 2017). Gender-nonconforming children are also reported to score lower in well-being assessments (Zenter & von Aufsess, 2020), although from a critical psychology perspective we could also question such surveys (see, for example, Prilleltensky & Stead, 2013). Further, parents might also impose essentialized gendered views upon their children, based on their own gender and sexuality (Kane, 2006). Children's bodies and gender identifications and performativities have been regulated by coercive and regulatory devices, including family, state, medical and psychological knowledge and the educational system towards the reproduction of cisgender and heterosexual structures (Preciado, 2020). Under such regulation, gender nonconformity is used as an argument *against* children's competence for autonomous decision-making in relation to gender-affirming healthcare (Moscati, 2022), thereby highlighting how fears around gender nonconformity in childhood works in harmful ways that can limit those children's access to support.

In this chapter rather than discussing children's experiences or their (so-called) well-being and mental states, we use Child as method, alongside, and in relation to, Butler's ideas,[2] to consider the use of images and fears surrounding those experiences and how these work as a means of imposing gender normativity. Therefore, when we mention representations of childhood throughout this chapter, we are using what we will explain as a Child as method perspective to analyze the sociopolitical engagements of ideas and practices, on, for or around childhood. We argue that, by understanding and challenging the way those discourses take place (and produce harm, including but not only to children), we can support resistances and resources to make those lives recognizable as legitimate and more livable.

9.2 Anti-Butler (anti-gender) demonstrations in Brazil

Butler has visited Brazil twice as an invited speaker at conferences. In 2015, Butler visited Salvador[3] and São Paulo for conferences in queer studies, with hundreds of attendees (including the first author of this very chapter), gaining a very positive reception (an understatement, to say the least) by the academic community. Butler enacted practices of solidarity through discourse and speeches, reaffirming that 'all bodies matter' in order to confront contemporary contexts of highly lethal violence, particularly evident against women in Latin America (Butler, 2016, p. 22). Indeed, they affirmed how gender and sexuality are ethical and political projects concerned with how people live

2 For a discussion on connections between Butler and Burman, see Cassal (2024, chapter 9).

3 The presented paper was published in Portuguese discussing trans-feminicide in Brazil and challenges for recognition and solidarity (Butler, 2016). All quotes from texts in Portuguese were translated by this book chapter's authors.

their lives individually and collectively, and how social movements have been reshaping what their objects are (such as 'women' as an object [see also Butler, 1993] but also the concept of violence). Meanwhile, at the entrance of one of the conferences, around 10 demonstrators chanted against Butler's allegedly 'homosexual ideology' and 'gender aberrations', albeit with little visibility.[4]

Then, in 2017, Butler returned to São Paulo to launch the Brazilian edition of the book *Parting Ways: Jewishness and the Critique of Zionism* (Butler, 2012) and co-host a conference on democracy and politics.[5] However, anti-gender demonstrations took place at the conference entrance while Butler was there, with many more protestors in attendance (Correa, 2017; Jaschik, 2017) and a change in tone. They particularly targeted Butler through public demands for the academic to 'leave children alone'; making declarations such as 'Butler [is a] paedophile' and 'Gender Ideologist'. They also orchestrated an online petition against Butler's visit, publicly burnt an effigy of them and accosted Butler at the airport (Jaschik, 2017; Correa, 2017; Miskolci & Pereira, 2018; Butler, 2024). This demonizes Butler, an anti-Zionist Jewish queer activist academic, in addition to mobilizing longstanding anti-Semitic associations surrounding nonnormative gender positionings and Jews (Harrowitz & Hyams, 1995). Combined with a connection with childhood this is also reminiscent of blood libel claims against Jews in medieval Europe (whose relation to European racism in general and as informing the emergence of scientific racism is discussed elsewhere, including Burman, 2024; Harrowitz, 1994).[6] Those attacks show a myriad of anti-gender discourses, configuring 'gender' as a vague and amorphous category, subjected to projections and political uses (Butler, 2024). Nevertheless, the challenges for democracy and politics were enacted as anti-gender demonstrations, taking Butler as the targeted object of hate speeches, particularly in the name of the absent children – or the ideas of childhood that inform and engage acts of injury and destruction.

Moreover, ideas of child protection are, firstly, formulated by ultraconservatives as children's rights, as they might see them and then, secondly, weaponized against trans and gender-nonconforming people – children but also adults, such as Butler themselves. Thirdly, they also mobilize a long-standing trope of enacting practices of racialized othering by positioning those 'others'

4 https://m.folha.uol.com.br/ilustrissima/2015/09/1683172-sem-medo-de-fazer-genero-entrevista-com-a-filosofa-americana-judith-butler.shtml. Retrieved on 2 May 2021.

5 We leave for another space the significance of this topic in igniting the particular and particularly hostile responses, but clearly this has relevance in terms of how the politics of Israel/Palestine has been configured alongside and, within, mainstream discourse, in feminist and queer debates (see also Butler, 2012). For an analysis of the Zionist Left and its links with colonialism in Brazil and Palestine, see Huberman (2024).

6 Claims that Jews abducted and murdered children to drink their blood were widespread throughout medieval Europe. No case was ever proven but the myth circulated powerfully and was used to warrant pogroms on, and murders of, Jews (see Burman, 2024 for a more extensive analysis).

as a threat to children and childhood reminiscent of the blood libel claims of medieval Europe that continued until modern times to be revived as a major trope in Nazi ideology. It is necessary to engage with these arguments, tracing the complex ways notions of childhood are mobilized, in order to not only critique and disarm them, both for children and children's rights, but also to better understand the political agendas that claims about children and children's rights are used for. Taking the specific example of Butler's Brazilian reception, we will discuss the project of gender normativity that lies within the demonstrators' discourses and the connections between gender, childhood and nation. Finally, we present some alternatives to prompt rethinking of children's rights to enable consideration of gender nonconformity not as a threat (as often portrayed) but rather as possibilities for those marked as children and adults.

9.3 Butler, a 'gender ideologist'[7]

In pictures from the demonstrations that are largely available online,[8] Butler is named a witch,[9] a pedophile and a 'gender ideologist', in addition to calls for them to be sent to hell. Let us just pause to note the intersectional, racialized as well as homophobic and transphobic misogyny at play in these claims, fueled by ultraconservative Christian anti-Semitism. These attacks, discussed at length by Butler in their most recent book, *Who's afraid of gender?* (Butler, 2024) as well as via her well-known critical analyses of the construction and functioning of hate speech, can be seen as acts of injury (Butler, 1997a). These words impose an identification on a person who might disagree with it, while at the same time they also have material effects on how others see, and treat, them, and what institutions do. Surely, Butler pointed to the absurdity

7 This is a sarcastic use of accusations made against Butler, which, nevertheless, had very material effects, as we will see shortly (as explained in Jaschik, 2017). Calling Butler a 'gender ideologist' in this chapter is an irony, twisting established discourses of injury (Butler, 1993; 1997a).

8 Some references are in English and others in Portuguese:

- www.theguardian.com/artanddesign/2018/nov/07/brazil-artists-death-threats-censorship-intimidation-jair-bolsonaro;
- www.frieze.com/article/looking-back-2017-judith-and-holofernes-brazil;
- https://vejasp.abril.com.br/cidades/boneco-com-rosto-de-judith-butler-e-incendiado-em-protesto/;
- www.cartacapital.com.br/sociedade/judith-butler-e-agredida-ao-embarcar-no-aeroporto-de-congonhas;
- https://brasil.elpais.com/brasil/2017/11/07/politica/1510085652_717856.html;
- www.cartacapital.com.br/diversidade/judith-butler-11-tiros-no-rosto-aborto-e-a-semana-no-patriarcado-do-brasil/;
- https://brasil.elpais.com/brasil/2017/11/07/opinion/1510088225_560754.html;
- https://pleno.news/brasil/cidades/judith-butler-e-recebida-com-protestos-em-sao-paulo.html

9 Category turned into an insult and reason for persecution to regulate women's bodies, autonomy and knowledge. See Federici (2014).

of being called a pedophile, 'which I strongly and absolutely oppose, as would any feminist scholar and activist' (Butler cited by Jaschik, 2017). The epithets 'Gender ideologist' and 'witch' were also shouted as insults, to diminish Butler based on their gender (assigned as a woman at birth) and their position (a White Jewish US scholar). In both cases, the expressions indicate a hidden agenda or force which Butler was presumed to be following, so echoing a dominant anti-Semitic theme of conspiracy theory combined with disturbances of gender roles.

Although this may not be so evident, the demonstrators were engaging ideas of childhood by calling Butler a 'Gender Ideologist'. As has been studied by gender scholars based in Latin America (see Junqueira, 2017; Prado & Correa, 2018; Chiaradia & Cassal, 2019), and as Butler (2024) also recently reviewed, 'Gender Ideology' is a pseudoscientific concept that was created by ultraconservative sectors of the Catholic Church (across the world but especially in Brazil) to oppose the growth of pro-feminist and pro-LGBTQI+ movements and debates in international organizations and conferences in the 1990s. From this view, 'gender' is taken as a social construct, but only in the sense that it is an artificial imposition over the allegedly natural character of body, sex and heterosexual relationships and procreation. Gender is portrayed as a category that threatens (a presumed gender-free or natural) childhood (Butler, 2024) which then makes it a key target for conservatives to tackle in order to protect children from its underlying logic. This rapidly became a question of the protection of (what is considered) childhood and family, as the content of demonstrations made clear.

Interpretations of the reasons for these particular attacks have also been already offered by Brazilian scholars (Correa, 2017; Miskolci & Pereira, 2018) and by Butler themselves (Jaschik, 2017; Butler, 2024). They point out the unity forged by several conservative and authoritarian forces with different political agendas,[10] all using Butler as a symbol of evil, object of hate and alleged threat to children. As a vague category, 'gender' was a suitable receptacle for anxieties, fears and hatred (Butler, 2024), while being configured in opposition to the idea of (naturalized) childhood. Those discourses portrayed Butler, a foreign scholar, as an interventionist agent pursuing 'shadow' (i.e. hidden, nefarious or otherwise undeclared) interests. Concerns about gender ambiguity speak of the fear of Butler's ideas (especially in books like *Gender Trouble* [Butler, 1990]), their political positions (for democratic speech, freedom and recognition) and the power of their notions of performativity (historically as a lesbian feminist and more recently as a nonbinary person). Hence, Butler was portrayed as an enemy of childhood, which is idealized as generic, universalized and naturalized.

10 For instance, supporters of military coups, anti-internationalists, ultraliberals, anti-leftists, religious ultraconservatives, anti-LGBTQI+ and feminist rights, extreme rights, monarchists, neofascists.

As Butler discussed, acts of speech are a force exercised according to certain frames of recognition (Butler, 1997a, 2005, 2010). Calling someone by a certain name is an act of speech that fixes and interpellates the subject. Although the act of speech happens in a specific moment – such as those anti-Butler demonstrations – it contracts and expands past and future, since it recovers a history of meanings and conflicts and directs toward expected outcomes and possibilities. Therefore, previous speeches about gender (such as conservative anti-gender discourses) are here re-enacted and connected with others (such as those of monarchists and militarists) towards an expected outcome (Butler's disappearance or destruction). They are, therefore, building a narrative around Butler, with material consequences – the misrecognition of Butler in the name of children. Children's rights, then, are weaponized against both children and adults – whether gender-nonconforming people or their allies.

Calling Butler a witch intends to offend, using a history of citations to wound and cause harm. As Butler (1997a) analyzed, an injury diminishes the addressed subject, trying to establish a relation of domination from the addresser to them. Still, the binding effect established by an injury is a form of recognition which, although not mutually agreed, still has commonly understandable meaning, and engages in an act of speech. Hence, the act of recognition is a dependent boundary since 'existing' depends on being recognized by others – being taken care of, protected, introduced to the language and seen as a singular and continuous person. For the same reason, injurious speeches threaten the boundaries which might keep us alive and together (Butler, 1997a, 2005, 2010, 2020). In addition, the figure of the child also appears as a hidden object – the one threatened by an absurd allegation of Butler as a pedophile. Some posters reproduce Butler's picture to create a certain narrative: a pedophile who went, or should go, to hell; being or becoming a witch (with an effigy burnt); and a horned demon (note the anti-Semitism here of imaging a self-identifying Jew with the devil as well as the homophobic elision of queer or gender nonconforming with pedophile). An injury does not only name a subject but also tells a story creating potential effects and actions. In name of a figuration of the threatened child, Butler could be attacked, symbolically and physically – in racialized as well as homophobic ways, and in name of an idealized childhood.

The injuries against Butler united people seeking the destruction of the scholar on different levels – intellectually, symbolically and even physically; academia was also threatened especially because of its position as an arena for free speech. Challenging the history of injuries is necessary to disrupt its repetition and established authority, producing alternative modes of understanding the world – including children's rights.

9.4 Injury and misrecognition

Agitators did not stop at the conference venue. Some of them followed Butler to the São Paulo airport, once again carrying posters and calling the scholar a pedophile, besides accosting them and their partner, Wendy Brown (Miskolci & Pereira, 2018; Jaschik, 2017; Butler, 2024). One protester used a poster with Butler's faces to push the academic,[11] which we can see as the realm of discourse and the materiality of bodies showing their interconnectedness, in which an injury has performative effects. The witch, the demon and the pedophile are those who could be threatened with destruction for alleged legitimate reasons. The so-called enemy of children would be one to be targeted and destroyed, whether preventively or as a punishment.

We can see some of those elements in those attacks. When Butler stood up and continued with their keynote on democracy despite hostile demonstrations outside the conference venue, they were resisting imposed silence and refusal about their words and presence. After being harassed at the airport, they still addressed their attackers' actions rather than identities (cited by Jaschik, 2017), avoiding the tendency to individualize (and perhaps to pathologize) acts of violence. This is not about passively forgiving the aggressor (as it could be in some Catholic traditions) but rather as Butler calling for a public debate and a mourning for the violence (Butler, 2016). This approach presents an alternative for the realm of rights that moves from adversarial to relational and even transformative models to consider the collective responsibility shared towards nonconforming people – including children. Indeed, Butler (2024) explicitly addresses the problem of weaponizing children's rights to block gender-affirming care; the lack of access to healthcare is seen by them as a harm to gender-nonconforming children's lives and rights.

In the name of children, Butler was misrecognized (a recognition being cast upon them). Even a *mis*recognition is a form of recognition because it creates, at least, some degree of social and discursive engagement (Butler, 1997a, 1997b). Nonetheless, demonstrators were not only affirming an 'anti-gender' position, but they also had their own agenda around gender and childhood, as discussed next.

9.5 Gender and childhood

Some of the hostile posters specifically address issues around gender and childhood. One of those says 'Judith Butler's dream: to destroy your sons' sexual identity'[12] and the pictures portray a girl and a boy in traditional gender roles (clothes, toys and play), and the same images with swapped heads on the right. Noticeably, those children are White, as the blonde demonstrator depicted appears to be as well. Gender and childhood can be seen as part of colonial processes of domination – those who are marked as children, and those who can

11 Butler said that neither they nor their partner were physically harmed in the event (cited by Jaschik, 2017).

12 Although 'children' might sound more adequate in this sentence, the protestor used a word meaning 'sons', with a masculine marker as it is traditionally used for plurals in Portuguese.

be gendered, resemble colonial ideals, including Whiteness (Bernstein, 2004; Lugones, 2016; Kilomba, 2020; Cannella & Viruru, 2004; Rollo, 2018).

Of course, we acknowledge these are demonstration posters, and the authors of the signs might have used the simplest and more accessible visual language. Nevertheless, this discourse resonates with some important issues about the images of childhood. Those posters have some presumptions: first, that girls and boys have different roles; second, these roles should be 'sexual identities'; third, 'sexual identities' risk being inverted (rather than becoming something else). If Butler allegedly threatens 'sexual identities', as the sign claims, those identities would surely have to exist in the first place. The demonstrator, therefore, recognizes something other than sex. What she calls 'sexual identity' could be assumed as 'gender identity'. Moreover, Butler (and consequently gender studies and/or activism) is presented as affecting such identities, turning girls into boys and boys into girls. The protestor's worries appear to suggest that identities are not fixed since the beginning, even for those who strictly argue for its essentialism. Also, the use of 'to destroy' stresses a threatening dimension of 'Butler's alleged dream'. This is a key problem because it topicalizes whose 'dream' this would be; hence, the conservative position projects the idea of a plan for children, which then appears to warrant them to act with their own response, plan or agenda. This position relates to what Preciado (2020) points out as a system of violence and torture imposed upon children to produce cis-heteronormativity as the expected result, while trying to eliminate potential dissidences. Therefore, what is erased in the demonstrations is not Butler, but the possibility of self-determination in childhood and its collective recognition – which can be an alternative to children's rights. These are the implicit fears arising in those debates and weaponized against the philosopher.

On ultraconservative signs, children are configurated as part of an idealized royalty – or, returning to a previous work by the second author of this chapter (Burman, 2019), an 'idiotic child' – living in a fairy-tale separate world because of being unable to cope with societal demands and challenges. Not by chance, that context might apply to upper-class White children, just as those portrayed; for all the other chronological (i.e. actual currently living, rather than recalled or imagined) children, they must find a way to deal with inequities, racism, ableism, gender discrimination or poverty, while not being recognized as 'proper' children exactly for the same reason. Butler being attacked after a conference on democracy shows that the threat is not simply their concept of gender performativity, but their position in favour of individual and collective self-determination.

9.6 Notes towards gender-nonconforming children's rights

Gender nonconformity and childhood are not the mutually exclusive topics that they might initially seem; on the contrary, they are connected by an artificially imposed opposition. Sedgwick (1991) explained the fears of 'lesbian and gay' movements (as LGBTIQ+ rights were called at the time) in discussing childhood in the 1990s, prompting academics and social movements to avoid this topic, and to focus particularly on adults' rights. The challenges and barriers to speak about gender-nonconforming children's rights in a public arena remain evident (Halberstam, 2018; Favero, 2020), because of the anxieties it arouses (Breslow, 2021). What we address here is that the restrictions, or prohibition, on debates on gender nonconformity and children's rights leaves an empty space that was occupied, as Butler (2024) argues, by phantasmatic fears of threat and danger. Therefore, while 'queer children' become objects of heavy emotional investment by public authorities, their existence is also systematically denied.

As has long been discussed (in both queer theory and childhood studies), the idea of childhood holds social (and unconscious) expectations of futurity and reproducibility in a capitalistic system (Roberts-Holmes & Moss, 2021), alongside the nostalgia for a world before its alienations and damage (see also Steedman, 1995; Taylor, 2013) which are challenged by gender nonconformity in childhood (Edelman, 2004; Breslow, 2021). Hence, gender-nonconforming childhoods are at once rendered nonexistent (by this denial) while only allowed to appear exceptionally, and in a pathologized way, in a search for origins and destiny for those marginalized or 'deviant' (adult) subjects (Favero, 2020). The word *gender* incites a trail of socially unconscious fears and anxieties, including about what childhood is and could be.

We have discussed elsewhere how unconscious motifs prevent debate connecting gender nonconformity, development and childhood, with profound impact in restricting legal gender recognition rights (Cassal, 2024; Cassal et al., 2024). Here we highlight how children's rights are a conflictual space in which gender nonconformity can be seen either as a right or as a threat. To challenge the exclusion of gender-nonconforming children, one has to criticize the underlying idea of childhood as object of protection. The destructive reaction to Butler could only take place because gender nonconformity and childhood are entangled in sociocultural fantasies as mutually exclusive, and as the object of projections *even if children themselves might not even be mentioned*. Moreover, conservatives 'claim paternalistically to know the true existential reality of trans people better than trans people do themselves' (Butler, 2024, p. 138), rendering gender-nonconforming experiences unthinkable (Butler, 2024). Therefore, to imagine them arouses anxieties and fears around gender, when nevertheless, it is gender-nonconforming people (including children) who effectively lose access to their rights because of conservative discourses (Butler, 2024). The acts of injury and aggression against Butler are, therefore, connected to the lack of care to children; by destroying one, the other can be threatened. Our first conclusion is that, drawing on the perspective of Child as method (Burman, 2019, 2023, 2024), in exploring how claims and discourses of childhood work geopolitically, from children and the politics of childhood to politics more generally, (ideas of) children's rights can be used, directly or indirectly, against adults, not only because they share common needs, characteristics or identities, but as a preventive measure in name of an idealized figuration of childhood. In other words, the implicit claim about children and childhood anchors the social anxiety within conservative discourses that adults could be destroyed while, materially, gender-nonconforming children risk being rendered nonexistent.

Moreover, in some sense the ultraconservative demonstrators could have been right in saying that Butler's framework threatens ***the naturalized figuration of childhood*** when this means normalized forms of existence (as also discussed by Preciado, 2020). The problem highlighted by demonstrators – more precisely, in what they did not say – relates to the right of self-determination. This last point connects with previous research on the allegedly limited capacity of children to decide about gender-affirming care (Moscati, 2022; Paechter, 2021), based on developmentalist ideas that also engage essentialized perspectives of gender (Cassal, 2024).

However, the rights of gender-nonconforming children can be defended as a good rather than a threat. Coupet and Marrus (2015) defend considering children as rights holders, rather than objects of protection, centering the debate on their agency. Importantly, Coupet (2015) highlights the need to consider the suffering of gender-nonconforming children and young people as an effect of social exclusion, rather than as a characteristic of their gender nonconformity. Hence, self-identification, social transitioning and even biomedical transitioning could be supported as measures that challenge this exclusion. In the Norwegian context, Sorlie (2015) considers that the Convention on the Rights of the Child (the UNCRC) gives enough evidence to protect children's autonomy, privacy and self-determination – although not explicitly mentioning gender identity. On the other hand, international regulations concerning children are often produced from adults' perspective (Sandberg, 2015), with particular implications for a history of erasure of gender-nonconforming childhoods and their right for gender self-determination. Our second conclusion, then, is the need to follow Butler's (2020, 2024) example in engaging in nonviolent forms of resistance, producing discourse on this often-avoided link between gender nonconformity and childhood.

Gender-nonconforming rights, then, create problems in the field of children's rights. On the one hand, as we have seen, when the idea of childhood is opposed to gender nonconformity the latter is portrayed as a threat to the former. In those terms, gender-nonconforming children would be a mistake or a deviance to be corrected. On the other hand, the rights of gender-nonconforming people are often focused on adults, involving such debates and measures as legal gender recognition (Cassal, 2024), mirroring debates on LGBTIQ+ rights across the decades. Nonetheless, in this chapter we argue that the problem to be addressed involves children's self-determination. Hence, the problem of gender nonconformity is not isolated (although specific), but links back to other challenges involving children's self-determination (individually but also engaged in collective claims such as the rights of Palestinian people, which also were part of Butler's discursive intervention that generated so much hostility – see Butler, 2012). Butler's theoretical framework is important here because the acts of injury are accomplished often on behalf of others. Injury is not just destruction per se, but the destruction of self-determination rights. Not only was Butler attacked physically, symbolically and materially but so also were children. Child as method shows that the images and ideas of childhood are engaged while also challenging how children are represented, and for what purposes. When ultraconservatives accuse Butler of imposing their 'dream' onto allegedly 'innocent' children, they reveal projected feelings, including their desires for normalized childhoods and fears of self-determination. Hence, our third conclusion is that the problem of self-determination is a key to link back gender-nonconforming childhoods to the field of children's rights and improve practices on, and from, gender-nonconforming children's (but also adults') rights. If this is the object of fear, it is also what needs (in Butler's [1997a] terms) repetition and re-signification towards what we might call transformation through collective debate and action.

Butler's nonviolent responses include their latest book (Butler, 2024) and further efforts of solidarity by feminist and LGBTIQ+ movements. Nonviolent response implies also collective response, which also took place by Butler's supporters leading a counter-demonstration. Therefore, this book chapter is an invitation for academics and practitioners in childhood studies to also make a collective stand in favor of self-determination.

References

Ammaturo, F. R., & Moscati, M. F. (2021). Children's rights and gender identity: A new frontier of children's protagonism? *Nordic Journal of Human Rights*, *39*(2), 146–162. https://doi.org/10.1080/18918131.2021.1997028

Bernstein, R. (2004). *Racial innocence: White supremacy and the performance of American childhood.* Yale University.

Braun, S. S., & Davidson, A. J. (2017). Gender (non)conformity in middle childhood: A mixed methods approach to understanding gender-typed behavior, friendship, and peer preference. *Sex Roles*, *77*, 16–29. https://doi.org/10.1007/s11199-016-0693-z

Breslow, J. (2021). *Ambivalent childhoods: Speculative futures and the psychic life of the child.* University of Minnesota Press.

Burman, E. (2017). *Deconstructing developmental psychology.* Routledge.

Burman, E. (2019). *Fanon, education, action: Child as method.* Routledge.

Burman, E. (2020). *Developments: Child, image, nation.* Routledge.

Burman, E. (2023). Child as method and/as childism: Conceptual–political intersections and tensions. *Children & Society*, *37*(4), 1021–1036. https://doi.org/10.1111/chso.12615

Burman, E. (2024). *Child as method: Othering, interiority and materialism.* Routledge.

Butler, J. (1990). *Gender trouble: Feminism and the subversion of identity.* Routledge.

Butler, J. (1993). *Bodies that matter: On the discursive limits of 'sex'.* Routledge.

Butler, J. (1997a). *Excitable speech: A politics of the performative.* Psychology Press.

Butler, J. (1997b). *The psychic life of power: Theories in subjection.* Stanford University Press.

Butler, J. (2005). *Giving an account of oneself.* Fordham University Press.

Butler, J. (2010). *Frames of war: When is life grievable?* Verso.

Butler, J. (2012). *Parting ways: Jewishness and the critique of Zionism*. Columbia University Press.
Butler, J. (2016). Corpos que ainda importam [Bodies that still matter]. In L. Colling (Org.) *Dissidências sexuais e de gênero* (pp. 19–42). EDUFBA.
Butler, J. (2020). *The force of non violence: An ethico-political bind*. Verso.
Butler, J. (2024). *Who's afraid of gender?* Allen Lane (an imprint of Penguin Books).
Cannella, G. S., & Viruru, R. (2004). *Childhood and postcolonization: Power, education and contemporary practice*. Routledge.
Cassal, L. C. B. (2024). *Age, development, nation: Child as method and legal gender recognition in the UK*. Unpublished thesis, University of Manchester.
Cassal, L. C. B., Christinaki, A., & Burman, E. (2024). Who counts as child? Using child as method and Fanon to challenge figurations of childhood. *Cultural Studies – Critical Methodologies*, *0*(0), 1–9. https://doi.org/10.1177/15327086241272015
Cassal, L. C. B., Christinaki, A., Burman, E., Black, L., & Wu, W. (eds.). (2023). *Child as method international symposium conference proceedings 5th–7th June 2023*. University of Manchester. https://doi.org/10.48420/24073236.v1
Chiaradia, C. F., & Cassal, L. C. B. (2019). Ressonâncias educativas de um conceito pseudocientífico: "Ideologia de Gênero" e sexualidade na sociedade brasileira [Educational resonances of a pseudo-scientific concept: "Gender Ideology" and sexuality in the Brazilian society]. *Perspectivas de la comunicación*, *12*(1), 227–258. https://doi.org/10.4067/S0718-48672019000100227
Correa, S. (2017, December 11). *Gender ideology: Tracking its origins and meanings in current gender politics*. LSE Blog. https://blogs.lse.ac.uk/gender/2017/12/11/genderideologytracking-its-origins-and-meanings-in-current-gender-politics/
Coupet, S. M. (2015). Policing gender on the playground: Interests, needs, and rights of transgender and gender non-conforming youth. In S. M. Coupet & E. Marrus (eds.) *Children, sexuality, and the law* (pp. 186–223). New York University Press.
Coupet, S. M., & Marrus, E. (2015). Introduction. In S. M. Coupet & E. Marrus (eds.) *Children, sexuality, and the law* (pp. 1–5.). New York University Press.
Edelman, L. (2004). *No future: Queer theory and death drive*. Duke University Press.
Favero, S. (2020). *Crianças Trans: infâncias possíveis* [Trans children: Possible childhoods]. Editora Devires.
Federici, S. (2014). *Caliban and the witch*. Autonomedia.
Halberstam, J. (2018). *Trans: A quick and quirky account of gender variability*. University of California Press.
Haraway, D. (1988). Situated knowledges: The science question in feminism and the privilege of partial perspective. *Feminist Studies*, *14*(3), 575–599. https://doi.org/10.2307/3178066
Harrowitz, N. A. (1994). *Antisemitism, misogyny, and the logic of cultural difference: Cesare Lombroso & Matilde Serao*. University of Nebraska Press.
Harrowitz, N. A., & Hyams, B. (eds.). (1995). *Jews and gender: Responses to Otto Weininger*. Temple University Press.
Huberman, B. (2024). Why the Brazilian Jewish left is not Anti-Zionist: The politics of the Zionist left as counterrevolutionary gatekeepers in Brazil. *Historical Materialism*, *32*(1), 58–89. https://doi.org/10.1163/1569206x-bja10044
Jaschik, S. (2017, November 12). *Judith Butler on being attacked in Brazil*. InsideHE. Retrieved June 30, 2024, www.insidehighered.com/news/2017/11/13/judith-butler-discusses-being-burnedeffigy-and-protested-brazil
Junqueira, R. (2017). "Ideologia de Gênero": a invenção de uma categoria polêmica contra os direitos sexuais ["Gender Ideology": The invention of a polemic category against sexual rights]. In M. M. Ramos, P. A. G. Nicoli & G. C. Alkin (eds.) *Gênero, sexualidade e direitos humanos: perspectivas multidisciplinares* (pp. 221–236). Initia Via Editora.

Kane, E. W. (2006). No way my boys are going to be like that!. *Gender & Society*, *20*(2), 149–176.

Kilomba, G. (2020). *Plantation memories: Episodes of everyday racism*. Unrast.

Lugones, M. (2016). The coloniality of gender. In W. Harcourt (ed.) *The Palgrave handbook of gender and development: Critical engagements in feminist theory and practice* (pp. 13–33). Palgrave Macmillan.

Mannoni, O. (2003). 'I know well, but all the same . . .' In M. A. Rothenberg, D. A. Foster & S. Zizek (eds.) *Perversion and the social relation* (pp. 68–92). Duke University Press.

Mattos, A. R., & Moura e Silva, G. D. (2023). "To be treated as a thing": Discussing power relations with children in a public school in Rio de Janeiro. In E. L. Zurbriggen & R. Capdevila (eds.) *The Palgrave handbook of power, gender, and psychology* (pp. 63–75). Palgrave Macmillan. https://doi.org/10.1007/978-3-031-41531-9_5

Millei, Z., & Imre, R. (eds.). (2016). *Childhood and nation: Interdisciplinary engagements*. Springer.

Miskolci, R., & Pereira, P. P. G. (2018). Who's afraid of Judith Butler?: The moral crusade against human rights in Brazil. *Cadernos Pagu*, *53*, e185300. https://doi.org/10.1590/18094449201800530000

Moscati, M. F. (2022). Trans* identity does not limit children's capacity: Gillick competence applies to decisions concerning access to puberty blockers too! *Journal of Social Welfare and Family Law*, *44*(1), 130–132. https://doi.org/10.1080/09649069.2022.2028410

Paechter, C. (2021). The rights and interests of trans and intersex children: Considerations, conflicts and implications in relation to the UNCRC. *Journal of Gender Studies*, *30*(7), 844–854. https://doi.org/10.1080/09589236.2021.1888285

Prado, M. A. M., & Correa, S. (2018). Retratos transnacionais e nacionais das cruzadas antigênero [Portraits of transnational and national antigender cruizades]. *Revista Psicologia Política*, *18*(43), 444–448.

Preciado, P. B. (2020). *An apartment on Uranus*. Fitzcarraldo Editions.

Prilleltensky, I., & Stead, G. B. (2013). Critical psychology, well-being, and work. In D. L. Blustein (ed.), *The Oxford handbook of the psychology of working* (pp. 19–36). Oxford University Press.

Riggs, A. E., Kinard, D., & Long, M. (2023). Children's evaluations of gender non-conforming peers. *Sex Roles*, *88*, 17–34. https://doi.org/10.1007/s11199-022-01322-0

Roberts-Holmes, G., & Moss, P. (2021). *Neoliberalism and early childhood education: Markets, imaginaries and governance*. Routledge.

Rollo, T. (2018). The color of childhood: The role of the child/human binary in the production of anti-Black racism. *Journal of Black Studies*, *49*(4), 307–329.

Sandberg, K. (2015). The rights of LGBTI children under the convention on the rights of the child. *Nordic Journal of Human Rights*, *33*(4), 337–352.

Sedgwick, E. K. (1991). How to bring your kids up gay. *Social Text*, *29*, 18–27.

Steedman, C. (1995). *Strange dislocations: Childhood and the idea of human interiority, 1780–1930*. Virago.

Sorlie, A. (2015). Legal gender meets reality: Socio-legal children's perspective. *Nordic Journal of Human Rights*, *33*(4), 353–379.

Taylor, A. (2013). *Reconfiguring the natures of childhood*. Routledge.

Zentner, M., & von Aufsess, C. (2022). Is being gender nonconforming distressing? It depends where you live: Gender equality across 15 nations predicts how much gender nonconformity is related to self-esteem. *Psychological Medicine*, *52*(10), 1857–1865. https://doi.org/10.1017/s0033291720003645

10 Child, early, and forced marriage from a critical children's rights perspective[1]

Wouter Vandenhole and Yitaktu Tibebu

10.1 Introduction

The mainstream approach to, and legal human rights framework on, child, early, and forced marriage (CEFM) is geared towards abolition. It focuses on prohibiting underage marriage, which is defined as marriage below the age of 18. This chapter presents five critiques on CEFM and current intervention strategies: the neglect of the complex interaction of socio-economic structural factors and social norms as drivers of CEFM; the universalist assumption of the chronological age of 18 as the marker of adulthood; the neglect of a gender perspective; the theoretical grounding in the neocolonial savage-victim-saviour paradigm; and the naive belief in legal change as a driver of social change. Those critiques have been distilled from a literature review and empirical research that was conducted in Quarit Woreda[2] in the Amhara region in Ethiopia which is a State Party to all relevant international and regional human rights instruments and has a robust legal framework that denounces CEFM as a harmful practice and criminalizes it. In what follows, we first introduce the methodology used for the empirical research. The mainstream approach is discussed in section 3. In section 4, we unpack our five critiques. We critically reflect on those critiques in section 5, after which we conclude in section 6.

10.2 Methodology

The data collection was conducted in Quarit (district) Woreda in the Amhara region in Ethiopia between March and August 2022. Woreda is one of the child marriage 'hot spot' areas in Ethiopia with 32.1% married girls aged between 10 and 17 and 51.6% married girls aged between 15 and 17 (Jones et al., 2016, p. 6; Central Statistical Agency (CSA) & ICF, 2016).

1 In line with the Contributor Roles Taxonomy (CRediT), developed by the National Information Standards Organization (https://credit.niso.org/), the following roles were played by the contributors: conceptualization and drafts were mainly done by Vandenhole. Tibebu wrote the sections on empirical research in Ethiopia and on the gender perspective, and reviewed drafts.

2 Woreda is a district.

DOI: 10.4324/9781003510284-11

In-depth interviews were carried out with various local respondents, including 12 adolescent girls, 10 mothers, 17 fathers, 5 priests, 3 male elders, and 11 adolescent boys. Additionally, semi-structured interviews were conducted with 124 local government stakeholders (36 F, 88 M). Twelve key informants were involved in the study, including school principals (4 M), gender club focal teachers (2 F), health extension workers (2 F, 1 M), a health centre head (1 M) and UNICEF/UNFPA focal persons (2 M). Further, 15 focus group discussions (FGDs) were conducted, involving 104 community members (41 F, 63 M). These FGDs comprised four groups with adolescent girls, two with boys, two with mothers only, two with fathers only, as well as separate FGDs with teachers, Orthodox Tewahido Christian priests, and elders.[3]

The data were analyzed utilizing a qualitative case study research design. A qualitative approach was used to uncover meanings and discover reasons (Creswell & Creswell, 2018). After securing data collection clearance from the required regional and district stakeholders, data were gathered in the selected *Kebeles* (the smallest administrative unit) with due respect and recognition of participants' autonomy (Ulrich, 2017, pp. 203–207). The tools were translated into Amharic before the data collection. All of the primary data collected through multiple sources were audio recorded after securing consent (and assent) from the participants. Further, the risk of vulnerability was carefully evaluated to ensure that participants were not exposed to any potential harm.

10.3 Mainstream approach

CEFM has been addressed in two core children's rights instruments – the Convention on the Rights of the Child (UNCRC) and the African Charter on the Rights and Welfare of the Child (ACRWC). For instance, Article 24(3) of the UNCRC obliges states to abolish traditional practices prejudicial to children's health. In turn, Article 21(2) of the ACRWC requires states to prohibit child marriage, to set the minimum age of marriage at 18, and to make registration of all marriages compulsory.

The main human rights instrument on women's rights, the Convention on the Elimination of All Forms of Discrimination against Women (CEDAW), imposes an obligation on states to ensure, in particular, free choice and full

3 Pseudonyms were used to identify study respondents during citation. Adolescent girls were labelled as AG, adolescent boys as AB, female parents as FP, male parents as MP, priests as P, elders as E, community facilitators as CF, school principals as SD, Gender Club Focal Female Teachers as GCFFT, Health Extension Workers as HEW, Health Centre Head as HCH, and UNICEF/UNFPA focal persons as IGO. As for the local government stakeholders, the pseudonyms used for identification were A01-A011 for *Kebele* level stakeholders, A001-A021 for Quarit Woreda informants, AA01-AA10 for Zonal level stakeholders, AA001-AA008 for regional level stakeholders, and AD1-AD12 for federal level stakeholders.

consent to enter into marriage as well as the same rights in marriage (Art. 16.1). Art. 16.2 of CEDAW prohibits child marriage and requires states to specify a minimum age for marriage, without any particular age suggestion. The CEDAW Committee has read into this provision that the minimum age for marriage should be 18 years, arguing that 'marriage should not be permitted before [individuals] have attained full maturity and capacity to act' (CEDAW Committee, 1994, para. 36). In their joint General Comment, the CRC Committee and CEDAW Committee have submitted that 'child marriage is considered to be a form of forced marriage, given that one and/or both parties have not expressed full, free and informed consent' (CEDAW & CRC Committee, 2019, para. 20). Article VI of the Protocol to the African Charter on Human and Peoples' Rights on the Rights of Women in Africa (the Maputo Protocol) repeats the elements of free and full consent and 18 as the minimum age of marriage. In sum, a globally uniform marriageable age of 18 is put forward, and child marriage is equated with forced marriage. The legal human rights framework on CEFM is geared towards abolition: underage marriage must be legally prohibited.

However, predominantly legalistic and repressive strategies to address CEFM have failed (Cislaghi et al., 2020; Collin & Talbot, 2017). More recently, in the advocacy space a shift in framing CEFM from 'age to agency' has taken place (Barney et al., 2022). The traditional poverty/underdevelopment, health, or education frame has been substituted by a feminist sexuality frame, which argues that the lives of adolescent girls are often characterized by the 'management of their sexuality.' Their lack of autonomy regarding sexuality is 'a core aspect of patriarchy' (Greene et al., 2018, pp. 4–5). A feminist sexuality frame requires broader social transformation that addresses patriarchy and gender inequality. A key element in such an approach is empowerment, including that which relates to the control of adolescent girls' sexuality (Barney et al., 2022, pp. 524–525).

A 2023 report by UNICEF showed that the global prevalence of CEFM has declined in the last 10 years, but that the decline is uneven. In sub-Saharan Africa, overall progress in CEFM reduction is due to advances in the richest families. By contrast, rising levels of CEFM on the continent have been noted among the poorest families (UNICEF, 2023, pp. 10–12). Those findings raise questions about not only the intervention strategies and the legal human rights framework they build on, but also about their theoretical groundings: if a causal relation between law and intervention strategies and CEFM prevalence can be assumed, it can only be done with regard to the richest families.

10.4 Critical perspectives

The dominant approach to CEFM, informed by children's and women's rights, can be critiqued on five counts (see the introduction). In what follows, we will develop each of those critical perspectives.

10.4.1 Complex interaction of socio-economic structural factors and social norms

There seems to be no single driver of CEFM, and it is also not always clear how drivers intersect, or reinforce, one another. Some are more structural, others more individual. Psaki et al. (2021) have identified five interrelated CEFM drivers: poverty (and economic factors); lack of opportunity; social norms and attitudes; lack of agency; and fear of girls' sexuality and pregnancy. Poverty and lack of opportunity are closely related, and we, therefore, group them together. A second cluster of drivers revolves around social norms and fears of girls' sexuality and pregnancy. The latter clearly speak to the control and management of girls' sexuality.

Poverty is one of the major factors underpinning CEFM (Bunting, 2005, p. 29; Bakta et al., 2022). Lack of education, job opportunities, or alternative pathways to independence from parents may be other reasons for CEFM (Psaki et al., 2021, p. S14). The Woreda study similarly indicates that poverty and the economic value associated with child marriage are key factors that motivate both parents and adolescent girls. Parents dispute the value of educating their daughters as a result of the prevalence of unemployment (AA2, 15 April 2022; A1, 29 March 2022 and A2 & A3, 31 March 2022; GFFT2, 13 April 2022 and HE 3 M, 8 April 2022). Marriage is viewed as a means of economic advancement for girls who are 15 years of age or older who choose labour migration in adjacent localities. Specifically, when girls' school performance declines, they drop out and start looking for assets that they can own themselves. In such situations they consider marriage to be the only option (AG6, 1 April 2022 and AG8, 12 April 2022).

Social norms are particularly relevant as a driver of CEFM (Cislaghi et al., 2020). Gender norms inhibit adolescent girls' access to schooling (particularly beyond primary school) and employment opportunities (UNICEF, 2008, p. 33). This is especially so when poverty intersects with gender dynamics in the family, which, in turn, affects choices about education and marriage. Gender stereotypes about women's roles in society manifest themselves amongst others in cultural and religious social norms about sexuality (Bunting, 2005, p. 29). A reason put forward for marrying girls at an early age is that it helps prevent premarital sex. Many societies prize virginity before marriage and this can manifest itself in a number of practices designed to 'protect' a girl from unsanctioned sexual activity (Steinhaus et al., 2019) and transactional sex (Stark, 2018). The Woreda study uncovered deeply ingrained misconceptions about female sexuality and gender stereotypes, as well as the widely held belief in the protective factor of *chagula merget* (i.e. marrying off girls during childhood) as the primary drivers of the persistence of CEFM in the area. *Chagula merget* is considered a protective practice, in particular, in cases where girls are subjected to rape, or when no betrothal request has been made at their socially expected age of marriage (Tibebu et al., 2023).

Likewise, the empirical study in Woreda has uncovered the prevailing misconceptions about girls' sexuality, a widely shared belief that girls tend to develop sexual ideation at an earlier age than boys, and confirmed that the prevailing view on underage marriage is that of the importance of preserving the virginity of child brides (A001, 29 March 2022; A002 & A003, 31 March 2022; A005, A009 & A010, 29 March 2022; A007 & A008, 2 April 2022; A013, 28 March 2022). Participants informed us that

> the age beyond 16 is frustrating for parents due to the widely held belief that girls will lose their virginity, locally known as *wedket* [meaning 'loss']. Rather than letting them lose their virginity, parents often prefer to marry them early.
>
> (A005, A009 & A010, 29 March 2022)

The study further unveiled two culturally assigned markers based on misconceptions of girls' sexuality. First, when girls exhibit biological changes in their bodies, parents tend to view it as an indication of womanhood and readiness for marriage (HE 1, 31 March 2022 and HE 2, 3 April 2022). Adolescent girl FGD informants shared that 'when girls attain 10 years, most parents usually believe that she has [a] sexual urge' (FGD 5, 13 April 2022). The second misconception is the assumption that a girl's 'impoliteness,' by, for example, responding 'without respect', is indicative of maturing sexual interest and the need for marriage (P2 and P3, 9 April 2022).

Age disparity at marriage between men and women is rooted in stereotypical gender roles that remain in most cultures, which hold that women are to be mothers and wives and men are to be providers for the family unit (Bunting, 2005). Consequently, women are deemed to be ready for marriage at an earlier age than men, who are accorded the opportunity to finish their professional training and, ideally, be financially secure before marrying (Bunting, 2005). The Woreda study identified two important ages attached to girlhood that resulted in the persistence of child marriage among girls: 12 as a 'socially appropriate' age for marriage and 15 as their 'age of consent.' A consistent finding from the local community elder informants shows that young girls often develop a desire to wed by the time they reach the age of 14 (E 1, 6 April 2022; E 2, 11 April 2022; E 3, 15 April 2022). Similarly, nearly all study informants highlighted that adolescent girls who attained the age of 14 or 15 consent to marry. Accordingly, the age beyond 15 is commonly viewed as threatening for the families of many girls due to the possibility of self-arranged marriage. As a result, girls as early as four years old are married off in their 'childhood' or later when they are in their 'young' age (12/13 years) which is known as '*akeme hewan*' (appropriate marriageable age for girls). In sum, CEFM seems to be driven by the intersection of structural socio-economic factors (poverty, lack of opportunities) and social norms related to gender stereotypes and the urge to manage, and control, girls' sexuality.

10.4.2 *Diversity of childhoods*

A second critique is that the dominant approach to CEFM erroneously takes 18 as a global marker of adulthood. Indeed, there is a risk that a 'strategy based on a uniform marriageable age as suggested by the CEDAW Committee (1994) and a narrow rights-based analysis misses the complexity of both marriage *and* age' (Bunting, 2005, p. 18). Moreover, when childhood is defined solely by age, 'it downplays the importance of other salient actors such as culture, gender, and socioeconomic status' (Campbell et al., 2011, p. 4). This concern with the Eurocentric nature of the image of childhood used in the UNCRC more generally is shared by many. One consequence is that it has limited application in other cultures (Campbell et al., 2011, p. 4). Abebe (2013, p. 72) adds to this by depicting children's rights as an:

> Hegemonic model in which selected ideals from a once localised Western construction of childhood being exported to the rest of the world gains momentum [references omitted], a model premised on the idea that children should have a safe and happy existence, and childhood is seen as a work-free and care receiving phase of the life course.

There is a clear need to decolonize conceptualizations of childhood and give space to pluralities and multiplicities in the ontologies and epistemologies of childhood (Abebe et al., 2022). Considering diverse cultural constructions of childhood in analyzing CEFM is only possible by moving beyond chronological age. Vandenhole (2020) has proposed, therefore, to shift the focus in CEFM away from age to agency (and consent) while, at the same time, acknowledging thorny questions regarding degrees of agency (and consent). Agency is not an individual characteristic, but 'depends largely on, and is regulated by, family contexts, livelihood opportunities/constraints and interpersonal relationships' (Abebe, 2013, p. 75). Hence, girls are

> simultaneously dependent and independent with respect to different aspects of their social worlds including their ability . . . to marry. . . . Their growing competencies – economic, cultural, and social – are not simply linked to chronological age but are born of social experiences and interactions, enhanced by exposure and practice.
>
> (Abebe, 2013, p. 75)

10.4.3 *A gender perspective*

A third critique on the dominant approach to CEFM is its exclusive focus on childhood, to the exclusion of a gender perspective. In line with recent advocacy, we argue that the approach to CEFM must move from viewing it narrowly as an age or protection issue to incorporating a gender perspective. CFEM primarily affects *girls'* lives. Greene et al. (2018) have argued that sexuality is key to understanding CEFM. By taking a gender-focused approach, one of the root causes (i.e., social norms on gender inequality) contributing to the practice of CEFM can be identified. CEFM is a means of the manifestation of patriarchy while controlling girls' sexuality is the result. Accordingly, addressing CEFM necessitates going beyond a child protection framework towards 'a more feminist gender-transformative framework' (American Jewish World Service, n.d., pp. 1). Adopting a feminist, rights-based perspective entails recognizing adolescent girls as individuals endowed with agency, encompassing their capacity to make decisions regarding their sexuality (American Jewish World Service, n.d, pp. 1).

In Woreda, the authority of adolescent girls to make decisions regarding their own marriages is linked to reaching the socially prescribed age of 15 or older. At this age, the girls are no longer compelled to marry. They are provided with the freedom to either accept or reject arranged marriage. When girls accept arranged marriages, they are regarded as being married by 'their own choice' (FP1, 4 April 2022; FP2, 4 April 2022; FP8, 8 April 2022; AB1, 12 April 2022; AB2, 12 April 2022 and AB8, 15 April 2022). According to adolescent girls, some parents resort to marrying off their daughters secretly if they believe the girls (at the age of 12/13) will resist the arranged marriage. Furthermore, the girls stated that 'parents will inform those girls who are assumed to be willing to accept an arranged marriage, but they will not inform those who are suspected to resist, usually those who are 15 years old or more' (FGD 5, 13 April 2022). They also confirmed that: 'parents will not request girls' consent before marriage. Nearly all girls have *"chagula regtewal"* [they're married in childhood]' (FGD 7, 30 March 2022). After attaining the age of 15 and older, they continued, 'the girls' choice is not uniform, some prefer marriage over education while others vice versa. However, most girls accept their parents' choice, will not resist. And those resisting girls will run away' (FGD 7, 30 March 2022).

By adopting a sexuality frame along with a gender lens, attention can be drawn to the agency of girls. Rather than focusing on their final decision, even if they choose to be child brides, their intention and motivation to exert the limited agency they can exercise is what matters.

Perhaps a rather surprising element of the gender perspective is the emphasis on the role of adolescent boys. They have the power and authority to establish appropriate marriageable ages for girls in their local community as they actively participate in selecting their future spouses (Tibebu et al., 2023). Additionally, their fathers seek their input and often allow them to see the potential bride before finalizing the betrothal agreement. Their inclination towards girls who are virgins explains their preference for marrying girls below the legal age of majority. On the other hand, their need for a wife who can manage household responsibilities leads to a preference for girls between the ages of 15 and 18 (FGD 001, 7 April 2022; FGD 004, 13 April 2022; E 02, 11 April 2022 and A005, A009 & A010, 29 March 2022).

10.4.4 A neocolonial savage-victim-saviour paradigm[4]

A fourth critique on the dominant children's rights discourse on CEFM is that it employs a neocolonial savages-victims-saviours (SVS) metaphor. Makau Mutua (2001, p. 245) has argued that the 'human rights movement must abandon the SVS metaphor if there is going to be real hope in a genuine international discourse on rights.' In the SVS metaphor, the state or the cultural foundation of the state is the savage, the 'human being whose "dignity and worth" have been violated by the savage is the victim' (Mutua, 2001, p. 203), and the human rights corpus the saviour (Mutua, 2001, pp. 202–204). Applied to CEFM, the social norms that form the cultural foundation of the state are the savage. Girls are the victims. And CEFM human rights norms and advocacy are the saviours.

The problem with the CEFM human rights norms is that they are fundamentally Eurocentric and suffer from five interdependent flaws:

> First, the corpus falls within the historical continuum of the Eurocentric colonial project, in which actors are cast into superior and subordinate positions. . . . Second, the SVS metaphor and narrative rejects the cross-contamination [footnote omitted] of cultures and instead promotes a Eurocentric ideal. The metaphor is premised on the transformation by Western cultures of non-Western cultures into a Eurocentric prototype. . . . Third, the language and rhetoric of the human rights corpus present significant theoretical problems. . . . Fourth, the issue of power is largely ignored in the human rights corpus. . . . The fifth flaw concerns the role of race in the development of the human rights narrative. The SVS metaphor of human rights carries racial connotations in which the international hierarchy of race and color is reintrenched and revitalized.
>
> (Mutua, 2001, pp. 204–207)

10.4.5 Legal change as the main driver of social change

A fifth and final critique of the dominant approach to CEFM is that it over-relies on legal reform to change the practice. A study of over 60 countries found that the introduction of age legislation is not enough on its own to prevent CEFM, in the absence of law enforcement (including capacity-building and resourcing) and of monitoring the efficacy of deterrence (Collin & Talbot, 2017). Another recent study found that legislative change was not effective in curbing CEFM in four out of the six countries studied, and that

4 This section draws on Vandenhole (2020).

their effectiveness in the two other countries was doubtful as well (Batyra & Pesando, 2021). Admittedly, other studies suggest that

> consistent laws against child marriage are negatively associated with the prevalence of child marriage. . . . The prevalence of child marriage was 40% lower among women in countries with laws that consistently set the minimum marriage age for girls at 18 or older than among women in other countries.
>
> (Maswikwa et al., 2015, p. 64)

In much of the mainstream law and development literature, there is a belief in legal solutions to societal problems, that is, in social engineering through law (Vandenhole, 2019). However, most legislation is ineffective, in that it has either no effects, not the intended effects, or is symbolic (Cislaghi et al., 2019, 2020; Cislaghi & Heise, 2018; Griffiths, 1983). Fraser (2019, p. 983) has, therefore, advocated an approach that goes beyond legalism in the domestic implementation of international human rights law, including in relation to CEFM.

A legalistic approach backed by punitive measures like imprisonment and fines may not be suitable, and certainly not sufficient either (Bhuwania et al., 2023). Rather than bringing an end to prohibited practices, punitive measures tend to either transform them or drive them underground (Grijns & Horii, 2018; UNFPA & UNICEF, 2020). Research conducted in Woreda has shown the same. The community devised innovative strategies and impeded the local government's ability to enforce the punitive measures. Two distinct types of covert underage marriages among girls can be pointed to as examples. First, the local government requires age estimation before marriage celebrations. As a result, parents marry off all their underage girls secretly, utilizing the marriage ceremony of the eldest daughter who meets the age requirement. This underground marriage practice is locally known as *chefeleko medar* (hiding the underage marriages). Second, other parents resort to deception regarding their plans to marry off their underage daughters. Instead of submitting the girls for age assessment, they avail themselves of other social gatherings (referred to locally as *maheber* and *senbete)* to conceal the weddings or surreptitiously dispatch underage girls at night without any formal ceremony. This form of underage marriage is locally known as *shuleklek* (sneak away) (FGD014, 05 April 2022; FGD017, 12 April 2022; AA09, 21 April 2022).

It is doubtful that a categorical legal prohibition of CEFMs yields the desired result of addressing human rights violations that come with CEFMs (Mwambene, 2010, p. 103). CEFM can be a response to poverty and be viewed by community members as a charitable act. In such instances, there may be resistance to minimum age in marriage laws (Kim et al., 2013, p. 596). But also, when CEFM is primarily understood as a gendered issue as it is in Woreda, community resistance to minimum age in marriage laws and those who advocate for them has been noted. The community resistance encompasses various forms of social sanctions. For instance, individuals who advocate for the minimum age of marriage may face exclusion from valuable local social networks during funerals, known as *Edir*, and prohibition from participating in collective cattle-herding activities. Also, local government officials, including police, administrators, and gender-focal representatives, as well as school deans and female teacher gender club leaders, who aim to protect underage girls, have been subject to intimidation and even threat of armed attacks (SD01, 30 March 2022; A014, 15 April 2022; A01, 3 April 2022; A02, 5 April 2022; A03, 7 April 2022; A09 & A011, 4 April 2022; GFT01, 18 April, 2022 and CF01 M, 30 March 2022).

Identifying a specific practice for elimination, without considering children's wider social and economic circumstances, risks neglecting the most critical problems they face (Boyden et al., 2012, p. 520). For example, enforcing the legal age of marriage in contexts where adolescents are sexually active well before the age of 18 and where there is a shortage of contraception, lack of abortion facilities, and low support for young women who bear children out of wedlock and then often face divorce and/or become single parents can result in serious adverse outcomes for girls and young women and their offspring (Boyden et al., 2012, p. 520). Moreover, in areas where prospects for girls to continue their education at secondary and tertiary levels as well as seek meaningful employment opportunities are limited, girls are unable to remain at school. Intervention programmes must seek to empower girls with information and support networks, ensure their access to quality education, engage and educate parents and community members about child marriage, and provide economic incentives and other forms of support to girls' families (Malhotra et al., 2011), and not just establish, and implement, a strong legal framework, such as a minimum age of marriage. On the other hand, and somewhat puzzling, multicomponent programmes seem less effective than stand-alone interventions (Malhotra & Elnakib, 2021).

10.4.6 Intermediate conclusion

The critical perspective on the legal human rights governance of CEFM that we have presented here calls, first of all, for a recognition of the diversity and intersectionality of CEFM drivers, in which structural factors ranging from poverty to societal gender stereotypes play an important role. Second, it emphasizes the need to acknowledge a diversity of childhoods and thereby problematizes the emphasis on chronological age (18 years) in children's and women's rights law. It proposes, instead, to focus on maturity, agency, and hence, consent. Third, it criticizes the absence of a gender perspective. Fourth, from a decolonization perspective, any framing of CEFM in human rights law should stay away from the SVS metaphor. Finally, our critical approach is sceptical of legal engineering and proposes, instead, a multipronged strategy in which law may be one element, but is certainly not the most important element.

10.5 Self-critical reflections on our critical perspective

In this section, we reflect on the critical stance we took previously. In particular, we consider the risk of depriving children from protection through our critique, and the questions of agency and a gender perspective.

10.5.1 Deprivation of children of special protection

A first element of self-critique is whether the criticism of the dominant approach to CEFM and, in particular, the rejection of a straight-18 approach, does not deprive girls from much needed special protection. A clear tension exists between decolonization of human rights law and depriving children from the special protection they may need. That tension has been studied and demystified with regard to working children (Okyere, 2014; Omoike, 2014; Hanson & Vandaele, 2013) and child orphans (Cheney, 2014), but much less for other groups of children such as those who end up in CEFM. Elsewhere, Vandenhole has suggested the use of the difference dilemma framework developed by Hanson and Vandaele (2013), which would allow us to reconcile general human rights such as the right to marry and rights in marriage with children's special rights to protection against harmful practices. At the very least, that would mean that forced marriage is never acceptable, and that full and free consent is required for any marriage to be human rights compliant.

A closely related critique is that 'local interpretation and definition . . . can also be a slippery slope – and in practice, varied understandings mean that we can easily speak at cross purposes' (Shetty, 2018, p. 2). Therefore, the question is whether there are red lines that should not be crossed in any vernacularization or localization exercise, who decides on them, and on which grounds. The difference dilemma framework may again be useful: it would not allow for any forced marriage, and hence, would require, again, free and full consent. Ultimately, it may be that questions about red lines in human rights vernacularization and localization cannot be given definite answers in the abstract, but should be resolved in the specific local contexts where they arise. However, one should not ignore the power dynamics at play in any (local) context. There are multiple forms, levels, and spaces of power. Power may manifest itself in visible, hidden, and invisible forms. Invisible forms, which refer to internalized beliefs and norms, play an important role (Gaventa, 2019).

Another risk of the critical perspective is that it may let children down in practice. A well-meant attempt to move beyond Western conceptions of childhood and children's rights and beyond legalistic approaches may lead to backlash and deprive children from much needed protection in their day-to-day lives. We could counterargue that the implication of the critical perspective is not deprivation of protection, but a shift from paternalistic protection to acknowledgement of agency. That agency can be used to claim protection when and where needed. But is that turn to agency not equally problematic?

10.5.2 Agency

Cross-cutting the rebuttal to the aforementioned critiques on our critical approach to CEFM is the emphasis on agency. In practice, that agency may be very minimal to nonexistent though in light of the structural drivers of CEFM, as well as due to (sexist and ageist) power relations in local communities. In that sense, agency is unlikely to be full, but will be constrained – hence the language of tactical or thin or circumscribed agency that has been used to frame such discussions (see Erdem Türkelli & Vandenhole, 2022).

More fundamentally, an emphasis on agency, in particular when equated with, or related to, autonomy may turn out to be part of a Western and liberal image of childhood. This leads to a situation whereby this critical perspective reinforces, rather than challenges, a neocolonial and universalist approach to children's rights. Any turn to agency would, therefore, need to engage with relationality and be understood as relational agency, as pointed out in critical childhood literature (Abebe et al., 2022).

Interviews in Woreda showed that 7 out of 12 adolescent girl informants agreed with arranged marriages. Three merely adhered to societal norms. They married someone they had not previously known, following the prevailing cultural norm of child marriage (AG2, 5 April 2022 AG9, 31 March 2022 and AG12, 14 April 2022). However, four of the seven informants provided reasons that could be considered reasonable justifications for their preference for underage marriage, highlighting relational agency. They explained that two of them had dropped out of school (AG5, 10 April 2022 and AG8, 12 April 2022); one had lost hope in education because of an existing conflict (AG3, 6 April 2022); another was overwhelmed by the domestic workload imposed by her stepmother and changed her attitude towards education when she noticed the existing unemployment in the local area (AG6, 1 April 2022). As a result, these four child brides exhibited 'constrained' agency, despite ultimately becoming child brides.

10.5.3 Gender perspective

A further critique on our critical perspective on CEFM may be that although girls are disproportionately affected by CEFM, there are instances where boys too are married off during their childhood, and that they remain invisible in the gendered critique that CEFM is first and foremost about managing and controlling girls' sexuality. In Woreda, when negotiating a betrothal agreement, it is customary for the two families to discuss the possibility of exchanging children, with the intention that a boy from the groom's family will wed another girl from the bride-to-be's family (A001, 29 March 2022; A002 & A003, 31 March 2022; A005, A009 & A010, 29 March 2022; A007 & A008, 2 April 2022). However, that drive to marry off young boys does not stem from concerns about controlling their sexuality, but more from economic considerations. If the two marrying families can exchange a female and a male from each family, neither party is required to pay a bride price. However, in cases where there is a single marriage involving a bride and groom, the groom's family is obligated to pay a bride price in the form of either money worth approximately ETB 5,000 to 6,000 (equivalent to USD 40–50), or gold. The marriage of the bride and groom who have married in childhood will often soon come to an end, following the celebration. However, such marriage in childhood (*chagula merget/daweja mdqedqe)* relieves the groom's family of the societal obligation to host his wedding celebration at his socially expected marriageable age (20–25 years old). One of the adolescent boys recounted the effects of child marriage, stating 'since my parents already celebrated my wedding in childhood, they are no longer responsible for my wedding expenses. So, when I intend to marry, then I shall be in a position to cover the cost myself' (AB5, 11 April 2022). Although the prevalence of CEFM among boys is much lower than among girls, this reality nevertheless raises the question about whether CEFM of boys needs a separate theoretical framework of analysis and a separate treatment (and possibly legal rules) in children's rights.

10.6 Conclusion

The dominant human rights framework on CEFM focuses on establishing a minimum age for marriage at 18 and is geared towards abolition through legal prohibition. This chapter has introduced a critical children's rights perspective on CEFM and current intervention strategies. Five critiques were presented: the neglect of the complex interaction of socio-economic structural factors and social norms as drivers of CEFM; its universalist assumption of the chronological age of 18 as the marker of adulthood; its neglect of a gender perspective; its theoretical grounding in the neocolonial savage-victim-saviour paradigm; and its naive belief in legal change as a driver of social change.

In the self-critique, three points stand out. First, the risk of depriving children who are exposed to CEFM from the special protection they need as children, both at the conceptual level (by ignoring special protection needs and by advocating through vernacularization or localization an anything-goes approach) and in practice. In an attempt to engage with that self-critique, we highlighted the importance of full and free consent to marriage, drawing on difference dilemma framework (see section 5.1). This brought us to the notion of agency and the second point of self-critique: how much agency can there be in light of the structural drivers of CEFM and the ageist and sexist power relations in families and communities, and do we not run the risk of agency taking us back to a Western and liberal notion of childhood in which autonomy plays a key role? Finally, the limitations of a gender analysis were borne out in instances in which underage boys are married off, and for reasons other than the management and control of their sexuality.

In the alternative approach to CEFM that we propose, a decolonized approach leads to a shift in emphasis away from chronological age to consent, with due attention though for ageist and sexist power. Likewise, a gender perspective necessitates a shift from protection to agency, with due acknowledgement, though, of the structural causes of CEFM, which allow only for constrained agency. One-sided attention for girls, at the expense of boys, should be avoided. Finally, intervention strategies should not be legalistic, but, instead, seek to address CEFM's root causes, including socio-economic factors as well as social norms.

References

Abebe, T. (2013). Interdependent rights and agency: The role of children in collective livelihood strategies in rural Ethiopia. In T. Abebe, K. Hanson & O. Nieuwenhuys (eds.) *Reconceptualizing children's rights in international development: Living rights, social justice, translations* (pp. 71–92). Cambridge University Press.

Abebe, T., Dar, A., & Lyså, I. M. (2022). Southern theories and decolonial childhood studies. *Childhood*, *29*(3), 255–275.

Bakta, S., Mchomvu, F., Warioba, I., Jonas, B., Erdem Türkelli, G., Dozsa, K., & Vandenhole, W. (2022). *A human rights-based approach to health challenges associated with child marriage in Tanzania: Research report.* Unpublished.

Barney, M., Murdie, A., Park, B., Hart, J., & Mullinax, M. (2022). From age to agency: Frame adoption and diffusion concerning the international human rights norm against child, early, and forced marriage. *Human Rights Review*, *23*(4), 503–528.

Batyra, E., & Pesando, L. M. (2021). Trends in child marriage and new evidence on the selective impact of changes in age-at-marriage laws on early marriage. *SSM – Population Health*, *14*, 100811.

Bhuwania, P., Huh, K., & Heymann, J. (2023). Impact of tuition-free education policy on child marriage and early childbearing: Does secondary matter more? *Population & Development Review*, *49*(1), 43–70.

Boyden, J., Pankhurst, A., & Tafere, Y. (2012). Child protection and harmful traditional practices: Female early marriage and genital modification in Ethiopia. *Development in Practice*, *22*(4), 510–522.

Bunting, A. (2005). Stages of development: Marriage of girls and teens as an international human rights issue. *Social & Legal Studies*, *14*(1), 17–38.

Campbell, K., Denov, M., Maclure, R., & Solomon, I. (2011). Introduction. In M. S. Denov, R. A. Maclure & K. M. Campbell (eds.) *Children's rights and international development: Lessons and challenges from the field* (pp. 1–14). Palgrave Macmillan.

CEDAW Committee. (1994). *General recommendation No. 21: Equality in marriage and family relations* (A/49/38).

CEDAW Committee & CRC Committee. (2019). *Joint general recommendation/general comment No. 31 of the committee on the elimination of discrimination against women and no. 18 of the committee on the Rights of the Child (2019) on harmful practices* (CEDAW/C/GC/31/Rev.1 CRC/C/GC/18/Rev.1).

Central Statistical Agency (CSA), and ICF. (2016). *Ethiopia demographic and health survey*. Retrieved January 28, 2025, from https://dhsprogram.com/pubs/pdf/FR328/FR328.pdf

Cheney, K. E. (2014). Conflicting protectionist and participation models of children's rights: Their consequences for Uganda's orphans and vulnerable children. In A. Twum-Danso Imoh & N. Ansell (eds.) *Children's lives in an era of children's rights: The progress of the Convention on the Rights of the Child in Africa* (pp. 17–33). Routledge.

Cislaghi, B., & Heise, L. (2018). Theory and practice of social norms interventions: Eight common pitfalls. *Globalization and Health*, *14*(83).

Cislaghi, B., Mackie, G., Nkwi, P., & Shakya, H. (2019). Social norms and child marriage in Cameroon: An application of the theory of normative spectrum. *Global Public Health*, *14*(10), 1479–1494.

Cislaghi, B., Nkwi, P., Mackie, G., & Shakya, H. (2020). Why context matters for social norms interventions: The case of child marriage in Cameroon. *Global Public Health, 15*(4), 532–543.

Collin, M., & Talbot, T. (2017). *Do age-of-marriage laws work? Evidence from a large sample of developing countries* (Nr. 458; CGD Working Paper). Retrieved January 20, 2025, from www.cgdev.org/publication/do-age-marriage-laws-work-evidencelargesampledeveloping-countries

Creswell, J., & Creswell, J. D. (2018). *Research design: Qualitative, quantitative, and mixed methods approaches.* SAGE Publishing.

Erdem Türkelli, G., & Vandenhole, W. (2022). *Advanced introduction to children's rights.* Edward Elgar.

Fraser, J. (2019). Challenging state-centricity and legalism: Promoting the role of social institutions in the domestic implementation of international human rights law. *The International Journal of Human Rights, 23*(6), 974–992.

Gaventa, J. (2019). Applying power analysis: Using the 'powercube' to explore forms, levels and spaces. In R. McGee & J. Pettit (eds.) *Power, empowerment and social change* (pp. 117–138). Routledge.

Greene, M. E, Perlson, S., Hart, J., & Mullinax, M. (2018). *The centrality of sexuality for understanding child early and forced marriage.* GreeneWorks and American Jewish World Service. Retrieved January 20, 2025, from https://sharenetinternational.org/resources/the-centrality-of-sexuality-for-understanding-child-early-and-forced-marriage/

Griffiths, J. (1983). Recht en ontwikkeling. *Recht en Kritiek, 9*(2), 175–191.

Grijns, M., & Horii, H. (2018). Child marriage in a village in West Java (Indonesia): Compromises between legal obligations and religious concerns. *Asian Journal of Law & Society, 5*(2), 453–466.

Hanson, K., & Vandaele, A. (2013). Translating working children's rights into international labour law. In K. Hanson & O. Nieuwenhuys (eds.) *Reconceptualizing children's rights in international development: Living rights, social justice, translations* (pp. 250–272). Cambridge University Press.

Jones, N., Emirie, G., Tefera, B., & Presler-Marshall, E. (2016). *Surprising trends in child marriage in Ethiopia.* ODI and UNICEF. Retrieved January 28, 2025, from www.unicef.org/ethiopia/media/1506/file/Surprising%20trends%20in%20child%20marriage%20in%20Ethiopia.pdf

Kim, M., Longhofer, W., Boyle, E. H., & Nyseth Brehm, H. (2013). When do laws matter? National minimum-age-of-marriage laws, child rights, and adolescent fertility 1989–2007. *Law & Society Review, 47*(3), 589–619.

Malhotra, A., & Elnakib, S. (2021). 20 years of the evidence base on what works to prevent child marriage: A systematic review. *Journal of Adolescent Health, 68*(5), 847–862.

Malhotra, A., Warner, A., McGonagle, A., & Lee-Rife, S. (2011). *Solutions to end child marriage: What the evidence shows.* International Center for Research on Women. Retrieved January 20, 2025, from www.icrw.org/publications/solutions-to-end-child-marriage/

Maswikwa, B., Richter, L., Kaufman, J., & Nandi, A. (2015). Minimum marriage age laws and the prevalence of child marriage and adolescent birth: Evidence from sub-Saharan Africa. *International Perspectives on Sexual and Reproductive Health, 41*(2), 58–68.

Mutua, M. (2001). Savages, victims, and saviors: The metaphor of human rights. *Harvard International Law Journal, 42*(1), 201–245.

Mwambene, L. (2010). Marriage under African customary law in the face of the Bill of Rights and international human rights standards in Malawi. *African Human Rights Law Journal, 10*(1), 78–104.

Okyere, S. (2014). Children's participation in prohibited work in Ghana and its implications for the Convention on the Rights of the Child. In A. Twum-Danso Imoh &

N. Ansell (eds.) *Children's lives in an era of children's rights: The progress of the Convention on the Rights of the Child in Africa* (pp. 92–104). Routledge.

Omoike, E. (2014). In the best interests of the child: The case of child domestic workers in Ghana and Nigeria. In A. Twum-Danso Imoh & N. Ansell (eds.) *Children's lives in an era of children's rights: The progress of the Convention on the Rights of the Child in Africa* (pp. 123–138). Routledge.

Psaki, S. R., Melnikas, A. J., Haque, E., Saul, G., Misunas, C., Patel, S. K., Ngo, T., & Amin, S. (2021). What are the drivers of child marriage? A conceptual framework to guide policies and programs. *The Diversity and Complexity of Child Marriage, 69*(6, Supplement), S13–S22.

Shetty, S. (2018). *Decolonising human rights.* Speech Delivered at the London School of Economics on 22 May 2018, https://www.amnesty.org/en/latest/news/2018/05/decolonizing-human-rights-salil-shetty/

Stark, L. (2018). Early marriage and cultural constructions of adulthood in two slums in Dar es Salaam. *Culture, Health & Sexuality, 20*(8), 888–901.

Steinhaus, M., Hinson, L., Rizzo, A. T., & Gregowski, A. (2019). Measuring social norms related to child marriage among adult decision-makers of young girls in Phalombe and Thyolo, Malawi. *Journal of Adolescent Health, 64*(4, Supplement), S37–S44.

Tibebu, Y., Zeleke, M., & Vandenhole, W. (2023). Socio-cultural and religious framings on marriageable age in Amhara Regional State. *Ethiopian Journal of Human Rights, 7*(1), 94–121.

Ulrich, G. (2017). Research ethics for human rights researchers. In B. A. Andreassen, H.-O. Sano & S. McInerney-Lankford (eds.) *Research methods in human rights: A handbook* (pp. 192–221). Edward Elgar.

UNFPA & UNICEF. (2020). *Child marriage and the law: Technical note for the global programme to end child marriage.* Retrieved January 20, 2025, from www.unicef.org/media/86311/file/Child-marriage-the-law-2020.pdf

UNICEF. (2008). *Child marriage and the law: Legislative reform initiative paper series.*

UNICEF. (2023). *Is an end to child marriage within reach? Latest trends and future prospects.* Retrieved January 20, 2025, from https://data.unicef.org/resources/is-an-end-to-child-marriage-within-reach/

Vandenhole, W. (2019). Children's rights and sustainable development from a "law and development" perspective. In C. Fenton-Glynn (ed.) *Children's rights and sustainable development. interpreting the UNCRC for future generations* (pp. 12–30). Cambridge University Press.

Vandenhole, W. (2020). Decolonising children's rights: Of vernacularisation and interdisciplinarity. In R. Budde & U. Markowska-Manista (eds.) *Childhood and children's rights between research and activism: Honouring the work of Manfred Liebel* (pp. 187–206). Springer.

11 Children's rights regimes and the political economy of children and childhood

A historical perspective of time in interpreting social change

Bengt Sandin

11.1 Introduction

In this chapter, I argue that we need to search for the broader historical, societal transformations that influence the rights that are ascribed to children if we are to understand children's rights in today's society. The contingent and situated character of children's rights and the negotiable, transformative, contested, and relational meaning of rights need to be analyzed with a historical perspective. A historical perspective open to the interaction between deep-rooted and slow-changing structures (*longue durées*), trends over medium-range periods, and temporally limited events makes it possible to understand how rights are configured in present day societies. Such approaches can disentangle changes that social science methodologies focused on contemporary society and current politic changes might surpass.

How societal structures influence children's rights and children's lives and shape generational orders, what and how rights are defined, and the relationship between different right holders are central to critical research on children and young people. Analyses of social, institutional, and economic systems need to focus on differences over time and space. Such analyses should ideally combine an understanding of structural changes with the lived experiences of children. The study of structure can be analytically distinguished from how the world is conceived or interpreted by children even though they are linked in political and social realms and central to understanding, for example, how the politics of children and family and generational orders have evolved.

Despite being an under-researched area in current childhood studies, society's generational order and structure (Zetterqvist, 2024; Punch, 2020; Alanen, 2020) hold immense potential. The permanence of the generational order underscores the importance of making children visible as a collective (Zetterqvist, 2024; Qvortrup, 2009) as well as the enduring nature of societal structures and diverse processes of change. Children's rights are intricately linked with institutional structures, governance systems, and specific rights regimes that define the generational order and structure the notions of rights.

DOI: 10.4324/9781003510284-12

Hence, we need to look for analytical tools to understand the linkage between children's rights and structure. This chapter argues that the notion of children's rights regimes is a helpful concept as it also incorporates dependence on a specific time and place. The Convention on the Rights of the Child (UNCRC) has been designated as a specific international children's rights regime (Pupavac, 2001; Grahn-Farley, 2024), but the concept can also be applied to how children's rights are structured on, for example, a national level. Maria Grahn-Farley discusses children's rights in Sweden and questions

> the very idea that child rights can be understood as free from the specifics of time and place, any more than they can be detached from the individual person claiming her rights. Neither can the role of the State be escaped. Place, time, and the State will continue to be the conditions upon which child rights gain their efficacy.
>
> (Grahn-Farley, 2024, p. 10)

By regimes, I refer to a complex set of beliefs and practices of a judicial and political nature that exhibit order, coherence, and persistence over time. Regimes of rights can be understood to represent norms and value structures of how the lives of children are best construed in different societies – living standards, protection, independence – thereby defining normality, family and child development. Consequently, rights also depend on the definitions of childhood as a structure shaped by gender, class, ethnicity – and age. They are intimately associated with how welfare regimes surrounding children are organized. The entanglement of law and society shapes how welfare regimes intertwine in the political economy of childhood and rights (Hassel & Palier, 2023; Jablonka, 2013; McCants, 1997). The relationships between states/governance, family, children, civil society organizations, religious institutions, and the local community embody conceptions of children's rights. While regimes express society's understanding of children's rights and reflect the processes through which they were established, regimes are, in turn, shaped by demographic, economic and social conditions, religion, political governance, professional responsibilities, and social relationships in society. Studies of regimes have a long historiography but have primarily been used to classify modern welfare systems. They are also criticized for not being sensitive to questions about gender (Esping-Andersen, 1990; Sainsbury, 1999; Foultier, 2015; Hearn et al., 2019).

In this chapter I will use regimes to understand how children's rights are constructed and changed historically as a consequence of age and generation, as the latter also are constituting aspects of regimes. Their relevance for the study of critical children's rights is dependent on their sensitivity to aspects with different temporalities: the structure of family, life course, legal traditions, the practice of law in different parts of the world, different court systems, the transformation of rights between different sectors of society, and political/institutional structures as space for the negotiation of rights. To that end, it is vital to also make a distinction between child perspectives on processes of change, and children's perspectives. Child perspectives differ from children's perspectives by emphasizing how childhood and children's rights depend on societal structure, institutional organization, and culture. By defining historical processes central to constructing children's rights regimes in the past, I contribute to understanding critical children's rights as I demonstrate how historical change evolves in different timeframes and, consequently, shapes children's rights regimes. In this way I foreground the value of historicizing understanding of rights.

I will start by discussing children's rights regimes and the link to child perspectives and different temporalities and then move on to historicized rights regimes and their relationship to differentiated understandings of historical change and children's rights. This discussion serves as a background for examples such as the significance of demography for children's and young people's rights and the consequence of the institutional location of children's rights negotiations. The following section uses the notions of governance to introduce a critical perspective on the modern study of children's rights and childhood – as a critical self-reflection. The last section provides a summary with a few concluding reflections on the necessary considerations in a critical analysis of children's rights when situating them in historical contexts.

11.2 Understanding children's rights regimes

Children's rights depend historically on developments in different institutional arenas and legal spheres, such as social work (poor law), education, criminal law, and family law. The social organizations and institutions and systems of governance in specific countries define these and situate where and how rights are defined. These are also a part of overall policies and welfare regimes targeting children nationally (Sandin, 2013, 2023). The makeup of what rights – the combination – has historically varied between different parts of the world, as children's rights regimes are entangled with economic developments that accept child labour or insist on school compulsion, for example (Hassel & Palier, 2023). Most critically, whereas rights regimes are consequential in determining the status of children, they reflect social changes that may escape the researcher if the focus is too narrowly on children. Equally important, children's rights regimes reveal how the political economy of childhood works and have limitations and consequences for children. However, the character of rights regimes varies in different parts of the world. Common societal challenges/problems are resolved in different ways because of different political and legal institutions, systems of governance, and institutions. The resulting regimes differ. They can be studied as a structure at a given instance but, most importantly, as dynamic and changing over time. Each nation/region experiences different cycles of change that form specific regimes of welfare and rights and historical dependencies. Also, critical political events can shape and influence regimes.

It is in this context that the usefulness of the distinction between the perspectives of the child as a holistic understanding of how society is structured and the child's perspective as an understanding of the voice and subjectivity of children is apparent. It also underwrites the need to see the context between the children's rights regimes and the political economy of children and childhood. Sociologist Gunnilla Halldén (2003) makes the distinction between the study of: a) a perspective of the child – the voice, agency, and interrelationship between individual children and the surrounding world; b) a child perspective – governance, regulation, policies, social and economic changes, i.e. structures that affect children and childhood as a cultural construct and the generational order, a structure of power that explicitly aims at the regulation of children's lives (cited in Zetterqvist, 2024). Often, however, societal changes do not explicitly address children or families but still have profound effects on the lives of children. For that purpose, a child perspective is needed to analyze an array of social and political changes that express the generational, gender, and class order of society, often without explicit reference to children or children's rights (Sköld, 2006, p. 40; Sandin, 2020a).

Institutional and legal developments are dependent on past institutions and are politically defined. The past; its regimes and institutions are not a homogeneous background setting to current events but a dynamic source of different legacies of law reflecting changes in different parts of society. This presumption of analytically different legacies also communicates how dependencies on historical institutions involve multiple causations that are not always (or rarely) in sync, but rather are responses to different, complementary, or conflicting historical structural changes or conflicting social changes. French scholars from the so-called Annales school such as F. Braudel distinguish between *la longue durée*, *la conjoncture*, and *les événements* in historical changes (Lee, 2013; Braudel & Reynolds, 1985, p. 1901) and show how these analytical distinctions also underwrite the different temporal processes that I would like to argue shape children's rights regimes.

The different causations, the lack of sync, the contradictory trends, and the lack of a homogenous past (Capoccia & Ziblatt, 2010) interact with these phenomena operating in different temporal systems and spaces. A time-space perspective can combine an understanding of how institutions and political decisions depend on earlier decisions and different temporal logics with analyses of individual life courses (Haraven, 1982; Pred, 2019). Such applications have broad relevance. The book, *Marginalizing Europe*, by Dipesh Chakrabarty (2000) argues that postcolonial history should be viewed as a conflict driven by social changes operating at different chronologies that are not cast in a linear Western developmental model. In turn, the French historian, Jean-François Bayart, demonstrates how an analysis of long trend changes can not only contribute to an understanding of African history (Bayart, 2009) but also illustrate the need to historicize regimes and social changes.

11.3 Historicizing children's rights regimes and different temporalities

Both the Global North and the Global South are defined by the differences among nations, regions, and cultures. The histories involved – of nation-building, of the family and children, of institutions of care and schooling, of work, of international cooperation, of imperialism and globalization – create a complex web of experiences that shape understandings of rights that are both unique and different from that of neighbours and, yet, are a part of a shared world experience. The regulation and system of governance of children's lives within families and definitions of rights feature both in a global and regional context and, most importantly, transform when borrowed or diffused between welfare regimes in different countries (Löw, 2020).

Therefore, from a historical perspective on children's rights, it is essential to uphold the distinction between different temporalities, long, medium, and short, as well as the difference between the temporality that marks a political sphere and the social changes that make up the regimes. Children's rights regimes depend on the complex interaction with many different sectors of society with different durations – and temporalities. The *durées* are different and on different clocks. The *longue durée* involves primary forms of social relations and means of production as they are shaped by geography, climate, natural and available technology, fundamental demographic transformations, and regimes. Medium-range societal changes include the development of institutions, school systems or poor laws/welfare systems, penal systems, and the like. The key point is that changes of *durées* are not linear, coordinated between regions and cast in one developmental model in different countries, which underwrites conflicts between societies in the Global South and the developmental logics that emanate from the Global North. That observation can be applied to postcolonial societies and the nations and rights regimes in the global system. Both traditional modernization theories and Marxist understanding of the logic of historical development can be questioned on these terms (Chakrabarty, 2000). In the remainder of this chapter, I will illustrate how structural changes in different temporalities influence regimes of children's rights.

11.4 Demographic transformation, children's rights, family, state, and welfare

Family historian Tamara Haraven (1982) demonstrated how industrialization operated on a different clock to that of the families that flocked to the emerging industrial sites in the east of the United States. Family life and the family cycle were still organized around a pre-industrial scheme and an agrarian background where families worked together and recruited family members to the factory. Family time is influenced by the pre-industrial organization and expectations of children as labourers under a family and household system. The lived family life was on a different temporal scheme, not always synchronized with the large-scale factory system and defined the usage of child labour and children's rights. At the same time, notions of childhood as an overall culture were established around romantic notions of the non-working schooled child with rights to an education and middle-class children as consumers in the market (Gillis, 1996; Sparrman et al., 2012). The different trajectories were not always successfully negotiated and demonstrate that children's rights in a regime can be based on incompatible notions of rights, formal and mainstream cultural defined rights, and lived rights of children.

Analyses need also to consider that children, on the one hand, are fundamental for the reproduction of societies but not necessarily a short-term social and economic asset. They are both a burden and a reward. This dilemma has demographic roots. We may take for granted that children are, or should be, welcome; consequently, we regard situations when children are not welcome as problematic. Importance is often placed on the parent–child relationship as the fundament of society (Pollock, 1983; Stearns, 2003). I want to stress three different complicating aspects.

First, there are not many examples of societies in which women reproduced at biological maximum. Avoiding having children was common in western societies, whether it was a consequence of a culture of late marriage or deliberate arrangements to keep fertility down. Avoiding having children was central to married and unmarried individuals' life choices, while health issues also contribute to the inability to bear a child. It was a demographic system in the West that characterized many European societies and had long-term consequences for how welfare societies were construed. Welfare systems and family policies aimed at women and families needed to negotiate conflicts between ambitions to build the demographic strength of a nation and the interests of the family to carve out a decent living with children. It was a conflict that underwrote many welfare projects for children. Underpinning this was the underlying need to support population growth for economic reasons or simply to deliver soldiers to the army that defined how welfare schemes and the character of support to families and children were designed and made a part of state systems of governance (Sandin, 2013; Luiten, 2019).

Furthermore, a second aspect is that the demographic regimes in Western Europe were generally based on late marriages, and a large proportion of the population did not marry or have children. Late marriages were also a central background to Western European economic development, capital formation, and the building of an economic infrastructure (Luiten, 2019). It also had institutional consequences for the interest in orphanages, worry about infanticide, regulation of marriage and households, and inheritance law (McCants, 1997; Harrington, 2009). It was reflected in the abundance of children born out of wedlock and a rising number of single providers in urban environments already during the early modern period. These problems seriously threatened the social fabric during the ensuing industrialization and urbanization, influencing the rise of a romantic notion of childhood

(Mueller, 2021), and formed the undercurrent of the child-saving and child-study movement. Governments countered the social problems by construing families, controlling childcare, and legislating about adoptions, fostering, and rules of inheritance (Lindgren, 2021; Sköld et al., 2014; Fuchs, 1984; Harrington, 2009; McCants,1997).

A third aspect of the demography of families influences definitions of children's rights. Families formed with two able providers ran into problems when they also had to support a growing number of children. Not only could the mother no longer support the children, but the children themselves could not help as infants until they were of a more mature age, when the family was burdened with still more children. At the same time, the plight of working families made authorities worry about the physical survival of children and that they would not be able to reproduce the value structure of society. Thus, it motivated education in religious or secular matters, depending on the context as well as the banning of child labour. School legislation had to accommodate the fact that children needed to support their families and attend school. Half-day schooling and long breaks during periods when children had work became a necessity. Here, the timing of education as a 'grammar' – often a full-time system and a right to education – came into conflict with the family's needs to use of child labour and, as a result, it needed to be negotiated. The temporality of children's schooling and family production was not synchronized (Sjöberg, 1997; Sjöberg & Dahl, 1999).

In the long run, the permanent, recurrent state of deprivation in the reproduction of families naturally also gave impetus to various social welfare initiatives, spanning from economic and institutional support through orphanages or systems of fostering in all the frequent cases when family/kin network or local community support did not suffice. In the Swedish case, researchers who looked at the development of welfare provisions as the expansion of the daycare for small children also noted that it enabled single mothers and low-income couples to keep their families together. The number of children placed in foster care or orphanages declined (Nyberg, 2000; Sköld et al., 2014).

Consequently, welfare institutions supported the cohesion of nuclear families in a two-provider family system rather than, as the American scholar Popenoe (1988) argued, undermined its stability. The family policy emphasized gender equality and encouraged women to join the labour market. These political processes had to negotiate and shift the borderline and limits of state authority over the family and children's rights to social support, even if it largely limited itself to propaganda and information on the benefits of gender equity. Children's rights were also defined as individual rights protected by the government rather than rights mediated through the family (Sandin, 2023). The children's right to physical integrity replaced the parents' right to punish children physically and was combined with a statute that children's rights included not being subjected to humiliating treatment (Sandin, 2023).

These critical events signify basic long-term structures that underwrite the life of family, youth, and children when they surface as political or economic problems, remedied by children's right to quality education/daycare and leading to a redefinition of the legal relation between parents, children, and the government. These historical legacies need to be integrated into the analyses of how children's rights have transformed. My account of these processes is grounded in the Western European experience, with, as mentioned, late marriages and small families, which is not the general experience in the Global South and in parts of Eastern Europe. That very difference underwrote the policies that framed family planning initiatives during the 1970s based on a Western model as a precondition for economic growth in, for example, India (Connelly, 2008).

The contingency of the notion of children and childhood and its dependence on complex long-term societal transformations can also be illustrated by how young people's citizenship, also an aspect of children's rights, can be understood. Around the turn of the 20th century, the young unmarried in Sweden began to be described as a generation to which various social problems could be attributed. Their presence in the urban environment changed the political dynamics when the chances to emigrate diminished, but it must also be understood from a longer perspective. With the electoral reforms of 1907–1921, the voting age in Sweden was raised from 21 years to 24 for the second chamber and the municipalities and to 27 for the county councils and the first chamber. The political pressure can be seen as a long-term consequence of the demographic transition from 1819 to 1830 that had long-lasting effects and shaped the demographic and political development for at least 100 years (Sandin, 2024).

The conflicts over voting age limits are examples of how social transformation and demography conflicted with the institutional systems created by the constitutional reforms of the mid-19th century. They were a reaction to the youth cohorts under 25 years of age that were particularly noticeable from the 1890s to the early 1920s in the expanding urban environments. The expansion of democracy was thus intimately linked to measures to limit the electorate by excluding the young and unmarried from the right to vote. It meant maintaining continuity with older institutional regulations and prioritizing married and older, socially stable, and established populations. The demographic transformation set the pace of the democratic reforms. The border between adulthood and youth was shifted, and a notion of youth was established – an age between the time an individual leaves home, around 15/16 years of age, and marriage from ca 25 years of age (Sandin, 2024; Sandin & Josefsson, 2022).

11.5 Families according to the law and location of rights negotiations

The different strategies the European governments deployed to address social problems were also shaped by the different legal traditions that had evolved in Europe. Sociologist Göran Therborn (1993, p. 240) distinguishes between four 'families according to the law': the common-law family, the family under Roman law, the Germanic family, and the Nordic family. In parts of Europe dominated by Roman legal patriarchy, the authority of the household head defined children as wards of the patriarch only as long as the child did nothing criminal. The ability of the state to intervene against abusive parenting was limited, but once the state intervened, it also took over the role of the parent. Children taken care of by the state were strictly defined as wards of the state and placed in foundlings or orphanages (Fuchs, 1984). In other parts of northern Europe, children were supported by the local government, but fathers were charged with the costs for the support (McClure, 1981; Harrington, 2009). The nature of the treatment and status of such children differed and indicated variances in the commitment to the well-being of different categories of children and definitions of family. In Catholic countries, foundlings were mainly established with the ambition to hide out-of-wedlock births. In Protestant countries, orphanages often were oriented to care for older children, to discipline the emerging urban streets, or care for orphaned middle-class children, based on the premise that the parents/fathers were identified and could contribute or that inheritance could provide financing for the child's education and upkeep (Harrington, 2009). The role and character of institutions that provided help differed throughout Europe and reflected the changing institutional structures on which the governance systems were built, including secular and religious institutions (Jablonka, 2013; Kertzer, 1993; Harrington, 2009).

Let me return to the national context and emphasize the complexity of paths that involve changes to children's rights (regimes) by using the example about the banning of physical punishment in families in Sweden. The understanding of children's rights to physical integrity travelled between legal arenas in the emerging Swedish welfare state. It transformed before it landed in a discussion questioning parents' right to discipline children. Before becoming an aspect of the relationship between parents and children, it was a part of a discussion about professionals and the role of government and governance of public institutions. It shifted from a discourse about gender, class, and older children to address parents' handling of young children. It also moved from being unacceptable when dealing with upper-class children and female servants to being more centred around public schools and working-class children (Sandin, 2023).

The banning of physical punishment was driven by numerous societal changes, which were not coordinated; they influenced each other in the terms children's rights were defined and discussed. It also signified an increased sensitivity about combining family upbringing for smaller children with public childcare and women's participation in the labour force. In the final stage of this process, the enquiry on children's rights, the discourse evolved – transformed – from a discussion of physical punishment to a question of children's rights as humans on par with the rights associated with adult citizens (Sandin, 2023).

The different changes refer to separate aspects of the transformation of society. The changes in criminal law in the 1950s reflected a long trend from the early 19th century. The changes in household master and servant legislation, not finalized until the 1920s, originated in the 18th century and mirrored the collapse of the remnants of a feudal society. The debates over disciplining children in schools and welfare institutions naturally reflected the evolution of the professionalization of childcare and the modern state. In contrast, the focus on younger children from the 1950s and 1960s mirrored the advent of a medical system that started diagnosing 'battered children'. In addition, immigration policies and the ambition to influence supposedly violent or 'backward' child-rearing practices in racially minoritized population groups played an important role. They signified a reaction to transforming a relatively homogeneous society into a multicultural one (Sandin, 2023). A child perspective can make us identify such complex, contingent processes with different historical durations.

The last example deals with another fundamental difference: different arenas of negotiation in parliaments or in court systems. An instructive comparison is between rights regimes in Sweden and the US since 1945. Such a comparison demonstrates both similarities and fundamental differences. The apparent similarities relate to the development of children's rights from an initial emphasis on providing elementary social services and protection to an expansive conception of rights that stressed children's participatory rights. Asserting such a typical trajectory of change in both nations could adhere to the linear model that dominates most presentations of the development of rights in the era, particularly those based on the history of the conventions and the philosophical notions that underpin the UNCRC in most nations and events such as the periodic White House conferences on children in the US.[1] The earlier period of Child Saving and Child Study involved both liberating and disciplinary changes and precise definitions of children's rights, which also entailed a specific understanding of the nature of childhood that, in many ways, was similar in the two nations. However, at an early stage, the understanding of the role of child-saving organizations, civil society, and government differed (Lindenmeyer & Sandin, 2008; Sandin, 2013), which had consequences for the following developments.

The most consequential site for such negotiations of children's rights in Sweden was Parliament and the commissions/enquiries it authorized. In the case of the US, courts were the most critical sites for negotiating children's rights. The role of civil society organizations was not straightforward but was less important in the Swedish welfare state and more critical in the US (Lindenmeyer & Sandin, 2008; Löw, 2020). In the court proceedings and the development of legal practice, legally trained personnel played the most critical

1 The White House Conference on Children and Youth was a series of meetings hosted by the President of the United States of America over 60 years from 1909 to 1971 about different child welfare issues. (https://en.wikipedia.org/wiki/White_House_Conference_on_Children_and_Youth, retrieved 15 January 2025.

role in the US. In Sweden, on the other hand, in enquiries and commissions, as well as in public and parliamentary discussions, a wide array of actors appeared including psychologists, authors, and social workers (Lindenmeyer & Sandin, 2008; Schmidt, 2010; Sandin, 2023). Similar concerns about children and rights claims can be identified in both cases, but different professionals and political establishments negotiated these and came to varying conclusions. The definition and application of children's rights in relationship to the rights of parents and the distinctions between the rights of children and rights of adults, and the role of the government differ significantly, as a consequence.

Also important is that the trajectory of the process in the US had the potential to change or reverse the definition of rights, while in Sweden, the foundation in parliamentary decisions and consequent establishments of administrative routines, government regulations, and ombudsmen were resistant to change once established. In the US, there has been a significant rollback of children's rights after an initially advanced position (Grossberg, 2012), while in Sweden, no such tendencies are noticeable except in the context of the current discussions about underage criminals in the Swedish parliament and changing legal procedures (Motion, 2013/14; ju 417, Riksdagen.se[2]).

The negotiating sites are significant in determining the fundamental character of specific rights and their continuing saliency or decline. A closer look also reveals that definitions of rights expressions as 'the best interests of the child' differ, as studies have demonstrated in migration courts cases and related legal processes (Josefsson, 2016). These cases also illustrate how varying and sometimes vague notions of children's rights were established as instruments for governing society (Holtzscheiter et al., 2019). In that process, the establishment of research on children's rights also played a role, as the following section demonstrates.

11.6 Governing welfare society and child research

An important example is the establishment of research centres that focus on children at universities. In Scandinavia, Norway and Sweden were the first to establish academic multidisciplinary research centres focusing on children during the 1980s. In the Swedish case, the research programme was explicit that research must focus on both a child perspective and a perspective of children. The programme was expected not to take the perspective of professionals, adults, or institutions but the perspective of children and the broader social changes. Hence, it also involved historical studies (Sandin et al., 2025). One background is the interest in exploring a novel field emerging around the discussion of children's rights and the opinions building towards a new convention on children's rights. Sweden had just a few years earlier banned physical punishment in families, which marked the conclusion of over a century

2 A proposal to the parliament to change the law of criminal responsibility for minors.

of discussions (see section 5 previously). It was a way of clarifying children's rights, perspectives, and voices.

However, it was also a part of the transformation of the welfare system and the establishment of a new regime of children's rights (Sandin, 2023). There was a striking need for knowledge about children's outlook and culture, it was argued, to support an institutional change in the educational system, social work, and family law, which also manifested itself in new policies on parent education, divorce legislation, and children's cultural expressions (Littmarck et al., 2018; Sandin, 2023). The role of child studies scholarship is to serve both the voice of children and contribute to a system that controls and regulates children and, at the same time, aims for the emancipation of children. That is a multilayered legacy that a critical children's rights scholar must take to heart.

11.7 Conclusion – historicizing children's rights

This chapter has argued that the conflict between the different temporality of long and short processes of change leads to the redefinition of regimes of rights, rights claims, and childhoods. The interaction between national, regional, and international transformations has been contradictory and conflict-ridden. It is not a homogeneous historical process. Analyzing long and medium structures and changes that do not directly address children/young people but shape the politics and economy that affect children give us tools to better understand the role of children's rights in society. We cannot limit our interest to children's rights in legal terms or the present. The study of rights must be set in a historical context with a sensitivity to the construction of historically defined welfare – and children's rights – regimes.

The first important aspect is that children's rights do not operate in a vacuum. Specific rights for children are not always expressed in legal terms. We must look for other concepts – control and surveillance, for example, and the transformation of the meaning of concepts between nations or societal and legal realms – as well as mundane popular culture notions of children's needs and interests. Legal rights cannot be understood independently from, for example, mundane types of expression of children's rights and clusters of right and 'right looking' expressions in discourses such as 'best interests', 'needs', and 'interests' that motivate welfare provisions or schooling and family support. Furthermore, rights to, for example, an education were historically influenced by rights definitions that originated as part of the expansion of health care or family support (Sandin, 2023).

A second point is, therefore, that rights are relational to notions of compulsion and obligations. The right to education was linked to education as a compulsion. Historically, such rights emerged locally from an interest to control families and children or the lower classes. Later, or partly in parallel, it was integrated into a national rights discourse. Such legacies have a bearing on current rights discourses and applications but are often not made explicit – but, instead, mobilized when children deviate from established social norms, or are put at risk (Sandin, 2020b; Paglayan, 2024).

The third point is that children's rights in different regimes transform in relation to the rights of other rights holders as they are ingrained in the notions of parental authority and what obligations are incumbent on the state and governments. Parents or governments can lose rights when children gain rights or when rights are transformed. Parents' rights and obligation to discipline children are questioned when children gain a right to physical integrity and can be replaced with other obligations to, for example, participate in parental educational activities and an expansion of government rights to intervene in families for the protection of children (Sandin, 2023; Littmarck et al., 2018).

The fourth point is that the governance of children and families is double-edged and provides regulation, control, and support (Holtzscheiter et al., 2019). This is the nature of welfare society. Rights are also used to govern and control children. The evolution of rights for children also makes them visible and governable subjects, evaluated as objects of research, and, as a consequence, available for social administration and governance. Children's rights come with a price – visibility and control.

References

Alanen, L. (2020). Generational order: Troubles with a "travelling concept". *Children's Geographies*, *18*(2), 141–143.

Bayart, J. (2009). *The state in Africa: The politics of the belly* (2nd ed.). Polity.

Braudel, F., & Reynolds, S. (1985). *The structures of everyday life: The limits of the possible.* Fontana.

Capoccia, G., & Ziblatt, D. (2010). The historical turn in democratization studies: A new research agenda for Europe and beyond. *Comparative Political Studies*, *43*(8–9), 931–968.

Chakrabarty, D. (2000). *Provincializing Europe: Postcolonial thought and historical difference.* Princeton University Press.

Connelly, M. (2008). *Fatal misconception: The struggle to control world population.* The Belknap Press of Harvard University Press.

Esping-Andersen, G. (1990). *The three worlds of welfare capitalism.* Polity.

Foultier, C. (2015). Regimes *of hospitality urban citizenship between participation and securitization – the case of the multiethnic French banlieue.* Linköpings Universitet.

Fuchs, R. G. (1984). *Abandoned children: Foundlings and child welfare in nineteenth-century France.* State University of New York Press.

Gillis, J. (1996). Making time for family: The invention of family time(s) and the reinvention of family history. *Journal of Family History*, *21*(1), 4–21.

Grahn-Farley, M. (2024). *Child rights, legal theory and social advocacy.* Cambridge University Press.

Grossberg, M. (2012). Liberation and caretaking: Fighting over children's rights in postwar America. In P. Fass & M. Grossberg (eds.) *Reinventing childhood after World War II* (pp. 19–37). University of Pennsylvania Press.

Halldén, G. (2003). Barnperspektiv som ideologiskt och/eller metodologiskt begrepp. *Pedagogisk forskning i Sverige*, *8*(1/2), 12–23.

Haraven, T. K. (1982). *Family time and industrial time: The relationship between the family and work in a New England industrial community.* Cambridge University Press.

Harrington, J. F. (2009). *The unwanted child: The fate of foundlings, orphans, and juvenile criminals in early modern Germany*. University of Chicago Press.
Hassel, A., & Palier, B. (2023). Same trend, different paths: Growth and welfare regimes across time and space. *Annual Review of Political Science, 26*, 347–368.
Hearn, J., Humbert, A. L., Strid, S., Balkmar, D., & Delaunay, M. (2019). *Lost in translation. The connections and disjunctions between welfare regimes, gender regimes and violence regimes*. Paper presented at Gender Regimes Workshop, City University, Helsinki, Finland, 7 June 2019.
Holtzscheiter, A., Josefsson, J., & Sandin, B. (2019). Child rights governance: An introduction. *Childhood, 26*(3), 271–288.
Jablonka, I. (2013). Social welfare in the Western world and the rights of children. In P. S. Fass (ed.) *The Routledge history of childhood in the Western world* (pp. 80–99). Routledge.
Josefsson, J. (2016). *Children at the borders*. Linköping University Press.
Kertzer, D. I. (1993). Sacrificed for honor: Italian infant abandonment and the politics of reproductive control. Beacon Press.
Lee, R. (2013). *Fernand Braudel, the longue duree, and world systems analysis*. State University of New York Press.
Lindenmeyer, K., & Sandin, B. (2008). National citizenship and early politics shaping "the century of the child" in Sweden and the United States. *Journal of the History of Childhood and Youth, 1*(Winter 2008), 50–62.
Lindgren, C. (2021). Changing notions of "good parents" and "the child's best interest": Adoption in Sweden 1918–2018. *Annales de Démographie Historique, 142*(2), 51–80.
Littmarck, S., Lind, J., & Sandin, B. (2018). Negotiating parenting support: Welfare politics in Sweden between the 1960s and the 2000s. *Social Policy and Society, 17*(3), 491–502.
Löw, J. (2020). *Världen, Sverige och barnen: internationell påverkan på svensk barnpolitik under välfärdsstatens framväxt i mellankrigstidens tidevarv*. Linköpings universitet.
Luiten, J. (2019). *The patterns behind change: Origins and features of the European marriage pattern. Capital women: The European marriage pattern, female empowerment and economic development in Western Europe 1300–1800* (online ed.). Oxford Academic.
McCants, A. E. C. (1997). *Civic charity in a golden age: Orphan care in early modern Amsterdam*. University of Illinois Press.
McClure, R. K. (1981). Coram's children: The London foundling hospital in the eighteenth century. Yale U.P.
Motion 2013/14; ju 417. Kenth Ekeroth (SD). Sänkt straffmyndighetsålder. Swedish parliamentary records. Retrieved January 3, 2025, from www.riksdagen.se/en/
Mueller, A. (2021). Mozart and the mediation of childhood. The University of Chicago Press.
Nyberg, A. (2000). From foster mothers to child care centers: A history of working mothers and child care in Sweden. *Feminist Economics, 6*(1), 5–20.
Paglayan, A. (2024). *Raised to obey, the rise and spread of mass education*. Princeton University Press.
Pollock, L. A. (1983). *Forgotten children: Parent-child relations from 1500 to 1900*. Cambridge University Press.
Popenoe, D. (1988). *Disturbing the nest: Family change and decline in modern societies*. Aldine de Gruyter.
Pred, A. (2019). *Making histories and constructing human geographies: The local transformation of practice, power relations, and consciousness*. Routledge.
Punch, S. (2020). Why have generational orderings been marginalized in the social sciences including childhood studies? *Children's Geographies, 18*(2), 128–140.

Pupavac, V. (2001). Misanthropy without borders: The international children's rights regime. *Disasters*, *25*(2), 95–112.
Qvortrup, J. (2009). Childhood as a structural form. In J. Qvortrup, W. A. Corsaro & M.-S. Honig (eds.) *The Palgrave handbook of childhood studies* (pp. 21–33). Palgrave Macmillan.
Sainsbury, D. (1999). *Gender and welfare state regimes.* Oxford University Press.
Sandin, B. (2013). The history of children's well-being in the West. In A. Ben-Arieh, F. Casas, I. Frones & J. Korbin (eds.) *Handbook of child well-being: Theories, methods and policies in global perspective.* Springer.
Sandin, B. (2020a). History of children and childhood – being and becoming, dependent and independent, Exchange. *The American Historical Review*, *125*(4), 1306–1316.
Sandin, B. (2020b). *Schooling and state formation in early modern Sweden.* Palgrave Macmillan.
Sandin, B. (2023). Recognizing children's rights: From child protection to children's human rights: The 1979 Swedish ban on corporal punishment in perspective. In B. Sandin, J. Josefsson, K. Hanson & S. Balagopalan (eds.) *The politics of children's rights and representation* (pp. 31–58). Palgrave Macmillan.
Sandin, B. (2024). *Politikens åldersgränser: rösträtt och valbarhet i Sverige från 1840-tal till 1920-tal.* Makadam förlag.
Sandin, B., & Josefsson, J. (2022). Age as a yardstick for political citizenship: Voting age and eligibility age in Sweden during the twentieth century. *Continuity and Change*, *37*, 257–280.
Sandin, B., Sjöberg, J., & Sköld, J. (2025). Tvärvetenskap och barnperspektiv: Tema Barns uppstart vid Linköpings universitet. In. J. Larsson & E. Hellström (eds.) *The history of education in the Nordics* (in press). Westberg.
Schmidt, J. D. (2010). *Industrial violence and the legal origins of child labor.* Cambridge University Press.
Sjöberg, M. (1997). Working rural children: Herding, child labour and childhood in the Swedish rural environment 1850–1950. In N. de Coninck-Smith, B. Sandin & E. Schrumpf (eds.) *Industrious children: Work and childhood in the Nordic countries 1850–1990.* Odense University Press.
Sjöberg, M., & Dahl, T. (1999). Sommarlovets historia och framtid. *Tvärsnitt*, *1999*(2), 48–61.
Sköld, J. (2006). *Fosterbarnsindustri eller människokärlek: barn, familjer och utackorderingsbyrån i Stockholm 1890–1925.* Stockholms universitet.
Sköld, J., Söderlind, I., & Bergman, A.-S. (2014). *Fosterbarn i tid och rum: lokal och regional variation i svensk fosterbarnsvård ca 1850–2000.* Carlsson.
Sparrman, A., Sandin, B., & Sjöberg, J. (2012). *Situating child consumption: Rethinking values and notions of children, childhood and consumption.* Nordic Academic Press.
Stearns, P. N. (2003). *Anxious parents: A history of modern child-rearing in America.* New York University Press.
Therborn, G. (1993). Politics of childhood. In G. Therborn & F. G. Castles (eds.) *Families of nations: Pattern of public policy in Western democracies.* Dartmouth.
Zetterqvist Nelson, K. (2024). Anmält saknat! Ett strukturellt perspektiv på barndom (essä). *Barn*, *42*(2), 1–9.

12 The hidden histories of children's rights

Basia Vucic

12.1 Introduction

The United Nations Convention on the Rights of the Child (UNCRC) is a groundbreaking agreement in human rights history for defining the child as an autonomous person from birth (Łopatka, 1999). The Polish Chair of the UNCRC Drafting Committee, Adam Łopatka, fought for everyone's entitlement to citizenship regardless of age. He outlined categories of political, economic, social, and personal rights, different from the delineation of children's rights into protection, provision, and participation that are commonly used now (Balcerek, 1986). Although he featured prominently during the decade-long UNCRC debate before ratification, few accounts incorporate his views. Poland's pivotal role in advancing children's rights remains overlooked despite its status as the UNCRC's original proponent.

Today, Poland appears as an economic powerhouse of the European Union, but at the time of the UNCRC's drafting, Cold War geopolitics defined global divisions. As with other communist states, Western powers viewed Poland with scepticism and suspicion, often dismissing Eastern European innovation (Arat, 2009). Meanwhile, Poland sought to demonstrate itself as a trustworthy player within the human rights sphere and that there 'did not have to be a monopoly of Western States' (Łopatka, 2007, p. xxxviii). Indeed, the Polish delegation expected hostility from the mighty West but presumed support would come from 'developing countries' (Łopatka, 2007, p. xxxviii).

The superpowers were generally opposed to including human rights within the UN mandate, citing various reasons for their resistance related to losing power. The British feared colonial independence movements, and the new Soviet Union saw the potential for foreign interference (Łopatka, 2007). Such anti-rights sentiments represent future concerns and imperial histories where, at various historical moments, non-state actors had seized human rights as political and ethical weapons of disruption and revolutionary action.

Perhaps the Polish purpose emanates from its revolutionary motto, *za naszą i waszą wolność* [for our freedom and yours], to emphasize solidarity with emerging democracies and challenge Western states' monopoly on human rights discourse. The Polish people endured centuries of domination under

DOI: 10.4324/9781003510284-13

the Russian, Prussian, and Austro-Hungarian Empires. After two decades of independence following World War I (WWI), Poland was invaded by Nazi Germany and later subjected to Soviet Russian control during the communist era. Facing various oppressors and hostile states, Poland fashioned children's rights into tools for resisting authoritarianism and fostering democratic values from the ground up.

Legal documents, such as the French Declaration on the Rights of Man, nationally bound the individual to the State. In contrast, the legal discourse around the slave trade centred upon crimes against humanity, which is explored in greater detail by Martinez (2013). This distinction is essential in understanding the divergence of historical Polish ideas on universal rights that sound unexpectedly contemporary. Contextualizing the population as bound in servitude to powerful neighbours exposes the issues of labour and property rights as central to its fight for national independence.

Polish anarcho-cooperative traditions, rooted in mutual aid and decentralized governance, further shaped its contributions to children's rights. These principles prioritized grassroots action over the reliance on centralized state mechanisms, reflecting the country's historical resistance to imperial and authoritarian rule. Failed military uprisings taught Poles to focus on cultural and social reforms, fostering resilience and self-reliance. This ethos informed Poland's advocacy for the UNCRC, which sought to empower marginalized voices and refute Kant's cosmopolitanism with a more inclusive, communitarian vision of human rights (Vucic, 2022).

For example, the 1901–1904 Września Children's Strikes exemplify Poland's use of grassroots resistance in advancing their political and social rights. In these protests, Polish schoolchildren refused to read and speak German as mandated by the German government, enduring persecution and imprisonment (Kulczycki, 1981). These strikes highlight the role of children in challenging domination and underscore Poland's broader resistance to physical and cultural subjugation. The strikes also embodied the anarchist principle that society precedes the state, illustrating how collective action at the community level can drive systemic change, even under a hostile state (Vucic, 2022).

Revealing that such events are missing in the dominant history of children's rights makes room for the concept of prefiguration as understood in Polish anarcho-cooperativism. This knowledge gap in research has been identified previously, with Liebel (2016, p. 3) coining the term *the hidden history of child rights*. However, few political players consider children's involvement instrumental in their power struggles. Prefigurative practice directs activists away from protest or disruption and towards enacting their vision of change in the present rather than some utopian future as the means of societal change to align with the end goals.

Anarchists are distinguishable from other socialists through prefigurative practice (Gordon, 2018). Prefiguration, as both a theoretical and practical framework, offers a lens through which to understand Poland's approach to children's rights. Anarchist thinkers argue that social movements must embody the values they seek to promote, creating spaces for experimentation and innovation. The Polish revolutionary, Rosa Luxemburg, reiterated that all people must take part in transforming life oppressed for centuries (Le Blanc, 2009). Maeckelbergh (2011) emphasizes the importance of prefigurative practices in movements with diverse goals, as they allow for the development of alternative political structures and processes. In the context of children's rights, prefiguration involves creating environments where children can exercise agency via serious decision-making, fostering a culture of risk-taking and mutual respect.

This introduction provides a background to the East-West[1] tension and the role of anti-state movements. Revising grand narratives within a single text is virtually impossible, so the chapter integrates the critical framework elements (see Introduction, this volume), focusing on deconstruction-construction to challenge assumptions within children's rights history. The underlying argument is that adopting a critical position to weaken the UNCRC is premature and misguided regarding its origins and relationship with democracy. The overreliance on cosmopolitanism to understand the historical context obscures how Poland's commitment to children's rights stemmed from its location and experiences of oppression and resistance as non-Western. This chapter embraces situatedness and the complexity of lived experiences by unapologetically foregrounding often-overlooked philosophical, historical, and geographical perspectives to deconstruct the existing narrative and reveal multiple hidden histories that may be applied to construct new possibilities. The alternative frameworks are informed by anarchist concepts such as prefiguration, decolonization, and ethics of care. By intersecting clearly with political theory, there is potential for broader appeal beyond children's rights scholarship. Adopting such a lens acknowledges that we traverse contested territory and must accommodate the complexity, paradoxes, and inherent conflict within rights. It is also an attempt to question one's own assumptions about children and childhood. Using anarchism as an academic endeavour may be considered innovative; however, it is also risky and isolating as it challenges beliefs about people, places, and events that we may hold as fundamental truths.

12.2 War is the father

History acknowledges the Declaration of the Rights of the Child adopted by the League of Nations in 1924 as the work of Eglantyne Jebb, the founder of the Save the Children Fund (SCF) established in London after WWI (Marshall, 1999; Milne, 2008; Save the Children, 2019). However, Balinska (1998, 2018), Taouk (2003), Mahood (2009), Baughan and Fiori (2015), Liebel (2016), and Dunstan (2018) all suggest hidden histories within this sphere of 20th century international development. The issue is further complicated

1 For further exploration of Poland as non-Western, see Wolff, L. (1994). Inventing Eastern Europe: the map of civilization on the mind of the enlightenment. Stanford University Press.

by narratives only adopting the perspectives of distant donor countries rather than those undertaking action on the ground (for examples see Foster, 1981; Patenaude, 1992, 2007; Marshall, 2008; Mahood, 2009). These scholars seem unaware of the extent and longevity of the propaganda scam to represent the Poles as victims and passive aid recipients, much like the children. This section aligns with Huijsmans (2016) who points to the emerging interest in exploring rights and childhood with a post-colonialist lens and suggests alternatives outside the dominant position.

The geopolitics of wartime required depoliticizing humanitarian action. To dissipate English concerns about saving the 'enemy', aid organizations promoted a newly constructed narrative centred on 'the innocent, pre-political child' (Baughan & Fiori, 2015, p. 130). The falsified history persists due to the success of the functional rhetoric and propaganda used to obscure 'politics and ideology as the imagined driving force of humanitarian action' (Baughan & Fiori, 2015, p. 130). Although not explicitly named in their research on the SCF, Baughan and Fiori draw conclusions related to non-state actors, radical pacifism, and universal brotherhood, concepts found in the existing political networks of revolutionary Europe.

The Polish independence struggle yields a rich and non-Western source of information on overlapping spheres of action by non-state actors. Rather than espousing peace and stability, the underpinning principle is that *conflict is creative*. This uncommon approach to children's rights mirrors what Quennerstedt et al. (2018) and colleagues advocate in relation to the drafting of the UNCRC as a historic battlefield rather than a rapid consensus. This 'connection with agitation, protest, destabilization, even violence has always been part of the human rights story', asserts Gearty (2014, p. 37) in his elaboration on the foundation of rights in society. Although scholars may quote Korczak's (2017, p. 6) motto, 'there are no children, only people', it is unusual to situate the conception of children's rights as part of the revolutionary history of human rights. Even in Polish scholarship, this absence is surprising, as Balcerek (1986) closely related the genesis of children's rights within the UNCRC as a chapter in the human rights story.

Much historical methodology relies heavily on official documentation, often leading to a centre-periphery discussion of empires and their colonies (McCulloch, 2011). Tracing the origins of internationalisms contrasted by localized actions raises contested narratives between different geographic regions. For example, the narratives of humanitarian efforts related to children are top-down, articulated from the perspective and locations of the fundraisers and the expertise of figures such as Jebb or Herbert Hoover, the head of the American Relief Administration. These accounts pay limited attention to the Polish landscape where humanitarian action occurred during wars. Published reports and speeches by crucial individuals rarely include the views and experiences of those most affected (Vucic, 2022). Thus, the aim is to highlight the collective strategies of actors operating in the Polish periphery rather than the Western centres.

Today, Poland tries to claim its place in the history of children's rights via its initiative in proposing and drafting the UNCRC. Meanwhile, scholarship increasingly acknowledges the Polish-Jewish doctor and educator, Janusz Korczak (Dr Henryk Goldszmit, 1878/9–1942), as the inspiration behind Poland proposing the UNCRC (Veerman, 1992; Hammarberg, 2009; Eichsteller, 2009; Milne, 2015: Freeman, 2015). However, the cursory credit of Korczak's influence overshadows that children's rights movements involving both adults and children existed over a century ago. Further work is needed to raise awareness of Korczak as the spokesperson for a political movement rather than a lone educator.

Poland's revolutionary traditions ensured an anarchist influence, with prefiguration emphasizing the alignment of means and ends in social change. Prefigurative practices encourage activists to embody the values they seek to promote, creating new societal structures. This approach resonates with Korczak's philosophy, the rights pioneer who viewed children as active participants in shaping their lives and societies. Korczak's orphanages exemplified prefiguration by fostering democratic and cooperative environments where children could practice self-governance and mutual aid. Korczak's writings, notably, *How to Love a Child* (1919), underscore the relationships between children and adults as crucial to a nation's history and future. He frequently referred to children's experiences of slavery, arguing that societal transformation required addressing the chains imposed on both children and adults. The central hypothesis elevates the political and socio-economic dimensions as the defining features of Poland's perspectives on children's rights.

However, historians of children's rights overlook another Polish-Jewish doctor and Korczak contemporary, Ludwik Rajchman (1881–1965), the founder of UNICEF. Emigrating to London, he achieved a meteoric rise in the public health sector (Balinska, 1998). Appointed to the League of Nations as its new medical director, Rajchman used his in-country knowledge to amplify international relief efforts. These aid programmes built local capacity for governance in undertaking and sustaining comprehensive solutions with quarantine facilities, health clinics, and orphanages. Employing a decentralized model facilitated grassroots capacity for leadership, democracy, and economic development amongst some of the world's most oppressed people. Following this success, Rajchman and Hoover revisited these earlier lessons to establish UNICEF together during World War II (WWII). Such networks surrounding Korczak and Rajchman suggest they were not solitary figures, but, instead, engaged in a Polish school of thought debating children's rights.

Recent research outlines the circumstances of war that brought foreigners and exiles to the aid of Poland, combining a fight against Bolshevism with the local goals of independence and democratic government (Vucic, 2022). Operating within quasi-private, nongovernmental organizations and networks, Hoover and Rajchman welcomed crises to broaden their mandate with unprecedented international power immune to bureaucratic delay (Horwitz, 2011). Though not explicitly articulating anarchist arguments, Borowy's

(2008) article, 'Crisis as Opportunity', explains that these mechanisms serve as a motor of human progress as emergencies force governments and the public to be more receptive to new ideas than usual. In other words, collectivist revolutionaries rely upon the anarchy created by conflict and emergency to reorganize society and seize greater power (Hoover, 1952).

The activist poet Audre Lorde (2018) famously coined the phrase 'the master's tools will never dismantle the master's house,' meaning the tools reinforce social structures and processes. However, Lorde (2021) later contradicts her original position, advocating for the use of whatever resources are available, as the master's tools allow the powerless entry into the master's house to chip away at power from within. Indeed, the Polish networks co-opted the master's tools for decades in preparation for a crisis, such as WWI, to seize their opportunity for direct action and mutual aid. Loosely affiliated cooperative institutions dedicated to medicine, education, and commerce assisted sick and starving populations, often in dangerous circumstances and isolated locations. Graeber (2011) highlighted kitchens, libraries, and clinics as key mutual aid-based institutions (cited in Kinna, 2017). These focal points enabled revolutionary networks to leverage the contributions of women and children. The distinction between securing rights in the Washroom versus the Courtroom reflects the difference between declaration and implementation. This raises questions about whether law reform can succeed without cooperation from the masses within the organizational efforts required for implementing human rights (Vucic, 2022). Of all reforms, Korczak (1907/1998, p. 65) stated that kitchens, bathrooms, and laundries were 'the brightest examples' of where thousands of women's hands worked in service to create the moral and intellectual resources for humanity. Often, trivial matters affect the weakest members of society and persist without change unless those in power afford greater importance and attention (Goodman, 1960).

Fostering the anarchist principles of 'direct action, illegalism and the rejection of hierarchy' is necessary for challenging the legitimacy of foreign and state interference in everyday life to build a new civil society (Kinna, 2017, p. 198). Before Polish independence, welfare, health, and education endured cycles of freedom and suppression by the Prussian, Russian, and Austro-Hungarian Empires, building a complex civil society with varying structures based on what Kuninski (1997, p. 241) termed 'natural communities'. The resultant networks cross-pollinated between ethnicities and political leanings to survive foreign oppression and natural disasters, even thriving to accumulate sufficient strength to emerge during war and authoritarian weakness.

During WWI, the Poles quickly transformed the model of caring for orphans, the sick, and the hungry into a broad network of spies, collaborators, and sympathizers through existing revolutionary networks. The individuals of these revolutionary circles engage 'in the politics of urgent moments' (Snyder, 2017, p. xviii). The ingenious strategies to establish kitchens, orphanages, and clinics gained influence over towns that the Peace Treaty and the Polish army had tentatively won. An apolitical façade held Poland's position across unstable and dangerous territories, while the regaining of independence introduced into such communities and civil society 'its missing dimension' of the national state (Kuninski, 1997, p. 243). This radical approach of caring for one's enemies attempted to stamp out underlying dissent, radicalism, and those undermining Polish attempts at stable democratic government. The strategy facilitated self-government by allowing local people to gain valuable experience in governance and economic management, uniting diverse communities while the battles raged.

Years of revolutionary action made it clear there was little chance of success in direct competition with the empires, so Poles had to find opportunities to establish, and exercise, weak power through cooperation. Specifically, weak power refers to the different distributions of power created by moments of change that offer the weak party alternative opportunities to leverage its position. The balance is tipped, for example, when the more powerful parties become dependent on critical resources or processes controlled by the weak, which, if maintained, boosts their power in the network or organization (Gargiulo & Ertug, 2014). Such concepts decree that conflict is creative, mirroring the anarchist view that peace reinforces the existing hierarchy and maintains oppression. The destabilization of power via crisis, violence, or scandal affords the weaker parties opportunities for action, labelled in anarchism as the societal cycle of destruction and creation.

Examining the programme to save children reveals the anarchist features of a rapid decision-making process, avoidance of restrictive organizational structures, and willingness to dissolve the hierarchies, networks, and trade unions. Suissa (2006) clarifies that anarchists do not reject all authority, explaining their resistance to authoritarianism and settings that concede the nation-state. Such definitions sit well with the Polish form of anarchism as not necessarily anti-state or anti-authority but anti-hierarchical, significantly where centralization limits personal interaction, increasing the oppression of distance. Suissa (2006, p. 62) articulates an anarchist demand that accountability rests with the 'smallest unit of social organisation'. Korczak aims to awaken this smallest social unit among children.

12.3 The little brigand

At the turn of the 20th century, children were generally absent in discussions on rights, with Poland as a notable exception (Korczak, 1919/1993). Polish perspectives, specifically emerging from medical ethics, demonstrate an awareness of the difference between goodwill towards children and their status as citizens with social rights from birth. At the outbreak of WWI, revolutionaries recognized the opportunity of seizing rights during the conflict rather than solely declaring them from above. Various local and foreign organizations employed tactics to convince the West to care about the plight of children in Central Europe and secure financial and political support. The negative perception of propaganda that Bernays (1928/2005) attached to the public deceit during WWI is an apt description for disguising the political agenda. Rebranding the international machinations as neutral and secular allowed SCF to effectively sidestep political hostility towards feeding so-called enemy children. However, under its guise of philanthropy, Hoover's child-feeding programme facilitated political and economic strategies geared towards the independence of democratic nation-states and the stabilization of Europe (Kellogg, 1920; Buschman, 2013). As Kuźma-Markowska (2015) outlines, the appeals capitalized upon English beliefs about women and children. The imagery of childhood innocence left a legacy abroad, but by 1917, a local Save the Children campaign had already fashioned Polish children into patriots (see Figure 12.1).

Figure 12.1 Polish 'Save the Children' poster, 1917.

Source: National Library of Poland.

The Poles pioneered such appeals to children, eventually influencing others. For example, in his role as food administrator, Hoover recruited over 40,000 American boys and girls for the relief efforts (See Figure 12.2).

Patriotic imagery surrounding children appears deeply ingrained within the Polish psyche, with *The Little Insurgent* as the most famous and

Figure 12.2 US Food Administration Poster, 1918.
Source: Wikipedia.

controversial portrayal of a child wearing a German soldier's rifle, helmet, and boots (Figure 12.3).

Most Poles today wish to keep children away from violence and war, but this forms part of their historical experience of difficult childhoods. Scholars such as Tobin (2014) criticize the vulnerability most associated with children compared to adults. There remains a false image of children as only passive and traumatized victims. Meanwhile, repeated wars fashioned various roles for Polish children and youth as brave and capable revolutionary fighters, spies, couriers, traders, and smugglers, often saving their families, communities, and the nation during uncertain times (Vucic, 2023). Thus, innocence and

Figure 12.3 Monument to *The Little Insurgent*, Warsaw Old Town.

Source: Wikipedia.

Figure 12.4 Declaration of the Rights of the Child, 1930s, Polish Committee of Child Care.

Source: National Library of Poland.

weakness are often notably absent or exaggerated in the extremes of Polish sentiments. Portrayals of the little brigands are reminiscent of the rebellious children celebrated by Korczak whose publications were often at the forefront of participatory practice. During the interwar period, other Poles followed suit as it became increasingly popular for adults to seek, and promote, children's opinions through surveys, letters to newspaper editors, interviews, and even art analysis (*Polski Komitet Opieki nad Dzieckiem*, 1928). The movement successfully reinforced an image of Polish children as citizens demanding their rights, as seen in a 1930s government poster celebrating children's rights with a parody of English suffragettes (see Figure 12.4).

12.4 The Kingdom is a game

Scholars repeatedly present Korczak as a lone actor ahead of his time, assuming his contemporaries could not understand his philosophy and practice. For example, Stambler (1980) considers Korczak's objection to corporal and coercive punishments as 'too avant-garde to develop into a major movement in his lifetime' and a better fit with current ideas on children's rights (cited in

Borodo, 2020, p. 183). This statement is incorrect, as the post-independent Polish government quickly moved towards prohibition of institutional corporal punishment in 1918, citing its incompatibility with cultural goals (Kielski, 1930). Similarly, Świdwiński (1928) celebrates the interwar Polish school as providing political, economic, secular, and democratic freedom for all citizens regardless of societal, ethnic, or religious affiliations. Before the Geneva Declaration, the *Pedagogical Review* journal featured the headline 'Reform of Discipline or Declaration of Rights', debating the efficacy of top-down declarations versus reforming relationships between adults and children (Ostrowski, 1921). Nonetheless, denying Korczak's influence on the Polish conceptions of children's rights and self-governance would be difficult.

Before establishing his orphanages, Korczak must have been thrilled with the early outcomes of promoting his theories. Being hauled before the Polish Teachers' Union in 1910 would have reinforced this celebrity doctor's view that his efforts had the desired impact. In a piece of orchestrated theatre, the Union requested Korczak's presence to defend himself against charges surfacing due to the influence of his 1908 children's story about summer camp. The publication outlined how Korczak solved many of his problems as a camp counsellor by establishing a children's court (Falkowska, 1989). The narrative stressed that he could not have managed the massive, unruly group without introducing self-governance. In less than two years, schoolchildren around Poland spontaneously organized themselves to initiate Korczak-inspired experiments (Vucic & Sękowksa, 2020).

Contrary to simultaneous experiments in other countries, children, rather than adults, initiated the action. Even more remarkable, they did so without models to copy, as such political structures did not exist or barely functioned in Polish society under Imperial rulers. Thus, Korczak's work provides a concrete example of prefigurative practice in action. His Children's Homes operated as parallel societies where vulnerable children who had committed crimes were encouraged to take responsibility for their lives and contribute to their communities. This philosophy challenges traditional hierarchical models of education and caregiving, advocating for a more collaborative and inclusive approach.

A helpful description of Korczak's endeavours is as an ethicist, where ethics studies moral and social behaviour. He declared children human and defined pedagogy as the study of humanity. Therefore, each day, he studied what it meant to be a person and how people can and should act. The Children's Republics, as Korczak's orphanages became known, undoubtedly were the most famous child-led organizations in Europe; however, others existed across the country. Regarding broader attitudes to children's participation, the newly independent Polish government frequently addressed children directly. Official campaigns urged children to form Junior Red Cross associations dedicated to securing their right to health and that of their community (PAKPD, 1922). The outcome produced examples such as a sanitorium run for, and by, children recovering from illness, entrusted with handling medical records and dispensing medication to each other.

The history of such children's institutions and movements is strongly associated with Poland's highs and lows and the development of cooperative movements generally (Babis, 2016). Indeed, the Children's Cooperative movement dates back to the 19th century and belongs to a broader trend of participatory democracy, offering an alternative to capitalism and socialism (Cwynar, 2015). For example, in 1900, *Pszczelin* (The Bees) functioned as a business school for village girls to encourage rural innovation, facilitate industrial espionage, and discourage emigration. Numerous cooperative experiments fostered an image of children from different backgrounds as capable and interdependent citizens. The cooperatives aimed to extend the economic and political sphere to every member of society, with the consumer rather than the worker viewed as the universal figure (Błesznowski, 2018). Initially, the action sought to build solidarity between the worker, peasant, and intellectual, later extending to the child.

Curtailed by having to maintain secrecy, the cooperative network finally emerged during WWI and exploded when Poland gained independence. Out of the misery of war, cooperativism touted work as the path forward for a new future that gathered strength from the bottom up to become the basis for the new world order. In this conception of cooperativism, weak members of society could challenge the economic status quo. As Taylor (1916/2017, p. 226) noted, the distinguishing feature of such associations was an adaptation to the needs of 'the economically weak social strata and is thus conducted with small amounts of capital. Therefore, its social importance lies precisely in enabling "little people" to make advantageous use of their capital, their talents, and their personal prowess'. One observer described a community centre run entirely by a committee of children, with board members as young as seven (Głuchowski, 1917). The estimates suggest that over 1 million children joined and led cooperatives during the interwar period in free Poland.

School and bank cooperatives still exist; however, the historical connections to implementing economic and political rights are hardly known, even in Poland. The Poles' motivation for engaging in such grassroots politics targeted what Rowbotham (1979) labelled as the politics of deferment, dealing with problems or processes continually postponed until after a future revolution. Beginning from the local and using knowledge-practice strategies, cooperative action meets the criteria for prefigurative politics and the possibilities of spectacular outcomes that the mundane offers (Rowbotham, 1979).

In his book, *The Child's Right to Respect*, Korczak (1929/1993, p. 452) outlines the relationship between respect, labour, and property, in writing, 'child's property – not rubbish, but beggars' possessions and instruments of labour – hopes and souvenirs'. He asks the question, even of the tiniest infant – to what extent is the concept of property linked in the child's mind with the conception of enhanced power and strength? Korczak (1919/1967) disputes whether the child asserts the self or asserts possession, differentiating between 'I' and 'Mine'. Comparing a baby holding a rattle to the primitive man with a bow, he considers neither as possessing merely property but as having instruments of labour and power. The Children's Courts promoted by Korczak require adults to treat property disputes between young children seriously. The outcomes restore or abolish faith in the rule of law; thus, imperfect authority gains or loses consent from the individuals involved. As with Polletta's (2012) description of critical pedagogy incorporating prefigurative practice, such Polish institutions valued children's expertise and authority in the micro-political arena.

Likewise, creating a new discipline, the Pedagogy of Law, could aim to democratize legal structures, processes, and language. The purpose of such educational approaches mirrors those espoused by early anarchists, serving to 'demystify power and authority' while simultaneously 'fostering autonomy' (Kinna, 2019, p. 86). Korczak (1942/1967) defined children as representing one-third of humanity, stressing they deserve not what we deliver out of kindness or sympathy but their equal rights. He doubts whether adults understand this principle of equity once applied to the economic sphere and the division of wealth, with his questioning of ecological destruction pre-empting contemporary environmental movements (Korczak, 1942/1967). Revolutionaries frequently cite Proudhon's (1876, p. 33) reconciliation of political and social equality that 'men equal in the dignity of their persons, equal before the law, ought to be equal in their conditions'. Dividing the Earth's resources amongst the children of God, this French anarchist favoured only men of intellect, while Korczak declared these to be the rights of all children. Korczak claimed children's dignity is 'a component of human dignity' and not merely preparation for the future or the sake of a happy childhood (cited in Bauman, 2003, p. 93).

12.5 Conclusion

The historical course of political struggle reveals the significance of the Polish proposal of the UNCRC as emerging from the conflict present in lived rights – a milestone within a much older human rights story. The flaw in narratives of saving the children is in relegating Eastern Europeans to the roles of soldier or victim. Similarly, academics fail to recognize how foreign cooperation with existing sociopolitical movements favoured mutual aid and economic mechanisms such as consumer cooperatives. Alongside preventing epidemics and feeding starving populations, the cooperative networks prioritized economic self-sufficiency and supported the emerging governance capacity of local populations, including women, children, and ethnic minorities. The war created anarchic conditions that facilitated influential people and civil society to change political institutions, improve material conditions, rewrite legislation, and challenge existing hierarchies. Propaganda employed the language of emergency, child welfare, and cosmopolitanism to disguise localized political action, facilitating the breakup of colonialist empires and the emergence of democratic countries.

The Poles embraced the practices of self-government featuring mutuality and autonomy to demonstrate prefigurative practice with, and by, the child-citizen. Their strategy of building a grassroots alternative amongst the weakest members of society, based upon cooperatives, sits well with the direct action of anarchism. The weakest social strata developed into a democratic force through cooperation and consumption rather than competition and production. Rather than impose democratic and judicial systems that shift power and authority into the children's hands, the children could challenge the very principles of lawmaking and governance by actively researching the flaws of practice and implementation. Children's rights can be considered as weapons in the hands of the weak in their struggle against powerful oppressors. As Korczak would say, changing how we raise our children reforms society.

Poland's historical context – centuries of oppression under empires and authoritarian regimes – shaped its unique approach to children's rights. From resisting corporal punishment to fostering self-aid and decentralization, Poland's struggles set civil society on an international rights trajectory parallel to its goals of national independence and freedom. Their strategies mirror anarchism's rejection of control via a centralized government and insistence that the people gain governance experience at a community level. The examples in this chapter capture the jurisprudence process, requiring the justification of emerging rights created through the cooperation of others, institutions, and collaboration from the wider society. Rather than rights as legal and political instruments, this emphasizes how the social process that explores the norms, values, and customs of society or a social group establishes new ways of right acting in the lived ethical sense to shape society from below. The proposed element of deconstruction and reconstruction within the critical rights framework is evident here, appearing as a more moderate form of the revolutionary cycles of destruction and creation needed to evoke change and reform society.

Revisiting this overlooked history challenges dominant Western narratives and improves our understanding of struggles for human rights and democracy against a hostile state. This chapter delivers a new, usable past to children's rights studies and practical strategies for marginalized actors, organizations, and states to seize opportunities during crises and challenging times.

References

Arat, Z. F. K. (2009). Women's rights as human rights – the promotion of human rights as a counter-culture 60 years of the Universal Declaration of Human Rights, United Nations. *Chronicle*, *45*(3), 9–13. https://doi.org/10.18356/d16204cd-en

Babis, H. (2016). Tradycje i teraźniejszość polskiej spółdzielczości uczniowskiej. [Traditions and the present day of polish student cooperatives]. In H. Babis, A. Budziewicz–Guźleckiej, A. Drab–Kurowskiej & M. Janowskiego (eds.) *Spółdzielnia Uczniowska: Praktyczna nauka postaw kooperacji i przedsiębiorczości wśród uczniów. Przewodnik.* [*Student cooperative: Practical teaching of attitudes of cooperation and entrepreneurship among students. A guide*]. Polska Fundacja Społeczeństwa Przedsiębiorczeg. www.spoldzielniauczniowska.pl/pliki/przewodnik.pdf

Balcerek, M. (1986). *Prawa dzieci* (*Children's rights*). PWN.
Balinska, M. (1998). *For the good of humanity: Ludwik Rajchman, medical statesman.* Central European University Press.
Balinska, M. (2018). Rajchman, Ludwik Witold. In B. Reinalda, K. J. Kille, & J. Eisenberg, J (eds.) *IO BIO, Biographical dictionary of Secretaries-General of International Organizations.* Institute for Management Research. Retrieved January 20, 2025, from www.ru.nl/fm/iobio
Baughan, E., & Fiori, J. (2015). Save the children, the humanitarian project, and the politics of solidarity: Reviving Dorothy Buxton's Vision. *Disasters, 39*(2), 129–145. https://doi.org/10.1111/disa.12151
Bauman, Z. (2003). Childhood of human dignity. *Dialogue and Universalism, 6,* 93–103.
Bernays, E. (1928/2005). *Propaganda.* IG Publishing.
Błesznowski, B. (2018). Utopia in the service of modernity: On the sources of cooperativism. In B. Błesznowski (ed.) *Cooperativism and democracy: Selected works of polish thinkers* (Studies in Critical Social Sciences, Vol. 111, M. Granas, Trans., pp. 1–46). Brill.
Borodo, M. (2020). *English translations of Korczak's children's fiction: A linguistic perspective.* Springer Nature.
Borowy, I. (2008). Crisis as opportunity: International health work during the economic depression. *Dynamis, 28,* 29–51. http://scielo.isciii.es/scielo.php?script=sci_arttext&pid=S0211-95362008000100002
Buschman, N. O. (2013). *The United States Food Administration during world war I: The rise of activist government through food control during mobilization for total war.* Unpublished Master's thesis, Auburn University. Retrieved January 20, 2025, from http://hdl.handle.net/10415/3861
Cwynar, K. M. (2015). Kooperatyzm Edwarda Abramowskiego wobec liberalizmu i socjalizmu. [A comparative of the cooperatism of Edward Abramowski with liberalism and socialism.] *Filo-Sofija, 15*(29), 239–257.
Dunstan, P. (2018). *Campaigning for life: A biography of Dorothy Frances Buxton.* The Lutterworth Press.
Eichsteller, G. (2009). Janusz Korczak – his legacy and its relevance for children's rights today. *The International Journal of Children's Rights, 17*(3), 377–391.
Falkowska, M. (1989). *Kalendarz życia, działalności i twórczości Janusza Korczaka* [*A calendar of life, activities and works of Janusz Korczak*]. Nasza Księgarnia.
Foster, G. (1981). Typhus disaster in the wake of war: The American-Polish relief expedition, 1919–1920. *Bulletin of the History of Medicine, 55*(2), 221–232.
Freeman, M. (2015). A guide to resources. *The International Journal of Children's Rights, 23*(1), 241–242.
Gargiulo, M., & Ertug, G. (2014). The power of the weak. In A. Mehra, D. Brass, D. Halgin, G. Labianca & S. P. Borgatti (eds.) *Contemporary perspectives on organizational social networks* (Research in the Sociology of Organizations, Vol. 40, pp. 179–198). Emerald Group Publishing Limited. https://doi.org/10.1108/S0733-558X(2014)0000040009
Gearty, C. (2014). Human rights: The necessary quest for foundations. In C. Douzinas & C. Gearty (eds.) *The meanings of rights: The philosophy and social theory of human rights* (pp. 21–39). Cambridge University Press.
Głuchowski, B. (1917). *Zakładamy i popierajmy kooperatywy szkolne: do nauczycieli i rodziców.* [*We are organizing and supporting school co-operatives: To teachers and parents*]. Społem: tygodnik poświęcony sprawom kooperacji. No. 8/9, 274–279. https://polona.pl/item/spolem-tygodnik-poswiecony-sprawom-kooperacji-r-10-nr-8-9-20-wrzesnia-1917,NTYzMzU2Mzc/41/#info:metadata
Goodman, P. (1960). *Communitas means of livelihood and ways of life.* Random House.

Gordon, U. (2018). Prefigurative politics between ethical practice and absent promise. *Political Studies, 66*(2), 521–537.
Graeber, D. (2011). Consumption. *Current Anthropology, 52*(4), 489–511.
Hammarberg, T. (2009). Korczak: Our teacher on the rights of the child. In Council of Europe (ed.) *Janusz Korczak; the child's right to respect (Janusz Korczak's legacy – lectures on today's challenges for children)* (pp. 5–8). Council of Europe.
Hoover, H. (1952). *The memoirs of Herbert Hoover: The great depression 1929–1941.* Macmillan.
Horwitz, S. (2011). *Herbert Hoover: Father of the new deal.* Cato Institute Briefing Papers, No. 122. Retrieved January 20, 2025, from www.cato.org/publications/briefing-paper/herbert-hoover-father-new-deal
Huijsmans, R. (2016). Decentring the history of the idea of children's rights. *The International Journal of Children's Rights, 24*(4), 924–929. https://doi.org/10.1163/15718182-02404011
Kellogg, V. (1920). *Herbert Hoover: The man and his work.* D. Appleton & Company.
Kielski, A. (1930). *O istocie i granicach demokracji* [*About the essence and limits of democracy*]. Zakład Graf. Pracow.
Kinna, R. (2017). Utopianism and prefiguration. In S. D. Chrostowska & J. D. Ingram (eds.) *Political uses of utopia: New Marxist, anarchist, and radical democratic perspectives* (Vol. 26, pp. 198–216) Columbia University Press. https://hdl.handle.net/2134/19278
Kinna, R. (2019). *The government of no-one: The theory and practice of anarchism.* Penguin UK.
Korczak, J. (1907/1998). Szkoła życia [School of life], przegląd społeczny. In A. Lewin, H. Kirchner, S. Wołoszyn & M. Ciesielska (eds.) *Janusz Korczak – Szkoła życia; Obrazki szpitalne: Artykuły pedagogiczne i medyczne (1900–1912)* (Vol. 4, pp. 7–14). Oficyna Wydawnicza Latona.
Korczak, J. (1919/1993). *Jak kochać dziecko – Dziecko w rodzinie* (how to love a child – a child in the family). In A. Lewin, H. Kirchner, S. Wołoszyn & M. Ciesielska (eds.) *Jak kochać dziecko. Momenty wychowawcze.* (Vol. 7, pp. 8–136). Oficyna Wydawnicza Latona.
Korczak, J. (1924/1967). Theory and practice. (The special school). In M. Wolins (ed.) *The selected works of Janusz Korczak* (pp. 524–529). Scientific Publications Foreign Cooperation Centre.
Korczak, J. (1929/1993). Prawo dziecka do szacunku [The child's right to respect]. In A. Lewin, H. Kirchner, S. Wołoszyn & M. Ciesielska (eds.) *Jak kochać dziecko. Momenty wychowawcze D.* (Vol. 7, pp. 8–136). Oficyna Wydawnicza Latona.
Korczak, J. (1942/1967). Memoirs. In M. Wolins (ed.) *The selected works of Janusz Korczak* (pp. 569–682). Scientific Publications Foreign Cooperation Centre.
Korczak, J. (2017). *The child's right to respect.* Rzecznik Praw Dziecka.
Kulczycki, J. J. (1981). *School strikes in Prussian Poland, 1901–1907: The struggle over bilingual education.* East European Monographs.
Kuninski, M. (1997). Liberalism in Poland: What is left? *Studies in East European Thought, 49*(4), 241–257.
Kuźma-Markowska, S. (2015). Ideały polsko-amerykańskiej kobiecości: szare Samarytanki i Stowarzyszenie Młodych Chrześcijańskich Kobiet w Drugiej Rzeczpospolitej [Ideals of Polish-American femininity: Grey Samaritans and the association of young christian women in the second republic]. In L. Niewiński (ed.) *Czas wojny, czas pokoju: Stany Zjednoczone Ameryki w XX i XXI* (pp. 38–48). Napoleon V.
Le Blanc, P. (2009). Luxemburg, Rosa (1870–1919). In I. Ness (ed.) *The international encyclopedia of revolution and protest: 1500 to the present* (pp. 2142–2148). Wiley-Blackwell.
Liebel, M. (2016). The Moscow declaration on the rights of the child (1918): A contribution from the hidden history of children's rights. *The International Journal of Children's Rights, 24*(1), 3–28.

Łopatka, A. (1999). *Konwencja Praw Dziecka w Polsce* [*The convention of the rights of the child in Poland*]. In J. Bińczycka (ed.) Prawa dziecka: deklaracje i rzeczywistość (Child Rights: The Declaration and the Reality). Materials from the Conference Held in Rembertów 19–21 June 1996. Impuls, Kraków, 4–25.

Łopatka, A. (2007). Introduction by Adam Łopatka, chairman/rapporteur of the working group on a draft convention on the rights of the child. In UN. Office of the High Commissioner for Human Rights and Rädda Barnen (eds.) *Legislative history of the convention on the rights of the child* (Vol. 1, pp. xxvii–xliii). UN Office of the High Commissioner for Human Rights.

Lorde, A. (2018). *The master's tools will never dismantle the master's house*. Penguin Books Limited.

Lorde, A. (2021). *Age, race, class, and sex: Women redefining difference* (pp. 191–198). Routledge.

Maeckelbergh, M. (2011). Doing is believing: Prefiguration as strategic practice in the Alterglobalization Movement. *Social Movement Studies*, *10*(1), 1–20, https://doi.org/10.1080/14742837.2011.545223

Mahood, L. (2009). *Feminism and voluntary action: Eglantyne Jebb and save the children, 1876–1928*. Palgrave Macmillan.

Marshall, D. (1999). The construction of children as an object of international relations: The declaration of children's rights and the child welfare committee of League of Nations, 1900–1924. *International Journal of Child Rights*, *7*(2), 103–148.

Marshall, D. (2008). Children's rights and children's action in international relief and domestic welfare: The work of Herbert Hoover between 1914 & 1950. *Journal of the History of Childhood and Youth*, *1*(3), 351–388. https://doi.org/10.1353/hcy.0.0019

Martinez, J. S. (2013). The anti-slavery movement and the rise of international non-governmental organizations. In D. Shelton (ed.) *The Oxford handbook of international human rights law*. Oxford University Press.

McCulloch, G. (2011). *The struggle for the history of education*. Taylor & Francis.

Milne, B. (2008). From chattels to citizens? Eighty years of Eglantyne Jebb's legacy to children and beyond. In A. Invernizzi & J. Williams. (eds/) *Children and citizenship* (pp. 44–54). SAGE Publications.

Milne, B. (2015). *Rights of the child: 25 Years after the adoption of the UN convention*. Springer International Publishing.

Ostrowski, B. (1921). Reform of discipline or declaration of rights. *Przegląd Pedagogiczny. Organ Towarzystwa Nauczycieli Szkół Średnich i Wyższych*, *40*(6–7), 165–168.

PAKPD. (1922). *Do dzieci polski* [*To polish children*]. PAKPD.

Patenaude, B. M. (1992). Herbert Hoover's brush with Bolshevism. *Occasional Paper Series No. 248*. Woodrow Wilson Center, Kennan Institute for Advanced Russian Studies. Retrieved January 20, 2025, from www.wilsoncenter.org/publication/herbert-hoovers-brush-bolshevism-1992

Patenaude, B. M. (2007). Food as a weapon. *Hoover Digest*, 1. Retrieved January 20, 2025, from www.hoover.org/research/food-weapon

Polletta, F. (2012). *Freedom is an endless meeting: Democracy in American social movements*. University of Chicago Press.

Polski Komitet Opieki nad Dzieckiem. (1928). *'Deklaracja praw dziecka' w twórczości dziecięcej*. Polski Komitet Opieki nad Dzieckiem – State Publishing.

Proudhon, P. J. (1876). *What is property?* (Vol. 1). BR Tucker.

Quennerstedt, A., Robinson, C., & I'Anson, J. (2018). The UNCRC: The voice of global consensus on children's rights? *Nordic Journal of Human Rights*, *36*(1), 38–54.

Rowbotham, S. (1979). The women's movement and organising for socialism. In S. Rowbotham, L. Segal & H. Wainwright (eds.) *Beyond the fragments: Feminism and the making of socialism* (pp. 21–155). Merlin.

Save the Children. (2019). *Our history*. Retrieved May 1, 2019, from www.savethechildren.org.uk/about-us/our-history
Snyder, T. (2017). *Nationalism, Marxism, and modern central Europe: A biography of Kazimierz Kelles-Krauz, 1872–1905*. Oxford University Press.
Stambler, M. (1980). Janusz Korczak: His perspectives on the child. *The Polish Review*, *25*(1), 3–33.
Suissa, J. (2006). *Anarchism and education: A philosophical perspective*. Taylor & Francis.
Świdwiński. (1928). Z zagadnień wychowawczych szkolnictwa [On the educational issues of schooling]. In *1921 Rocznik Pedagogiczny* (pp. 136–149). Dickenstiena.
Taouk, Y. (2003). *The Roman catholic church in Britain during the first world war: A study in political leadership*. The University of Western Sydney.
Taylor, E. (1916/2017). The concept of cooperativism: Cooperativism as the organization of relatively weak economic elements. In B. Błesznowski (ed.) *Cooperativism and democracy: Selected works of polish thinkers* (pp. 226–232). Brill.
Tobin, J. (2014). Justifying children's rights. In M. Freeman (ed.) *The future of children's rights* (pp. 258–304). Brill Nijhoff.
Veerman, P. (1992). *The rights of the child and changing image of childhood*. Martinus Nijhoff Publishers.
Vucic, B. (2022). *(R)evolutionary rights and hidden histories: A new reading of Janusz Korczak*. Unpublished PhD thesis, University College London (UCL).
Vucic, B. (2023). Our home: A revolutionary case study in social pedagogy. *International Journal of Social Pedagogy*, *12*(1), 1–15.
Vucic, B., & Sękowska, Z. (2020). *Our home: Janusz Korczak's experiments in democracy*. Wyd. Akademii Pedagogiki Specjalnej.
Wolff, L. (1994). *Inventing Eastern Europe: The map of civilization on the mind of the Enlightenment*. Stanford University Press.

13 Historicizing rights subjectivities in postcolonial contexts

The right to education and the deregulation of child labour in India[1]

Sarada Balagopalan

13.1 Introduction

Contemporary logics of child rights governance not only risk reproducing the hierarchies that marked earlier governmental projects, but they also ironically serve to legitimize new exclusions within more neoliberal articulations that skillfully mobilize the futurity indexed in the child (Holzscheiter et al., 2019). Children's rights governance allows state power to renew itself through new legal guarantees, and in this chapter, I discuss the critical contribution that historicizing rights-subjectivities can make to understanding the current working out of children's rights governance as a complex, contradictory, and ahistorical sphere. To preclude a simplified reading of these new guarantees for children as always an improvement over what exists, we need to sharpen our analysis of how the differential working out of citizenship shapes the uneven working out of rights-subjectivities in postcolonial contexts. I am not making a broad-based argument focused on difference-centered theorizations of citizenship, which allow us to include the child as a citizen (Moosa-Mitha, 2005). Instead, my focus on differential citizenship is directed towards unsettling two underlying assumptions that mark the working out of children's rights governance within postcolonial contexts. First, I interrogate how the setting in place of new legal guarantees around children assumes the capacity of all citizens, including marginalized communities, to act upon these new rights. Second, with these new laws often framed as marking a fundamental difference from the past, this assumption around this capacity usually buoys the speculative realization of these guarantees. This future temporality of children's rights thereby helps mask existing structural exclusions and exploitation of these communities within a particular history of colonial and postcolonial capitalism. This differential working out of citizenship is a feature of liberal democratic governments worldwide but is particularly stark within

1 This chapter is an abridged and revised version of the following article: Balagopalan, S. (2019). Why historicize rights-subjectivities? Children's rights, compulsory schooling, and the deregulation of child labour in India. *Childhood*, *26*(3), 304–320.

DOI: 10.4324/9781003510284-14

postcolonial contexts. Drawing on the work of postcolonial scholars, I explore the differences that marked the historical emergence of citizenship in the postcolony. The chapter's central argument is that historicizing rights-subjectivities can help us critically engage with how the differential working out of citizenship in postcolonial contexts informs the rights-based claims made by subaltern children and their communities. I utilize Gayatri Spivak's (2004, p. 529) framing of the 'subaltern' to best characterize children and communities who 'are removed from lines of social mobility' and are usually 'the silent victims of pervasive rather than singular and spectacular human rights violations.' The normative framework of children's rights tends to ignore how communities are differentially positioned within national contexts to exercise their claims to legal justice and to participate fully and equally. To be recognized as a claimant implies knowledge of existing processes, namely to be a rights subject who can comply with arrangements and performances framed as legitimate within a liberal rights discourse.

Existing efforts to de-universalize children's rights have critiqued the normative assumptions that underlie these rights and argued for the need to contextualize their working out within varied cultural contexts. This focus on how subaltern communities interpret and rework children's rights in their everyday lives, as proposed by the 'living rights' framework, for example, has compellingly recalibrated the earlier, more deficit-based framings of these population's interactions with children's rights. By centering translation processes, broadly conceived, of children's rights, this framework highlights the meaning that communities make of rights as key to a broader imagination of social justice (Hanson & Nieuwenhuys, 2013). This aligns with David Engel's (2012) arguments on the need to move away from a 'vertical' perspective or that which tracks how legal forms and practices travel from 'authoritative centers' to instead incorporate a more 'horizontal' engagement focused on the more local and contextual working out of norms, practices, and beliefs. This shift in perspective to a 'bottom-up' approach is the fundamental recognition that the global circulation of children's rights discourses normalizes a particular rights-based subjectivity whose universalistic assumptions risk obscuring the multiple ways in which communities engage with rights discourses (Balagopalan, 2014; Liebel, 2012; Reynaert et al., 2012). Thus, by offering a nonhierarchichal reading of the differences that mark various subaltern communities' interpretations of rights, these frameworks compel us to ground the circulation of children's rights within the everyday working out of culture, sociality, and relationality. Within these debates, the contextualized 'child' pushes back against the dominant framing of a rights subject as an individuated, agentic actor exercising rights and is more as a member of a community whose lifeworlds inform their understanding of, and interaction with, the entitlements made available by this recent regime of children's rights (Balagopalan, 2014; Fay, 2021; Pells, 2012). However, what is surprisingly absent in these discussions is an effort to ground these everyday understandings within a more historicized framing of rights-subjectivities that engages more squarely with how the colonial past informs the uneven claim-making capacities of communities in national contexts.

The uneven working out of these liberal modalities is tied to this colonial past and the exclusions it set in place, which has shaped long-standing sociocultural hierarchies of citizenship within the postcolonial nation-state. Some aspects of the working out of children's rights in these contexts disclosing these hierarchies have been explored by scholars. They trace its travel across transnational, international, and domestic state and non-state actors and organizations to reveal how it materializes locally as an ambiguous node that aids in the increased surveillance and regulation of subaltern communities (Van Daalen et al., 2016; Viego & Manciavillano, 2014). Excellent examples of this include Olga Nieuwenhuys' (2001) pioneering ethnographic exploration of the contradictory role played by NGOs and the state in incentivizing self-exploitation as a necessary aspect of improving street children's chances of enjoying a decent childhood in Addis Ababa as well as Dana Aufseeser's (2014) critical discussion on how Peru's law to protect minors from begging served, instead, as a mechanism for increased social control.

However, this critical reading of children's rights governance as projects aimed at addressing structural issues through increased self-regulation and surveillance of subaltern communities does not adequately explore how the uneven ability of subaltern communities to act upon these new child rights claims is always already historically marked (Spivak, 2004, 1992). While subaltern communities are increasingly exposed to discourses of children's rights through their interaction with NGOs, teachers, and the state (Balagopalan, 2013; Cheney, 2007; Twum-Danso, 2013), this awareness does not necessarily enable them to substantively challenge prevailing exclusions that mark the working out of these rights.

With the majority of world governments increasingly adopting laws and policies linked to various aspects of 'provision,' 'protection,' and 'participation' as enshrined in the United Nations Convention on the Rights of the Child (UNCRC), children's rights governance risks working out as an ahistorical terrain. Put another way, governmental actions linked to children's rights allow the state to continually renew its commitment to equality and justice through new legal guarantees that draw on the speculative future of the child. This speculative future absolves the state from creating real sites and equitable structures through which these new entitlements might materialize as well as factoring in existing hierarchies and exclusions that mark the differential working out of citizenship. Instead, this ahistoricity is reflected in the myriad pedagogic efforts directed at subaltern populations to inform, teach, train, and sensitize them to the new rights their children now have in the expectation that they can now act on these entitlements. By assuming that it is only the content of these new rights or legal guarantees that need to be shared and transmitted, what these efforts miss, or rather, what the optimism of these efforts rests upon, is the assumed ability of all citizens to make these claims. This effectively produces subaltern communities within a transition narrative, as communities who are 'lagging' and are desirous of, but are as yet unable to, inhabit this universal subject-position.

To read children's rights against the grain and to better attend to the risk of its working out as a terrain of neoliberal exclusions, our scholarship needs to factor in how this sphere is always already marked by the vicissitudes of the differential working out of citizenship within Southern contexts. This becomes necessary to ensure that we do not naturalize a 'deficit' reading of subaltern communities that puts the onus on them not to act upon these abstract assurances around their children's rights. Moreover, historicizing rights subjectivities draws our attention to how the dominant children's rights regime de-historicizes subaltern communities' past struggles around gaining similar assurances. This regime thereby effectively reproduces, albeit through a new speculative language of improved futures, the earlier colonial asymmetry of ignorance that viewed these communities as 'lagging.' This flattening out of the past or the deliberate de-historicization set in place by children's rights governance also institutionalizes a general lack of accountability around policy and programmatic failures and the slow pace of existing reforms (Balagopalan, 2022).

This chapter argues that factoring in this historicization may help politicize as well as transform the terrain of children's rights in two ways: first, this historicization realigns the focus away from the newness of legal guarantees, like the right to education, that children's rights make available and, instead, serves to remind us of how long-standing socio-structural hierarchies of citizenship continue to mark the exercise of these rights. Second, through centering how the stickiness of this exclusionary past affects contemporary citizen subjectivities, this historicization impedes a simplified reading of these guarantees as always an improvement over what exists. It draws critical attention to transnational and national governance practices that continually renew the promise of progress through the futurity that the child figure embeds. This chapter does not argue against children's rights. It makes a case for why historicizing rights subjectivities is essential to ensuring greater accountability of children's rights regimes, narrowing the gap between these laws, and realizing justice for all children in the present.

The first section of this chapter discusses postcolonial theorizations around colonial and postcolonial modernity, including differences in the historical emergence of citizenship. To help situate this theorization, the next section of the chapter briefly explores the Indian postcolonial governmental apparatus and its assumptions around labouring children, including the recent, shocking deregulation of child labour seven years after all children were legally guaranteed their right to education.

13.2 De-universalizing rights-based subjectivities: postcolonial theorizations

For several decades now, postcolonial scholars have challenged the triumphant utopianism that often frames our construction of 'freedom' and 'rights' as an authoritative break from an oppressive past. By framing colonialism as having engendered a violent insertion into modernity for the majority of the world's peoples (Bhabha, 1994; Said, 1978; Spivak, 1993), they continually remind us that 'rights' discourses, practices, and institutions indelibly remain marked by that project of violence and conquest. Their tracing of the thick and continuing effects of colonialism on forms of knowledge and everyday cultural, social, psychic, and material practices in both ex-settler and non-settler colonies and the metropole compels us to acknowledge the more ambiguous working out of universal projects, as well as question the stability of meaning that usually underlies categories such as 'rights.' Their scholarship serves as a helpful reminder that universal assurances, irrespective of their efforts to incorporate previously excluded populations – such as children and their rights – are always at risk of being used to rationalize less-than-ideal ends.

Given that children worldwide do not share analogous histories, we can assume that the differences that mark their lives are very unlikely to produce all children as similar rights-bearing subjects. Postcolonial theorizations draw our attention to how children's rights discourses take liberal, rights-bearing subjectivities for granted as natural and inevitable. The normative children's rights discourse is marked by a hegemonic narrative of 'transition' within which these universal assurances are framed within a singular, linear, and predetermined trajectory. Postcolonial scholars productively disrupt this trajectory by alerting us to colonialism's continuing effects on contemporary racialized representations and the related epistemic devaluation of particular communities (Balagopalan, 2024). These effects include the differential working out of legal subjectivities in ex-colonial contexts. In decentering a historicist framing that would read this absence of liberal subjecthood as a 'lag' that reinforces the travel of 'civilizational imperatives' from the modern West to the Global South, postcolonial scholarship, instead, offers an explanation grounded in a more historicized reading of rights-subjectivities in ex-colonial contexts (Chatterjee, 2004, 1993). This historicized reading helps us critically unpack children's rights by alerting us to how postcolonial nation-states work to both invisibilize and perpetuate existing hierarchies, albeit in new ways.

In his comparative analysis of citizenship in the modern West and ex-colonies, Partha Chatterjee (2004) discusses that in the former, citizenship develops chronologically from the institution of civic rights in civil society to political rights in the nation-state. Thereby, citizenship as an ethical, normative category that implies participation in the sovereignty of the state historically precedes modern Western states securing their legitimacy through ensuring the well-being of populations. However, in former colonies, the creation of nation-states was preceded by colonial rule that produced its technologies of governmentality, which administered colonial subjects while not recognizing them as citizens (Chatterjee, 2004). Instead, the colonial state worked upon native populations through an elaborate apparatus that classified, categorized, and enumerated them as population groups for a range of purposes linked to concerns of colonial governmentality, including crime prevention and public health and hygiene (Bhattacharya, 2012; Cohn, 1996; Kupinse, 2004). In the modern West, the emergence of an apparatus of welfare provision in the 19th and 20th centuries was long after citizenship, as tied to state sovereignty, had been secured and was, instead, shaped around bourgeois social reform efforts focused on schooling, health, and employment, an apparatus that Nikolas Rose (1999, p. 126) has characterized as the 'familialization of society.'

After decolonization and with independence, India and several other ex-colonial countries adopted a democratic form of government with universal adult franchise. This meant that these national populations received the right to vote without necessarily embodying the particular citizen subjectivity that Western liberalism assumes (Chakrabarty, 2000). This absence of the hegemony of liberal norms in Global South contexts does not indicate a lack of modernity per se, but rather that modernity took a different form in the post-colony. Ranajit Guha (1998) discussed how the formation of modernity and citizenship in the colony emerged through splitting the political domain into two distinct sensibilities that get woven together continuously. While the first is the formal-legal, and secular networks of governance, which are predicated upon the sovereign subject of the citizen, the second is a different set of practices that index relationships of direct domination and subordination in which hierarchies like those of caste, ethnicity, language, and region play out in everyday lives.

Despite India's liberal Constitution with its surfeit of progressive legislation that upholds the figure of the individual citizen subject, the everyday lives of subaltern populations are rarely structured around such a figure. While the Constitution regards all citizens as members of civil society able to contractually, and thus freely, interact with each other and the organs of the state, the actual relationship between the state and these populations is built on a vastly different history of the modern (Chatterjee, 2004). As 'governed' populations, subaltern communities are engaged with, recognized, and provisioned by various governmental and nongovernmental agencies. This is the sphere of postcolonial development. This relationship does not entirely conform to the exercise of individuated rights-subjectivities as constitutionally depicted in the ideal relation between the state and members of civil society (Chatterjee, 2004). This analysis helps explain why the working out of children's rights governance in Southern contexts should be framed less as a clash between 'tradition' and 'modern/liberal' assurances. Instead, much like the earlier and continued travel of human rights and women's rights discourses, children's rights work to link, and help renew, existing entanglements between subaltern populations and the state's welfare apparatus (Dhawan, 2014).

Existing research in critical human rights studies, as well as feminist engagements with women's rights, have built upon, and reaffirmed, postcolonial interrogations of liberalism's transhistorical essence and have used these insights to be more attentive to policies that adopt an 'add women and stir' approach (Parisi, 2017). Their broad recognition that formal equality before the law also requires equality of opportunity, access to resources, and the dignity to participate as full community members instructively tie together issues of representation, recognition, and redistribution (Fraser, 2005). Their research foregrounds how rights-subjectivities are complexly mediated by the oppressive working out of intersectional hierarchies, including race, class, caste, religion, gender, region, and so on, within these national contexts. Similarly, children's rights risk reifying existing hierarchies through its ahistorical framing of rights subjectivities. In the next section, I demonstrate how this happens by discussing the Indian state's paradoxical move to deregulate child labour seven years after all children in India were legally guaranteed their right to free and compulsory education. Not only has the state failed to set up the equitable infrastructure required for subaltern children to exercise their right to mandatory elementary schooling, but it obfuscates these inequities by deploying an abstract idea of citizenship, or namely, the equal ability of all citizens to act upon their entitlements, and by so doing, it effectively shifts onto subaltern communities the responsibility of their children's labour.

13.3 Understanding the paradox of compulsory schooling and the deregulation of child labour

India's status as a rising economic powerhouse has not significantly diminished its woeful distinction as the country with the highest number of child labourers in the world (UNICEF/ILO, 2021). The phenomenal growth of the Indian economy from the late 1980s overlaps with India's ratification of the UNCRC in 1992. The country more formally adopted several legal and policy measures to implement children's rights. Of these, the 2009 Right to Education Act (RTE), which made schooling compulsory for 6 to 14 years of age, is viewed as exercising a very significant role in reducing child labour (Government of India, 2009). However, despite the phenomenal increase in enrollment figures in primary schools, the continued persistence of child labour is disconcerting, as it also raises fundamental questions about the Indian state's priorities given the assumed correlation between rapid economic growth, compulsory schooling, and the elimination of child labour.

These tensions were starkly exposed in 2016 when the Indian government approved two significant amendments to the country's child labour laws. At a superficial level, the 2016 Child Labour (Prohibition and Regulation) Amendment Act appears to be a much-needed step in the right direction, as it not only prohibits all children under 14 years of age from engaging in labour, but it also prevents all adolescents aged under 18 from undertaking labour in 'hazardous' occupations. A more careful reading, however, reveals how it permits the continuing use of the labour of children under 14 in 'family or family enterprises,' with the latter defined as any work, profession, or business in which a family member works with other persons. This legalization of the bulk of child labour is further augmented by the absence of regulation around how many hours these children should work. Instead, the amendment states that children may work 'after school hours or during vacations' (Government of India, 2016, p. 2). When read together with the amendment's drastic reduction of 'hazardous' work from 83 prohibited activities to only three, what becomes clear is that the previous ban on children's work in brick kilns, cotton farms, restaurants, and domestic work because of the specific dangers that these trades pose (Ramanathan, 2009) has now been nullified. Given that roughly 80% of child labourers in India are involved in caste-based work (including the persistence of inter-generational debt bondage) in farms, forests, and home-based assembly and that children are often employed in domestic work, eateries, street vending, and roadside garages with the consent of their families, the government's recent move to legitimize child participation in 'family enterprises' as well as minimize what counts as 'hazardous' work effectively deregulates the bulk of child labour in the country (Mander, 2016).

The Indian state's paradoxical legalization of child labour, seven years after it passed a law making schooling free and compulsory from 6 to 14 years of age, is in stark contrast to the 'civilizational' trajectory through which children's permanent separation from wage work has been achieved. This trajectory is of increased regulation of labour within the democratization of schooling. Despite the deregulation of child labour, the Indian state retains its moral legitimacy at this current moment through two main moves. First, it mobilizes phenomenal statistics around primary school enrollment to discuss the success of the new legal guarantee. These statistics help flatten out and obscure the ongoing exclusions that subaltern populations face within a highly segregated and increasingly privatized landscape of poor-quality schools. Second, the state invokes the 'duty' of subaltern parents to enroll children in schools, and then it uses this moment of legal guarantee to shift the onus of schooling onto parents. It effectively privatizes a more extended history of social and economic exclusions by invoking 'duty' as a parent's individuated, autonomous, moral-behavioural response to the new legal guarantee of free and compulsory elementary schooling. Past committees, including the Gurupadaswamy Committee on Child Labour, set up in 1979, did not automatically expand the existing apparatus of formal education to include these children.

Moreover, the first consolidated legal measure to address child labour, namely the Child Labour (Prohibition and Regulation) Act of 1986, which adopted a uniform age threshold across different sectors and banned the employment of children under 14 years of age in multiple hazardous industries, would technically have freed a large population of children to attend school (Ramanathan, 2009). Instead of working to enroll these children in schools, the central government worked to provide incentives to voluntary organizations to establish 'child labour cells.' At a time when it was widely recognized that less than half of the country's children were formally enrolled in schools (Sadgopal, 2006), nonformal education and vocational training continued to mark the lives of labouring children. The deep embeddedness of caste hierarchies within these politics of exclusion (Weiner, 1991) has meant that the empathetic framing adopted by these policies in naturalizing children's labour as crucial to their family's subsistence has helped produce a national common sense that essentially reproduces and preserves upper-caste hegemony and material interests.

Though the 2006 right to free and compulsory schooling is indeed a landmark legislation that has initiated coalition-building around children's rights discourses (Bajpai, 2003; Bhabha, 2014; HAQ Centre for Child Rights, 2011), a closer look reveals that a majority of these efforts play out within the more restricted civil social sphere and involve national elites. For the subaltern majority, this new legal guarantee often materializes through sensitization campaigns undertaken by local NGOs (Balagopalan, 2013; Cheney & Sinervo, 2019). A more historicized framing of rights-subjectivities disrupts the current fetishization of this law by the state and this upper-caste elite and instead highlights the constitutive ambivalence that has marked postcolonial policymaking on education with regard to labouring children. With the recent amendment privatizing child labour and thereby further reducing the state's role in addressing this scourge, this moment of child rights governance and the new legal guarantee around compulsory schooling is also paradoxically one in which Dalit and other subaltern populations are being asked to manage their economic precarity.

In a stark departure from standard economic theory that views the phenomenal expansion of India's informal economy as incidental to India's spectacular economic growth, some economists have argued that the Indian economy thrives on a deliberate inability to accommodate most of the country's population in the formal economic sector (Bhattacharya & Sanyal, 2011; Sanyal, 2007). According to them, the Indian economy – as part of a postindustrial global economy – works through two parallel registers of 'accumulation' and 'need.' As Sanyal (2007) discusses, the 'economy of accumulation' is an exclusionary apparatus centered on the desire to create surplus wealth for industrial development. Its requirements for an unending supply of land and mineral wealth are met by dispossessing subaltern populations in rural and urban areas using colonial laws of 'eminent domain' that continually usurp resources. Economic development in India continues to rely on processes of primitive accumulation as a constitutive element of postcolonial capitalism. The governmental apparatus provides some economic relief for most of the population that cannot be accommodated within this 'accumulation economy,' given limited employment in the formal sector. While these state-run programmes help supplement their low wages, it is never quite adequate to propel these populations outside of futures within the growing informal sector.

The working out of the right to education in India is marked not only by persistently high rates of children being pushed out of school but also by an assemblage of technocratic expertise that naturalizes, through multiple modalities, the increased privatization of public education as the ideal solution (Balagopalan, 2019; Juneja, 2010; Kingdon, 2007; Subramanian, 2018). However, the continued recognition of this right as a decisive milestone within children's rights governance relies on its ability to deploy the abstract equality written into this new law, marking an authoritative break from their earlier exclusion from formal schooling. Only through historicizing rights-subjectivities are we alerted to the limits of these new assurances in terms of their entanglements in earlier and more entrenched processes and priorities of 'national development' (Ludden, 2005).

13.4 Conclusion

Historicizing rights-subjectivities allows us to gauge whether marginal populations' 'access to lines of social mobility' (Spivak, 2004) is substantively altered as compared to their past histories of exclusion and thereby continues to foreground the structural exclusions that often underwrite abstract assurances of equality. As victims of 'pervasive rather than singular or spectacular human rights violations' (Spivak, 2004, p. 529), the inability of marginal populations in the Global South to effectively deploy discourses of children's rights has less to do with the newness of these abstract assurances and more to do with a different historical path through which such populations have emerged in modernity. By assuming rights-subjectivities as universal, children's rights governance in the Global South ignores, and thereby reproduces, the fundamental difference in how elite and marginal communities have engaged their rights-subjectivities as citizens of liberal democracies and been worked upon by postcolonial development. Stark differences mark this exercise of citizenship, including the ability to make claims on the state, all of which continue to leave their strong traces on the more recent and paradoxical working out of children's rights in these contexts.

References

Aufseeser, D. (2014). Control protection and rights. *International Journal of Children's Rights*, *22*, 241–267.

Bajpai, A. (2003). *Child rights in India: Law, policy and practice.* Oxford University Press.

Balagopalan, S. (2013). The politics of failure. In K. Hanson & O. Nieuwenhuys (eds.) *Living rights: Theorizing children's rights in international development* (pp. 133–151). Cambridge University Press.

Balagopalan, S. (2014). *Inhabiting 'childhood': Children, labour and schooling in postcolonial India.* Palgrave Macmillan.

Balagopalan, S. (2019). Afterschool and during vacations: On labor and schooling in the post colony. *Children's Geographies*, *17*, 231–245.

Balagopalan, S. (2022). The politics of deferral: Denaturalizing the 'economic value' of children's labor in India. *Current Sociology*, *70*(4), 496–512.

Balagopalan, S. (2024). Theorizing 'difference'. In S. Balagopalan, J. Wall & K. Wells (eds.) *The Bloomsbury handbook of theories in childhood studies* (pp. 44–58). Bloomsbury Academic.

Bhabha, H. (1994). *The location of culture.* Routledge.

Bhabha, J. (ed.). (2014). *Coming of age: Reframing the approach to adolescent rights.* University of Pennsylvania Press.

Bhattacharya, N. (2012). *Contagion and enclaves.* Liverpool University Press.

Bhattacharya, R., & Sanyal, K. (2011). Bypassing the squalor: New towns, immaterial labour and exclusions in postcolonial urbanisation. *Economic & Political Weekly*, *XLVI*, 27–40.

Chakrabarty, D. (2000). *Provincializing Europe: Postcolonial thought and historical difference*. Princeton University Press.
Chatterjee, P. (1993). *The nation and its fragments: Colonial and postcolonial histories*. Princeton University Press.
Chatterjee, P. (2004). *Politics of the governed: Popular politics in most of the world*. Columbia University Press.
Cheney, K. (2007). *Pillars of the nation: Child citizens and Ugandan national development*. The University of Chicago Press.
Cheney, K., & Sinervo A. (eds.). (2019). *Disadvantaged childhoods and humanitarian intervention*. Palgrave Macmillan.
Cohn, B. (1996). *Colonialism and its forms of knowledge*. Princeton University Press.
Dhawan, N. (2014). *Decolonizing enlightenment: Transnational justice, human rights and democracy in a postcolonial world*. Verlag Barbara Budrich.
Engel, D. (2012). Vertical and horizontal perspectives on rights consciousness. *Indiana Journal of Global Legal Studies*, *19*(2), 423–455.
Fay, F. (2021). *Disputing discipline: Child protection, punishment, and piety in Zanzibar schools*. Rutgers University Press.
Fraser, N. (2005). Reframing global justice. *New Left Review*, *36*, 69–89.
Government of India. (2009). *The right of children to free and compulsory education act*. Ministry of Law and Justice.
Government of India. (2016). *The child labour (Prohibition and Regulation) amendment act*. Ministry of Law and Justice.
Guha, R. (1998). *Dominance without hegemony: History and power in colonial India*. Harvard University Press.
Hanson, K., & Nieuwenhuys, O. (eds.). (2013). *Living rights: Theorizing children's rights in international development*. Cambridge University Press.
HAQ Centre for Child Rights. (2011). *Twenty years of the CRC: A balance sheet* (vols. 1–3). CRC20BS Collective.
Holzscheiter, A., Josefsson, J., & Sandin, B. (2019). Child rights governance: An introduction. *Childhood*, *26*(3), 271–288.
Juneja, N. (2010). *Access to what? access, diversity and participation in India's schools*. (Research Monograph No. 32). NEUPA.
Kingdon, G. (2007). The progress of school education in India. *Oxford Review of Economic Policy*, *23*(2), 168–195.
Kupinse, W. (2004). The Indian subject of colonial hygiene. In W. Cohen (ed.) *Filth: Dirt, disgust and modern life* (pp. 250–272). University of Minnesota Press.
Liebel, M. (2012). *Children's rights from below: Cross-cultural perspectives*. Palgrave Macmillan.
Ludden, D. (2005). Development regimes in South Asia. *Economic & Political Weekly*, *40*, 4042–4051.
Mander, H. (2016). A law against children. *The Indian Express*. Retrieved April 22, 2017, from https://indianexpress.com/article/opinion/columns/child-trafficking-cases-law-bill-lok-sabha-parliament-5272206/
Moosa-Mitha, M. (2005). A difference-centred alternative to theorization of children's citizenship rights. *Citizenship Studies*, *9*(4), 369–388.
Nieuwenhuys, O. (2001). By the sweat of their brow? Street children, NGOs and children's rights in Addis Ababa. *Africa*, *71*(4), 539–557.
Parisi, L. (2017). Feminist perspectives on human rights. *Oxford Research Encyclopedia of International Studies*, 1–30. https://doi.org/10.1093/acrefore/9780190846626.013
Pells, K. (2012). Rights are everything we don't have: Clashing conceptions of vulnerability and agency in the daily lives of Rwandan children and youth. *Children's Geographies*, *10*(4), 427–440.
Ramanathan, U. (2009). Evolution of the law on child labour in India. In H. Hindman (ed.) *The world of child labour: An historical and regional survey* (pp. 783–787). M. E. Sharpe.

Reynaert, D., Bouverne-De Bie, M., & Vandevelde, S. (2012). Between 'believers' and 'opponents': Critical discussions on children's rights. *International Journal on Children's Rights*, *20*, 155–168.
Rose, N. (1999). *Governing the soul.* Routledge.
Sadgopal, A. (2006). A post-Jomtien reflection on the education policy. In R. Kumar (ed.) *The crisis of elementary education in India* (pp. 92–136). SAGE.
Said, E. (1978). *Orientalism.* Routledge.
Sanyal, K. (2007). *Rethinking capitalist development: Primitive accumulation, governmentality and post-colonial capitalism.* Routledge.
Spivak, G. (1992). *Thinking academic freedom in gendered postcoloniality.* T. B. Davie Academic Freedom Lecture Cape Town, 11 August 1992. University of Cape Town.
Spivak, G. (1993). *Outside in the teaching machine.* Routledge.
Spivak, G. (2004). Righting wrongs. *South Atlantic Quarterly*, *103*, 523–581.
Subramanian, V. (2018). From government to governance: Teach for India and new networks of reform in school education. *Contemporary Education Dialogue*, *15*, 1–30.
Twum-Danso, A. (2013). Children's perceptions of physical punishment in Ghana and the implications for children's rights. *Childhood: A Global Journal of Child Research*, *20*(4), 472–486.
UNICEF/ILO. (2021). *Child labour: Global estimates 2020, trends and the road forward.* UNICEF/ILO.
Van Daalen, E., Hanson, K., & Nieuwenhuys, O. (2016). Children's rights as living rights. *International Journal of Children's Rights*, *24*, 803–825.
Viego, V., & Manciavillano, P. (2014). Childhood rights in Argentina. *International Journal of Children's Rights*, *22*, 268–284.
Weiner, M. (1991). *The child and the state in India: Child labour and education policy in comparative perspective.* Princeton University Press.

14 The social construction of children's rights

Origins of, and developments in, the children's rights movement in Flanders

Didier Reynaert

14.1 Introduction

In this chapter, we examine children's rights through the lens of *social constructivism*. While it may seem self-evident to claim that children's rights are socially constructed, this perspective remains under-explored in contrast to dominant paradigms such as 'legal essentialism' or 'global constitutionalism'. These approaches often presume that children's rights possess inherent legal or moral properties, which are codified and institutionalized in international instruments (see Introduction, this volume; Nash, 2015; Reynaert et al., 2010; Stammers, 2009; Merry, 2006; Santos, 2002). Within this framework, children's rights are conceptualized as unambiguous, neutral claims, and aspirations. By contrast, recognizing children's rights as socially constructed emphasizes the importance of specific social, cultural, economic, and historical contexts that shape these rights. This process of construction originates 'from below' (Liebel, 2023; Ife, 2009), grounded in the everyday struggles children face when encountering injustice. Children's rights are continuously constructed, deconstructed, and reconstructed through a diverse range of practices. Rather than relying solely on the 'law in the books', a constructivist approach aims at understanding the contextual character of children's rights. However, how children's right are constructed still remains too much of a black box as a result of a myopic view in children's rights scholarship (Reynaert et al., 2012, 2010). This contribution seeks to provide a deeper understanding of this process of constructing children's rights. To achieve this, we draw upon insights from Social Movement Studies. Although this field of study encompasses diverse approaches, concepts, and models, it can broadly be described as the study of 'social mobilization' and 'collective action' by social movements (see, for example, Della Porta & Diani, 2015). Social Movement Studies critically contribute to the analysis of children's rights by focusing on the bottom-up agency of individual and collective action, while also addressing the complex patterns and configurations of power involved in challenging existing social and political orders (Stammers, 2015, 2009).

DOI: 10.4324/9781003510284-15

We investigate the social construction of children's rights in the context of the emergence and development of the Flemish children's rights movement. Flanders, the northern region of Belgium, has a population of over 6.7 million, with 19% under the age of 18. Within Belgium's federal state structure,[1] Flanders holds primary authority over policies related to children and youth. The region has a well-established tradition in developing a children's rights framework, in which the Flemish children's rights movement has played a pivotal role – one that predates the adoption of the Convention on the Rights of the Child (UNCRC). However, the UNCRC served as a significant catalyst in advancing Flemish children's rights policies. The Flemish government has implemented a comprehensive array of policy instruments that collectively shape its children's rights policies (see Desmet et al., 2015; Op de Beeck, 2015, and further discussion in this chapter). Within the European context, Flanders can be regarded as a front-runner in children's rights policymaking.

Beyond this substantive rationale, there is also a personal dimension to my focus on the Flemish children's rights movement, as I have been deeply involved in this field. In 2002, I began working for the Flemish Children's Rights Coalition, a network of organizations monitoring the implementation of the UNCRC from a nongovernmental perspective. Later, I combined this role with a position at the Child Legal Centre, an organization dedicated to enhancing the legal protection of minors. My position in the field of children's rights shifted in 2005 when I joined the Children's Rights Centre at Ghent University. Transitioning from a practitioner in the children's rights field to an academic researcher, I moved from activism and advocacy to critical scholarly enquiry – a transition that posed challenges in balancing engagement with analytical distance. In 2010, alongside colleagues from various universities, I co-founded the Children's Rights Knowledge Centre, succeeding the Children's Rights Centre of Ghent University. This interuniversity platform aims to collect, disseminate, and stimulate the production of critical scientific knowledge on children's rights. More recently, in 2022, the Children's Rights Knowledge Centre, of which I am currently the chair, was commissioned by the Flemish government to merge with the Flemish Children's Rights Coalition and the Child Legal Centre as part of a reform of Flemish children's rights policy. This merger, set to take effect in 2026, seeks to unite a network of NGOs, focused on advocacy, with a network of academics, dedicated to critical research – two objectives that often stand in tension. The analysis presented in

1 Belgium is a federal state, composed of three Communities (the Flemish Community, the French Community, and the German-speaking Community) and three Regions (the Flemish Region, the Brussels Capital Region, and the Walloon Region). The powers of the Communities are 'person-related', such as culture, education, child protection, youth care, social welfare, etc. The powers of the Regions are 'territorial-related' and include housing, mobility, agriculture, etc. The Flemish Government is authorized for both the powers of the Flemish Community and the Flemish Region. The federal government is responsible for matters such as national defence, justice, finance, social security, etc.

this contribution cannot be separated from my involvement in the children's rights movement in Flanders over the past few decades.

This contribution is organized into three sections, each analyzing a key period in the development of the Flemish children's rights movement. It draws upon a capita selecta of events and activities that hold particular significance in understanding the social construction of children's rights within the context of this movement. Each section highlights a distinct dimension of the construction process: the first focuses on *pre-institutionalized constructions* of children's rights, the second examines *interpretative constructions*, and the third addresses *institutionalized constructions* of children's rights. Building on this analysis, the conclusion advocates for a social constructivist ontology of children's rights.

14.2 *The power of the alternative*: pre-institutionalized constructions of children's rights

The Flemish children's rights movement found its 'breeding ground' in the alternative youth care movement of the late 1960s. This period marked a critical moment when the social position of children and young people came under scrutiny within the broader context of emancipation movements in Western countries. Although the alternative youth care movement was a diverse amalgamation of initiatives and ideas, certain defining characteristics can be identified (Werkgroep Bijzondere Jeugdzorg, 1981; Verzelen, 2009). Its alternative nature lay in its critique of the dominant, Christian-inspired, large-scale, and paternalistic forms of youth care that prevailed at the time. In contrast, the alternative youth care movement prioritized the principle of self-determination: children and young people were to participate actively in decisions about the care they received, as their status as minors should not negate their agency.

> Alternatives highly value independency, resilience and self-determination. Young people should get out of the institutional system and need to stand on their own two feet as soon as possible. The transition from institutions to independency has become huge due to the pre-structured nature of the institutions themselves. In those institutions, young people cannot decide what they want for themselves, how or when they want it.
>
> (Werkgroep Bijzondere Jeugdzorg, 1981, p. 240)

The principle of self-determination was reflected in efforts to recognize the legal capacity of minors, framing children as rights-bearers with the ability to exercise these rights independently. The movement sought to uncouple responsibility from age, challenging the traditional distinction between minors and adults. In the realm of child offending, this meant, among other things, recognizing the 'punishability' of minors, provided that the penalizing nature of the punishment encouraged young people to take responsibility.

In practice, the alternative youth care movement advocated for small-scale, community-based forms of care – 'in small groups in ordinary houses, in ordinary streets, with the café and shop around the corner' (Werkgroep Bijzondere Jeugdzorg, 1981, p. 21). This stood in stark opposition to large-scale, often geographically isolated institutions, that symbolically and physically segregated children from society. The movement's critique extended beyond the institutions themselves, to the unlimited power these organizations had, which enabled intrusive interventions in children's lives. At the time, youth protection measures lacked fundamental legal safeguards such as legality, equality, subsidiarity, and the right to protest (Dupont, 1979; Walgrave, 1979). This critique led to the establishment of Youth Advice Centres (YACs) in several Flemish cities in 1972. YACs provided low-threshold support to young people, focusing on their calls for greater freedom, safe spaces for experimentation, and the development of their own lifestyles, symbols, and social networks. These centres operated with horizontal organizational structures, sharing responsibility between young people and volunteer staff. Their approach was non-paternalistic, pluralistic, and deliberately distanced from the Christian morality that underpinned traditional youth care. In addition to their informational and supportive functions, the YACs developed a distinct pillar of social action with a politicizing objective, serving as the voice and advocate for young people within society. The establishment of the YACs can be regarded as the flagship initiative of the alternative youth care movement. Through the grassroots efforts of its pioneers, the foundational principles of what would later evolve into the Flemish children's rights movement began to take shape. These foundational principles included: (i) an alternative approach to engaging with children and young people, centred on the principle of self-determination; and (ii) the enhancement of the legal status of children and young people, particularly those in youth care, as a safeguard against unrestricted governmental intervention.

The genesis and early development of the alternative youth care movement reveal that children's rights in the Flemish context were constructed as a product of *contentious politics*. This term refers to the process of collective action that employs a variety of methods to challenge and transform existing power structures and societal norms. These methods range from playful actions, demonstrations, and strikes to legal actions and the creation of alternative practices exemplified by the YACs. The latter can be understood as forms of *prefigurative politics*, wherein 'movements adopting prefigurative practices work in local contexts, creating micro-utopias . . . and everyday forms of resistance that exist in parallel with, or in the course of, adversarial action' (Ishkanian, 2022, p. 588). These practices were developed on the margins of the formal institutional network of youth services, which often failed to meet the needs and expectations of children and young people. As such, these practices are sometimes categorized as belonging to the 'shadow state', a term that captures their position as informal, alternative structures operating alongside established institutions. Using Nancy Fraser's (Fraser, 2024, p. 67) lens, such initiatives can be understood as 'counter-public spheres', or discursive arenas 'where members of subordinated social groups invent and circulate counter discourses which in turn permit them to formulate oppositional interpretations of their identities, interests, and needs'.

However, Fraser's concept does not fully align with the Flemish children's rights movement, particularly regarding the participation of subordinated groups. A distinctive feature of the Flemish children's rights movement is its roots in youth care, rather than domains such as education or leisure, where government paternalism and unjustified exercise of power were a reality. Yet, despite its foundation on principles of self-determination and participation, the movement for alternative youth care – and later the children's rights movement – struggled to realize these ideals within its own practices. Children were not part of the rise and later development of the Flemish children's rights movement. This observation is notable for several reasons. First, although one of the foundations of alternative youth care, and later the children's rights movement, is precisely the recognition of their participation rights, it seems to be difficult for the movement for alternative youth care and the children's rights movement itself to get those participation rights realized in the work of its own movement. This is undoubtedly due to the context of youth care, which is characterized as a highly professionalized context of expert adults caring *for* children. Second, this disconnect is surprising given Flanders' long-standing tradition of participatory youth work, where children and young people voluntarily engage in organizing leisure activities for their peers (Redig & Coussée, 2017). Despite this rich tradition, the children's rights movement has struggled to connect with youth work, leaving the target group it aims to serve largely absent from its own activities. Today, the Flemish children's rights movement remains a social movement primarily composed of professional adults advocating on behalf of children, rather than one driven by the active participation of children and young people themselves (see also Stammers, 2009).

This initial period of the Flemish children's rights movement demonstrates that the social construction of children's rights possessed a pre-institutional character. Children's rights were not primarily a (legal) instrument embedded within an institutionalized framework of services, regulations, and policies as part of the social architecture of a particular welfare regime. Instead, children's rights were claims that challenged the dominant order and its institutionalized architecture, particularly its power dynamics in relation to children. Following Belgium's adoption of the UNCRC in 1991, the nature of this construction process of children's rights shifted. From that point onward, the construction of children's rights largely unfolded within the contours outlined by the UNCRC.

14.3 *Disqualifying parents in poverty*: interpretative constructions of children's rights

During the 1980s and 1990s, youth care remained the primary arena for advocating for the recognition of children's rights. Alongside the movement for alternative youth care, the family movement – although less prominent – also participated in this social struggle from its inception. The growing recognition of children's rights brought increased visibility to children and their interests within the family context. Policy focus shifted away from the family as the central reference point and instead emphasized the child as the primary subject of policymaking. This shift marked a move toward 'de-familiarization' in family policy, most notably seen in the abandonment of the traditional 'command household' model in favour of the 'negotiation household' model (Reynaert et al., 2009). Consequently, the family movement emerged as a second significant precursor to, and shaper of, the children's rights movement in Flanders.

While the family movement's origins can be traced back to the post-World War I period as an advocate for improved material conditions for families, it played a more prominent role after World War II. This role reached its peak with the expansion of the welfare state, which introduced a range of family-oriented measures such as maternity leave, school allowances, family-friendly taxation, and child benefits. From the outset, the family movement largely supported the demands of the alternative youth care movement for more respectful and rights-based approaches for supporting children and young people. However, this alignment was not without tension. Strengthening children's rights, particularly within youth care, was often perceived as being at odds with parental authority.

These tensions became especially visible in the early 1990s during parliamentary hearings on the General Report on Poverty (GRP). Following the electoral success of the extreme right on 'Black Sunday' in 1991, political attention turned to social discontent, including issues of poverty. The GRP, published in 1995, was groundbreaking, not only because the report outlined the contours of a future poverty policy, but even more so because of the fact that the realization of this report took place in close dialogue with people themselves living in poverty.

From the outset, a key theme emerged: the protection of family life. Parents in poverty expressed significant concerns about the excessive and inappropriate use of residential care placements for children growing up in poverty. They argued that such placements often occurred *due to* poverty-related conditions without adequately addressing the broader structural issues at play. As the GRP noted, 'Children are often placed for reasons related to poverty, either directly because of poverty itself, or indirectly because of behaviours or situations resulting from poverty' (Algemeen Verslag over de Armoede, 1994, p. 47). For parents, the fear of child placement was pervasive, as illustrated by testimonies such as: 'I have been removed from my home; will the juvenile court now place my children?' and 'When we are told that they will help us, we immediately become afraid that they will take away our children' (Algemeen Verslag over de Armoede, 1994, p. 48). Parents also shared experiences of coercion and threats: 'If we don't dare to go to the youth care organisations, it is because we are afraid of coercion and threats. We are afraid that we will be told, 'If things don't improve, we will place your children' (Algemeen Verslag over de Armoede, 1994, p. 48). When their children were placed, parents uniformly experienced this as punishment: 'Not having your children at home is the greatest humiliation inflicted on you as a mother or father. It is being destroyed in your own survival' (Algemeen Verslag over de Armoede, 1994, p. 48). It was very clear from the GRP report that parents living in poverty perceived the placement of their child as a total failure, sending the message that they were not considered capable of caring for their child. Furthermore, these interventions rarely addressed the broader socio-economic challenges facing families, leaving parents unsupported in their precarious living conditions. After all, an intervention of the youth care system is primarily focused on the situation of the children. To solve this, one places a child out of the family. But the family itself often experience being left on their own. They are left behind in the precarious situation of poverty that prompted the placement. Support in ensuring better housing or finding a place in the job market is not the mission of youth care. What families denounced was the lack of an integrated approach to the problems of families in poverty. In response to these concerns, the GRP took a firm stance, advising that:

> the placement of children for the sake of poverty should never happen. Family residence should remain the rule and placement the exception, the very last measure. Juvenile judges and social workers should be much more aware of this. However, it strongly seems that children from poor families are placed more easily than others and that their return to the family is made particularly difficult.
>
> (Algemeen Verslag over de Armoede, 1994, p. 42)

The report's publication closely followed Belgium's 1991 ratification of the UNCRC, making it impossible to separate the debate on child placements from discussions of children's rights. However, many parents in poverty perceived the recognition of children's rights as a threat to family life. Families in poverty feared that 'the recognition of children's rights only contributes to disqualifying those responsible for parenting' (Steunpunt tot bestrijding van armoede, bestaansonzekerheid en sociale uitsluiting, 2005, p. 2).

What was pointed out was that the UNCRC sees the best interests of the child as the central touchstone against which the living situation of children can be assessed. This leads to a very child-centred view of situations of poverty. At the same time, the UNCRC also recognizes the right to family life, with a mandate for states to support parents to live up to this family life. This, in turn, leads to a more family-oriented view of situations of poverty. This extremely difficult tension between the best interests of the child and the best interests of the family would be very much at the centre of the poverty debate with the adoption of the UNCRC. Notably, the Flemish children's rights movement was almost entirely absent from the poverty debate. This absence was evident in the mid-1990s when the Flemish Children's Rights Coalition published its alternative report for the UN Committee on the Rights of the Child. Poverty organizations did not participate in this coalition, unlike their French-speaking counterpart, which actively engaged with poverty-related issues and organizations. This lack of engagement reflected the broader disconnect between the children's rights movement and poverty organizations in Flanders, despite the foundational work of the GRP. It was not until the late 2000s that poverty was (re)discovered as an issue by the Flemish children's rights movement, prompted by the rising number of children living in poverty following the 2008 financial crisis. However, this renewed focus on 'child poverty' rather than 'family poverty' perpetuated a narrow, child-centred approach. Efforts to address child poverty emphasized improving conditions in areas such as education, childcare, and youth care, largely ignoring the structural challenges facing families. This is what we described elsewhere as the 'institutionalized youth land', those domains of social life that focus quasi-exclusively on children (Reynaert et al., 2023). This approach risks framing poverty as a problem of inadequate parenting, holding parents accountable for their perceived failures in fulfilling their children's rights. Consequently, the children's rights movement has yet to fully reconcile its history of individualization and recognition with the broader structural realities of family poverty, risking a continuation of the same controlling dynamics toward parents that it seeks to challenge (Reynaert et al., 2023).

The adoption of the UNCRC marked the beginning of a new phase of interest in children's rights in Flanders. The construction process of children's rights was no longer focused on 'rights-acquisition' through a politics of contention. Instead, it shifted predominantly towards the interpretation, and application, of the principles enshrined in the UNCRC. The poverty debate in Flanders sharply illustrates how the Flemish children's rights movement adopted a different interpretation of the UNCRC compared to the anti-poverty movement. The claims made by both social movements within the framework of the UNCRC retained their distinctly political nature: both the children's rights movement and the anti-poverty movement, each from their unique roles and positions, challenged societal power structures. As the UNCRC became further institutionalized within the Flemish welfare architecture, this dynamic underwent a significant shift.

14.4 *Advocacy with gloves on*: institutionalized construction of children's rights

From the 1980s, the ideas championed by the movement for alternative care began to exert a profound influence. In the reform of youth care, particular emphasis was placed on recognizing the legal capacity of young people. The 1985 decree on special youth assistance stipulated that children up to the age of 14 must be heard prior to the initiation of youth care, while children aged 14 and older were required to give their consent. Additionally, a preventive component was introduced to the youth care system, aiming to reduce the need for residential placements. Further reforms included a greater differentiation of measures, designed to curtail the interventionist nature of the former youth protection system. The mid-1980s reform of youth care marked the initial institutionalization of the ideas promoted by the movement for alternative youth care, which were later disseminated more broadly by the children's rights movement. This social mobilization around children's rights intensified following the adoption of the UNCRC by the United Nations General Assembly in 1989 and its ratification in Belgium in 1991. A significant entrenchment of minors' rights in youth care followed with the comprehensive reform of 2004. Practices developed earlier by various youth care organizations to enhance the legal position of minors were codified into law (Bosmans, 1996). Rights such as access to information, participation, complaints, visits, pocket money, privacy, and others for minors in (residential) care were formally established under the Decree on the Legal Status of Minors in Integrated Youth Care (2004). This decree is widely regarded as a groundbreaking development in the protection of children's rights in youth care (Desmet & Put, 2011). It demonstrates how the ideas initiated by the alternative youth care movement and later advanced by the children's rights movement gradually became mainstream and institutionalized. While children's rights in Flanders emerged 'from below' as a grassroots reaction to inadequate youth welfare provisions and through a politics of contention, they were eventually incorporated into the institutional framework they once challenged (Busso & De Luigi, 2019). The work of the children's rights movement thus at some point became instrumental to the construction of social policies for children and youth that grafted on children's rights (Martin, 2001). This is the process of institutionalization (Jensen et al., 2019).

The institutionalization of children's rights is even more pronounced in a second 'battleground' that emerged post-UNCRC adoption and evolved into what is now known as the 'horizontal child rights policy' or the 'child rights sector'. This encompasses an array of policy instruments and actors unified by an explicit focus on children's rights. In 1996, a loose coalition of actors from NGOs, academia, and government emerged as the Flemish Children's Rights Coalition. This coalition included researchers from the Centre for the Rights of the Child, established at Ghent University in 1978. By 1999, this informal network transformed into a formalized NGO-only structure, serving as a watchdog for children's rights vis-à-vis the government. The network was funded by the Flemish Government to prepare the NGO alternative report as part of Belgium's obligations under Article 44 of the UNCRC. In parallel, 1997 saw the establishment of the Flemish Children's Rights Commissioner within the Flemish Parliament and the appointment of a coordinating minister for children's rights within the Flemish Government. The minister was tasked with overseeing the implementation of children's rights across all policy areas. More recently, on 22 November 2023, a new Decree on Youth and Children's Rights Policy and Support for Youth Work was adopted, consolidating several existing regulatory frameworks into one integrated policy framework. Key components of this decree include: (i) a Flemish youth and children's rights policy plan; (ii) a network of 'contact points for children's rights' within Flemish Government departments; (iii) a child and youth impact assessment tool to evaluate new legislation against the UNCRC; (iv) a 'horizontal consultation' comprising contact points for children's rights, civil society, and academic actors; (v) a 'vertical consultation' in which each Flemish Government minister annually engages with the Children's Rights Commissioner and Flemish Youth Council to evaluate policy impacts on children; and (vi) the Flemish Youth Council as the official advisory body representing children and young people.

The 2023 Decree represents a new milestone in the decades-long effort to integrate children's rights into Flemish policymaking. This effort, which began in the late 1960s, gained a strong social and legal compass with the adoption of the UNCRC in 1989. Over decades, this movement evolved from grassroots activism into a broad social movement and eventually became institutionalized within policy frameworks. This process of institutionalization is not unique to Flanders but reflects dynamics characteristic of a neo-corporatist regime. In such regimes, civil society plays a significant role in shaping welfare state architecture. Belgium, in particular, is notable for its expansive nonprofit sector, with Flanders hosting the highest proportion of paid nonprofit professionals in the country (Pauly et al., 2021). Beyond these quantitative dimensions, the qualitative relationship between civil society and the state is crucial. In neo-corporatist systems, civil society organizations are not merely external advocacy groups; they are at the wheel of policy, often through consultative mechanisms aimed at achieving social consensus (Císař, 2015). This model also applies to the children's rights movement in Flanders.

The institutionalization of children's rights has altered not only the playing field but also the rules of the game. The movement's historical role as a challenger to the status quo now exists in tension with its incorporation into public policy systems, positioning it as part of the very institutional order it once contested. This tension, described by Stammers (2009) as the 'paradox of institutionalization', highlights the ambiguity of a movement that transitions from a politics of contention to a politics of institutionalization. The incorporation of children's rights into the welfare state is often assumed to be a neutral process that preserves its transformative potential. However, scholars like Busso and De Luigi (2019) challenge this assumption, arguing that institutionalization risks fostering a more sterile relationship between children's rights movements and governments, characterized by collaborative consensus. This dynamic, which they term 'advocacy with gloves on', can dilute dissident voices and lead to a homogenization of discourse, with all actors 'speaking the same language'. Similarly, Stammers (2009) warns that institutionalization may strip children's rights of their capacity to challenge the existing order, reducing them to tools of 'legal bureaucratization'.

14.5 Conclusion

In this chapter, we examined children's rights through the lens of social constructivism. The analysis was organized into three sections, in which we deconstructed the emergence, and development, of children's rights in Flanders over the past several decades. A central focus was the role played by the Flemish children's rights movement. We identified three distinct dimensions of this social construction process: pre-institutionalized constructions, interpretive constructions, and institutionalized constructions of children's rights. While each of these dimensions contributes individually to shaping children's rights, we also offered critical reflections on these distinct construction processes. In this conclusion, we revisit these critical reflections and propose a framework for a social constructivist ontology of children's rights. This framework comprises three key features.

The first feature is the ***contextual determinacy*** of the social constructionist process of children's rights. The understanding that children's rights are contextually constructed and must be interpreted through social, cultural, political, geographical, and historical lenses is well-established in the field of Children's Rights Studies (see Introduction, this volume). However, what remains under-explored is how a welfare state regime, as a macrostructural context, facilitates, mediates, and negotiates the realization of children's rights. Scholars such as Henry (2020) and Daly (2020), building on the pioneering typology of Esping-Andersen (1990), have identified different welfare regimes with distinct impacts on shaping national child policies. However, these studies have not directly linked this framework to children's rights or explored how children's rights might be differently shaped across various welfare regimes. Research in the area of social rights, however, suggests that different welfare regime types can have varying effects on the recognition and implementation of social rights for marginalized populations, such as immigrants or people living in poverty (Sainsbury & Morissens, 2012). Building on these insights, it is reasonable to assume that children's rights are negotiated differently within different welfare state regimes. A key actor in this negotiation process is civil society, which can function as a provider of 'welfare from below', complementing governmental efforts, or which can challenge existing policies, advocating for alternative approaches to children's rights (Barker & Lavalette, 2014). In our case of the Flemish children's rights movement, for example, we observed that, at its inception, the movement primarily played a political role by contesting existing policy, but over time, it shifted towards an extension of government provision in the context of a neo-corporatist welfare regime. Further research in the field of Critical Children's Rights Studies focusing on this macro-contextual dimension could reveal a more diverse social construction process of children's rights, offering a more nuanced and contextually rich understanding of the subject.

A second characteristic of the social construction process of children's rights is its ***political character***: children's rights are shaped through the contestation of oppressive power relations directed towards children, with the goal of improving their living conditions. As such, children's rights are primarily a political claim, rather than a legal or moral demand (see, for example, Stammers, 2015, 2009; Nash, 2015; Goodhart, 2013). They emerge as a result of social struggles and contestation, rather than originating from (international) legal frameworks such as the UNCRC. Focusing on the construction process of children's rights highlights not only the importance of the contextual agency of individual and collective actions, but also the complex power dynamics inherent in challenging the existing hegemonic order (Stammers, 2009). This was illustrated through the inception and development of the children's rights movement in Flanders. Indeed, the Flemish children's rights movement emerged from a social struggle that began in the late 1960s, long before the adoption of the UNCRC influenced the Flemish children's rights regime. The Flemish context demonstrates that a claim for children's rights is, at its core, a denunciation of existing conditions of oppression or inequality. Dembour (2010, p. 2) articulates the political nature of children's rights by stating that children's rights 'are fought for'. They arise from social contestation and mobilization by grassroots organizations seeking to make visible an underrepresented group of children and young people in society. This underscores the role of civil society organizations and social movements in advocating for children's rights (see also Rajagopal, 2009). Such an approach on children's rights from below warrants further exploration within the field of Critical Children's Rights Studies, as it remains an underdeveloped area in the theorization of children's rights.

A third and final feature of the social constructivist ontology of children's rights centres on its ***discursive disposition***. If children's rights can serve as a claim to denounce oppression and injustice, it is equally true that children's rights can also be used as an instrument of domination and oppression (Nash, 2015; Goodhart, 2013). In the context of human rights, Rajagopal (2009, p. 56) rightly asserts:

> And we should also start by recognising that 'international human rights' is a language, a language of both power and resistance. It is a language of hegemony and counter-hegemony, and we need to recognise the multiple uses to which it is put and the fact that it is a terrain of contestation.

In other words, a claim for children's rights can equally be employed to defend the interests of the powerful and privileged, thereby perpetuating or even exacerbating existing power relations in society. This is especially true for institutionalized forms of children's rights (Goodhart, 2013). Therefore, the construction process of children's rights is a discursive practice that can vary in its course and outcomes depending on its contextual embedding. This perspective aligns with the work of de Sousa Santos (2002), who, in his broader critical account of globalization, introduces the concept of 'subaltern cosmopolitanism'. He argues that human rights only hold value when understood in connection with the everyday realities in which they are situated. Human rights claims emerge in response to locally experienced injustices across different regions, resulting in diverse human rights movements worldwide, each with distinct political demands. Similarly, numerous children's rights movements exist, each with differing political agendas. Even within the context of a single nation-state, multiple, often conflicting, claims coexist. This was evident in the case of the Flemish children's rights movement, where, in the early 1990s, there was significant debate over the interpretation and impact of the recently adopted UNCRC on the situation of families living in poverty. In pluralistic societies with varying interests and power relations, children's rights can be viewed as a distinctly *contested terrain* (Reynaert et al., 2012), an arena of ongoing struggle and conflict where efforts to understand children's rights contextually and critically are constantly negotiated. Recognizing children's rights as a contested terrain is not only fundamental for practice and policy development but also for advancing Critical Children's Rights Studies as well. This recognition should guide our understanding of children's rights beyond the well-established consensual narratives that often dominate current discourse.

References

Algemeen Verslag over de Armoede. (1994). *General poverty report.* Koning Boudewijnstichting.

Barker, C., & Lavalette, M. (2014). Welfare changes and social movements. In D. Della Porta & M. Diani (eds.) *The Oxford handbook of social movements* (pp. 711–758). Oxford University Press.

Bosmans, J. (1996). Implementation of young people's rights in Flemish provisions for special youth welfare. In E. Verhellen (ed.). *Monitoring children's rights* (pp. 713–726). Brill Nijhoff.

Busso, S., & De Luigi, N. (2019). Civil society actors and the welfare state: A historically based analytical framework. *Partecipazione e conflitto, 12*(2), 259–296.

Císař, O. (2015). Social movements in political science. In D. Della Porta & M. Diani, (eds.) *The Oxford handbook of social movements* (pp. 50–67). Oxford University Press.

Daly, M. (2020). Children and their rights and entitlements in EU welfare states. *Journal of Social Policy, 49*(2), 343–360.

de Sousa Santos, B. (2002). Toward a multicultural conception of human rights. In B. Hernández-Truyol (ed.) *Moral imperialism: A critical anthology* (pp. 39–60). New York University Press.

Della Porta, D., & Diani, M. (2015). Introduction: The field of social movement studies. In D. Della Porta & M. Diani (eds.) *The Oxford handbook of social movements* (pp. 1–28). Oxford University Press.

Dembour, M. B. (2010). What are human rights? Four schools of thought. *Human Rights Quarterly, 32*(1), 1–20.

Desmet, E., De Beeck, H. O., & Vandenhole, W. (2015). Walking a tightrope: Evaluating the child and youth impact report in Flanders. *The International Journal of Children's Rights, 23*(1), 78–108.

Desmet, E., & Put, J. (2011). Het Decreet Rechtspositie Minderjarigen: een internationaalrechtelijke toetsing. *Tijdschrift voor jeugd en kinderrechten, 12*(2), 103–120.

Dupont, L. (1979). *Jeugdbescherming met mate Maatschappelijke funktie van de jeugdrechtbank.* Studiecentrum voor jeugdmisdadigheid.

Esping-Andersen, G. (1990). *The three worlds of welfare capitalism.* Polity.

Fraser, N. (2024). Rethinking the public sphere: A contribution to the critique of actually existing democracy. In A. Scott (ed.) *New critical writings in political sociology: Volume two: Conventional and contentious politics* (pp. 489–513). Taylor & Francis.

Goodhart, M. (2013). Human rights and the politics of contestation. In M. Goodale (ed.) *Human rights at the crossroads* (pp. 31–44). Oxford University Press.

Henry, C. (2020). Children and the welfare state: The need for a child-centered analysis. *Journal of Sociology and Social Welfare, 47*(2), 157–179.

Ife, J. (2009). *Human rights from below: Achieving rights through community development.* Cambridge University Press.

Ishkanian, A. (2022). Social movements and social policy: New research horizons. *Journal of Social Policy, 51*(3), 582–595.

Jensen, S. L., Lagoutte, S., & Lorion, S. (2019). The domestic institutionalisation of human rights: An introduction. *Nordic Journal of Human Rights, 37*(3), 165–176.

Liebel, M. (2023). *Children's rights from below.* Policy Press.

Martin, G. (2001). Social movements, welfare and social policy: A critical analysis. *Critical Social Policy, 21*(3), 361–383.

Merry, S. E. (2006). Transnational human rights and local activism: Mapping the middle. *American Anthropologist, 108*(1), 38–51.

Nash, K. (2015). Is it social movements that construct human rights?. In D. Della Porta & M. Diani (eds.) *The Oxford handbook of social movements* (pp. 743–752). Oxford University Press.

Op de Beeck, H. (2015). Children's rights indicators from theory to implementation: The Flemish case. *Child Indicators Research, 8*(2), 243–264.

Pauly, R., Verschuere, B., De Rynck, F., & Voets, J. (2021). Changing neo-corporatist institutions? Examining the relationship between government and civil society organizations in Belgium. *Public Management Review, 23*(8), 1117–1138.

Rajagopal, B. (2009). The international human rights movement today. *Maryland Journal of International Law, 24*(1), 56–62.

Redig, G., & Coussée, F. (2017). Youth work in Flanders – playful usefulness and useful playfulness. In H. Schild, N. Connolly, F. Labadie, J. Vanhee & H. Williamson (eds.) *Thinking seriously about youth work. And how to prepare people to do it* (pp. 27–37). Council of Europe and European Commission.

Reynaert, D., Bouverne-De-Bie, M., & Vandevelde, S. (2009). A review of children's rights literature since the adoption of the United Nations Convention on the Rights of the Child. *Childhood, 16*(4), 518–534.

Reynaert, D., Bouverne-De Bie, M., & Vandevelde, S. (2010). Children, rights and social work: Rethinking children's rights education. *Social Work and Society, 8*(1), 60–69.

Reynaert, D., Bouverne-De-Bie, M., & Vandevelde, S. (2012). Between 'believers' and 'opponents': Critical discussions on children's rights. *The International Journal of Children's Rights, 20*(1), 155–168.

Reynaert, D., Formesyn, N., Roets, G., & Roose, R. (2023). Combatting child poverty in the childhood moratorium: A representational lens on children's rights. In B. Sandin, J. Josefsson, K. Hanson & S. Balagopalan (eds.) *The politics of children's rights and representation* (pp. 227–249). Springer Nature.

Sainsbury, D., & Morissens, A. (2012). Immigrants social rights across welfare states. In D. Sainsbury (ed.). *Welfare states and immigrant rights: The politics of inclusion and exclusion* (pp. 113–134). Oxford University Press.

Stammers, N. (2009). *Human rights and social movements.* Pluto Press.

Stammers, N. (2015). Human rights and social movements: Theoretical perspectives. *Revue interdisciplinaire d'études juridiques, 75*(2), 67–89.

Verzelen, W. (2009). *De alternatieve hulpverlening van de jaren zeventig* (Welzijnsgids, Vol. 72, pp. 139–167). Welzijnszorg.

Walgrave, L. (1979). Op zoek naar een alternatief voor de jeugdbescherming. *Kultuurleven, 46*(9), 807–821.

Werkgroep Bijzondere Jeugdzorg. (1981). *Wablief alternatief? De werking van alternatieven in de bijzondere jeugdzorg.* Federatie werkgroep bijzondere jeugdzorg.

15 Strategic uses and redefinitions of children's rights

Violence against children in Argentina and Brazil

Valeria Llobet, Fernanda Bittencourt Ribeiro and Carla Villalta

15.1 Introduction

In the 1980s, the field of children's rights in the Southern Cone[1] became populated by activists who had constructed their interests and 'causes' in the heat of the resistance against dictatorships (Fonseca, 2004; Grinberg, 2013). Children's rights became a key framework for challenging authoritarian institutions and advocating for state reforms, especially for poor children in Argentina. In Brazil, activists extended the human rights narrative to historically excluded groups (Vianna, 2010). Children's rights provided a core language and a rhetoric that enabled critical discussions to take place on child poverty and the repressive nature of state interventions targeting specific demographics (Fonseca, 2004; Villalta, 2010).

We aim to analyze recent political developments in Argentina and Brazil and how they reframe and contradict the previous rights meanings. We focus on the parallel process of multiple uses of interpretation of violence as harmful to children's rights and promoting national laws protecting children in Brazil and Argentina. The debate on what counts as violence against children (VAC) has proven a fruitful scenario for gaining awareness of sexual abuse in the family and connecting those agendas with gender issues; it has also become a platform to question the veracity and quantity of declarations denouncing gender-based violence, domestic violence and child abuse. These opposite 'discursive fronts' (Fonseca & Cardarello, 2005), composed by local actors connected to international movements, mobilize meanings, morals and political power, and reinterpret and seek to transform what 'children's rights'

1 'Southern Cone' is the southernmost part of the Americas, comprising Chile, Argentina, Uruguay and the south of Brazil. All the countries comprised by 'Southern Cone' share similar historical processes on State and economic development as well as the dictatorial processes in the 1970s. The differences with, for instance, the 'Andean' countries (Bolivia, Peru, Colombia and Ecuador) in South America are quite relevant, as are those differences with Central America and the Caribbean. Hence, this makes it difficult for us to generalize our analysis to 'Latin America' as a whole.

DOI: 10.4324/9781003510284-16

means. Therefore, children's rights are understood as a strategic language that plays an important part in different regional disputes and conflicts. That strategic nature is indicative of the need for an analysis that focuses on the practices of rights and problematizes the idea of a unidirectional and homogeneous 'globalization of children's rights' or their straightforward emancipatory redefinition.

By focusing on their strategic uses, we move away from the core critique of children's rights as a product of Western ideas of childhood or Global North neo-imperialism, to focus on what we consider a more productive question: how, and through what practices, does the children's rights framework acquire political purchase? We argue that the categories 'North' and 'South' can obscure complex sociohistorical processes that are not originated in a single point of origin but are shaped by tensions that transcend these labels and by locally rooted political values.

We propose a view of children's rights that problematizes their diverse potentialities and their capacity to transmit different arguments and positions for examining the specific geopolitical agendas enacted by, and through, claims around children, childhood and children's rights (Merry, 2006, 2010). In doing so, we will not only depart from a dominant ontological vision of rights, but also problematize critical positions that, from our point of view, do not acknowledge the ambiguous nature of human rights.

Our argument is twofold. First, it is necessary to understand the specific ways in which different actors in each country strategically use the language of rights, and what locally charged meanings these rights acquire in specific institutional and sociohistorical contexts. Second, situatedness is a core point of departure for analyzing children's rights, particularly if we try to avoid reproducing inequalities, marginalization and injustices.

15.2 Children's rights as a field of dispute

In Latin America, particularly in the Southern Cone, children's rights were configured from an early stage as an arena of dispute in which different political philosophies held various interpretations on what is best for a child (Fonseca, 2004). By the first decades of the 20th century, the language of children's rights had acquired political efficacy by interweaving itself with the value and emotionality of childhood well-being, insofar as it portrayed children as inherently dependent, helpless and in need of protection from adults (Llobet, 2020). This language provided the basis for demanding social intervention by the state and sometimes its coactive intervention. But in certain situations, it also helped children themselves to be considered as political subjects and to achieve greater levels of protection and equality (Carli, 2002; Cosse, 2006).

Towards the end of the 20th century, the rhetoric of children's rights gathered renewed impulse in the region. At that time, human rights gained legitimacy as they made it possible to denounce the crimes committed by the numerous U.S.-backed dictatorships that ravaged the region after the 1960s and 1970s, and thus became a language for political struggle. Likewise, in the name of children's rights, the large juvenile institutes and the arbitrary and classist nature of the juvenile justice system were questioned. The approval of the Convention on the Rights of the Child (UNCRC) in 1989 was a catalyst for this criticism, and thus the language of rights made it possible to amplify and strengthen many of those protests.

By examining this process, it is possible to appreciate that rights, rather than as a language carrying a univocal meaning or an invention of the North that is imposed on the South and that only disseminates a 'universal conception of childhood', can be analyzed in terms of complex, contradictory and contested processes of production and transformation. These processes enable various courses of action, but also, they produce subjectivities and new social relationships which entail consequences that were initially unforeseen (Cowan, 2010).

From the perspective that we propose, even the idea that children's rights are a Western creation can be understood as an interpretation that was used strategically to denounce the gaps between global statements and local realities from an approach respectful of cultural diversity. But it is also necessary to recognize that this notion has been used by neoconservative movements that will take advantage of the 'foreign' or imposed character attributed to children's rights.

Similarly, the argument about the effectiveness of rights turns fruitless if it only centres on the opposition between the supposed protectionism or aristocratic character of the 'Northern' approaches (Hanson & Nieuwenhuys, 2020) and the protest-inspired, emancipatory approaches that are supposedly based on perspectives 'from the South' (Cordero Arce, 2015). Indeed, certain topics promoted by specific actors revitalize the old colonial 'salvationism', as critical approaches have pointed out (Hart, 2006). However, when analyzed from the experience of local activists in Argentina and Brazil, children's rights do not emerge only as external impositions. Rather, they emerge as constructs that have enabled activism to problematize the webs of power that sustain vulnerabilities and injustices as well as to challenge inequalities and hierarchies.

A central critique of the UNCRC highlights its universalization of a Eurocentric image of childhood, grounded in the dichotomy between adulthood and childhood. This critique exposes the limitations and hegemonic tendencies of children's rights, revealing the narrowness of such instruments in addressing the diversity of childhood experiences (Hanson, 2022; Roche, 1999; Cordero Arce, 2012). However, this perspective often overlooks how conceptions of childhood are reinterpreted in diverse contexts. Activists may strategically adapt and benefit from these discourses, even while engaging with their normative frameworks. The critique not only sometimes assumes a binary between a 'hegemonic' childhood in the Global North and 'other' childhoods in the Global South, inadvertently reinforcing static, dichotomous divisions and the 'othering' of non-Western experiences. Furthermore, this critical approach seems to *assume* the existence of a 'hegemonic' childhood in the North and 'other' childhoods in the 'majority world', thus repeating a reification of institutionalized categories and 'otherness', and a dichotomous and static division between a White West and 'the rest' (Cadahia & Coronel, 2023).

Now, in order to counteract this North-Atlantic vision of childhood spread by the UNCRC and for this to be a tool for emancipation, authors such as Cordero Arce (2012, p. 396) maintain that children's rights must 'amplify the oppressed voices of children of those [marginalized] childhoods'. Although this statement is widely adopted by critical rights scholars, we understand that it should be approached with caution. Our proposal is that even though it is essential to open our eyes to the variability of childhood experiences and listen to children, in theoretical perspectives such as Arce's, the emancipation seems to remain at a discursive or voluntaristic level. From this vision the specific political disputes in which this type of interpretation of rights are developed are not considered. In this sense, we understand that the decontextualization and romanticization of the forms – in which ambiguity is displayed in the formulation of rights in general and children's rights in particular – does not allow us to consider the variable and disputed meanings used by specific actors.

As we will attempt to show, the Northern, hegemonic, neo-salvationist or adult-centric character of the right to a 'life free of violence' is not what allows, or prevents, violences against childhood to be thematized, appropriated and redefined. Any analysis must consider the specific practices of human rights, since that is what enables us to examine in what ways rights are vernacularized and become effective (or not) in questioning hierarchies, injustices or inequalities (Merry, 2010).

A critical perspective on the practice of human rights (Merry, 2006) makes it possible to analyze the ways in which their effects vary according to the strategic configurations that play out in the interaction of different social groups (Reynolds et al., 2006; Ferreira & Schuch, 2010). Also, it enables us to divest rights of their usual traits centred around mystifying abstraction and exclusive universalism (Brown, 2020) to understand them as agreements, albeit partial ones – which are products of situated struggles.

This perspective reveals that the prioritization of rights is strategic, shaped by what different actors seek to highlight and challenge. The ways rights are combined, amplified or constrained are not fixed but emerge from symbolic struggles and political disputes over their interpretation and scope. These struggles determine which social groups are recognized – and legitimized – as *human* and, therefore, as rights holders (Fonseca & Cardarello, 2005). Thus, the visibility of certain rights, the marginalization of others and the use of depoliticizing or individualizing strategies within rights narratives are inherently political operations. In summary, a critical approach prompts us to ask: How, and through what languages, practices, and mechanisms, does the focus on children's rights gain traction in various forms of activism?

To explore this question, we will consider two 'hot scenarios' (Cosse, 2021): 1) the emergence of a neoconservative government in Brazil that sought to consolidate a 'traditional' model of family; and 2) disputes around the expansion of sexual and gender rights in Argentina. In both cases children's rights are configured as a field for disputing wider reconfigurations about the democratization of family relationships, parental authority and the role of the state. Likewise, the reinstallation of authoritarian processes in the Southern Cone and the negation of human rights offer a fruitful field for discussion about childhood and the nature and extension of children's rights.

15.3 The redefinition of childhood in Brazilian neoconservatism

In Brazil, the enactment of the Child and Adolescent Statute (*Estatuto da Criança e do Adolescente*, ECA; Law No. 8069/90), which is aligned with the principles of the UNCRC, is inseparable from the country's process of re-democratization that began in the late 1980s (see also Castro, this volume). Elaborating on the Federal Constitution of 1988, which marked the end of more than 20 years of military dictatorship, the ECA interweaves the language of children's rights with the ideals of building a democratic society. The so-called Guardianship Council created by this legislation is emblematic of this process. The ECA mandated the creation of, at least, one Guardianship Council in each Brazilian city. These institutions are constituted by five guardianship counsellors elected directly by the population to denounce violence against children. More than 30 years after the law went into effect, the positions within the Councils of Guardianship are disputed by candidates from a wide political and religious spectrum, from fierce defenders of the principles of the ECA to its opponents. Controversies on issues such as the decrease of the age of criminal responsibility – from 18 to 16 – and the legitimacy of physical punishment in children's education, core topics for neoconservative discourses, permeate the Councils. Among the proposals for modifying the ECA, these two issues have had the greatest repercussions through opinion polls published in the press and the dissemination of reports that put physical punishment at the centre of debates on children's rights in Brazil.

The draft law for the prohibition of physical punishment, known as the 'anti-spanking law',[2] was spread by conservative groups, mainly right-wing politicians and those linked to evangelical churches, who pointed to the loss of parental authority as a danger to society (Ribeiro, 2013, 2018). The catalyst for the law's eventual approval after four years of debate in Congress (2010 to 2014) was the murder of an 11-year-old boy, Bernardo. The son of a physician in a small city in the south of the country, Bernardo was murdered by his stepmother with the alleged complicity of his father. The case caused a huge public uproar, was widely portrayed in the media and hastened approval of the law, which became known as the 'Menino Bernardo Law' ('boy Bernardo's law').

2 The draft law is aligned with the Global Initiative to end all Corporal Punishment of Children, https://endcorporalpunishment.org/es/.

Until that moment, the informal name 'anti-spanking law' had been used as the way to point out, in a critical tone, the unimportant object of this law. The reconstruction of Bernardo's family life in the media, showing that he was a victim of multiple forms of violence, and that his pleas for help had not been heeded by the institutions that exist to protect children, created the conditions for the prohibition of physical punishment to be voted on, and approved by, the federal Senate, in a '*sessão de emergência*'.[3] Nevertheless, even after its promulgation the Menino Bernardo Law was not the subject of outreach campaigns or specific public policies. This would have been an important development, since the legal ban on corporal punishment, defended by the global initiative to abolish all forms of violence against children, claims to have a pedagogical objective in terms of spreading this ethical sensitivity (Segato, 2006).

Research conducted after the law came into effect (Multari, 2020; Santos, 2021; Oliveira, 2022) shows a significant lack of knowledge in Brazilian society about the law's contents, the persistence of the name 'anti-spanking law' and the link between criticism of what is interpreted as the state's interference in family life and the political polarization that marked the country in the last decade.[4]

During the presidential campaign and subsequent government of Jair Bolsonaro (2019–2022),[5] Bolsonaro showed his denial of childhood as a subject of law as formulated by the UNCRC and articulated in Brazilian law. Even before being elected president, when he was a federal deputy in Congress, his positions on diverse public debates were a step back from the rights affirmed in the ECA. He further opposed the expansion of rights: as a representative, he was in favor of decreasing the age of criminal responsibility and was against a project for banning physical punishment. Regarding this latter issue, his position is a good illustration of what we have previously pointed out as a collateral effect of the simplistic North-South opposition to promoting children's rights. Besides affirming that forbidding physical punishment impaired the right of families to educate their children, Bolsonaro also invoked nationalist reasons, taking issue with the foreign origin of the UNCRC which was being promoted worldwide by the United Nations and international NGOs such as Save the Children.

In the last few years Brazil witnessed an increase in all indicators of VAC: violent death, statutory rape, sexual exploitation and maltreatment. According to the Brazilian Public Safety Annual Report published as recently as 2023, 211 murders of children aged 0–11, and 2,278 murders of adolescents aged

3 '*Sessão de emergência*', or urgency call, is a special session called to discuss an issue of law in the parliament.

4 Since 2019, Draft Law No. 4275 has been under consideration in the House of Representatives. Written by a police representative, it proposes derogating the ban on physical punishment, arguing that the law was 'the product of the ideology that dominated the previous governments'.

5 Jair Bolsonaro, a former Brazilian Army captain, is an extreme right-wing politician. Before being elected President of the Republic in 2018, he was a federal deputy in Congress for 28 years.

12–17 had been reported (Reinach & Barros, 2023). Tragically, the promotion of children's rights seems to have been unable to reduce the indices of violence, and public debates with the greatest capacity for mobilization continue to be restricted to the issue of punishment. Today, a draft law (No. 4011/20) is being negotiated in the Chamber of Deputies that quotes the Menino Bernardo Law to justify the necessity of banning the sale, publication and diffusion of books or conferences that stimulate the physical punishment of children. This initiative is derived from the publication of the book *What every mother would want to know about biblical discipline* (*O que toda mãe gostaria de saber sobre disciplina bíblica*), in 2016, in which the author, Simone Quaresma, a supporter of Bolsonaro, uses the Bible to defend the use of the cane in child education.

During the last national administration in Brazil, the vindication of the use of firearms and the instrumentalization of childhood with this goal produced a specific articulation between the language of rights – in this case, the 'right to defense'- and the differentiation of children. In political events where Bolsonaro played the leading role, the presence of children in military dress, imitating firearms with their gestures or carrying toy guns, was common. The United Nations' Committee on the Rights of the Child expressed that these practices violate the international commitments ratified by Brazil regarding children's involvement in armed conflicts and should be penalized. This represents clashes between an authority that places itself at a distance from the sensibilities elaborated in the recent decades on childhood and children's rights and those actors who are committed to working within the framework of this language; this dissonance is evidence of a dispute in which one of the involved parties denies the universalist vision that defines, in terms of age, at least, the parameters around who is a child. The analysis of public scenes starring Bolsonaro encouraging the use of weapons highlights that, invariably, the children in these scenes are White and of a young age (Ulhôa et al., 2023). In opposition to these children who must 'learn to defend themselves' (Ulhôa et al., 2023), the social media accounts of supporters of the now-former president show images of Black and poor teenagers bearing firearms in order to depict them as criminals and produce postcards against the disarmament of the population as well as make a case in favor of a decrease in the age of criminal responsibility. Thus, the images of a president encouraging White children to bear arms is a discourse on violence that is authorized for White middle classes, reinforcing the distinction between innocent and dangerous childhoods, the critique of which was the basis for the elaboration of the ECA.

15.4 Violence against childhood and the anti-feminist debate in Argentina

In Argentina, women's and children's rights have a long history of spurring each other on following the enactments of the first laws for protecting working mothers and their offspring as well as policies aiming to protect the 'mother-son dyad', a concept that has also been called strategic maternalism (Nari, 2005; Llobet & Milanich, 2018; Llobet, 2020). In the early 1980s, during the post-dictatorship period, a new wave of secularization emerged, challenging the authoritarian Catholic moral framework that had prevailed under military rule. Feminist activism articulated the demand for the legalization of divorce and shared custody rights (Grammático, 2021). This legislative activism promoted specific strategies that tended to institutionalize gender equality agendas and sought to transform the ideological matrices of the judiciary's interventions in family conflicts.

The protection of children is embedded within an institutional framework where relationships of trust among specific actors play a crucial role in shaping dominant interpretations of issues related to childhood and in defining the resulting intervention routines. In many Argentinean provinces the interaction between the health system and the judiciary for declaring or disregarding emergencies related to violence against children, and for labelling 'good/bad' mothers, are more predominant than the interpretations and interventions of the various bodies for the protection of children's rights (Grinberg, 2010; Villalta & Llobet, 2014).

Since 2015, the rise of the mass movement of #NiUnaMenos ('Not one [woman] less') against gender-based violence translated into a territorial activism that reinforced organizational webs, and into legislative lobbying that consolidated numerous laws that brought a strong problematization to gender-based violence and linked it with violence against childhood. This activism was strengthened by the increased visibility of cases that were constructed as exemplary or emblematic, and which made it possible to pass various laws. These norms postulated the obligation to train state workers in gender-based violence (Micaela Act, Law No. 23592); it provided financial assistance to children of victims of femicide (Brisa Act, Law. No. 27452).[6]

The struggles to bring to light the diverse manifestations of gender-based violence led to also problematizing violence in upbringing and sexual abuse in childhood, which from the 1960s had been problematized almost exclusively in terms of psychopathology (Grinberg, 2010). These activisms became focused on producing a combined narrative that would make it possible to interpret VAC as an expression of patriarchal violence. Organizations such as UNFPA, UN Women and UNICEF began to question the separate treatment of gender violence and VAC. In this way they focused on promulgating a redefinition of institutional categories to allow articulated interventions that do not revictimize adult and child victims.

6 Both laws are the result of the activism derived from 'cases' of extreme violence that had enormous repercussions and were constructed as emblematic: the femicides of Micaela García in 2017, and of Daiana Barrionuevo in 2014; the latter was the origin of the Brisa Act, so called in honour of one the victim's daughters.

In turn, this context saw the emergence of groups self-designated as 'Protective Mothers' (*Madres Protectoras*), which problematize the relationship between gender-based violence and the violence, abuse and maltreatment of children, denouncing different forms of 'vicarious violence' – the maltreatment of children by their fathers to intimidate and hurt their mothers. And they criticize the judiciary, pointing out that magistrates were forcing child victims to re-establish bonds with the father-perpetrator. These feminist groups were opposed by other organizations – such as 'Shared Childhoods' (*Infancias compartidas*) and the Association of Parents Far from their Children (*Asociación de Padres Alejados de sus Hijos*, APADESHI) – which disputed this formulation and accused mothers of using their children against them. To this end, they mobilized ideas about family authority, heterosexual relationships and intergenerational hierarchy as bases for 'the family', using the figure of the 'Parental Alienation Syndrome' to legitimize their demands. At the same time, they identify feminism as their contender and point out that the struggle for legal abortion and the Comprehensive Sex Education Act are examples of a kind of double standard put in motion by feminism, since they intentionally interpret both laws as contrary to the rights of children and the 'asexual nature' of childhood.

In November 2021, public opinion in Argentina was shocked by horrific news: Lucio Dupuy, a five-year-old child, was battered to death by his mother and her female partner, who then took him to a hospital when he was suffering convulsions.[7] The painful details of the case, the repeated situations of maltreatment and abuse that the child had suffered, as well as his tender age and state of helplessness, painted an abject portrait that was emphasized by successive news reports highlighting the monstrous character of the women perpetrators and the inefficiency of the state. The 'Lucio case', as it was known, exacerbated readings that situate VAC within the realm of the pathological and moralizing. On the other hand, these arguments gave apparent legitimacy back to neoconservative positions against the expansion of gender rights. Public indignation and the general uproar caused by this case enabled the passage of Law No. 27709 on the Creation of the Federal Training Plan on Rights of Children, which established mandatory training in detecting and responding to violence against children. It also fueled heated criticism by neoconservative actors who alleged that 'gender ideology' (see Cassal & Burman, this volume) damaged the state's capacity for action. In this regard, they maintained that a female judge, biased by this approach, determined that after his parents' separation Lucio should live with his mother, and did not see the danger that

7 Lucio Dupuy was murdered on 26 November 2021 in Santa Rosa, Province of La Pampa. He had repeatedly suffered violence, as was shown during the trial which found his mother guilty of 'murder in the first degree, triple aggravated by cruelty, malice and kinship', and her partner guilty of 'murder in the first degree aggravated by cruelty, malice and seriously outrageous sexual abuse'.

the child was in. Similarly, since the mother's partner was a woman, virulent criticism was directed against the expansion of rights that these neoconservative actors sought to delegitimize, such as same-sex marriage, adoption by gay couples or contesting the continuation of the relationship with the male progenitor in cases of gender violence. This case was even used to invent a demonizing campaign against CELS (Centro de Estudios Legales y Sociales), a human rights organization that emerged during the resistance to the military dictatorship, but which now works with a broad human rights agenda. This attack against CELS was primarily due to the fact that the executive director (a woman) was falsely accused of having called for the acquittal of the women accused of killing Lucio.

Attributing 'gender ideology' to foreign activism, delegitimizing human rights tout court and assimilating the protection of childhood to traditional forms of familial authority are central axes in the positions held by conservative actors (Vaggione & Campos Machado, 2020; Morán Faúndes, 2023). These collectives built micro spaces with regional and international connections which circulate discussions, strategies and resources. Local actors put into motion various meanings on rights and on childhood. If, in some debates – such as same-sex marriage – the rights of children were used as a restraint against the rights of LGBTQ+ individuals, in others they were considered as subsidiary to the rights of fathers, and, secondarily, of mothers. Likewise, an ensemble of rights linked to gender equality is assigned to a 'foreign' and imperialist sphere, while other rights are inscribed in the defence of nationalist interests linked to 'traditional' families.

The instrumental character of children's rights in the last decade is now maximized in a new political scenario dominated by an extreme right-wing government that calls into question the basic consensuses that were reached after the worst and most violent dictatorship in Argentina's history and lasted for decades. Indeed, as we write this chapter, the current president, who came into office in December 2023 as leader of an extreme right libertarian party, affirms, without hesitation, the possibility of the sale of children by their parents if need be, the need to revert women's right to abortion and the denial of the very idea of social rights. Further, he claims that the 2030 Agenda for Sustainable Development is 'foreignizing', and in public statements that would have been unthinkable only a few years ago, he vindicates the repression experienced during the last dictatorship, affirming that the crime of child appropriation (that is, kidnapping the children of political enemies and changing their identities) was only 'an excess' on the part of the military or a good deed aimed at saving those children.

15.5 Final considerations

A decade ago, Reynaert et al. (2012. p. 166) called for an agenda for the field of critical thinking about children's rights, one that would be oriented to 'critically analysing social constructions of children's rights in a diversity of practices and analysing the diverse interpretations that are given to the underlying logics'. Nevertheless, the underlying approach to critique has focused on the 'conceptual anomalies' of the UNCRC. The limitations in inscribing the research in their situatedness and historicity may be the culprit of the establishing of uncritical consensus around what it means to be critical.

Critical perspectives have characterized children's rights as Northern, Western-centric and neocolonial, unidirectionally imposed from the North to a South that is barren and empty of political traditions. In this chapter, our goal was to displace ourselves from these perspectives, considering that while human rights constitute a cosmopolitan language, they acquire practical senses that are imbricated in local cultures and specific social relationships (Merry, 2006), and, therefore, their meaning is neither static nor ahistorical.

In the context of a marked neoconservative offensive linked to reactionary postures that, until a short time ago, were in the minority in democratic societies, our aim was to reflect on the possibilities of contributing a critical viewpoint on rights that allows both a reassessment and deeper understanding of how human rights in general, and children's rights in particular, are practiced and used.

In this regard, we ask ourselves in what ways can a critical perspective on children's rights shed light on the complex political processes and social practices in which rights come into being? We believe that an approach that focuses exclusively on the incidence and reception of campaigns by the UN and NGOs against violence, documenting only their insistence in promulgating the passing of laws against physical punishment, would not allow for an understanding of the precise web in which, in local contexts, it may or may not be possible to thematize VAC as a human rights issue. It would not be possible to shed light on disputes between opposing political projects and the catalyzing features projected onto these debates by the characterization of the morally intolerable VAC (Bourdelais & Fassin, 2005; Grinberg, 2013).

The perspective we present emphasizes activism and the actions undertaken by political and social actors, rather than focusing solely on the subjects of rights. Furthermore, it does not consider children's rights in isolation, but, instead, examines them in connection with other issues, creating a complex field of disputes that encompasses social and generational relations. This does not imply including childhood in a depoliticizing invisibility but understanding that the whole field of activism is produced by strategic practices that include thematizing social problems in concrete scenarios. In that sense, displacing the 'child-centred' perspective to include these rights in connection with others seems a necessary process.

Our proposal is simple. A critical stance on rights requires building a perspective that not only understands the unequal relationships underlying the production of rights and unjust global processes but also has the capacity to examine how rights are used by specific political actors in local contexts. We believe this approach makes it possible to avoid taking for granted what rights are and to refrain from claiming a priori that they are inherently Western-centric and neocolonial.

The approach we propose also allows for distancing from a perspective that merely portrays the Global South as a homogeneous and unequivocally subordinated entity, overlooking and disregarding the capacity of local political actors, as well as children themselves, to make creative and strategic use of rights.

We have used the idea of vernacularization as a tool to understand the active role of local actors in giving shape, meaning and political value to children's rights. That helps to understand that rights constitute a contested field: they can be transformed into a language of political struggle, and in these specific uses, they are shaped, transformed and acquire diverse meanings.

The idea shared by Sousa Santos (2002) and Cordero Arce (2012) about the value of participation to ensure that human rights are emancipatory rather than exclusionary have, as a prerequisite, the ideological agreement that excludes the possibility of the instrumentalization of the rights. The processes we are analyzing here show the opposite to be plausible. Human rights, as fields of political dispute, not only show their historicity and contextuality, but also indicate that such a contested nature implies paradoxes that are not resolvable through the moral and ideological resources that we have put into play up to this point to support the interpretation of human rights closer to its origins and to the 'spirit of the legislator'.

Finally, we must reflect on how our position as critical children's rights scholars, committed to the idea of justice, has created a conflict within us when confronted with the setbacks of the critiques on the hegemonic ideas of children's rights in contexts in which human rights are being put into question. The current context of debates – and setbacks – must alert us to the relevance of expressly considering these issues in our theoretical developments, especially if we still believe that human (and children's) rights are a toll to protect people from state authoritarianism.

References

Bourdelais, P., & Fassin, D. (2005). *Les constructions de l'intolérable*. La Découverte.

Brown, W. (2020). *En las ruinas del neoliberalismo*. Tinta Limón.

Cadahia, L., & Coronel, V. (2023). Volver al Archivo. De las fantasías decoloniales a la imaginación republicana. In M. Marey (ed.) *Teorías de la República.- y prácticas republicanas*. Editorial Herder.

Carli, S. (2002). *Niñez, pedagogía y política*. Mino y Dávila.

Cordero Arce, M. (2012). Towards an emancipatory discourse of children's rights. *The International Journal of Children's Rights*, *20*(3), 365–421. https://doi.org/10.1163/157181812x637127

Cordero Arce, M. (2015). El derecho de las niñas y niños al trabajo: un derecho secuestrado por el adultismo y el capitalismo hegemónico. *Anales De La Cátedra Francisco Suárez*, *49*, 87–127. https://doi.org/10.30827/acfs.v49i0.3279

Cosse, I. (2006). *Estigmas de nacimiento: peronismo y orden familiar, 1946–1955*. Fondo de Cultura Económica.

Cosse, I. (2021). Jerarquías sociales, familia y niñez. In I. Cosse (ed.) *Familias e infancias en la historia contemporánea: jerarquías de clase, género y edad en Argentina* (pp. 13–49). Eduvim.

Cowan, J. (2010). Cultura y derechos después de Culture and Rights. *Revista de Antropología Social*, *19*, 67–101.

Ferreira, J., & Schuch, P. (2010). *Direitos e Ajuda Humanitária, perspectivas sobre família, gênero e saúde*. Editoria Fiocruz.
Fonseca, C. (2004). Os direitos da criança: Dialogando com o ECA. In C. Fonseca, V. Terto & C. F. Alves (eds.) *Antropologia, diversidade e direitos humanos: diálogos interdisciplinares* (pp. 103–115). Editora da UFRGS.
Fonseca, C., & Cardarello, A. (2005). Derechos de los más y menos humanos. In S. Tiscornia & M. V. Pita (eds.) *Derechos humanos, tribunales y policías en Argentina y Brasil* (pp. 9–41). Antropofagia.
Grammático, K. (2021). La campaña feminista por la reforma de la patria potestad durante la última dictadura militar argentina. In I. Cosse (ed.) *Familias e infancias en la historia contemporánea: jerarquías de clase, género y edad en Argentina* (pp. 313–363). Eduvim.
Grinberg, J. (2010). De "malos tratos", "abusos sexuales" y "negligencias". Reflexiones en torno al tratamiento estatal de las violencias hacia los niños en la Ciudad de Buenos Aires. In C. Villalta (comp.) *Infancia, justicia y Derechos Humanos* (pp. 73–108). Editorial de la Universidad Nacional de Quilmes.
Grinberg, J. (2013). La recepción de los "derechos del niño" en Argentina: Trayectorias de activistas y conformación de una nueva causa en torno a la infancia. *Virajes, 15*(1), 299–325.
Hanson, K. (2022). Reinventing children's rights. *Childhood, 29*(2), 149–156. https://doi.org/10.1177/09075682221098593
Hanson, K., & Nieuwenhuys, O. (2020). A child-centered approach to children's rights law: Living rights and translations. In J. Todres & S. King (eds.) *The Oxford handbook of children's rights law* (pp. 100–118). Oxford University Press.
Hart, J. (2006). Saving children: What role for anthropology? *Anthropology Today, 22*(1), 5–8. https://doi.org/10.1111/j.1467-8322.2006.00410.x
Llobet, V. (2020). Tensiones entre derechos de las mujeres y protección de la infancia. *Estudos Feministas, 28*(3), 1–20. https://doi.org/10.1590/1806-9584-2020v28n365412
Llobet, V., & Milanich, N. (2018). Stratified maternity in the barrio: Mothers and children in Argentine Social Programs. In R. Rosen & K. Twamley (ed.) *Feminism and the politics of childhood: Friends or foes?* (pp. 172–190). UCL Press.
Merry, S. E. (2006) Transnational Human Rights and Local Activism: Mapping the Middle. *American Anthropologist, 108*(1), 38–51.
Merry, S. E. (2010). *Derechos humanos y violencia de género: el derecho internacional en el mundo de la justicia local*. Siglo del Hombre Editores.
Morán Faundes, J. (2023). La tercera ola neoconservadora en Latinoamérica: ofensivas contra los derechos sexuales y reproductivos. *Iztapalapa, 44*(95), 349–376. https://doi.org/10.28928/ri/952023/aot9/moranfaundesj
Multari, P. (2020). *A educação dos filhos na palma das mãos: análise dos discursos sobre a Lei da Palmada no Facebook*. Master's dissertation, Pontifícia Universidade Católica de São Paulo. Digital Repository PUCSP. https://tede2.pucsp.br/handle/handle/23181
Nari, M. M. (2005). *Las políticas de la maternidad y maternalismo político, Buenos Aires, 1890–1940*. Biblos.
Oliveira, R. T. de. (2022). *Legitimidade da autoridade familiar e modos de poder parental: Um estudo longitudinal (2017–2019)*. Doctoral thesis, Universidade de São Paulo. Digital Repository USP. www.teses.usp.br/teses/disponiveis/8/8132/tde-14022023-115147/pt-br.php
Reinach, S., & Barros, B. W. (2023). O aumento da violência contra crianças e adolescentes no Brasil em 2022. In *17º Anuário Brasileiro de Segurança Pública* (pp. 188–203). Fórum Brasileiro de Segurança Pública. https://forumseguranca.org.br/wp-content/uploads/2023/07/anuario-2023.pdf
Reynaert, D., Bie, M. B., & Vandevelde, S. (2012). Between 'believers' and 'opponents': Critical discussions on children's rights. *The International Journal of Children's Rights, 20*(1), 155–168. https://doi.org/10.1163/157181812X626417

Reynolds, P., Nieuwenhuys, O., & Hanson, K. (2006). Refractions of Children's Rights in Development Practice: A view from anthropology - Introduction. *Childhood: A Global Journal of Child Research, 13*(3), 291–302. https://doi.org/10.1177/0907568206067476

Ribeiro, F. B. (2013). Governo dos adultos, governo das crianças: agentes, práticas e discursos a partir da 'lei da palmada'. *Civitas: Revista de Ciências Sociais, 13*(2), 292–308. https://doi.org/10.15448/1984-7289.2013.2.15480

Ribeiro, F. B. (2018). Le nom de la loi: violences, protection et différenciation sociale des enfants. *Problèmes d'Amérique latine, 108*(1), 19–36. https://doi.org/10.3917/pal.108.0019

Roche, J. (1999). Children: Rights, participation and citizenship. *Childhood, 6*(4), 475–493. https://doi.org/10.1177/0907568299006004006

Santos, R. M. dos. (2021). O debate sobre a "lei da palmada" na Câmara dos Deputados. *Revista Brasileira de Ciência Política, 36*. https://doi.org/10.1590/0103-3352.2021.36.247860

Segato, R. L. (2006). Antropologia e direitos humanos: alteridade e ética no movimento de expansão dos direitos universais. *Mana, 12*, 207–236. https://doi.org/10.1590/S0104-93132006000100008

Sousa Santos, B. de. (2002). Hacia una concepción multicultural de los derechos humanos. *El Otro Derecho, 28*, 59–83. ILSA.

Ulhôa, L. M., Silva, M. B. d. N., & Dorne, V. D. (2023). Gesto de arma com as mãos e/na produção de subjetividades da infância. *Policromias - Revista de Estudos do Discurso, Imagem e Som, 8*(1), 156–180. https://doi.org/10.61358/policromias.v8i1.54974

Vaggione, J., & Campos Machado, M. (2020). Religious patterns of the neoconservatism in Latin America. *Politics & Gender, 16*(1), 6–10.

Vianna, A. (2010). Derechos, moralidades y desigualdades. Consideraciones a partir de procesos de guarda de niños. In C. Villalta (comp.) *Infancia, justicia y derechos humanos* (pp. 21–72). Editorial de la Universidad Nacional de Quilmes.

Villalta, C. (2010). La administración de la infancia en debate. Entre tensiones y reconfiguraciones institucionales. *Estudios en Antropología Social, 1*(2), 81–99.

Villalta, C., & Llobet, V. (2014). Los heterogéneos significados de la 'protección'. Un análisis de los nuevos circuitos y dispositivos de protección de los derechos de niños, niñas y adolescentes. *Derecho de familia. Revista Interdisciplinaria de Doctrina y Jurisprudencia, 64*, 293–317.

16 Beyond implementation

A critical children's rights-based approach to the experiences of neurodiverse justice-involved youth

Daniella Bendo, Dustin Ciufo and Christine Goodwin-De Faria

16.1 A critical children's rights-based approach to the experiences of neurodiverse justice-involved youth

An analysis of the historical trajectory for children's rights and its academic study reveals parallel stories at play. As the United Nations Convention on the Rights of the Child (UNCRC) is the most widely ratified international human rights treaty in the world (UN, 1989), it may be assumed that consensus has been reached on what children's rights are and how best to secure them. For instance, within the field of children's rights studies, the UNCRC is the predominant frame by which to evaluate children's rights and, therefore, a legal disciplinary approach is often adopted to analyze the extent to which children's rights are being upheld. This is the prevailing paradigm in children's rights studies that came into prominence as a result of the UNCRC (see Price Cohen & Naimark, 1991) and continues to persist (see Howe & Covell, 2018; Waldock, 2020). It is a top-down understanding of children's rights that advocates for robust implementation of the UNCRC that will ultimately lead to more fully realizing children's rights. This is not surprising considering the UNCRC is rooted in a social movement (the children's rights movement) rather than an academic field of study; as such, the prevailing paradigm is closely linked to advocacy, practice, and implementation (Bendo, 2020). While scholarship focusing on the UNCRC is important, a critical turn for the discipline is paramount; this is because rather than simply defining children's rights from legal viewpoints, and unpacking complexities associated with implementation, the UNCRC (and children's rights more broadly), must be critically problematized to expand possibilities for children's rights.

Therefore, central to a Critical Children's Rights Studies paradigm is to prevent the children's rights debate from devolving into a 'technocratic discourse' (Reynaert et al., 2009). As its ontological starting point questions claims to an objective truth, it interrogates a singular vision of children's rights. What it, instead, offers is a 'framework of children's rights as a "sensitizing concept;" a frame of reference that appeals to fundamental principles of human dignity' (Reynaert et al., 2015, p. 10) – this framework may operate differently across a range of children's lived realities. Critical Children's Rights Studies question

DOI: 10.4324/9781003510284-17

the prevailing legal perspective and its prioritization of the implementation gap. It challenges the notion that such standard setting is appropriate, understandable, and has the capacity to uphold children's rights by critically analyzing the underlying norms, values, and principles that placed such standards in their position of prominence (Vandenhole et al., 2015). While the paradigm acknowledges that children's rights 'are undeniably codified in international and legal documents[,] . . . children [only] . . . become aware of their rights as they struggle with their families and communities to give meaning to their daily existence' (Hanson & Nieuwenhuys, 2012, p. 4). This ontological position that Critical Children's Rights Studies takes is equipped to reconceptualize children's rights as a *contested terrain*. Therefore, this chapter seeks to advance understandings of the field by moving beyond implementation and toward a thorough problematization of children's rights. It is only in so doing that the rights of children in their varied situatedness may become more fully realized.

Given this academic pursuit, this chapter explores children's rights within the context of neurodiverse youth and their experiences with the law. Neurodiversity is a term that was first proposed in the 1990s and emphasizes that neurological differences are to be celebrated, honoured, and valued (Day, 2022). Considering the term is centred on acknowledging the range of differences in thinking, learning, and behaving, when we use the term neurodiverse in this chapter, we are acknowledging that all youth included in our sample may identify as neurodiverse (since all human beings may think, learn, and behave differently). In addition, it is important to note that the term neurodivergent encompasses a range of characteristics, with no universally accepted definition (Criminal Justice Joint Inspection, 2021). The term neurodivergence may commonly include intellectual and developmental disabilities (IDD) which, oftentimes, is associated with cognitive and adaptive functioning differences (meaning challenges with everyday living skills). Youth with an IDD may have difficulties in problem-solving, concentrating, and learning new things. Cognitive disabilities, organic brain injury (for example, Fetal Alcohol Spectrum Disorders – FASD), and traumatic brain injury (for example an accident in childhood) are a few examples. Intelligence or IQ is an important criterion in an intellectual disability. A young person can have a developmental disability without an intellectual disability (for example, high-functioning autism spectrum disorder or cerebral palsy). In addition, IDD is characterized by adaptive functioning based on the following primary areas: conceptual, social, and practical.

It is of further importance to note that caution is required when relying on a medicalized model to understand and define neurodivergence. Doing so may result in a focus on individual deficits that must be corrected through treatment, and ignores wider environmental and social factors, as well as institutional processes that serve to further disable and exclude individuals (Day, 2022). Our study therefore includes both neurodiverse and neurodivergent youth who may, or may not, have received a formal diagnosis. We focus on this population as research demonstrates that neurodivergent youth are disproportionately overrepresented in, and susceptible to, the complexities of the youth justice system (Day, 2022; Marinos, 2017).

This chapter adopts an empirical approach that focuses on the experiences of 21 neurodiverse justice-involved youth aged 14–20 years old in Ontario, Canada.[1] As a signatory to the UNCRC, Canada is responsible for upholding the rights of children in relation to the law (see Article 40) and in conjunction with Article 2 which requires that 'States Parties shall respect and ensure the rights set forth in the present Convention to each child within their jurisdiction without discrimination of any kind . . . [including] disability' (United Nations, 1989). Moreover, Canada's *Youth Criminal Justice Act* (YCJA) broadly stipulates that 'special requirements' of youth (including disability) must be responded to. However, questions abound as to the effectiveness of the UNCRC and YCJA in upholding the rights of justice-involved neurodiverse youth. This chapter aims to show how a legal approach remains lacking in addressing children's rights. It will therefore proceed to demonstrate how a critical approach may provide a pathway to better facilitate the realization of children's rights.

The chapter's critical children's rights analysis applies both critical disability theory and a feminist ethics of care approach respectively to not only deconstruct obvious beliefs of the legal paradigm by drawing out injustices in the case of the former, but this is followed by constructing alternative pathways through the critical children's rights paradigm as potential solutions from the latter. It will also offer a critique to the critical children's rights perspective itself all while infusing the voices of neurodiverse justice-involved youth throughout to highlight how Critical Children's Rights Studies analyze the legal system in a manner that goes beyond implementation toward a thorough problematization of these youths' rights.

16.2 Sample, methods, and recruitment of neurodiverse justice-involved youth

A critical children's rights approach informed the methodological decision-making processes that were drawn up for conducting field work. Non-probability and snowball sampling techniques were employed to recruit participants for online semi-structured interviews. Various youth justice organizations across Ontario were sent the project information and circulated a project poster to help recruit interested participants. A selection criterion was developed for recruitment purposes which focused on: youth aged 14–20 years old, youth with previous or current experiences in the Canadian criminal justice system, and participants residing in Ontario. While Canada's Youth Criminal Justice Act responds to youth between the ages of 12–17, it is possible that

1 Pseudonyms are used throughout the chapter to protect the identities of the participants. This research was supported by a SSHRC Partnership Development Grant.

youth are still dealing with their charges past their 18th birthday. Therefore, these youth were included as they were able to give insight into their experiences in the youth system. As each youth participant was above the age of 14, they could consent for themselves without needing their parents or service providers as outlined by the Research Ethics Board approval for this project. Participating youth who met this criterion were asked if they were neurodivergent (diagnosed or undiagnosed); they were also asked if they have an individualized education plan (IEP) at school or if they receive assistance from an educational assistant. Due to the barriers and complexities surrounding assessments and diagnoses for neurodivergence in the criminal justice system (Day, 2022; Lunsky et al., 2024), we cannot officially confirm that each participant has a formal diagnosis. Moreover, it is important to note the complexity around disclosure and questions youth face concerning potential benefits and consequences of sharing formal diagnoses. Societal stigma creates hesitation to share this information not only with justice professionals but also within research contexts. Despite these barriers, every participant shared experiences and insights on the realities and complexities of navigating the criminal justice system as neurodivergent (both diagnosed and/or undiagnosed).

Interviews were carried out online via Zoom by trained research assistants between October 1, 2023, and May 11, 2024. On average, the interviews ranged in length from 30 to 60 minutes. Interviews were conducted in private spaces selected by the participants. Interviewers followed a semi-structured interview guide which included open-ended questions pertaining to youth rights, the police, court, outcomes of court, proposed solutions, and viewpoints on accommodations for neurodivergence. While most of the participants were only involved with the justice system once, some of the participants were involved multiple times. In total, 21 participants were recruited from across Ontario, Canada. Despite the mutual viewpoints that many of the youth share, their unique individual experiences showcase the importance of embracing situatedness when thinking about children's rights in the context of the youth justice system.

16.3 Critical Children's Rights Studies and critical disability theory – critical as deconstructing obvious beliefs

Critical Children's Rights Studies can importantly include critical disability theory in deconstructing the 'obvious' beliefs of the prevailing legal approach to children's rights. This is because both the field and theory situate children and persons with disabilities as experiencing marginalization and, therefore, emphasize the importance that they both exercise enhanced agency (Watson, 2012). While disability proves a multidimensional concept, critical disability theory has drawn attention to the socially constructed experiences of disabled people (Watson, 2012). What this means is that actors and institutions that operate according to a biological model of disability and that locate impairment within the individual need to relocate it across society. In so doing, what may prove an obvious belief for societal norms broadly, and children with disabilities specifically, may encounter an important challenge to ultimately enhance children's rights.

16.3.1 Critiquing the implementation gap

As a critical approach to children's rights is tasked with contesting the dominant legal approach to the field, analytical deconstruction of its obvious beliefs is best suited to begin by addressing the implementation gap. This is because for legal children's rights scholars, the UNCRC acts as an international north star that countries around the world have agreed to set their metaphorical compass to. Therefore, because consensus has been reached on what children's rights are, the mission is to now overcome the implementation gap by aligning what is stated in the law with the experiences of children's rights worldwide (Vaghri et al., 2022). In response, critical children's rights scholars problematize this static interpretation of children's rights by recognizing their dynamic nature. They call into question a top-down, adult-centric, and universal approach by advancing a bottom-up, child-centred, and relative response (Vandenhole et al., 2015). This unsettles the legal view that simply requires filling the gap.

The importance of challenging this implementation gap can be seen in the context of children with disabilities. While Article 23 of the UNCRC outlines the rights of children with disabilities, critical scholars reveal that there is a disproportionate focus on the right to protection when contrasted with the right to participation (Sabatello, 2013; Schneider, 2018). In this manner, the UNCRC may be problematically operating within the medical model, where disability lies with the individual, rather than the social model, where disability lies in the environment (Schneider, 2018). Therefore, if the rights of children with disabilities were to be solely achieved by upholding Article 23 of the UNCRC, it would perpetuate a needs-based approach. This is because the prevailing legal approach may see neutral institutions (i.e. courts) deliberate upon, and determine, children's rights in order to arrive at an objective outcome (Reynaert et al., 2015). However, not only do such circumstances strip away the rights of children themselves, but this lends itself to an adversarial process devoid of truly understanding children's situated experiences. This is because the legal approach fails to fully understand children's agency broadly and neurodiverse youth in particular. For instance, the competency children may have to show in order to exercise agency may not be evaluated at all. Instead, a legal threshold based upon biological age creates one law for all children. As such, it clearly disregards each child's unique capacity (O'Neill, 2012). There are implications of this in practice; consider the following interview excerpts:

Zoe: I wish I felt heard. I did not feel like my feelings were listened to or heard or even acknowledged. Like I felt so unseen and so unheard. I felt like I was just talking just so that there's some words on a piece of paper. I felt like nothing I said was actually gonna help . . . I didn't feel like a human. I didn't feel my feelings mattered. I felt like they were just asking their basic questions, following basic routine because that's what they get paid to do. I didn't feel like they wanted to know what happened. I didn't feel like they wanted to see if that's actually who I was or if it was just a one-time thing. . . . I felt upset by that, I was like this is not who I am, this is literally a one-time-only thing . . . I've never been charged since and I wasn't before that because I'm an academic student, I'm a good friend, I'm a good person. Like I've never ever done anything like that. . . . So, when I'm trying to explain myself and prove to myself that this is not who I am, I just felt so ridiculous.

Laura: I guess the one thing I would say is having it [the justice system] be more accessible and the language . . . it just felt like everyone was talking around me and I was not really sure what was going on. And then after leaving I was given a debrief of like, okay, this is what just happened. It would have been nice to, I guess, be more involved in the actual experience in court or have a better idea of what's going on. So maybe that is the judge talking to me more directly like a human being rather than everyone talking around me. I think that would have been nice just because it felt so impersonal. I was just so disassociated from the actual conversations, I was kinda looking in and I wasn't actually present.

As these insights demonstrate, the sweeping generalizations that a legal approach applies limits children's agency to secure their rights. This is because it has a particularly difficult time accounting for the distinct circumstances of these neurodiverse justice-involved youth. Consider how Zoe never felt her feelings mattered while Laura shared no one really informed her of what was going on. The prevailing paradigm's narrow focus on Article 23 is unable to account for the restrictive norms inherent in legal proceedings. There is a problematic objectification of youth that is compounded by the marginalization they experience due to both their neurodiversity as well as involvement with the justice system. This is emblematic of legally prioritizing protection at the expense of participation. Therefore, the prevailing legal approach designed to fill a gap does not solve the issue. But instead, a critical children's rights approach is essential for mainstreaming the participation of neurodiverse justice-involved youth experiences. Consequently, these respondents show how reconceptualization is essential to shift the focus away from individual impairments and instead shine light on how standard institutional and legal frameworks infringe upon neurodiverse justice-involved youth.

16.3.2 Critiquing the siloing of children's rights

A second area where the critical children's rights approach may deconstruct the obvious beliefs of the prevailing legal children's rights approach is by analyzing the place of children in international law. While the UNCRC asserts that children hold rights by virtue of their status as children (Archard, 2015), the question that this, in turn, leads to, however, is whether the UNCRC may serve as a supplement to other human rights law, or should it be the sole decider on matters of children's rights? This is the question posed by Quennerstedt and colleagues (2018, p. 52), who argue that there 'is no discernable closure in relation to this particular issue'. As such, it speaks to the dual limitations of the legal approach. First, it has failed to conclusively assert the UNCRC's legal responsibilities, while second, on account of the prominence it invests in the UNCRC, it may silo children's rights from other human rights law.

This siloing process may have a deleterious effect on ensuring the rights of children with disabilities. On account of the fact that such children may exercise their rights solely under the UNCRC, they would fail to incorporate advances made within the United Nations Convention on the Rights of Persons with Disabilities (UNCRPD). As this international law incorporates a more relational approach (Sabatello, 2013), it better aligns with a sociological understanding of disability (Schneider, 2018). This is made apparent in a variety of ways, including the preamble where subsections draw attention to collaborative involvement in decision-making processes, emphasizing experiences across intersecting identities, and situating persons with disabilities within their communities (UN, 2006). Even more specifically, Article 7(3) of the UNCRPD states that 'children with disabilities have the right to express their views freely . . . on an equal basis with other children, and to be provided with disability and age-appropriate assistance to realize that right' (UN, 2006). This is a significant advancement from the protectionist, needs-bearing, service-providing emphasis of Article 23 in the UNCRC. Should the siloing of rights unfold where the UNCRC rather than the UNCRPD informs the experiences of neurodiverse justice-involved youth, there remains a great deal of limitations to these youths' rights. Consider the following interview excerpts:

Zoe: I have really bad ADHD and when I go to ask [police officers] a bunch of details just to get to one point, they're not very good listeners. . . . Every time that I've ever talked to a police officer, they're not very happy to talk to me if I just pinpoint like this is point A point B point C. . . . Every time I go off into little blurbs (and I consider them necessary points to get to my main point), but if I go off and explain every little detail, I kind of get cut off and I don't really get listened to . . . they give me a confused look. So, I get a little annoyed when I try to explain where I was getting to or they'll just kinda jump to the next question, they won't let me finish what I'm saying.

Kathy: The cops were not understanding in the slightest. At least my lawyer said I was treated very aggressively considering the severity of my case. They didn't really offer me any support; they gave me the sheet that I could read on my own about Legal Aid, and all of that, but they didn't offer me anything personally . . . when I went to the station to speak with the police, they weren't friendly.

These insights showcase the importance of critically deconstructing obvious beliefs in relation to moving beyond Article 23 of the UNCRC and highlighting the importance of the relational approach that is advanced by the UNCRPD. Zoe and Kathy demonstrate the lack of supportive communication between police officers and neurodiverse justice-involved youth. These findings are relevant to the UNCRPD which focuses on relationality and the impact of the social model of disability which highlights the effect of systemic barriers and social exclusion. As both participants outline, they were not adequately assisted when the UNCRDP clearly outlines not only their right to voice their views but that both youth and disability-adaptable measures are required to facilitate such viewpoints. In Zoe's case, she acknowledges that while she has ADHD and sometimes provides longer detailed explanations to get to her key point, she did not feel listened to. Comparably, in Kathy's case, she found that police officers were unkind, unsupportive, and unfriendly. Despite the unresolved nature as to whether the UNCRC should supplement other human rights law or act as the ultimate arbiter, the hegemonic status it has attained requires interrogation. There is a clear need to broaden out the rights of children to go beyond the UNCRC by truly working in concert with all other international human rights laws. Failing to do so has marginalized the rights of these neurodiverse justice-involved youth simply based on the limitations of the legal approach.

16.4 Critical Children's Rights Studies and feminist ethics of care – critical as constructing alternative pathways

Critical Children's Rights Studies can also benefit from collaboration with a feminist ethics of care in constructing alternative pathways to securing children's rights. This is because the heightened attention to children's agency that critical children's rights provide finds resonance with the analysis of power and emphasis upon relationships and responsibility in care that a feminist ethic offers (Cockburn, 2010). For instance, Carol Gilligan (2011, p. 177) argues that the feminist ethics of care can 'frame [social] struggle[s] in a way that clarifies what is at stake and . . . illuminate a path of resistance grounded not in ideology but in our humanity'. Therefore, the inherent nature of these critical theoretical approaches opens space for new ways of being. In the context of neurodiverse justice-involved youth, this becomes even more pressing given the inherently ageist and ableist actors and institutions they encounter. It speaks volumes to the pressing need for alternative pathways that prioritize the dignity of the individual to secure their rights.

16.4.1 A feminist ethics of care and the law

While a critical approach to children's rights importantly critiques the prevailing legal approach to children's rights, it is imperative that the former simultaneously construct an alternative pathway to the latter. By integrating a feminist ethics of care, Critical Children's Rights Studies can benefit from among many positive attributes, how it reveals the 'myth of the unembodied subject' (Kittay et al., 2005, p. 445). This is a vital theoretical frame through which to analyze the law due to this subject's intrinsic place within the legal approach. For instance, the prevailing legal approach to the study of children's rights sees the child of the UNCRC as a universal figure with rights and entitlements insofar as experts in the field permit (Cockburn, 2010). However, a feminist ethics of care highlights the ways in which this fails to recognize the diversity of experiences that children have. This is because such standard operating procedures prove unwilling to grasp the complexity of the human condition, and, therefore, must be replaced by individualized solutions guided by care (Cockburn, 2010). As such, a feminist lens when combined with a child-centred approach 'can be symbiotic allies in creating a better world for women, children and men' (Cockburn, 2010, p. 35).

The theoretical depth and practical application that a feminist ethics of care may have on children is relevant to study law and disabilities. For instance, Kelly (2005) uses this approach to reveal both the paternal protectionist nature and limited resonance with universalism that defines the legal approach to children's rights. Given these theoretical weaknesses, she makes clear that children involved with the law should operate in accordance with the 'principle of actuality, [where] . . . decision-making about children would focus on the actual circumstances of the child's life, rather than an abstract and often essentialist test' (Kelly, 2005, p. 391). Such an approach may decentre adults from decisions related to children and children with disabilities. Moreover, it may specifically move toward 'co-constructi[on] . . . [in a] rights-respecting context and environment' (Schneider, 2018, p. 372). In the following excerpts, consider the importance of relationality and the positive impact it had on neurodiverse justice-involved youth:

Zoe: When I got charged, I walked in having no idea who I was gonna be talking to, where I was walking, what room I was going to. . . . I didn't know anything. And then when I was in my trial, there was this girl, and she was like the greatest help ever . . . 'This is this room, this is where you're sitting, this is who you're talking to, this is who's gonna be beside you'. Like she told me every little tiny detail that I would need to know. . . . That's just a nice thing to know especially with the way my brain is wired because I also have OCD. . . . It felt like somebody was in my corner and actually believed what I was saying, wanted to hear what I was saying, and that was the first and last time that I'd ever had any type of help when it came to that type of stuff.

Kathy: I don't remember what her job title was but she kind of worked with the Crown. She had access to this service dog, and I was able to have the dog when I was in my trial. I'm just a huge animal person and it was just really nice because she sat right behind me and the dog sat

> right beside me and so not only did I have her and the cutest dog ever but it really helped me realize that 'I'm not lost in the moment, I don't have to get in my mind to where I'm frozen and I get scared'. I have a dog to continuously pet . . . it's not as scary as it was before.

Clearly, these types of individualized, contextualized, and supportive interactions reflect a feminist ethics of care that can have a significant impact supporting neurodiverse justice-involved youth in intimidating courtroom situations. It does so by not only drawing attention to the fallacy of the universal subject but instead reconceptualizing possibilities for the unique context of each individual youth. When Zoe conveys that she had 'someone in her corner', it entails a partnership designed to ensure a more holistic realization of her rights. For Kathy to navigate the youth justice system with a service dog is to position her as a rights-bearing individual, hear her concerns, and support her through this process so that 'it's not as scary as it was before'. Collectively, these insights show how a feminist ethics of care emphasizes the importance of relationality and the impact of encouragement from, and communication with, youth justice officials.

16.4.2 Feminist ethics of care, marginalized intersecting identities, and youth voices for change

A further manner by which to extend a feminist ethics of care is to shine a light on how marginalized intersecting identities can negatively impact youth. From here, space can be given to listen to how they feel adult institutions and actors could better support them. For instance, the prevailing legal approach to children's rights may situate children with disabilities as experiencing a compounding infantilization. This is because they may be viewed as 'objects of charity and as passive recipients of welfare' (Sabatello, 2013, p. 468) due to assumptions about their 'immatur[ity] [i.e. child] or incompeten[ce] [i.e. person with a disability]' (Schneider, 2018, p. 370). This unjust conception requires contestation through advancing a reconceptualization of their identities.

Such rearticulation brings to the forefront how a legal approach may essentialize who children with disabilities are and what their lives consist of. It is particularly the case as these children so frequently are 'characterised by lacks and difficulties' (Wickenden, 2019, p. 124). For Wickenden (2019, p. 133), this problematic view means 'we should see childhoods and children as diverse and, therefore, embrace the differences that children called disabled have, not as deficits, but in positive, celebratory, and inclusive ways.' These arguments are relevant to insights the participants shared about their treatment throughout the justice process:

Michael: If you're gonna judge someone for something they did, you should at least know the whole person. . . . I wish the police heard my side of the story . . . I get that they want me to stay silent but if you're gonna hear the other person's side, at least hear my side so you can decide if you want to take me down [to the police station], you know?

Claire: When I was giving my last statement at court, they asked me if I wanted to say anything. I wouldn't say I didn't feel heard, but I didn't really feel personal to them. . . . It's really important the judges or crowns connect with younger people.

Clearly, a feminist ethics of care is importantly equipped to provide a platform for neurodiverse justice-involved youth. Michael's sentiment highlights the desire for the chance to share his side of the story with police officers who are failing to acknowledge his basic humanity. Claire also indicates that she could learn from her experiences in the court setting if justice professionals made an effort to 'connect' with her. A feminist ethics of care approach draws attention to eliciting the viewpoints of neurodiverse justice-involved youth and in so doing can reconceptualize possibilities in children's rights. For instance, Patrick draws attention to the importance of justice professionals knowing that neurodiversity is present:

Patrick: It would help them [justice professionals] understand case by case why someone did something. It would probably give them a better way to give a more detailed program and maybe they would be able to make accommodations in the court. Maybe make a different court that's less stimulating . . . people with autism, if there's too much stimulation it starts to bother them right? They can make a different court room where it would be for people with disabilities that would be more quiet or one person at a time.

Overall, these situated viewpoints from young people exemplify how a feminist ethics of care approach in conjunction with a commitment to disability rights would help to better serve neurodiverse justice-involved youth and, therefore, provide an alternative pathway forward: one where they may name, explain, and proclaim their rights.

16.5 Conclusion – 'critical' as expressing critique to the critical perspective

This chapter has sought to provide a critical children's rights approach to children, the law, and neurodiversity. In so doing, it has served as an important challenge to the prevailing paradigm within children's rights studies. Critical scholarship emphasizes the importance of separating the lawyers and policymakers who implement children's rights (Hanson, 2014) from the scholars who utilize critique to 'make implicit knowledge underlying children's rights practices explicit and therefore subject to debate' (Reynaert et al., 2015, p. 10). This approach has profoundly advanced the field, but like all research paradigms, it is not above reproach. Our critique of Critical

Children's Rights Studies is not so much a challenge to its underlying ethos, but rather a paradigmatic assertion to push itself further. In order to do so, it must not only deconstruct the dominant discourse, but also reconstruct 'difference-responsive[ness]' (Wall, 2022, p. 267) *within* childhood categories while 'interpret[ing] hegemonically suppressed lived experiences into more expansive social understandings for *all*' (Wall, 2022, p. 267 emphasis added). This critique of the critical approaches' application to children, the law, and neurodiversity means that while identifying children as neurodiverse to better address their rights is important, the emancipatory principle that has come to define Critical Children's Rights Studies cannot solely rest with the specific population under consideration. Instead, it must extend outward to the people with whom they are in relation who may, in turn, influence the institutions they collectively come up against. In so doing, this paper echoes Spyrou et al. (2018) call for a reimagining of childhood studies. They explain that research should focus on decentring childhood studies by moving beyond the narrow confines of the concept of the *individual child*. This can in turn facilitate wide-scale institutional change that is child rights-based, disability-informed, and rooted in a feminist ethic of care because as the following excerpt shows, the status quo is a gross violation of neurodiverse justice-involved youth's rights.

As demonstrated throughout this chapter, Critical Children's Rights Studies provide an important contestation for the legal approach to children's rights. This is because it moves beyond implementation to provide a thorough problematization of children's rights. By drawing into dialogue both critical disability theory and a feminist ethics of care approach within Critical Children's Rights Studies and applying it to neurodiverse justice-involved youth, we have attempted to not only deconstruct obvious beliefs but also provide alternative pathways that may decentre children's rights studies from the 'narrow confines of the individual child'. In so doing, this may help to promote a critical approach to the field of children's rights studies that may ultimately advance the state of children's rights.

References

Archard, D. (2015). *Children: Rights and childhood* (3rd ed.). Routledge. https://doi.org/10.4324/9781315740676

Bendo, D. (2020). Parallel lines? Childhood discourses emphasized by the children's rights movement and the emerging field of children's rights studies. *Childhood*, *27*(2), 173–187.

Cockburn, T. (2010). Children, the feminist ethic of care and childhood studies: Is this the way to the good life? In T. Cockburn, I. Diehm, U. Sander, H. Ziegler & S. Andresen (eds.) *Children and the good life* (pp. 29–39). Springer. https://doi.org/10.1007/978-90-481-9219-9_3

Criminal Justice Joint Inspection. (2021). *Neurodiversity in the CJS: A review of the evidence.* Retrieved January 17, 2025, from www.justiceinspectorates.gov.uk/cjji/wp-content/uploads/sites/2/2021/07/Neurodiversity-evidence-review-web-2021.pdf

Day, A. (2022). Disabling and criminalising systems? Understanding the experiences and challenges facing incarcerated, neurodivergent children in the education and youth justice systems in England. *Forensic Science International: Mind and Law*, *3*, 1–9. https://doi.org/10.1016/j.fsiml.2022.100102

Gilligan, C. (2011). *Joining the resistance*. Polity Press.

Hanson, K. (2014). 'Killed by charity' – towards interdisciplinary children's rights studies. *Childhood*, *21*(4), 441–446. https://doi.org/10.1177/0907568214547453

Hanson, K., & Nieuwenhuys, O. (eds.). (2012). *Reconceptualizing children's rights in international development: Living rights, social justice, translations*. Cambridge University Press.

Howe, R. B., & Covell, K. (2018). *Education in the best interests of the child: A children's rights perspective on closing the achievement gap*. University of Toronto Press. https://doi.org/10.3138/9781442666108

Kelly, F. (2005). Conceptualising the child through an 'ethic of care": Lessons for family law. *International Journal of Law in Context*, *1*(4), 375–396. https://doi.org/10.1017/S1744552305004039

Kittay, E. F., Jennings, B., & Wasunna, A. A. (2005). Dependency, difference and the global ethic of long-term care. *The Journal of Political Philosophy*, *13*(4), 443–469. https://doi.org/10.1111/j.1467-9760.2005.00232.x

Lunsky, Y., Matheson, F. I., Kouyoumdjian, F., Whittingham, L., Lin, E., Durbin, A., Calzavara, A., Moser, A., Dastoori, P., Sirotich, F., & Volpe, T. (2024). Intellectual and developmental disabilities in Ontario's criminal justice and forensic mental health systems: Using data to tell the story. *Criminal Behaviour and Mental Health*, *34*(2), 197–207. https://doi.org/10.1002/cbm.2331

Marinos, V. (2017). *Persons with intellectual disabilities and false guilty pleas*. Retrieved January 17, 2025, from https://vimeo.com/236598427

O'Neill, T. (2012). Young carpet weavers on the rights threshold: Protection or practical self determination? In K. Hanson & O. Nieuwenhuys (eds.) *Reconceptualizing children's rights in international development* (pp. 93–112). Cambridge University Press. https://doi.org/10.1017/CBO9781139381796.007

Price Cohen, C., & Naimark, H. (1991). United Nations Convention on the Rights of the Child: Individual rights concepts and their significance for social scientists. *The American Psychologist*, *46*(1), 60–65. https://doi.org/10.1037/0003-066X.46.1.60

Quennerstedt, A., Robinson, C., & I'Anson, J. (2018). The UNCRC: The voice of global consensus on children's rights? *Nordic Journal of Human Rights*, *36*(1), 38–54. https://doi.org/10.1080/18918131.2018.1453589

Reynaert, D., Bouverne-de-Bie, M., & Vandevelde, S. (2009). A review of children's rights literature since the adoption of the United Nations Convention on the Rights of the Child. *Childhood*, *16*(4), 518–534. https://doi.org/10.1177/0907568209344270

Reynaert, D., Desmet, E., Lembrechts, S., & Vandenhole, W. (2015). Introduction: A critical approach to children's rights. In W. Vandenhole, E. Desmet, D. Reynaert & S. Lembrechts (eds.) *The Routledge international handbook of children's rights studies* (pp. 1–24). Routledge. https://doi.org/10.4324/9781315769530-1

Sabatello, M. (2013). Children with disabilities: A critical appraisal. *The International Journal of Children's Rights*, *21*(3), 464–487. https://doi.org/10.1163/15718182-02102007

Schneider, C. (2018). Between children's rights and disability rights: Inclusion and participation of children and youth with disabilities. In X. Chen, R. Raby & P. Albanese (eds.) *The sociology of childhood and youth in Canada* (pp. 360–377). Canadian Scholars.

Spyrou, S., Rosen, R., & Cook, D. (2018). *Reimagining childhood studies*. Bloomsbury Publishing.

United Nations. (1989). *United Nations Convention on the Rights of the Child.* Retrieved January 17, 2025, from https://treaties.un.org/Pages/ViewDetails.aspx?src=IND&mtdsg_no=IV-11&chapter=4&clang=_en

United Nations. (2006). *United Nations Convention Relating to Persons with Disabilities.* Retrieved January 17, 2025, from https://treaties.un.org/pages/viewdetails.aspx?src=treaty&mtdsg_no=iv-15&chapter=4&clang=_en

Vaghri, Z., Zermatten, J., Lansdown, G., & Ruggiero, R. (2022). *Monitoring state compliance with the UN Convention on the Rights of the Child: An analysis of attributes* (1st Edition 2022, Vol. 25). Springer Nature. https://doi.org/10.1007/978-3-030-84647-3

Vandenhole, W., Desmet, E., Reynaert, D., & Lembrechts, S. (eds.). (2015). *Routledge international handbook of children's rights studies* (1st ed.). Routledge. https://doiorg.proxy1.lib.trentu.ca/10.4324/9781315769530

Waldock, T. (Ed.). (2020). *A question of commitment: The status of children in Canada* (2nd edition). Wilfrid Laurier University Press.

Wall, J. (2022). From childhood studies to childism: Reconstructing the scholarly and social imaginations. *Children's Geographies, 20*(3), 257–270. https://doi.org/10.1080/14733285.2019.1668912

Watson, N. (2012). Theorising the lives of disabled children: How can disability theory help? *Children & Society, 26*(3), 192–202. https://doi.org/10.1111/j.1099-0860.2012.00432.x

Wickenden, M. (2019). 'Disabled' versus 'nondisabled': Another redundant binary? In A. Twum-Danso Imoh, M. Bourdillon & S. Meichsner (eds.) *Global childhoods beyond the north south divide. Palgrave studies on children and development.* Palgrave Macmillan. https://doi.org/10.1007/978-3-319-95543-8_7

17 A critical perspective on children's right to play

Anandini Dar

17.1 Introduction

Play is considered a natural and spontaneous part of human and animal life (Huizinga, 1949). The significance of play in childhood garners distinct attention as it is an innate part of children's lives, which can occur involuntarily, begets fun, and does not have to be taught per se, although different rules of games are defined by children as they play along (Caillois, 2001; Corsaro, 2003). In other ways, play is also part of children's everyday life (Bowen, 2015), and is a negotiated act from which they develop cognitively (Piaget, 1965) as well as learn about, and make meaning of, their social and material worlds (Katz, 2004). Such dynamics between play and childhood have now been sufficiently discussed and debated in the field of child development and childhood studies. However, the relationship between childhood and play, and how it relates to children's right to play, has not been adequately explored in the existing scholarship.

In this chapter, I examine the play activities and daily experiences of play of children growing up in an urban slum in Delhi, India, to make meaning of children's right to play. These children's play activities are set within the context of recent trends of urban development and urbanization. There has been large-scale migration of families from villages to urban centers of India in the hopes of a better life for their children and families, but instead, most migrant families live in displaced urban settlements in cities where they face constant fear of eviction and lack basic facilities of water, sanitation, electricity, and adequate living and leisure spaces. Hence, the everyday possibilities for play for these children in urban slums are charged by processes of modernity and development and affect how, and where, marginalized children can play, since both the city and their neighbourhoods lack adequate and inclusive spaces for play and for playgrounds. Children's games, thus, emerge in the context of constraints, marginality, and negotiations – for space and materials required in play. By unpacking these marginalized children's daily experiences of play, their negotiations for materials for play, their co-generational aspect of play, and the challenges they face as a result of growing up in a displaced informal urban settlement, I argue that children's play and their right to play is intrinsically linked

DOI: 10.4324/9781003510284-18

to their childhoods, affected by the sociopolitical and economic contexts in which they grow up. The universal right to play legislation, enshrined in the United Nations Convention on the Rights of the Child (UNCRC), sidesteps the questions of political economy and the co-generational production of play. However, I locate the right to play, children's daily experiences of play, and their experience of childhood as deeply embedded within the sociopolitical and economic contexts of their lives. These everyday lives of children, and children's experiences of daily play activities, illuminate how children's social and material worlds come to life. In other words, how, where, and in what ways children engage with games render meaning to their rights, and it is through a contextual understanding of play that their right to play manifests. Such a framework on the right to play, which is tuned into children's meanings of play, their experiences, challenges, and negotiations in their daily life, departs from the imagination of the right to play enshrined in the individualistic and universal notion of the children's rights convention. This chapter contributes to the scholarship on Critical Children's Rights Studies, by drawing on the framing of 'critical as embracing situatedeness' as discussed in the introduction to this volume, wherein the 'situatedness of the experiences of children and their environment in their daily life' offer a more nuanced understanding of the rights of children.

My arguments about play and the right to play also demonstrate alternative pathways to thinking about children's rights, in that the material challenges faced by children and the gender discriminations experienced by girls, highlight the need to reflect on issues of equality and address existing exclusions in the discourses on children's right to play. In this way, this chapter contributes to the field of Critical Children's Rights Studies, and in particular offers a new approach in comprehending the right to play for all children. For a more critical perspective on children's right to play, I opine that the right to play discourse ought to account for everyday situated realities and how these affect children's play and their childhoods in the Global South, resulting in possible alternative pathways to imagine equality and justice for children.

17.2 Theories on play and urban development

Play is an essential way through which children learn. It fosters their cognitive, physical, and socio-emotional learning (Hughes, 2010). Children also learn about their environment, and about their social roles in society through play. This indicates an intrinsic link between their right to play and their childhoods. Cindi Katz (2004) has, for example, discussed the transformative power of play in her research with children in rural Sudan in the 1980s. Katz explores how, through play, children mimic their future adult roles, as they play games such as 'house' or 'setting up a shop.' While doing work, such as herding sheep or fetching water for the house, children also play along the way and demonstrate behaviours and skills necessary for them as adults. Yet, they also transform these roles in their play as some girls enact slightly different gender roles from what their mothers perform. Overall, Katz's research suggests that play is not taught nor is it claimed as a right; rather, it emerges in spontaneous moments of the everyday and can have a transformative role wherein children learn, perform, and transform gendered and future roles and behaviours. In other words, play can be understood as an innate part of the everyday lives of children.

At the same time, play requires both materials and space. Since play can be transformative and play is also 'transformed in the course of political-economic and social transformation(s)' (Katz, 2004, p. 107), children often find innovative ways to adapt their environments for play as well as employ materials for their games that are accessible in their everyday environs. In sites where capitalism has recently entered the region, or in contexts of postcolonial inequality and poverty, marginalized children find various resources from their daily lives to carve out play spaces and devise play materials for their games. In several anthropological works on play, scholars have discussed how the resources in the environment are employed by children to create games and play materials, and through it they learn about their surroundings and roles in society. For instance, David Lancy (1996) and Zazie Bowen (2015) discuss how the resources from the soil and earth become play materials for children in rural areas, and through this they also learn about their environment and generational roles. In other words, play is part of culture (Schwartzman, 1978, p. 4). However, for many marginalized children living in urban centres, play is marred by their context of marginality, depravity, and precarity. This chapter also urges us to move beyond a romanticized idea of play and understand the limits of the transformative power of play, so as to imagine a more critical perspective on the right to play.

In the context of neoliberal policies on urban development, urban centres in the Global South are witnessing a shrinking of playground spaces (Chaturvedi, 2024). This results in greater inequalities in access to play spaces if they are available. For instance, children living in urban slums find it difficult to play games in open public areas, if there are any, as these are often occupied by adult men and youth. This poses a specific challenge for marginalized young girls, who end up playing largely in their homes or right outside in narrow street areas (Dar & Chopra, 2024). While there are studies promoting the need for child-friendly cities, and urban playgrounds in the light of increasing urbanization (Ekawati, 2015; Gill, 2021; Gleeson & Sipe, 2006), there is little discussion around the challenges facing marginalized children growing up in cities and their depleting play spaces. Migrant children in India are often restricted from accessing neighbourhood parks available in high-rise building complexes adjacent to their slums, and some of the schools they attend lack playgrounds despite laws such as the Right to Education Act, 2010, which mandate that all schools include a playground (Ravishankar, 2022). These interconnected issues of urban development, marginalization, poverty, and play spaces are often overlooked in debates on national and global children's rights. Understanding the everyday reality of marginalized children's lives and their play contexts highlights the need to reimagine a critical concept of the right to play. In the subsequent sections I present empirical data and analysis from a research study about the everyday contexts of play of marginalized migrant children growing up in New Delhi, India.

17.3 Research site, participants, and methodology

I draw on a study I conducted between 2019–2022, as part of a collaborative research project with architects and social scientists entitled 'Displacement, Placemaking and Wellbeing in the City.'[1] While the larger study explored questions around how displaced communities make use of places across four global cities, the data for this chapter specifically focus on interviews and fieldwork conducted with children in a slum in Delhi to understand their living conditions, education, and play. Due to the COVID-19 pandemic, the fieldwork and informal interviews were conducted between September to December of 2019, and then the in-depth interviews were conducted at the end of 2021 and early 2022. While pre- and post-COVID contexts altered the circumstances of children to some extent, including a greater dropout rate from school and more time for play, this study does not aim to capture a difference between pre-and post-COVID contexts. Play for the children was largely observed and discussed in the context of where they lived. For this chapter we draw on interviews conducted with 25 children, including 14 boys and 11 girls, between the ages of 9 and 15 years, living in an informal settlement in Delhi.

This urban settlement hosts a 200-household complex, located in the heart of south Delhi, surrounded by several government residential quarters and a market, neatly hidden behind tall trees from four sides. The residents began living in this unoccupied plot of land in 2004. Most of the families at the time were engaged in painting work, as they were part of the 'safedi community' (whitewashers/housepainters), and they were mostly second-generation migrants. There are, however, many recent migrant families who reside here as well, who have arrived through kin and work networks, largely from the states of Bihar and Rajasthan. Most of the new arrivals build their own temporary house with the support of a local resident in the neighbourhood who also runs a tent business and provides them with temporary roofing and building materials for a cost of approximately INR 20,000.[2] This local resident is referred to as the unofficial *pradhan* (local leader) of the area and resides in the neighbouring government residential quarters allotted to janitors/grade D-level government employees, many of whom are Dalit and from 'Other Backward Castes,' the most disadvantaged groups in India. The *pradhan* keeps

1 This project, based in Delhi, was funded by the Indian Council of Social Science Research (ICSSR).

2 Approximately 250 USD.

a close watch on the settlement, ensuring that no new residents enter the space and that no one can expand their facilities or build encroachments beyond what he permits. In this way the slum has developed and grown amidst a very busy and bustling market and a complex residential area. Unlike other slum areas where families mostly come from the same region of India and make a home, here, the families have arrived from different states of the country (Bihar, Rajasthan, Jharkhand) but mostly through networks of caste and work. Only three families are Muslim, while the rest are from disadvantaged castes. Despite no running water supply and no drainage system in place, families live in this slum because of its location, with access to work and services in the neighbourhood. There is no government-provided child care facility nor any toilets in the settlement. While this slum meets all the criteria under the Delhi Slum & JJ Rehabilitation and Relocation Policy 2015 for adequate in situ rehabilitation, the residents have not been relocated to more permanent housing and, instead, have received notices for eviction by the Central Public Works Department (CPWD), which owns the land. Apart from three or four households that managed to build their own toilets, the rest of the residents use the Municipal Corporation's built toilets, two blocks away in the market area. This results in substantial anxiety around hygiene and safety, particularly for girls and women as they have to walk a long distance away from their houses every time they need to use the toilet facility at all hours of the day and night. Most of the adult women are occupied as domestic workers or street vendors, and men are engaged in day wage work as rickshaw pullers, street vendors, chefs, and drivers. Some men also work and live away from their family as they are engaged in contractual work for construction or painting. During the COVID pandemic many families sent their children to live with their grandparents as they were unable to support them and take care of them while searching for livelihoods. This resulted in their names getting struck off the school register. However, most of the children we interviewed attend the neighbouring government New Delhi Municipal Council (NDMC) and Sarvodaya schools. To understand where and how children spend their time and to get a sense of when and where they play, we conducted a time lapse mapping exercise, and also frequently observed how children use the spaces in the settlement. The 25 in-depth interviews with the children also revealed what and where they play and why they prefer to play at home or in the slum, as opposed to in their schools.

When we began our fieldwork, we obtained permission to do so by first discussing with the community details about the research and the research team. After receiving their consent, we began initial interactions with the elders of the community to understand the site more broadly. With frequent visits subsequently, along with MA students from my university who were conducting a class project on ethnography of play, we were able to build rapport and position ourselves objectively as researchers, distinct from the social workers and political party representatives who visit the slum to interact with them for other purposes.

We obtained consent for interviews from parents and children and followed necessary ethical protocols for data collection as per the university rules on research. Interviews and focus group discussions (FGDs) were conducted by me, and two research assistants, one of whom had previously worked in the community for their MA thesis, and one activist who was also working with an NGO to ensure that families are not evicted from the slum. Positioning ourselves as allies and researchers who support their right to better living conditions overall helped to build a relationship of trust, after which we conducted interviews. At the same time, the data collection and analysis also involved a process of reflexivity wherein the inequality in power relations between the researcher and the researched are acknowledged as we gained far more from the interactions than did those with whom we conducted the research (England, 1994). Yet, by giving voice to children's own experiences and expressions of play, this study is able to capture a child-centred and situated understanding of children's play and demonstrate what ought to constitute their right to play.

17.4 Spatial mapping of children's daily play

To comprehend how children play in an urban slum, it is essential to make sense of the physical landscape. The slum is surrounded by trees on all sides with a small public milk dispensary at one end that connects the slum to the streets in the neighbourhood. Most children play within the boundary of the slum which is demarcated by streets on each side. Children either played right in front of their houses or in the six or seven play areas marked in Figure 17.1.

Girls from the slum rarely went to play in the areas that go beyond the boundary of the settlement. However, many of the boys, particularly those

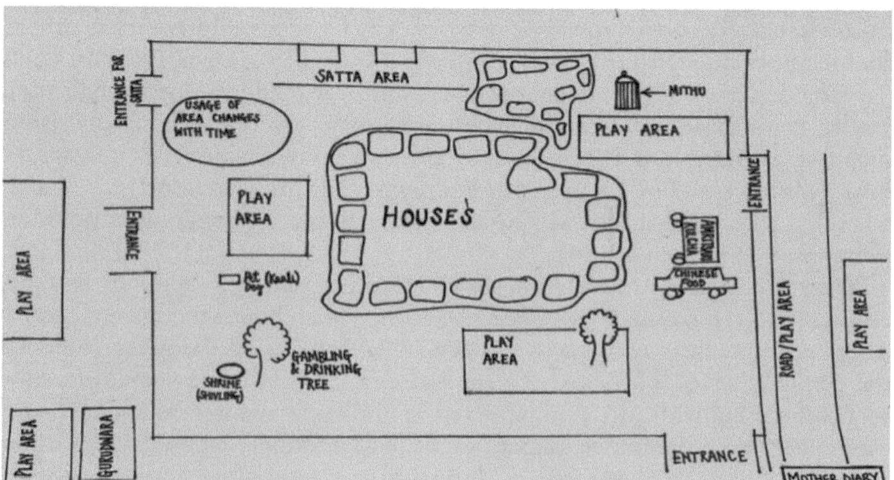

Figure 17.1 Hand-drawn map of the settlement capturing the dominant play areas.

above the age of 11, played near the *gurudwara* (Sikh temple) across the street (on the bottom left of the map), and oftentimes on the road in the large open land to the east of the settlement. This open land space is also used by neighbouring residents, particularly young boys and men for sports like cricket or football. Some boys also venture into the market on the west side beyond the milk booth, to play on the streets and sidewalks.

The young boys from the settlement are particularly drawn to the play area near the *gurudwara* as they are able to access the free Wi-Fi network of the temple. Prior to the national ban of the famous online game, *PUBG*, most of the young boys would be found playing this single-player game either alone or collectively on a shared device (usually belonging to a parent) in the area adjacent to the temple. Girls were rarely found playing in this area as they were either not allowed by their parents to go where only boys were found playing, or they were not interested in the game. Parents would also be concerned about their daughters' safety and restrict them from going alone to the nearby market area or neighbouring streets. While girls would sometimes flout parental restrictions on other matters, they were often hesitant about playing outside of their settlement. Some of the girls would express concerns around safety in open public areas or streets, as these are largely dominated by men or male youth, and those spaces are not welcoming to women and girls, a sentiment that resonates with scholarship in gender studies (Phadke et al., 2011). While both boys and girls also played together, this was mostly within the settlement. It was only when the entire family went to local public parks in Delhi that girls had an opportunity to play in grounds beyond their neighbourhood. Most of the children of the settlement reported that they had visited Central Park or Lodhi Garden, Delhi's large public parks, with their parents and siblings on days their parents had time off from work, and they thoroughly enjoyed their time playing with the animals in these large public parks, chasing their siblings, or playing with their parents. None of the children spoke about school as a space for play. Although one or two children shared that they have some friends at school, the rest of the children explained that they did not feel they had any 'real' friends at school and preferred playing with their friends in the settlement, or with peers with whom they went to tuition classes after school.

17.5 Inter-/co-generationality and play

In the discourse on children's right to play, the poor or marginalized parents or caring adults hardly figure, and if they do, it is in the context of lacking any ability to support children's play. Rarely is the right to play imagined as intergenerational or existing beyond an individualistic frame. Children of migrants growing up in urban slums, however, experience play not just with their peers or in schools but also, and more frequently, in their everyday living environments and with their parents. Many of the parents played with their children both as a way to pass the time and as a family activity.

Take, for instance, Rajeev, who explains how his family plays games together both offline and on a single shared mobile phone:

Q: Do you play any games on the mobile phone?

A: Yes. I play games like carrom board and ludo on my father's phone. My mom, me, and I also play ludo offline as well. Then there is this game called *PUBG*, I also play that. I play all of this at night.

While playing online games tends to be viewed as a solitary and an individual experience, this child explains how sometimes he plays online games on his father's phone at night along with him. On further discussion he explained that his parents would also chip into what moves he should make next on the game and despite the fact that he was playing as an individual player in an online game, he had an offline team supporting him. Play and games, hence, became a family activity at night before sleeping.

Similarly, another participant, Surbhi, shared how she enjoys watching cartoon films with her family at night. She found this to be a form of play. For children, play or leisure may not necessarily be only a child-related activity, to be either performed or experienced alone or with other children. Instead, they recalled, very enthusiastically, moments when they played with their parents or that they would play in the presence of their parents. A 9-year-old female participant, Rekha, while recounting her daily activities excitedly, shares that she enjoys playing when she goes to the public Central Park with her parents in the early hours of the morning:

A: Yes, we have to go down to the market area to the public toilet. My father, me and my mother go together. Then from there we go to the public park. We go jogging together. Mother, father and I go together. We go every morning for a jog. Kishan (brother) does not go because he's sleeping. We also jog in the Central Park. Father also exercises and builds his body and then we also play on the merry go round swing. We go when it's early morning. Very few people are there at that time. It is a lot of fun.

According to Roger Caillois (2001), a key characteristic of play is 'fun' or, as Rekha puts it, *'mazaa.'* Going to the park is fun particularly because they can access the merry-go-round, a play equipment not otherwise available to the children in their neighbourhood or school, and because Rekha is able to play along with her parents. That her family follows this routine together indicates how play is produced co-generationally in the everyday, not accounted for in the discourse on the right to play. This co-generationally produced aspect of play also includes moments where children have to manoeuvre and negotiate time for peer play with their parents. Many parents consider peer play a waste of time, which can lead to 'bad influences' in terms of resulting in romantic relationships or substance addiction, and many generally believe that free play can be a distraction from their schoolwork and household responsibilities.

Given this context, many of the girls, in particular, negotiate time to play by trying to quickly complete their house chores and homework and then find time to play while their parents are still at work. Therefore, play encounters are possible when children refute parents' restrictions on play.

Q: Okay. So, do you enjoy staying at home when your parents are not at home?

A: Yes. Because first we quickly finish all our work and then we come outside of the house and start playing. We send two or three kids to go keep a look-out for our mother in case she is returning home. If she is coming home we quickly throw away the stones and ball we are playing with. Mummy scolds us if she sees us playing *'pithoo'* (stone-ball game), and says we keep playing this game all the time. Plus, if we are playing a match of girls vs. boys, she scolds us for playing with boys (Chaaya, age 13 years).

Oftentimes, parents restrict children from playing because they want them to complete their homework and fear that mix-gender play will result in romantic relationships and elopement. In her research with children in a slum of Kolkata, Kabita Chakraborty (2015) similarly shares that parents place many restrictions on their daughters' mobility, and even monitor their movement closely as they were particularly concerned about premarital sexual interactions. These fears are largely related to daughters choosing to marry outside their castes. Hence, to avoid this, restrictions on the mingling of girls and boys begin early and is carefully imposed during playtime. However, many children shared how they would, like Chakraborty's interlocutors, negotiate time for interacting with the opposite sex.

Many children in the slum shared that as soon as their mothers left for work, they would start playing. They would also sometimes play badminton with boys on the road adjacent to the settlement but make sure their parents did not find out. Radha, another 11-year-old girl, shares how they play *pithoo paala* when their mother leaves for work, and stop playing as soon as she returns in the afternoon. They then go and spend time watching some shows on the television with their mother and when she becomes engrossed in her TV show, they quietly step out to play again. These forms of negotiations for play with parents demonstrates that play is set within the embedded contexts of their living conditions, wherein children need to navigate their time for work and time with family, alongside play. Play is not a right they can claim for themselves, nor is it obtained in institutional and individualized sites; rather, it is co-generationally produced in the negotiations of everyday pressures of work, schooling, parental expectations, rules, gender, and their own desires.

17.6 The material realities of play

The material resources children have at hand determine what, and how, children can play. While not studied extensively, a few scholars in South Asia have now examined children's play materials, which reveal the socio-economic and cultural history of children's playthings and their society, the benefits of artefacts for children, and also how children make do with their material realities during play. Sudarshan Khanna (1981), for instance, has documented extensively the craft of wooden and traditional toys in India, while Supriya Varma (2018) explores how toys and other play materials were used in childhood in the Harappan Civilization. More recently, scholars have argued that play materials and built play areas are more accessible to children from middle and upper classes, whereas children from disadvantaged families tend to be more 'innovative' in their use of play materials, depending on what is available around them (Oke et al., 1999). Children growing up in marginalized contexts have limited access to open public spaces for play, and also limited resources for play materials. When we asked children in the settlement what they would like to change in the neighbourhood, many of them shared that they would like some play equipment, such as swings, more open and safe spaces to play in the settlement, and a children's park. Such a desire indicates two things: 1) that children imagine and wish for facilities for play as those they witness in areas outside the settlement; and 2) that there is lack of access to playgrounds and play materials in their schools, neighbourhood, and city. Children had reported that when they visit the parks in their neighbourhood, some families and even the guards would tell them to leave the parks since they do not live in the high-rise buildings adjacent to which these parks are constructed. While one or two girls would try to reach their schools early so that they could play in the playground, others either do not go to school, or their schools do not have playgrounds. Many children also do not like attending their school since they do not have friends there. Migrant children face distinct challenges in schooling as some families migrate seasonally and their children need to change schools according to their parents' movement, making it difficult for them to adjust to a new system (Dyer & Rajan, 2023). Hence, inventiveness vis-à-vis play materials is not something to be considered as a celebration of their childhood; rather, it is to be understood in the context of necessity, negotiation, and challenges, and beckons the question of equality for play. Although not ideal for them, the children in the settlement also employ innovative methods to develop their own play materials and transform certain spaces in the slum into their own playgrounds.

Risha, an 8-year-old girl, shares how one of her friends has a hand-me-down dollhouse set; however, many of the parts are missing and hence, they had to use their own household items for their game 'house-house' rather than store-bought miniature household toys.

> I have more friends in the village than here. Chaaya and Samira are my friends here. We mostly play house-house. We play it both inside the house and outside. Samira had a doll set that we used to play with. But when we play house-house we also use the caps from plastic bottles lying around and also bring bowls from our house. We would make vegetables by using a small earthen lamp as our wok for cooking.

Another makeshift game for children was swinging on the tree. Sonu, a 10-year-old boy, shares that they would mostly like to swing on the tree, since they did not have a built swing like in most playgrounds. He added that 'actually it isn't really a swing, it's just a broken tree on which we sway. This way it becomes our swing.' There was another big tree in the front of the settlement on which the children climbed and played often. This outdoor play became even more frequent for children in the settlement during the pandemic. One child shared that, in fact, they played more often than usual as a result of the lockdown and closures of schools. This was unlike children in middle-class homes who were distanced from greenery and parks and had to play in their cemented homes during the COVID-19 stay-at-home state order (Chaudhary et al., 2021).

Most marginalized children, such as those in my study, do not have the resources to purchase basic play materials such as balls, bats, rackets, etcetera. For *pithoo pala*, a game which they played often, children would collect marble pieces strewn around in the settlement and break them according to the size they required with some bricks. After arranging these pieces in a height order starting from the ground, they would then require a ball to be thrown at it to dismantle it and topple all the pieces over, indicating a win. Children would take turns to break the arrangement, and whoever dismantled the greatest number of pieces would win. However, having a ball to play this with is not common for them; hence, children would stuff paper inside socks that they would bring from their homes and then wet the socks, making it into a packed ball. This way, they always had access to a ball. Stacks of marbles were collected from trash materials strewn around in the settlement, making it possible to play whenever they wanted. Therefore, these games were possible for children despite the limited material resources at hand. At the same time, these games indicate how situated contexts deeply impact children's play and, therefore, must be addressed and thought about in any discourse on the right to play.

17.7 Discussion and conclusion

Whereas play has been studied as an innate part of childhood and as emerging in any environment that children occupy, an ethnographic study of the everyday lives of migrant children growing up in a slum indicates how everyday urban environments result in shaping the games children are able to play, who they can play with, and how, and when, they play. Restrictions on children's play, playtime, and play spaces are intrinsically linked to the larger political economic conditions in which they are growing up. Informed by urban development agendas and myth of modernity, families and their children migrate to cities, and live in informal settlements that lack the most basic facilities, let alone adequate spaces for play. Concerns for safe spaces in the settlements also result in parental restrictions on where girls can play. Thus, studying the everyday situatedness in which marginalized children play offers a reading of the challenges and inequalities in their lives vis-à-vis access to play materials and spaces. Such examinations around the centrality of political economy and gender in play are absent from discourses on children's right to play and this chapter argues that it must be prioritized in a critical perspective on children's rights. Hence, to understand what constitutes children's right to play, there is a need for a deeper examination of the link between childhoods and children's everyday play contexts. It also requires us to move beyond a romanticization of the transformative power of play, and reckon with the unequal structures of society that enable some children to access play materials while others have to innovate based on whatever limited resources are available in their environments.

Children in this study not only play with peers but also with their parents, or oftentimes play games on their parents' mobile phones, along with them. On other occasions, children would navigate parents' restrictions on the time for play, and in this way, play, as this chapter has argued, is produced inter-generationally. Adequate literature in childhood studies demonstrates how childhoods are embedded in interdependent and inter-generational relations (Abebe, 2013; de Castro, 2022; Twum-Danso Imoh, 2022); however, this understanding of how children navigate possibilities for play inter-generationally remains unexplored. Therefore, equally essential to a critical perspective on children's right to play is the discussion of inter/co-generationality of children's play, as it offers a reading of play as going beyond the individualized model of the universal convention on children's rights.

Overall, the empirical data of this chapter highlights two distinct points that contribute to a critical understanding of children's right to play: 1) that the materiality of the lived contexts of children's lives informs how, and what, they can play; and 2) that gender and co-generationality defines children's play. When such an understanding of play and childhood surfaces, a critical perspective on their right to play is possible; one that is arrived at through 'embracing situatedness' and that opens up pathways for justice for all children's right to play.

References

Abebe, T. (2013). Interdependent rights and agency: The role of children in collective livelihood strategies in rural Ethiopia. In K. Hanson & O. Nieuwenhuys (eds.) *Reconceptualizing children's rights in international development: Living rights, social justice, translations.* (pp. 3–25) Cambridge University Press.

Bowen, Z. (2015). Play on the mother-ground: Children's games in rural Odisha. *South Asian History and Culture*, *6*(3), 330–347.

Caillois, R. (2001). *Man, play and games.* University of Illinois Press.

Chakraborty, K. (2015). Bollywood as a role model: Boyfriends, dating and negotiating romance. In C. Bradford & M. Reimer (eds.) *Girls, texts, cultures* (pp. 238–263). Wilfred Laurier University Press.

Chaturvedi, M. (2024). Lost playgrounds: How metro cities are failing their children. *India Today.* Retrieved June 18, 2024, from www.indiatoday.in/educationtoday/featurephilia/story/lost-playgrounds-howmetrocities-are-failing-their-children-2554669-2024-06-18

Chaudhary, N., Kapoor, S., & Pillai, P. (2021). 'It was peers and playgrounds that were missing, not play': Young children in northern Indian homes during the pandemic. *International Journal of Play*, *10*(4), 405–419.

Corsaro, W. (2003). *We're friends right? Inside kids' culture.* Joseph Henry Press.

Dar, A., & Chopra, D. (2024). Participatory and co-design approaches for migrant girls' wellbeing: A study in an urban informal settlement of Delhi. *Wellbeing, Space and Society, 6*, 100201.

de Castro, L. R. (2022). Righting adults' wrongs: 'Generationing' on the battlefield: The decolonial approach. *Childhood, 29*(3), 355–370.

Dyer, C., & Rajan, V. (2023). Left behind? Internally migrating children and the ontological crisis of formal education systems in South Asia. *Compare: A Journal of Comparative and International Education, 53*(2), 287–304.

Ekawati, S. A. (2015). Children-friendly streets as urban playgrounds. *Procedia – Social and Behavioral Sciences, 179*, 94–108,

England, K. (1994). Getting personal: Reflexivity, positionality and feminist research. *The Professional Geographer, 46*(1), 80–89.

Gill, T. (2021). *Urban playground: How child-friendly planning and design can save cities* (1st ed.). RIBA Publishing.

Gleeson, B., & Sipe, N. (Eds.). (2006). *Creating child-friendly cities: New perspectives and prospects.* Routledge.

Hughes, F. P. (2010). *Children, play, and development.* Sage Publications.

Huizinga, J. (1949). *Homo Ludens: A study of the play element in culture.* Routledge and Kegan Paul.

Katz, C. (2004). *Growing up global: Economic restructuring and children's everyday lives.* University of Minnesota Press.

Khanna, S. (1981). *Dynamic folk toys: Indian toys based on the simple application of principles of science and technology.* www.arvindguptatoys.com/arvindgupta/dynamicfolktoys.pdf

Lancy, D. (1996). *Playing on the motherground: Cultural routines for children's development.* Guilford Press.

Oke, M., Khattar, A., Pant, P., & Saraswathi, T. S. (1999). A profile of children's play in urban India. *Childhood, 6*(2), 207–219.

Phadke, S., Khan, S., & Ranade, S. (2011). *Why loiter? Women and risk on Mumbai streets.* Penguin Books.

Piaget, J. (1965). *The moral judgement of the child.* Norton.

Ravishankar, R. (2022). *Over 23% schools in India have no playground: Report.* EducationWorld. www.educationworld.in/over-23-schools-in-indiahave-no-playground-report/#:~:text=The%20UDISE%2B%20report%20for%202021,Meghalaya%20have%20a%20designated%20playground

Schwartzman, H. (1978). *Transformations: The anthropology of children's play.* Plenum.

Twum-Danso Imoh, A. (2022). Framing reciprocal obligations within intergenerational relations in Ghana through the lens of the mutuality of duty and dependence. *Childhood, 29*(3), 439–454.

Varma, S. (2018). Material culture and childhood in Harappan South Asia. In S. Crawford, D. Hadley & G. Shepherd (eds.) *The Oxford handbook of the archaeology of childhood* (pp. 179–196). Oxford Handbooks Online.

18 Children's rights implementation as a lived practice

An ethnography of implementation in India and its potential for Critical Children's Rights Studies

Therese Boje Mortensen

18.1 Introduction

We were having lunch at one of the many nongovernmental organization-run (NGO) branches of India's national child helpline in the state of Madhya Pradesh where I worked as a researcher and volunteer for three months. The talk fell upon the topic of child marriages, and I asked the social workers whether they managed to stop them. One of the social workers in attendance, Radha, responded:

> The truth is that 99% will not be stopped, even if they are legally stopped. In the best cases, they will wait until the girl is old enough, but the day she turns 18, she gets married. Other times they will not get legally married, but send the girl to live with the in-laws anyways and then get her married when she is old enough.
>
> (fieldnotes, 14 February 2019)

According to India's Prohibition of Child Marriage Act (2006), it amounts to child marriage if a girl below 18 years gets married. As an employee of the state-sponsored child helpline, it was Radha's job to ensure that this legal act was 'implemented.'

The aim of this chapter is to critically and ethnographically unpack the notion of 'children's rights implementation' by de-emphasizing its legal aspects and, instead, highlighting its social, interactive, and informal character. The key question is how we, as critical children's rights scholars, who seek to go beyond critiquing a 'gap' between law and practice, can study the everyday implementation of children's rights. The first section of the chapter sets the intellectual context for this endeavour by demonstrating how ethnographic studies of implementation can be a methodological tool for critical children's rights researchers. Then, I showcase my own ethnography by narrating stories of how children's protection rights were implemented in Madhya Pradesh. Finally, I conceptualize implementation as a 'lived practice' and draw out methodological and theoretical implications for Critical Children's Rights Studies.

DOI: 10.4324/9781003510284-19

18.2 'Implementation ethnographies' as tools for critical children's rights researchers

Critical Children's Rights Studies seek to deconstruct 'obvious' assumptions in children's rights law. One such assumption is that if laws are consistent with children's rights, but rights are not fulfilled, the reason is poor implementation. The 'implementation gap approach' has already been critiqued (Reynaert et al., 2012; Vandenhole et al., 2015), and alternatives have been suggested, such as 'localising' (De Feyter, 2007; see Vandenhole's chapter in Liebel, 2012) or 'vernacularising' (Levitt & Merry, 2009) children's human rights. These approaches have brought out the social contexts that law exists in, but they have not critically interrogated the notion of 'implementation' itself. Is it a superfluous legal and policy-related concept with no relevance for 'real' children's rights? Or can a detailed study of what exactly 'implementation' involves help us to understand why some rights seem unimplementable? What happens if instead of disregarding 'implementation,' we dive ethnographically into it and study it as a lived practice?

In order to deconstruct the idea that children's rights implementation simply equals the application of law, we first need to acknowledge that children's rights law does not necessarily reflect the same ideals as their advocates intended. Indeed, scholars have emphasized how legal institutionalization and bureaucratization of rights can work counter to the emancipatory ideals that inspired the advocacy for these laws (Stammers, 2009; Reynaert, 2025). Second, those who try to 'teach' rights to children (and by extension, those who *implement* such laws on the ground) significantly affect the ultimate enjoyment, and understandings, of children's rights in a given context (Balagopalan, 2014). However, discrepancies between the original intent of a law and its implementation should not, I argue, amount to simply blaming lower-level bureaucrats for not implementing the laws well enough. Instead, they should make us question whether laws are not, in fact, 'products of a crazed imagination and of an elite disconnection from the labours of real implementation' (Mathur, 2016, p. 7). What makes good policy on paper is often the most unimplementable (Mosse, 2004). My intention in this chapter is, therefore, to move 'away from the disjuncture between the plan and its realization to elaborate the process through which this realization happens' (Mathur, 2016, p. 16). In other words, there may be an 'implementation gap,' but this gap is filled with rich social situations worth unpacking.

I argue that we should conceive of children's rights implementation as a *lived practice*. Here, it is useful to recall Karl Hanson and Olga Nieuwenhuys' (2013, p. 6) concept of 'living rights' which 'highlights that children (amongst other people), while making use of notions of rights, shape what these rights are – and become – in the social world.' Building upon this but also going further, my purpose is not only to highlight *children's* agency in using, and shaping, the children's rights concept but also to emphasize other actors who participate in children's rights implementation, and their roles and interdependency. In the spirit of Critical Children's Rights Studies, I seek to avoid messianic beliefs in the child's voice as the only key to understanding the practice of children's rights, and, rather, examine how children and adults, and the power dynamics between them, together, shape children's rights practice. Conceptualizing implementation as a lived practice consisting of negotiations between bureaucrats, NGOs, families, and children thus reflects the interdependency of human relations that Critical Children's Rights Studies and, in particular, childism emphasize (Wall, 2025).

18.2.1 Implementation actors for children's rights in India: the importance of the NGO sector

Just like Critical Children's Rights Studies, ethnography emphasizes context. In this chapter, I focus on the role of NGOs in implementing children's protection rights in India, and it is, therefore, necessary to first provide some contextual background.

India's so-called 'voluntary' sector has overlapped with the state since independence (Sen, 1992; Srivatsan, 2015). With the liberalization of the Indian economy in the early 1990s, the role for NGOs as subcontracted service providers of the state's social policies has been dominant (Mortensen, 2023), as mirrored in many other neoliberal contexts (Pradhan et al., 2023). This chapter's empirical focus is one such NGO-contracted service: India's erstwhile national helpline for children, CHILDLINE. From 1996 to 2022, CHILDLINE was funded by the central government, managed by a foundation in Mumbai, and implemented by hundreds of small NGOs across the country.[1] Anyone could call the free number 1098 with a problem related to children. The calls were first handled by regional call centres, and then transferred to subcontracted NGOs whose staff would meet and help the child at hand within one hour. NGO employees were thereby indirectly representing the state and the law: they answered calls on the 'government helpline,' identified which law was being breached, counselled families and children, and connected them to authorities.

CHILDLINE's setup raises broader questions about whether it is really 'rights implementation' if it is not 'official' state actors, but NGOs, who are the performers. The fact that NGOs with state-like practices implement rights is indeed a global phenomenon (Bernal & Grewal, 2014; Ferguson & Gupta, 2002; Trouillot, 2001). When becoming part of the governance apparatus (Sharma, 2006) and of the developmental state (Corbridge et al., 2005, p. 7), NGOs are certainly implementers of law if we define implementation as 'the series of tasks undertaken by individuals and groups for achieving the state's

1 CHILDLINE does not exist in this form anymore due to political changes in India. My fieldwork reflects the state of things in 2019. The points about implementation as a lived practice, however, are relevant beyond CHILDLINE.

policy objectives over its territory' (Mangla, 2022, pp. 37–38). Through the example of CHILDLINE, this chapter, thus, expands understandings of implementation actors beyond bureaucrats, to also include NGO workers, families, and children. This is not to say that 'official' state actors are irrelevant, but rather reflect an ambition to focus on an understudied aspect of implementation which recognizes the plurality of the state (Randeria, 2007). In such set-ups, the subjectivities of 'half-state, half-NGO' workers become critical in children's rights implementation, as we saw previously with the NGO worker, Radha, who questioned whether she was really stopping child marriages when she was only 'legally' doing so, as I will return to in the discussion.

18.2.2 Ethnography and the positionality of the foreign researcher

If we conceptualize children's rights implementation as a lived practice, ethnography is an apt methodological approach. Ethnography requires that the researcher place herself in the studied social situations. Participant observation and in-depth interviews are used to document 'what people do routinely – practices – the way they talk about their social world – meanings and modes of discourse – and the social structures within which they live and work – social networks and institutions' (Merry, 2017, p. 141). Inspired by legal anthropology, the ethnography of implementation is interested in what is practiced (which actors are engaged in implementation, and how?) rather than taking its point of departure from 'the state' because it is legally responsible for human rights implementation. For this study, I spent three months with a CHILDLINE-implementing NGO in Madhya Pradesh, India. Seven case workers, one counsellor, and one volunteer were employed there. As a PhD student from a Swedish university, I had negotiated with the NGO's director to work as a volunteer for the NGO while observing their practice, writing fieldnotes, talking informally to employees, and conducting semi-structured individual and group interviews with employees of the NGO and local child protection authorities. My interest was in observing children's rights implementation as social workers performed their everyday work. Ethnographic findings then become an entry point for grounding new normative children's rights theory. For my case, such theory concerns the conceptualization of 'children's rights implementation,' but ethnography is more widely applicable for eliciting the situatedness and contextuality of children's rights practice.

One of the reasons why ethnography is an apt approach for Critical Children's Rights Studies is its mature scholarship on positionality. Children's rights researchers – also non-ethnographers – have a 'position' towards their topic which determines their analytical lenses (Alcoff, 1991; Cerwonka & Malkki, 2007). This can relate to the scholar's education, upbringing, citizenship, or identities. For my case: I have been interdisciplinarily and critically schooled in human rights studies in Europe; I have professional experience in children's rights NGOs; and I have studied Hindi and traveled extensively in India prior to the fieldwork. Yet, I do not have a diasporic or personal relationship to the country. Therefore, I am a critical and privileged outsider who shared the professional field of child rights with the research participants. As a participant observer, I engaged wholeheartedly in the NGO's work, but in my analyses, I maintained a critical distance, placing myself neither as a 'believer' in nor an 'opponent' of children's rights (Reynaert et al., 2012).

Another aspect of positionality, which is pertinent in ethnographic, and similar, research, concerns how the researcher's physical presence affects situations and how that could impact findings. For my case, traveling from Europe to India to 'work with NGOs' or to 'do anthropology' carries with it expectations and connotations that tap uncomfortably into the colonial past. Colonialism made a kind of human intimacy possible through anthropological fieldwork that was rather one-sided (Lemons, 2017). Being cognizant of this history, I was careful not to place myself in situations where my presence could do harm. For instance, the presence of a foreign researcher in case visits or counseling of children could create misconceptions that the NGO had more resources than it did and place unfulfillable expectations upon them. At the beginning of my stay, the NGO's director and I agreed that I would only participate in outreach, awareness activities, and office work. Thus, the most intimate parts of CHILDLINE's work, such as phone calls, case visits, and counselling, are not considered in my findings through firsthand experience, but through secondhand information. I only met CHILDLINE's most vulnerable target groups in unforeseen situations, such as when they came to the office unexpectedly or when we met them during 'outreach.' As will be evident from the upcoming empirical section, such situations turned out to provide some of the richest findings, a fact which reflects the difficult balance between not doing harm to participants and still contributing to knowledge advancement (Traianou, 2020). Furthermore, my presence may have led the social workers to seek to 'perform' their job in order to show their visitor best practices, but the length of my stay minimized this tendency because they inevitably fell into regular routines as they got used to me being there.

My main points regarding the positionality of critical children's rights ethnographers are that we should begin with a reflection on the 'location' we write from and the consequential perception we have of what children's rights are, and what they should be; then, in ethnographic research situations, we should negotiate our presence with a gatekeeper, and carefully balance knowledge gains with avoiding direct and indirect harm to participants.

18.3 Children's rights law meets complex social realities: the case of implementing a child helpline in India

In this section, I will illustrate what implementation as a lived practice looked like in the case of one CHILDLINE branch. While CHILDLINE was mandated to help any children who called, at times simply through phone counselling, I will here focus on the part of the helpline's work that consisted of implementing a specific number of rights-based legal acts: the Prohibition of Child Marriage Act, 2006; the Right of Children to Free and Compulsory Education Act, 2009; the Protection of Children from Sexual Offences Act, 2012; the Juvenile Justice Act, 2015; and the Child Labour (Prohibition and Regulation) Amendment Act, 2016. It is important to underline that the NGO workers did not have a *legal* mandate to implement these acts (apart from the Juvenile Justice Act, in which CHILDLINE is mentioned), but studying implementation as a lived practice is exactly about studying *how* rights are implemented, whether as legally intended or not. A key finding from my ethnography was, indeed, that NGO workers were central in implementing the mentioned acts, and thus part of the governance apparatus of 'state-like' practices as discussed previously.

I will highlight how implementation for NGO workers consisted of interacting and negotiating with parents in need of 'convincing,' with children as simultaneous 'rights holders' and 'rights violators,' and with local state authorities, which switched between acting as allies and antagonists to rights implementation. Through these meetings between different implementation actors, I show how India's well-meaning children's rights laws met complex social realities. This serves as an illustration of the informal, nonlegal implementation work that becomes evident if we do not strictly study a law, but rather the people who implement rights.

18.3.1 Implementation as convincing parents to act differently

On one of my first days of fieldwork, the NGO staff took me to do 'outreach' in the outskirts of the town where a group of Adivasi ('tribal') communities lived along the road. We all sat down outside the house – Radha and I on something that looked like a bed without a mattress, the male CHILDLINE workers and the father of the family on plastic chairs put out for the occasion, and the mother on the elevated clay entrance to the house. Jagadish, the NGO director, small talked with the parents before beginning his social work exercise: he called the oldest daughter as she was walking across the courtyard doing some domestic work – 'child, sit!' She sat down next to her mother, looking down. Jagadish asked questions like 'how old are you, do you go to school, when did you finish school, do you want to work?' etc. She had finished eighth grade and was now about to get married. Most answers came from the mother. Jagadish asked the parents about their jobs. They were day labourers. He explained about a sewing course that would enable their daughter to earn an income. But getting into the sewing course required her to finish tenth grade. She could live at a girl's hostel in Indore, and he would find a way to cover the fees. The parents were quiet. The girl was looking at the ground, only answering if asked directly. But through his insisting economic arguments, Jagadish managed to get the parents responding, and when an older brother showed up, he agreed to enroll his sister in ninth grade (fieldnotes, 3 February 2019).

This is an example of how a key part of children's rights implementation, in this context, was for NGO workers to get families 'on board.' If parents did not subscribe to the values implicit in children's rights legislation, then implementation would be a futile exercise. Jagadish had here appealed to the economic improvement the family could achieve by sending the daughter to school, but depending on the case, the social workers skillfully chose what to appeal to. For instance, social worker Aditya told me how many parents in villages feared that their teenage girls would elope with a boy from a different caste and, therefore, they married them off early. These parents, he said, should be provided with the statistic that most 'eloping girls' had left school before tenth grade: educated girls would not do this (interview with Aditya, 4 March 2019, Madhya Pradesh). The last resort in these convincing exercises was to appeal to parents' fear of authorities and the law. As social worker Kunal said: 'Some people will not listen to you. [But] if we say that we are sent from the Government of India . . . then everyone will listen and agree to what we say' (group interview with Kunal, Pradeep & Basanti, 23 April 2019, Madhya Pradesh). I now turn to an example of the interaction between social workers and children.

18.3.2 Implementation as helping and scolding children

India's Child Labour Act mandates that children under 14 years of age are not allowed to work. Implementing this act, however, is much more than the police punishing employers and parents as the act proclaims. It also consists of NGO workers' negotiations with working children who learn how not to 'get caught.' Consider this situation:

> Two girls came by the CHILDLINE office, selling mangos. Radha and Pradeep, allegedly interested in mangos, invited the girls inside. The girls were offered to sit down, but they refused. 'Do you go to school?' 'Yes.' 'What grade?' '10th.' 'How old are you?' '10.' '10 years old and you are in 10th grade?' '10–11 . . .' one of them said. They looked like they were beginning to realize that something was going on. Pradeep and Radha explained about the free number 1098, made them repeat it, and explained about child labour: 'You should not do this kind of work. You should not roam around the streets like this.' Radha got out a pen and paper and got their names and their parents' names. 'Now you have to go home,' she said. 'And tell them that you got caught. If you do it again, we will send you to an *aashram* [a residential institution for children]. That's what we'll tell your parents.'
>
> 'Which year were you born in?' Aayushi, a trainee, asked to ascertain their ages. 'Two thousand . . .' one of the girls began, then stopped and hesitated. 'Five,' she finished. 'What kind of office is this?' the other asked. 'CHILDLINE,' Radha and Pradeep repeated. 'We work for children. If someone is in trouble, then we help them. We are a child helpline. Like the police helpline. Also at night, if there is any trouble, you can call.'

Slowly, through more questions, we found out that the girls went to sell mangos because their mum told them to. The money went to their family. Radha warned them again: 'if we see you working! Don't go selling now, go straight home.' Pradeep said that if they needed anything for school, they could just call.

Then the staff took photos of the girls one by one. 'It's forbidden to work for children under 14,' Pradeep said as the last thing before letting the girls go.

(fieldnotes, 17 April 2019)

In this scene, as in others I observed, the interaction with children was a constant switching of hats for the social workers: with their 'NGO hat,' they demonstrated a kind willingness to help children; simultaneously, with their 'government hat,' they underlined the illegality of an activity. As a result, children were treated as subjects of rights one second, and as indirect violators of their own rights the next. The children, quickly realizing what was going on, were understandably skeptical, and everyone present probably knew that the immediate result of this interaction would be that the mango sellers would change their route to avoid CHILDLINE's office. This case could hardly be considered a successful implementation of the Child Labour Act. However, it demonstrates two key difficulties of implementation: the impossibility of implementing an act that prohibits activities that families and children are compelled into due to economic hardship; and social workers' troubles with being both 'helpers' and law implementers. I now turn to the final example of implementation as a lived practice, namely the NGO's interactions with local authorities.

18.3.3 Rights implementation with, or despite, the state

While the NGO workers considered themselves as upholding the aforementioned child protection laws, their belief in the local authorities to do the same was mixed. Most often, the authorities were considered allies. For a single child marriage case, CHILDLINE would involve the District Women Empowerment Officer, the police, the Integrated Child Protection Services, the Child Welfare Committee, and *Anganwadi*[2] workers (fieldnotes, 26 March 2019). The police and other local authorities often referred cases directly to CHILDLINE (fieldnotes, 4 March 2019; 3 April 2019), signifying that much of implementation happened as a collaboration between authorities and NGOs. This is a reflection of the significant role NGOs play as service implementers and as a part of rights governance in India (see Balagopalan, 2019; Sharma, 2006).

2 *Anganwadis* are local centres for early childhood care, which also work with teenage girls and mothers.

However, while I witnessed many friendly meetings between CHILDLINE's social workers and the local authorities, the NGO workers also held some skepticism towards the police:

> Let's say that a child marriage is happening somewhere, and someone calls the police. Then the police will not take action on its own. Only when the call reaches CHILDLINE, action will be taken. [The police] won't do anything. . . . A lot of police just go there, take a bribe. They let the marriage happen.
>
> (interview with Bhavesh, 28 March 2019, Madhya Pradesh)

Aditya similarly explained that in reality, families would find ways to do the marriage anyways, often through the local police, who would take bribes to give the family the 'right' advice: don't do it in this village, go to another temple in a neighbouring village, don't invite anyone, just the girl and boy. And then take the girl back home for a while so it looks like she is living at home (fieldnotes, 1 April 2019). Kunal added that it was not only corruption, but also political clout that mattered, as he explained how certain people would be able to refuse the intervention of CHILDLINE in child marriage cases if they had the right connections to local politicians or authorities (interview with Kunal, 3 March 2019, Madhya Pradesh). The NGO's director exhibited the common perception that as NGO workers, they were not as corruptible and had some higher sense of purpose than those who were directly employed by the state. He regularly mentored his staff along the lines of: 'Are we here to make the CWC [Child Welfare Committee] happy? To make the police happy? No, we are here to work for children! We are not here to make the system happy, but to make the system work' (fieldnotes, 6 April 2019).

The NGO's collaboration with, but simultaneous skepticism towards, the local authorities is evidence that children's rights implementation in many cases only happens when authorities are given a push and kept under scrutiny by other actors through their conviction and identity as part of the 'social sector.' The ways in which NGOs have become part of children's rights governance, thus, turned out to be key to understanding implementation as a lived practice in India.

18.4 Conceptualizing implementation as a lived practice

I now return to the theoretical ambition of the chapter, namely, to deconstruct the idea that 'children's rights implementation' equals a technical application of children's rights law. The ethnographic findings presented previously instead suggest that children's rights implementation is the outcome of the interactive social meeting between children's rights law, its official and unofficial implementers, its beneficiaries (children), and their immediate relations (most often families). Conceptualizing implementation as lived practice, thus, highlights social situations and the roles that these interdependent actors play.

Within the implementation exercise, it is particularly important to analyze who is perceived to represent the state, and thereby who has the authority to enforce rights. In the case of CHILDLINE, it was not simply local authorities, but also the 'semi-governmental' helpline workers who were perceived as 'state like' (Ferguson & Gupta, 2002; Trouillot, 2001). We saw, for instance, how children and parents seemed to perceive the helpline workers as 'the state,' and, consequently, were skeptical towards their intentions. Acknowledging this role of NGOs is not to say that 'official' steps such as appointing Child Marriage Prohibition Officers or upholding the law through police work should not also be considered 'implementation' – but rather that we lack an acknowledgement that implementation includes what happens in informal and unintended ways. Some of these observations are specific to CHILDLINE and India, but the fact that NGOs are increasingly becoming implementers of children's rights is, as discussed previously, a global phenomenon, especially in neoliberal contexts, and these findings, therefore, have broader relevance.

Another important role in rights implementation is that of the perceived 'violator' of a right. By conceiving themselves as 'implementers,' NGO workers, at times, ended up making villains of the parents who 'violated' their children's rights. Their discourses indicated that some parents seemingly would do anything to get around the law to marry off their daughters. Similarly, they, at other times, made villains of children themselves by threatening to send them to *aashrams* if they continued engaging in child labour. The social workers meant well, but this could lead to turning parents and children against the NGO workers and the authorities. The ethnography has, thus, shown how, in practice, implementation can risk losing the engagement of adults who are close to children, or of children themselves.

Then there is the role of the rights holder, who risks being left without much agency in the lived practice of implementation. We saw, for instance, how social workers used their social capital towards the Adivasi family to argue why education was better than early marriage. It was, ultimately, the brother who agreed to enroll his sister in school. While the right to education was achieved in this case, the girl at the heart of the discussions barely uttered a word, meaning that gender-based discriminatory social norms were not challenged. As such, implementation of progressive laws does not always consist of challenging the root causes of structures in society.

Finally, there is the role of the advocate or critic, which, in the case I have analyzed, overlapped with the 'state-like' authority role. To illustrate the NGO's advocate or critic role, we can recall the situations in which NGO workers questioned state authorities, like when Jagadish encouraged his employees to help *children*, not the Child Welfare Committee. We can also recall the introductory vignette of this chapter in which Radha questioned whether she was really stopping child marriages if she were only stopping them 'legally.' Stopping a child marriage 'legally' means to adhere to the age limit of 18 years as defined in the Child Marriage Act. Radha, on the other hand, was aware of the 'social age' (Clark-Kazak, 2009) of young married women which defined their life situation more than their chronological age did. Radha's reflections on social age, thus, demonstrate the difficult 'hat switching' exercise for social workers like herself who are both implementers and critics of child rights law. Where NGO workers' conceptions of rights come from is a complex question which cannot be fully answered here. Elsewhere, I have shown how the values held and practiced in NGOs like Radha's are a complex patchwork consisting of both 'vernacularized' (Levitt & Merry, 2009) ideas about rights from national and international frameworks, from the employees' degrees in social work, and from personal and inter-relational experiences of rights violations – but also new and proactively developed ideas by subjects like Radha. For instance, a combination of 'social service' values intertwined with rights values in Radha's NGO and gave rise to particular understandings amongst NGO workers of their role as a 'provider' of rights (Mortensen, 2024).

18.4.1 Learnings for Critical Children's Rights Studies

A key contribution of this chapter has been to, by way of example, demonstrate how ethnography can be used for Critical Children's Rights Studies. While I have identified the actors relevant in the Indian child helpline context specifically, the thought behind a critical children's rights ethnography is that each contextual study leads the researcher to determine which actors are part of the implementation practice. In other contexts, it could be religious institutions, courts, informal communities, or children's groups. I have also demonstrated some challenges with ethnography, such as balancing between access to vulnerable children and doing no harm to research participants. Finally, I have shown that if we ethnographically study and take seriously the interpersonal interactions that constitute implementation, we will be able to empirically ground new normative conceptions of children's rights.

Thus, the second key contribution of this chapter has been the conceptualization of implementation as a lived practice. This is not a theory for an ideal world, but rather a recognition that implementation has a meaning beyond law. Understanding this enables us to gain conceptual tools to explain, for instance, the dual roles of NGOs as both critics and implementers in concrete children's rights cases, or the tensions between 'social' and 'legal' ages. These types of conclusions reverse the unconvincing idea that the 'implementation gap' is due to corrupt bureaucrats not understanding the real intentions of a progressive law. Instead, we have filled this vaguely understood 'gap' with concrete content: the implementation gap consists of social situations in which state employees, NGOs, children, and families negotiate which practical changes can and cannot be 'implemented' to make their lives more consistent with children's rights – a set of norms which is continuously redefined by the very same actors.

18.5 Conclusion

This chapter has suggested the importance of conceptualizing children's rights implementation not as a technical application of law, but as a lived practice. It has done so by emphasizing the benefits of ethnography for the emerging field of Critical Children's Rights Studies. First, 'implementation' has been deconstructed in order to understand it as a lived practice. Second, I have suggested a method that allows for understanding the nitty-gritty everydayness of implementation, which, in turn, can help ground new alternative pathways for children's rights. Third, I have emphasized that context and situatedness are crucial in order to understand implementation ethnographically. Finally, I have argued that ethnography is beneficial for a critical approach because the ethnographer by definition scrutinizes her own 'gazes' to a given topic or situation.

References

Alcoff, L. (1991). The problem of speaking for others. *Cultural Critique*, *20*, 5–32. https://doi.org/10.2307/1354221

Balagopalan, S. (2014). *Inhabiting 'childhood': Children, labour and schooling in postcolonial India*. Palgrave Macmillian.

Balagopalan, S. (2019). Why historicize rights-subjectivities? Children's rights, compulsory schooling, and the deregulation of child labor in India. *Childhood*, *26*(3), 304–320. https://doi.org/10.1177/0907568219856077

Bernal, V., & Grewal, I. (2014). *Theorizing NGOs: States, feminisms, and neoliberalism*. Duke University Press.

Cerwonka, A., & Malkki, L. H. (2007). *Improvising theory: Process and temporality in ethnographic fieldwork*. University of Chicago Press.

Clark-Kazak, C. R. (2009). Towards a working definition and application of social age in international development studies. *Journal of Development Studies*, *45*(8), 1307–1324. https://doi.org/10.1080/00220380902862952

Corbridge, S., Williams, G., Srivastava, M., & Véron, R. (2005). *Seeing the state: Governance and governmentality in India*. Cambridge University Press.

De Feyter, K. (2007). Localising human rights. In W. Benedek, K. De Feyter & F. Marella (eds.) *Economic globalisation and human rights* (pp. 67–92). Cambridge University Press.

Ferguson, J., & Gupta, A. (2002). Spatializing states: Toward an ethnography of neoliberal governmentality. *American Ethnologist*, *29*(4), 981–1002.

Hanson, K., & Nieuwenhuys, O. (2013). Living rights, social justice, translations. In K. Hanson & O. Nieuwenhuys (eds.) *Reconceptualizing children's rights: Living rights, social justice, translations* (pp. 3–26). Cambridge University Press. https://doi.org/10.1017/CBO9781139381796

Lemons, K. (2017). the ethics and politics of NGO-dependent anthropology. In A. Lashaw, C. Vannier & S. Sampson (Eds.) *Cultures of doing good: Anthropologists and NGOs* (pp. 194–211). University of Alabama Press.

Levitt, P., & Merry, S. E. (2009). Vernacularization on the ground: Local uses of global women's rights in Peru, China, India and the United States. *Global Networks*, *4*, 441–461. https://doi.org/10.1111/j.1471-0374.2009.00263.x

Liebel, M. (2012). with contributions by K. Hanson, I. Saadi, & W. Vandenhole. *Children's rights from below: Cross-cultural perspectives*. Palgrave Macmillan.

Mangla, A. (2022). *Making bureaucracy work: Norms, education and public service delivery in rural India*. Cambridge University Press.

Mathur, N. (2016). *Paper tiger: Law, bureaucracy and the developmental state in Himalayan India*. Cambridge University Press.
Merry, S. E. (2017). The potential of ethnographic methods for human rights research. In B. A. Andreassen, H.-O. Sano & S. McInerney-Lankford (eds.) *Research methods in human rights* (pp. 141–158). Edward Elgar Publishers.
Mortensen, T. B. (2023). *NGOs as child rights implementers in India: How NGO workers negotiate human rights responsibility in 'partnership' with a neoliberal and restrictive state*. PhD dissertation, Lund University.
Mortensen, T. B. (2024). Human rights as social service: Vernacular rights cultures and overlapping ethical discourses at an Indian child rights NGO. *Nordic Journal of Human Rights*, *42*(2), 234–251. https://doi.org.ludwig.lub.lu.se/10.1080/18918131.2024.2326784
Mosse, D. (2004). Is good policy unimplementable? Reflections on the ethnography of aid policy and practice. *Development & Change*, *35*(4), 639–671. https://doi.org/0.1111/j.0012-155X.2004.00374.x
Pradhan, S., Norman-Tichawangana, V., & Kamat, S. (2023). NGOs in international development: Ongoing trends and new architectures. In *International Encyclopedia of Education* (4th ed., pp. 565–573). Elsevier. https://doi.org/10.1016/B978-0-12-818630-5.010629
Randeria, S. (2007). The state of globalization: Legal plurality, overlapping sovereignties and ambiguous alliances between civil society and the cunning state in India. *Theory, Culture & Society*, *24*(1), 1–33. https://doi.org/10.1177/0263276407071559
Reynaert, D. (2025). The social construction of children's rights: Origins of, and developments in, the children's rights movement in Flanders. In V. Llobet, D. Reynaert, A. Twum-Danso Imoh & W. Vandenhole (eds.) *Critical Children's Rights Studies: A research companion*. Routledge.
Reynaert, D., Bie, M. B.-D., & Vandevelde, S. (2012). Between 'believers' and 'opponents': Critical discussions on children's rights. *International Journal of Children's Rights*, *20*(1), 155–168.
Sen, S. (1992). Non-profit organisations in India: Historical development and common patterns. *Voluntas: International Journal of Voluntary and Nonprofit Organizations*, *3*(2), 175–193.
Sharma, A. (2006). Crossbreeding institutions, breeding struggle: Women's empowerment, neoliberal governmentality, and state (re)formation in India. *Cultural Anthropology*, *21*(1), 60–95.
Srivatsan, R. (2015). *Seva, saviour and state: Caste politics, tribal welfare and capitalist development*. Routledge.
Stammers, N. (2009). *Human rights and social movements*. Pluto Press.
Traianou, A. (2020). The centrality of ethics in qualitative practice. In P. Leavy (ed.) *The Oxford handbook of qualitative research* (2nd ed., pp. 86–110). Oxford University Press.
Trouillot, M.-R. (2001). The anthropology of the state in the age of globalization. *Current Anthropology*, *42*(1), 125–138. https://doi.org/10.1086/318437
Vandenhole, W., Desmet, E., Reynaert, D., & Lembrechts, S. (Eds.). (2015). *Routledge international handbook of children's rights studies*. Routledge.
Wall, J. (2025). Children's rights from a childist perspective: Theorizing social empowerment. In V. Llobet, D. Reynaert, A. Twum-Danso Imoh & W. Vandenhole (eds.) *Critical Children's Rights Studies: A research companion*. Routledge.

19 Critique after inclusion

Three pathways towards a Critical Study of Children's Rights

Jonathan Josefsson

19.1 Introduction

On 19 May 2022, Elana Wong, Global Focal Point of the Migrant Youth and Children Platform, climbed onto the podium at the General Assembly taking place at UN Headquarters in New York during the general debate organized by the International Migration Review Forum (IMRF).[1] Her speech followed the speeches of UN Secretary General António Guterres, and General Secretary of the International Organization of Migration António Vitorino, and addressed all UN member state delegations representatives from civil society, business, and mayors. In her speech, Elana Wong stated that she did not only speak on behalf of the over 556,000 children and youth across 36 countries who participated in the Migrant Youth and Children Platform's self-organized consultations in the progress of the Global Compact for Safe, Orderly, and Regular Migration (GCM; United Nations, 2019) but also took on the impossible task of representing the diverse collection of global migrant voices and communities generally. While celebrating the fact that she, as a representative of the young migrant community who was standing in front of the UN General Assembly, was a sign of the increasing recognition that migrants are experts on migration issues, she also pointed to a shrinking civil society space in the GCM process and called for an acknowledgment of the struggles against injustice and the suffering that migrant communities face around the world.

In one sense, Elana Wong's entrance onto the symbolically powerful podium could be regarded as formal success after decades of mobilization

1 UN Headquarters May 19, 2022, International Migration Review Forum 2022, General Assembly, Opening Segments, Min. 26.44, Speech of Elana Wong. Global Focal Point of The Migrant Youth and Children Platform, Link: https://media.un.org/en/asset/k1i/k1iezn9rhm. The International Migration Review Forum serves as the primary intergovernmental global platform involving the participation of all relevant stakeholders to discuss and share progress on the implementation of the Global Compact for Safe, Orderly, and Regular Migration (www.iom.int/international-migration-review-forum-2022).

DOI: 10.4324/9781003510284-20

for the recognition of children and youth as subjects of international politics. Since the latter part of the 20th century, the world has witnessed the unprecedented mainstreaming of children's rights in international law; new norms have developed for the inclusion of young people's experiences in administrative and political processes, and institutions have been established to open up space for the participation of children and youth to represent their interests at international, national, and regional levels (Holzscheiter et al., 2019, 2025; Josefsson, 2023; Kwon, 2019). On the other hand, her speech also illustrates with significant clarity how, despite this formal breakthrough, injustices, domination, inequalities, and lack of access to fundamental rights continue to characterize the lives of young people around the globe.

This has hardly passed unnoticed by researchers and children's rights advocates. Migration is only one of the domains where knowledge production on children's lives and rights has grown exponentially since the 1990s parallel to increasing public awareness and an expanding children's rights field (Brittle & Desmet, 2020; Quennerstedt, 2013; Reynaert et al., 2012). Critiques of the failures of states, international institutions, and business have often been sharp, and the key recipe to remedy these failures, it seems, has been to promote 'even more inclusion' of young people in political, legal, and administrative procedures by calling for new children's rights' strategies, the strengthening of child-sensitive policy frameworks, better participation models, more child-friendly justice systems, and the reconstruction of democratic institutions. Although this critique has taken various forms and built on different ideational legacies, it shares – I suggest – the conviction that even more inclusion of children's voices and rights will lead to societal transformations, children's emancipation, and access to justice.

However, while the paradigm of 'children's inclusion' appears not only to have a weak political force in transforming society, it also hides central epistemological and normative problems and actually risks reinforcing orders of power and structural injustices. The question I seek to ask is: if the calls for more, and better, inclusion of children and their rights and experiences have constituted a central element in public and scholarly critique for decades, what are its political and social effects, and what is left of its radical potential for societal transformation? And can we build a critique which, instead of taking the idea and practice of children's inclusion for granted, can help us enquire about the conditions and social forces that uphold this paradigm and explore alternative pathways for a critical study of children's rights? In the first section of the chapter, 'Inclusion as Critique', I want to point to how the field of children's rights studies has come to embrace the conviction that more inclusion of children's voices, participation, and experiences in political, legal, and administrative procedures can offer a radical social critique. In the second section, I want to critically scrutinize this conviction and outline some pathways forward in the study of children's rights along the lines of what I refer to as 'critique after inclusion'. I will situate my argument mainly in the context of international politics, building on our recent studies on children and youth representation in global politics,[2] with the hope that it will also be useful across a much broader range of domains in society and childhood.

19.2 Inclusion as critique

The ideational roots of including children as members of society and recognizing them as rights bearers as a way of transforming society can, in its modern form, be traced back to, at least, the child-saving movement of the early 20th century (Platt, 1969; Rizzini, 2002). In this context, childhood was seen as a social problem and the separate treatment of children and youth was propelled by an elite group who, through humanitarian efforts, education, and close supervision, sought to expand societal control over children as a way of building a modern nation. When Ellen Key published *The Century of the Child* (1900) at the turn of the 20th century, she put the child at the centre of the public agenda to offer a set of radical visions to fundamentally transform Western societies in the domains of childhood, education, and family life as well as to critique rearmament and imagine a world free of war. And when the Geneva Declaration on the Rights of the Child (1924) was adopted in the wake of the First World War, the inclusion of children as a group within the framework of international human rights fed into an agenda of Western humanitarianism that was closely linked to the emergence of international nongovernmental organizations working specifically with children and to the building of a new international liberal order (Baughan, 2021).

In the 1960s and 1970s, child liberationists wanted to strengthen the inclusion of children in society through abolishing the difference between children and adults by allowing children to make decisions concerning their own lives, giving them political citizenship and protecting them from parental and state paternalism (Margolin, 1978). This kind of critique that has been further developed more recently by children's rights studies is often based on the idea that children are competent actors with agency and, therefore, ought to be better included or empowered to participate in decision-making processes on matters that concern them (Lundy, 2018; Josefsson & Wall, 2020; James, 2007).

In the 1980s and 1990s, the international children's rights movement picked up the overarching idea that children ought to be entitled to universal rights, but emphasized, in contrast to the child liberationists, the recognition of the special nature of children as dependent and vulnerable, their rights

2 In our project, ***Youth Representation in Global Politics: Climate, Migration and Health Governance Compared***, we have compared how, and by whom, young people are represented in contemporary global governance institutions and what the effects of such representations are in three salient domains; climate, migration and health. The project is funded by ***Riksbankens Jubileumsfond*** (P19–0845:1, https://liu.se/en/research/youth-representation-in-global-politics). See, for example, Buhre & Josefsson, 2024; Holzscheiter et al., 2025; Josefsson, 2023; Josefsson & Löw, 2024; Stadelmann et al., 2025.

to a family, and that the state must take responsibility for children as right-holders (Minow, 1995; Bendo, 2020). Since children's rights studies emerged as a separate field of study in the wake of the adoption of the UNCRC in 1989, it has been concerned with the efforts (or lack thereof) to study how standards of children's rights, as expressed in the UNCRC, are implemented in legal and administrative procedures. This line of critique typically rests on the assumption that children's rights are an outcome of international negotiations that took place during the decade leading up to the adoption of the UNCRC, and that children's inclusion in society should be secured through mainstreaming human rights for children and an increased focus on implementation and monitoring (Holzscheiter et al., 2019; Quennerstedt, 2013; Reynaert et al., 2012; Vandenhole, 2015). At the same time, the so-called New Sociology of Childhood and Childhood Studies emphasized the need to include children in new forms of knowledge production as a way of contesting taken-for-granted, and essentialist, understandings about children's lives (Alanen, 2011). The examination of children's experiences and agency in diverse contexts was used as an entry point to question taken-for-granted norms about children, childhood, and children's rights. In this way, scholars took on the role of the critical scientist seeking to make a political difference and improve the social standing of children in society (James et al., 1998; James & Prout, 1990; Liebel, 2012; Hanson & Nieuwenhuys, 2013; Reynaert et al., 2015; Wall, 2019).

19.3 Critique after inclusion

In the following I would like to outline a set of possible pathways for a 'critique after inclusion' that moves beyond a focus on 'the more and better inclusion of children'. While children's rights studies have significantly increased the empirical study of children's rights and experiences across the world (albeit with an emphasis on Global North childhoods, cf. de Castro, 2020; Twum-Danso Imoh et al., 2022) as a way of fostering 'critical awareness' of children's living conditions (Alanen, 2011), I seek to strengthen the theoretical and methodological side of 'critical activity'. I don't propose that children's rights studies have not engaged in critique before. On the contrary, parts of the field have been closely intertwined with the project of the 'critical social sciences' in recent decades (Sayer, 2009). Yet, the notion of the 'critical' has often either been concerned with children's rights advocacy to critique current political orders (Reynaert et al., 2012) or 'reduced to little more than scepticism, coupled with a concern to be "reflexive"' (Alanen, 2011, p. 149). And as the prefix 'critical' has become more frequently used, many times it offers poor analytical and explanatory force, works primarily to sell titles for publication, or is used to signal moral credibility. The typical critical activity in the field has focused on empirically exploring children's voices and lives as a starting point for contesting taken-for-granted norms about childhood (Reynaert et al., 2015) or pointing to the 'implementation gap' (Vandenhole, 2015) and to 'translations' (Hanson & Nieuwenhuys, 2013) between the lived experience of children and international commitments to children's rights.

In recent scholarly conversations about Childism, emphasis has been placed on the relational aspects of childhood, how membership is shaped by patterns of exclusion and inclusion in mainstream society, and how rights are grounded in the responsibility to construct ever more 'other-inclusive societies' (Biswas et al., 2023; Josefsson & Wall, 2020; see also Wall, this volume). Building on post-structural traditions in feminism, critical race theory, and decolonial studies, this scholarship argues that social critique should not only focus on the point that young people ought to acquire the same rights as adults within existing institutions but also on how childhood poses a critique of the way the idea of rights is constructed and can be used to more fundamentally transform societal norms and institutions. Other scholarship has explored how the hegemonic status of children's rights can also reproduce injustices and work as instruments of governance to advance various political visons and agendas (Holzscheiter et al., 2019; James, 2007; Wells, 2011). We can, therefore, not assume that 'the implementation of more children's rights is logically better for children' (Reynaert et al., 2012, p. 155). Instead, these may work to uphold hierarchies, domination, and reinforce human suffering (Lind, 2019; Nieuwenhuys, 2001; Fay, 2019; Pupavac, 2001).

In Max Horkheimer's seminal essay 'Traditional Theory and Critical Theory' from 1937, he outlines some of the fundaments of the influential Frankfurt School of critical theory (Celikates & Flynn, 2023; Horkheimer, 1972). Horkheimer's programme for the social sciences was hardly intended to deepen our understanding of childhoods or children's rights. Instead, it was developed as a response to the social realities of capitalism, human suffering, and the search for emancipation in the first half of the 20th century. Still, some of its building blocks are relevant to this chapter. Horkheimer argued for the risk of scientific specialization and the need for an interdisciplinary social science that moves between theoretical and empirical work to productively analyze society's conflicts, contradictions, and tendencies. In the essay, he reflects on the necessity of a methodology and critical theory that not only aims to describe social reality but also generates insights into the forces of domination that operate in society and seek to stimulate change. Further, he argues, although critical activity

> itself emerges from the social structure, its purpose is not, either in its conscious intention or in its objective significance, the better functioning of any element in the structure. On the contrary, it is suspicious of the very categories of better, useful, appropriate, productive, and valuable, as these are understood in the present order, and refuses to take them as non-scientific presuppositions about which one can do nothing.
>
> (Horkheimer, 1972, p. 207)

While the field of children's rights studies often recognizes and stresses the value of interdisciplinarity, it has, in recent decades, developed into its own field of sciences with journals, conferences, and institutions. With this follows an apparent risk that the theories, methods, and empirical focus of the field are being shaped by certain kinds of interdisciplinarity, where some scholarly traditions are taken for granted while others appear 'strange' to mainstream debates in children's rights. Children's rights studies have, for example, had difficulties finding a way beyond the taken-for-granted elements of the UNCRC, which have resulted in a strong focus on the 'implementation gap', where the use of the UNCRC as analytical framework has led to under-theorization in the field (Quennerstedt, 2013). To counter these lock-in effects, we need to foster a self-critical discussion of how those theories, methods, and empirics that appear strange can offer productive impetus spurring on new advancements in the field. Analogous to the thoughts of Horkheimer, in order to enquire about the hegemonic assumption in children's rights studies that 'more', 'deeper', or 'better' inclusion of children can emancipate young people from domination and injustices, we seem to be in a moment where we need to re-examine what underpins our scientific analysis and what alternative pathways we may tease out.

19.4 Inclusion as a politics of exclusion

An initial pathway for critique rests on the insight that with children's inclusion also come exclusions. The exclusionary effects of children's inclusion affect not only young people themselves as individual subjects and groups but also other individuals and groups based on categorizations such as age, ethnicity/race, citizenship, class, educational background, geographical dynamics, and gender. Further, these exclusions are manifested in various ways, from processes of co-optation, disciplining, silencing, and through the reproduction of systems of governance that reinforce domination and injustices at the structural level. Thus, when studying processes of children's inclusion and the expansion of rights, we need to also explore the exclusionary dynamics and political effects underpinning these processes.

To illustrate this, we can make use of the institutionalization and mainstreaming of children's and youth's participation in international decision-making processes (Josefsson, 2023; Knappe & Smith, 2021; Kwon, 2019). After the United Nations' recognition of children and youth as one of the 'major groups' in Agenda 21 (United Nations, 1992), we have witnessed a significant growth in the organization of youth constituencies, working groups for children and youth, child rights strategies, and youth forums in international institutions (Holzscheiter et al., 2025; United Nations, 2018). Although this has resulted in a significant increase in the number of young representatives at global summits and the strengthening of the access of some groups of young people, studies show how young people, at the same time, experience that their voices and actions are recurrently being co-opted, disciplined, and silenced (Buhre & Josefsson, 2024). We can note how youth keep witnessing the problem of 'youth washing' or 'youth-tokenism'. While 'youth participation' has become highly prioritized at a rhetorical and symbolic level (and thus is seldom rejected formally), studies illuminate the extent to which young people's voices are being transformed and used for purposes other than those intended by young people themselves (Bullon-Cassis, 2024; Holzscheiter et al., 2025), and how the UN system effectively disciplines young activists into professional insiders (Marquart et al., 2023) who feed into neoliberal models of global governance (Kwon, 2019). The problems and pitfalls of using young people's voices for different political and commercial purposes is hardly news to a field such as childhood studies, but a critical agenda would need to deepen the efforts to study the political and economic dynamics of the uses and representations of young people's voices beyond claims of 'authenticity' and 'innocence' and explore them as sites of contestation (Holzscheiter et al., 2025; James, 2007; Josefsson et al., 2023). Along this line, the inclusion of young people cannot be reduced to a process of identifying and transmitting interest from a constituency to its representatives, but also needs to be examined as a constructive process of making claims and as a constitutive force that facilitates the formation of political groups, identities, and agendas (Disch, 2019).

Another aspect of the exclusionary effects relates to the silencing of constituencies, interests, and voices. For example, our recent studies on children and youth representation in international institutions demonstrates how youth face significant bureaucratic, financial, and competence barriers that follow certain socioeconomic and postcolonial patterns (Buhre & Josefsson, 2024; Josefsson & Löw, 2024). The institutional designs and the selection procedures of global summits limit who can attend these meetings, how constituencies are made present or absent, and what voices are heard or silenced. The structural inequalities and silencing mechanisms especially hit youth who are younger, lack educational or professional backing, and originate outside Europe and North America. Hence, a productive way forward could be to advance the empirical and theoretical study of silence and representation at a claim and system level (Vieira, 2020). Taking silence as the site of a potential presence, rather than meaningless absence, and distinguishing between the multiple functions and uses of silence would be a first step from which a critical agenda in children's rights studies could benefit. For example, by treating silence as a nonlinguistic form of communication, silence could be interpreted as either a negative decision, as neglect, or as an internalized sense of powerlessness that results from experiences of alienation, apathy, or inertia. Alternatively, it can be interpreted as a positive decision 'not to do', a form of non-locutionary speech that can mark an absence where presence is expected and that represents dissent or a particular political will or function (Vieira, 2020). From a political-theoretical level, scholars have pointed to how the inclusion and visibility of some subjects come hand in hand with the simultaneous exclusion and invisibility of others (Lindahl, 2013; Young, 1997). Thus, when including some young people into a circle of membership, this is also conditioned by a structural asymmetry and a prior closure of community and deliberations that determine who counts as members of society and who does not (Josefsson,

2019; Lindahl, 2013). What I then suggest is further research into inclusion as a politics of exclusion at a practical and system level that, on the one hand, focuses on the exclusion of subjects, actions, and claims *through visibility*, and on the other hand, centres on exclusion *through invisibility*.

19.5 Institutionalized inclusion: time, space, and materiality

In this second pathway of critique, I argue for a research agenda that scrutinizes children's institutionalized inclusion. To make a more systemic critique of societal organization possible, children's rights' scholars would benefit from strengthening their temporal, spatial, and material analysis of how institutions of childhood have become integrated into the structure of society and become a bearer of certain values, cultures, and dynamics that open up – or shut down – certain kinds of politics (Josefsson et al., 2023; Pierson, 2004). Educational systems, social and health care services, foster care, children's rights, family law, asylum procedures, children's ombudspersons, international bodies such as the Committee on the Rights of the Child, the UN Youth Envoy, and the UN Youth Office are just a few examples of these 'systems of established and prevalent social rules that structure social interactions' (Hodgson, 2006, p. 2) that have emerged, developed, and transformed in parallel with changing norms around childhood (Holzscheiter et al., 2019).

To illustrate what I mean, let's return to the scene of international politics. When Elana Wong stepped onto the podium of the UN General Assembly in New York, this was definitely not the first time children and youth had been recognized by, and invited to, the UN. In fact, the history of international institutions has been closely tied to the recognition of young people as objects of concern in, for example, international peace and humanitarian movements and the building of international organizations such as the League of Nations and the United Nations (Baughan, 2021; Holzscheiter et al., 2025; Marshall, 1999). Having young people invited to the UN – as speakers, participants in negotiations, or as symbolic figurations for visions of a new world order – follows a longer historical script and institutional legacy. By the end of the 1940s when the UN was established, youth were identified as key partners (Roosevelt & Ferris, 1950), and in subsequent decades, various efforts were made to institutionalize the involvement of children and youth by offering them a place in government missions, giving youth organizations consultative status, and adopting resolutions and conventions specifically targeting young people. Starting in the 1990s, the adoption of the UNCRC and the identification of children and youth as a 'major group' in Agenda 21 set in motion a range of institutionalizing processes to include children and youth in the global governance of issues such as migration, climate, peace and security, and the Sustainable Development Goals.

Thus, when young people's involvement in international politics in the present – such as the global youth climate strikes in recent years – is described as 'a historical turn' and as 'a new form of resistance pursued by children' that is unique in its expression of agency and global scope (Holmberg & Alvinius, 2020, p. 78), it lacks a historicization of how the institutionalization of child and youth engagement in global politics have become bearers of ideas and practices that are constitutive of what kinds of politics of young people are made possible today. For example, the ways in which young people have engaged in environmental movements since the middle of the 20th century are key to understanding continuity and change in norms about young people's agency, the historical scriptures contemporary protest strategies build on, and how previous experiences of transnational organizations have laid the ground for effective mobilization today. Furthermore, the formative events at the end of the 20th century, when the UNCRC was adopted and children and youth were formally recognized as stakeholders in Agenda 21, are central in seeing how institutional path-dependencies can explain in what ways global summits, youth constituencies, child and youth strategies, leadership programmes, innovation contests, and the establishment of a UN Youth Envoy and Youth Office have conditioned the inclusion/exclusion of children and youth in international politics. To explain young people's involvement in international politics, the historical path-dependencies, discursive and ideological shifts, periods of change, and critical junctures can help us reveal some of the complex relationships between the institutionalization of childhood, young people's agency, and processes of inclusion (Holzscheiter et al., 2019).

In addition, in our recent studies on youth representation at climate summits, we demonstrate how the participation of children and youth are constrained by certain spatial and material conditions (Buhre & Josefsson, 2024). These conditions shape who becomes a representative, what claims are made possible, and ultimately, what relationships are formed between the representatives on site and the larger global populations of young people who they are supposedly representing. By focusing on the socioeconomic structures, material resources, and the role of objects and space in international politics (Lambach, 2022), we can, therefore, see how the institutionalized inclusion of children and youth in international politics is conditioned by specific bureaucratic, financial, and competence barriers as well as the spatial organization of summit venues and meeting rooms. These dynamics reflect long-standing structural injustices and postcolonial relationships in international politics that not only affect young people due to their young ages but also cut across populations with unequal access to power, financial means, visas, bureaucratic competences, symbolic capital, and language skills (Chowdhry & Nair, 2013; Getachew, 2019). Hence, we should be cautious about making assumptions about 'youth' or 'children' as pre-political subjects that should be included 'simply' by making participatory processes of institutions more efficient. Rather, it is central to study institutionalized inclusion as temporally, spatially, and materially situated processes that produce political claims, subjects, and agendas on behalf of children and youth (Holzscheiter et al., 2025; Josefsson et al., 2023), and which we can use as analytical entrance points to explain how the inclusion of young people also risks reproducing hierarchies, maintaining power imbalances, and upholding political status quo (Hanson, 2023).

19.6 Claims for inclusion at the outfields of children's rights regimes

A third pathway for critique takes its point of departure from those claims for inclusion that can be found at the outfields of current regimes of rights for children. By starting our inquiry into claims from the margins or outside children's rights regimes (Grahn-Farley, 2024; Holzscheiter et al., 2019; Pupavac, 2001), we can get vital analytical impetus to understand the exclusionary side of inclusion and to grasp the societal currents and underlying political processes that would otherwise be hidden. Historically, we have many examples of groups of children and youth who have claimed rights and fought injustices from the margins in areas such as labour, migration, climate, and democracy (Hanson & Nieuwenhuys, 2013; Josefsson & Wall, 2020; Liebel, 2012; Sandin et al., 2023). These actions were not primarily about the means available within existing institutions or in reference to rights as enshrined in domestic law or international treaties; instead, these claims made reference to ideals as formulated outside law and were facilitated through social movement mobilization (Dembour, 2010). These claims might appear 'alien' to current legal and political regimes at a specific time and place in the sense that they are made invisible and pushed out from discourse or political regimes as such, or that they are visible but appear so 'strange' that they cannot be recognized as a 'right' (Lindahl, 2013; Josefsson, 2019).

To illustrate this, let's go back to the speech of Elana Wong in the UN General Assembly and the issue of global migration. While positioned as a representative of a global community of young migrants at the symbolic heart of international politics, she was apparently well aware of all the experiences and claims of migrants regarding decent living conditions that couldn't find any room in the discourse of the General Assembly. After Elana Wong's speech, about 150 of the member state missions each used their three minutes for interventions over the course of two days to highlight their achievements in the Global Compact on Migration. Sitting as an observer at the grandstand I saw how, in principle, all other stakeholder representatives, youth included, left soon after Wong's speech. Apparently, they did not feel that it would be meaningful to passively listen for two days to the member states without any opportunity to respond from the floor. Instead, they used the cafeteria, corridors, or meeting rooms, or crossed the street from the UN Headquarters, to gather in parallel forums where they could engage in what appeared to be more productive dialogues with other stakeholders. So, while the very purpose of this International Migration Review Forum was to create room for dialogues between civil society, business, cities, and UN member states, the institutional design and routines of the UN made such dialogues impossible and pushed stakeholders elsewhere.

I think a couple of lessons can be learned from this episode. First, in the most immediate context of our study on youth representation in global migration governance (Josefsson, 2023; Josefsson & Löw, 2024), it becomes evident that the dominant political discourses of the speeches, background papers, or progress declarations offer only glimpses of the experiences and claims of young migrants. To gain nuances and more in-depth understandings of young people's struggle for inclusion in global governance of migration, it has been key to study the 'outfields' of international institutions. Through interviews, analyses of social media posts, and background papers produced by children and youth themselves as well as observations of meetings online, in cafeterias, and in locations outside the official conference venues, we could trace the various routes and barriers to institutional access, historical breakthroughs and the effects of young people's mobilization in global governance. This analysis could not have been done if we had stuck to a study of dominant political discourse or the practice of 'youth inclusion', as they appear at the symbolic centre of international institutions. Secondly, a central observation is that these kinds of high-level meetings make little room for children and youth of lower age, with weaker educational backgrounds, fewer communicative skills, and those who are undocumented or who more radically contest the very legitimacy of state authorities and current migration regimes (Josefsson, 2023; Josefsson & Löw, 2024). In this sense, there is a striking difference in character between the claims and actions for rights, recognition, and inclusion of migrants at the international institutional level on the one hand, and at national and local levels on the other (Josefsson, 2019). We know from previous studies that many of the right claims of young migrants to residence permits, health, security, and education find poor or no normative resonance in either national or international law (Bhabha, 2015). Instead, their normative source is grounded in public reasoning and political mobilization at the margins or outside legal frameworks (Josefsson, 2019).

Theoretically, this takes us back to the question of asymmetric relationships and normative questions about claims of inclusion. At the structural level, asymmetry is always established by prior closure about who counts as a member of society and who does not (Lindahl, 2013). Thus, in a liberal international order of human rights in which the opening up of international institutions to new stakeholder groups such as children and youth have become central features, we need to remind ourselves that what counts as a 'whole-of-society approach', or 'inclusionary space' is dependent on the premise that a non-deliberative closure has already taken place. Enquiring into 'alien' claims that disrupt, or have no place in the dominant normative order or regimes of rights (Josefsson, 2019), can open up new avenues for analyzing gaps, limits, and the fluidity of legal concepts around childhood in a direction that differs from some of the dominant traditions of cosmopolitanism, positivism, and notions of the 'ever-inclusiveness' of human subjects (Lindahl, 2013, p. 266; Rancière, 2001; Grahn-Farley, 2024).

19.7 Conclusion

In this paper I have suggested that children's rights studies, to a large extent, share the conviction that the inclusion of children can constitute the very foundation of a radical critique of societal norms, practices, and structures. This conviction seems to be underpinned by an assumption that more or better inclusion of children in social and political life will lead to societal transformations, children's emancipation, and access to justice. As an alternative, I have sketched a set of pathways to critically scrutinize this conviction, its underlying premises, and outline some routes forward in the study of children's rights along what I refer to as: 'critique after inclusion'; inclusion as a politics of exclusion; institutionalized inclusion: time, space, and materiality; and claims for inclusion at the outfields of regimes. The scholarly drive for the more and better inclusion of young people's experiences and rights, mainly framed within, or in relation to, the UNCRC, has certainly served an important function for societal critique in the children's rights field in recent decades. Yet, in order to release a more radical agenda, my argument is that a study of 'children's inclusion' should not be reduced to a specialized and micro-oriented enquiry of children's experiences or to close analysis of the correct interpretations of legal provisions or philosophical principles as bases of critique. Rather, it needs to be accompanied by a historicization of its ideational roots, an analysis of its structural conditions and effects, and a theorization of its normative potential for transforming societies. For this endeavour, we already have a rich palette of resources within the field of children's rights; nonetheless, we will have to reinvent an interdisciplinary methodology and critical theory that constantly work in dialogue with other disciplines and traditions, and which, in the words of Max Horkheimer (1972, p. 207), move beyond a focus on 'the better functioning of any element in the structure', and which do not merely aim to describe social reality but also to generate insights into the forces of domination that operate in society.

References

Alanen, L. (2011). Critical childhood studies? *Childhood*, *18*(2), 147–150.

Baughan, E. (2021). *Saving the children: Humanitarianism, internationalism, and empire*. University of California Press.

Bendo, D. (2020). Parallel lines? Childhood discourses emphasized by the children's rights movement and the emerging field of children's rights studies. *Childhood*, *27*(2), 173–187. https://doi.org/10.1177/0907568219896610

Bhabha, J. (2015). Arendt's children: Do today's migrant children have a right to have rights? In M. Crock (ed.) *Migrants and rights* (pp. 221–262). Routledge.

Biswas, T., Wall, J., Warming, H., Zehavi, O., Kennedy, D., Murris, K., Kohan, W., Saal, B., & Rollo, T. (2023). Childism and philosophy: A conceptual co-exploration. *Policy Futures in Education*, *22*(5). https://doi.org/10.1177/14782103231185178

Brittle, R., & Desmet, E. (2020). Thirty years of research on children's rights in the context of migration: Towards increased visibility and recognition of some children, but not all?. *The International Journal of Children's Rights*, *28*(1), 36–65. https://doi.org/10.1163/15718182-02801008

Buhre, F., & Josefsson, J. (2024). The materiality of youth representation at climate summits: Navigating barriers, routes, and spaces. *Globalizations*, 1–15. https://doi.org/10.1080/14747731.2024.2404285

Bullon-Cassis, L. (2024). A game show at the end of the world: The currency of youth in UN climate summitry. *Journal of Youth Studies*, 1–18. https://doi.org/10.1080/13676261.2023.2296667

Celikates, R., & Flynn, J. (2023). Critical theory (Frankfurt school). In Edward N. Zalta & Uri Nodelman (eds.) *Stanford encyclopedia of philosophy* (Winter 2023 edition). https://plato.stanford.edu/archives/win2023/entries/critical-theory

Chowdhry, G., & Nair, S. (eds.). (2013). *Power, postcolonialism and international relations: Reading race, gender and class.* Routledge.

de Castro, L. R. (2020). Why global? Children and childhood from a decolonial perspective. *Childhood*, *27*(1), 48–62.

Dembour, M. B. (2010). What are human rights? Four schools of thought. *Human Rights Quarterly*, *32*(1), 1–20.

Disch, L. (2019). Introduction: The end of representative politics? in L. Disch, M. van de Sande & N. Urbinati (eds.) *The constructive turn in political representation.* Edinburgh University Press.

Fay, F. (2019). Decolonizing the child protection apparatus: Revisiting child rights governance in Zanzibar. *Childhood*, *26*(3), 321–336.

Getachew, A. (2019). *Worldmaking after empire: The rise and fall of self-determination.* Princeton University Press.

Grahn-Farley, M. (2024). *Child rights, legal theory and social advocacy.* Cambridge University Press.

Hanson, K. (2023). Children's representation in the transnational mirror maze. In B. Sandin, J. Josefsson, K. Hanson & S. Balagopalan (eds.) *The politics of children's rights and representation* (pp. 181–201). Springer International Publishing.

Hanson, K., & Nieuwenhuys, O. (2013). Living rights, social justice, translations. In K. Hanson & O. Nieuwenhuys (eds.) *Reconceptualizing children's rights in international development: Living rights, social justice, translations* (pp. 3–26). Cambridge University Press.

Hodgson, G. M. (2006). What are institutions? *Journal of Economic Issues*, *40*(1), 1–25.

Holmberg, A., & Alvinius, A. (2020). Children's protest in relation to the climate emergency: A qualitative study on a new form of resistance promoting political and social change. *Childhood*, *27*(1), 78–92.

Holzscheiter, A., Josefsson, J., Lövbrand, E., & Pantzerhielm, L. (2025). In-between worlds: The unsettled politics of child and youth representation in international institutions. *Globalizations*, *22*(3), 343–357. https://doi.org/10.1080/14747731.2025.2471705

Holzscheiter, A., Josefsson, J., & Sandin, B. (eds.). (2019). Child rights governance: An introduction. *Childhood*, *26*(3): 271–288.

Horkheimer, M. (1972). Traditional and critical theory. In M. J. O'Connell (ed.) *Critical theory: Selected essays, translation.* Herder and Herder.

James, A. (2007). Giving voice to children's voices: Practices and problems, pitfalls and potentials. *American Anthropologist*, *109*(2), 261–272.

James, A., Jenks, C., & Prout, A. (1998). *Theorizing childhood.* Polity Press.

James, A., & Prout, A. (eds.) (1990). *Constructing and reconstructing childhood: Contemporary issues in the sociological study of childhood.* Falmer.

Josefsson, J. (2019). Non-citizen children and the right to stay: A discourse ethical approach. *Ethics and Global Politics*, 12(3), 1–18.

Josefsson, J. (2023). The representative breakthrough? Children and youth representation in the global governance of migration. In M. Beier & H. Berents (eds.) *Children, childhood and global politics* (pp. 87–100). Bristol University Press.

Josefsson, J., & Löw, J. (2024). Representing children and youth in global governance of migration: Mobilization, corporatist representation and partnerships. *Globalization*, 1–16. https://doi.org/10.1080/14747731.2024.2416341

Josefsson, J., Sandin, B., Hanson, K., & Balagopalan, S. (eds.). (2023). Representing children: Introduction. In B. Sandin, J. Josefsson, K. Hanson & S. Balagopalan (eds.) *The politics of children's rights and representation*. Palgrave Macmillan.

Josefsson, J., & Wall, J. (2020). Empowered inclusion: Theorizing global justice for children and youth. *Globalization, 17*(6), 1043–1060.

Knappe, H., & Schmidt, O. (2021). Making representations: the SDG process and major groups' images of the future. *Global environmental politics, 21*(2), 23–43.

Kwon, S. A. (2019). The politics of global youth participation. *Journal of Youth Studies, 22*(7), 926–940.

Lambach, D. (2022). Space, scale, and global politics: Towards a critical approach to space in international relations. *Review of International Studies, 48*(2), 282–300. https://doi.org/10.1017/

Liebel, M. (2012). *Children's rights from below: Cross-cultural perspectives*. Basingstoke: Palgrave Macmillan.

Lind, J. (2019). Governing vulnerabilised migrant childhoods through children's rights. *Childhood, 26*(3), 337–351.

Lindahl, H. (2013). *Fault lines of globalization: Legal order and the politics of a-legality*. Oxford University Press.

Lundy, L. (2018). In defence of tokenism? Implementing children's right to participate in collective decision-making. *Childhood, 25*(3), 340–354.

Margolin, C. R. (1978). Salvation versus liberation: The movement for children's rights in a historical context. *Social Problems, 25*(4), 441–452.

Marquardt, J., Lövbrand, E., & Buhre, F. (2023). The politics of youth representation at climate change conferences: Who speaks, who is spoken of, and who listens? *Global Environmental Politics, 24*(2), 19–45.

Marshall, D. (1999). The construction of children as an object of international relations: The declaration of children's rights and the child welfare committee of league of nations, 1900–1924. *International Journal of Children's Rights, 7*(2), 103–148.

Minow, M. (1995). What ever happened to children's rights? *Minnesota Law Review, 80*, 267–298.

Nieuwenhuys, O. (2001). By the sweat of their brow? 'Street children', NGOs and children's rights in Addis Ababa. *Africa, 71*(4), 539–557.

Pierson, P. (2004). *Politics in time: History, institutions, and social analysis*. Princeton University Press.

Platt, A. M. (1969). *The child savers: The invention of delinquency*. University of Chicago Press.

Pupavac, V. (2001). Misanthropy without borders: The international children's rights regime. *Disasters, 25*(2), 95–112.

Quennerstedt, A. (2013). Children's rights research moving into the future – challenges on the way forward. *International Journal of Children's Rights, 21*(2), 233–247.

Rancière, J. (2001). Ten theses on politics. *Theory & Event, 5*(3).

Reynaert, D., Bouverne-De Bie, M., & Vandevelde, S. (2012). Between 'believers' and 'opponents': Critical discussions on children's rights. *International Journal of Children's Rights, 20*(1), 155–168.

Reynaert, D., Desmet, E., Lembrechts, S., & Vandenhole, W. (2015). Introduction: A critical approach to children's rights. In W. Vandenhole, E. Desmet, D. Reynaert & S. Lembrechts (eds.) *Routledge international handbook of Children's Rights Studies* (pp. 1–24). Routledge.

Rizzini, I. (2002). The child-saving movement in Brazil: Ideology in the late nineteenth and early twentieth centuries. In T. Hecht (ed.) *Minor omissions: Children in Latin American history and society* (pp. 165–180). University of Wisconsin Press.

Roosevelt, E., & Ferris, H. J. (1950). *Partners: The United Nations and youth*. United Nations.

Sandin, B., Josefsson, J., Hanson, K., & Balagopalan, S. (eds.). (2023). *The politics of children's rights and representation*. Springer Nature.

Sayer, A. (2009). Who's afraid of critical social science? *Current Sociology*, *57*(6), 767–786.

Stadelmann, F., Kramer, N., Pantzerhielm, L., & Holzscheiter, A. (2025). Reckless subjects, future capital? 'Youth' as an object of concern in international health organizations' discourse. *Globalizations*, *22*(3), 358–377. https://doi.org/10.1080/14747731.2024.2414688

Twum-Danso Imoh, A., Rabello de Castro, L., & Naftali, O. (2022). Studies of childhoods in the Global South: Towards an epistemic turn in transnational childhood research? *Third World Thematics: A TWQ Journal*, *7*, 1–16.

United Nations. (1992). *Agenda 21. United Nations conference on environment and development.* https://sustainabledevelopment.un.org/content/documents/Agenda21.pdf

United Nations. (2018). *UN Youth Strategy 2030.* https://www.un.org/youthenvoy/wp-content/uploads/2018/09/18-00080_UN-Youth-Strategy_Web.pdf

United Nations. (2019). Global Compact for Safe, Orderly and Regulated Migration. Resolution adopted by the General Assembly on 19 December 2018. A/RES/73/195.

Vandenhole, W. (2015). Children's rights from a legal perspective: Children's rights law. In W. Vandenhole, E. Desmet, D. Reynaert & S. Lambrechts (eds.) *Routledge international handbook of children's rights studies* (pp. 27–44). Routledge.

Vieira, M. B. (2020). Representing silence in politics. *American Political Science Review*, *114*(4), 976–988.

Wall, J. (2019). From childhood studies to childism: Reconstructing the scholarly and social imaginations. *Children's Geographies*, *20*(3), 257–270.

Wells, K. (2011). The politics of life: Governing childhood. *Global Studies of Childhood*, *1*(1), 15–25.

Young, I. M. (1997). Asymmetrical reciprocity: On moral respect, wonder, and enlarged thought. *Constellations: An International Journal of Critical & Democratic Theory*, *3*(3), 340.

Conclusion

Afua Twum-Danso Imoh, Valeria Llobet,
Didier Reynaert and Wouter Vandenhole

Introduction

The introduction to this volume comprehensively tracked the evolution of discourses that have framed children's rights research and highlighted the pinpoints that led to the development of the field of critical children's rights in particular (see Introduction, this volume). This concluding chapter aims to build on that foundation and explore, drawing on the themes emerging from the chapters included in the volume, the future directions of the field of critical children's rights and address any gaps that may otherwise hinder attempts to strengthen the field and its relevance to broader discourses around children's rights and childhoods more generally.

The suitability of our five-pronged framework

As outlined in the introduction, in developing the book proposal we, as editors, produced five themes to frame the volume and which all contributors were expected to address in their respective chapters. These five themes can be summarized as follows: deconstructing 'obvious' beliefs and assumptions underpinning dominant discourses of children's rights; constructing alternative pathways to understandings of rights as outlined in dominant discourses; situatedness; consideration of our own positionality as critical scholars; and the need to remain critical of the critical perspective itself. It is important to note that these themes did not simply emerge at the whim of the editors, nor were they a top-down typology developed, and then imposed, on contributors to the volume. Instead, the themes framing the volume were the by-products of the process underpinning our development of the book project which has already been outlined in the introduction (see Introduction, this volume). In particular, they emerged from our first seminar series organized in 2023 with a range of children's rights scholars focusing on meanings, ambiguities, contradictions, and unwanted outcomes of the uses and practices of children's rights, reflecting on the main critique of children's rights as well as the definitions of the critical children's rights field.

DOI: 10.4324/9781003510284-21

However, in addressing these themes, we note a significant unevenness, not just in relation to how each theme was addressed but also with regard to how fully they were incorporated into the contributing chapters by different authors. Of all the themes the first one (deconstructing 'obvious beliefs') was comprehensively addressed by all chapters. Josefsson (Chapter 19, this volume), for example, explicitly questions the generalized assumption that more inclusion of children as part of the critique of, or deconstruction of dominant discourses of, rights is equated with transformative change and children's emancipation. Added to this Dar (Chapter 17, this volume) makes the case that dominant discourses around children's right to play sidestep questions of political economy and the co-generational production of play by not focusing on everyday play. In turn, Wall (Chapter 5, this volume), in his chapter on childism, deconstructs the ways that existing human rights practices, frameworks, and theories marginalize children's experiences systemically. He takes as examples international frameworks such as the Convention on the Rights of the Child (UNCRC) and national and local law, which, he argues, are biased toward adult standpoints. Similarly, van Daalen (Chapter 2, this volume) exposes how mainstream children's rights scholarship has defined children's liberation as meaning the same thing as equal rights for children and adults, thereby stripping it of its feminist and revolutionary intent. Furthermore, in his chapter Hanson (Chapter 6, this volume) problematizes the notions of 'been', 'being', and 'becoming' of childhood, concepts that have, hitherto, framed some of the key discussions within childhood studies, and criticizes, somewhat implicitly, the relatively simple representation of the future in dominant conceptions of children's rights. Drawing on the case study of gender attacks against Judith Butler, a well-known American gender scholar, on their recent visits to Brazil, Cassal and Burman (Chapter 9, this volume) show how ultraconservative actors have weaponized the concept of children's rights against trans and gender-nonconforming individuals – be they adults or children. That all chapters effectively address our first theme is not too surprising as a review of the existing literature within the critical children's rights field illuminates the extent to which critiquing dominant rights discourses, especially those centred around the UNCRC, has, hitherto, formed the 'bread and butter' of much of the scholarship within this field.

In setting out the critique of dominant children's rights discourses, most authors also framed their argument around, or, at least, illuminated the importance of, context or the extent to which the situatedness of concepts such as rights were critical to analyses within this field. This is evidenced in Mortensen's chapter (Chapter 18, this volume) in which she adopts an ethnographic approach to situatedness that incorporates the researcher's perspective into the very definition of the notion of context – not merely in the framing of the research question. In turn, Llobet and colleagues (Chapter 15, this volume), in their chapter on the contested nature of children's rights in Argentina and Brazil, offer a critique of hegemonic understandings of rights which they assert overlook the complex nature of children's rights and, instead, call for the recognition of the way the concept is strategically deployed at national and local levels. Similarly, Liebel (Chapter 3, this volume) insists on the ideological situatedness of children's rights in the bourgeois-liberal form and the need to transform them into counter-rights. In addition, Vandenhole and Tibebu (Chapter 10, this volume) draw attention to the structural causes of child, early, and forced marriage and, thereby, illuminate the constraints on the agency that young people can exercise. In her paper, Rabello de Castro too (Chapter 4, this volume) underscores the need for a critical analysis of contexts that accounts for the enduring effects of colonialism, particularly in shaping contemporary patterns of racial and age-based discrimination. This analysis reveals how such forms of social organization often render 'rights' ineffective as tools for meaningful social change, especially in the Global South.

The remaining themes were more challenging for a number of chapters to address evenly. For instance, in relation to reconceptualizing an alternative pathway of rights, it was evident that most authors attempted to address this theme in one way or another. However, developing a fuller conceptualization as an alternative pathway was only elaborated in some depth by some authors (Brando, Chapter 1 this volume; Vandenhole and Tibebu, Chapter 10 this volume; Josefsson, Chapter 19 this volume; Wall, Chapter 5 this volume; Abebe, Chapter 7 this volume; Twum-Danso Imoh, Chapter 8 this volume; Bendo et al., Chapter 16 this volume; Vucic, Chapter 12 this volume). Drawing on his decades-long research in rural southern Ethiopia, Abebe, for instance, offers a pathway to a new way of thinking about rights which foregrounds interdependence between generations, relationality, and reciprocity and, thus, enables us to consider how rights are borne out of social, economic, political, and cultural relationships that are central to producing childhoods in a given context. In their chapter Bendo and her colleagues (Chapter 16, this volume) take their inspiration from the feminist ethics of care framework which they seek to utilize, and extend, to show how it can contribute to addressing the rights claims faced by marginalized young people who experience adverse challenges due to their intersecting identities. Adopting a historical lens, Vucic, in her chapter on the hidden histories of children's rights (Chapter 12, this volume), proposes a more inclusive historiography that integrates Eastern European perspectives. She highlights the transformative potential of crises in challenging and reshaping societal norms and structures. Ultimately, her chapter underscores the importance of recognizing the (r)evolutionary potential of children's rights as weapons for radical democratization from below. However, it is important to note that this process of constructing an alternative pathway is not one that can be claimed simply because one seeks to oppose dominant discourses of children's rights. In fact, Brando (Chapter 1, this volume) warns us that not all reconstruction exercises seeking to find an alternative pathway to rights are aligned with the notion of 'criticality'. Rather, he urges us to take into account the content and procedure within reconstruction processes and subject them to scrutiny by testing them against the five themes put forward in this volume.

The fact that not all chapters were fully able to articulate this alternative pathway of rights is an indication of the extent to which, as critical children's rights scholars, there is a need for us to, for example, move beyond critiquing the UNCRC and dominant children's rights scholarship more generally, and start considering how we can contribute more concretely to the development of alternative pathways to rights. This notwithstanding, we must also acknowledge that for some critical children's rights scholars this need to critique dominant children's rights scholarship and principles is firmly fixed as their primary research objective and, therefore, they are hesitant to turn their attention to efforts to construct alternative pathways to rights within their research agenda. Hence, there is a need to understand the critical children's rights field as operating on a continuum of sorts with scholars contributing in different ways, and to varying degrees, or points, to the key elements of the field. While some may critique dominant children's rights scholarship *and* also seek to engage in discussions about alternative possibilities, others may not see it as their task to take that additional step. This further points to the dynamism and openness of the field as already noted in the introduction to this volume.

Even if not all critical children's rights scholars see it as their 'job', so to speak, to engage in developing alternative pathways to rights following their deconstruction efforts, it is imperative that we do consider our positionality more as we frame our critiques of children's rights discourses as well as continually refine ways of being critical of our very own perspectives. Developing strategies to consider these elements of our framework is vital to ensure that we, as critical children's rights scholars, do not fall into the trap of overlooking certain perspectives and creating feedback loops which perpetuate a vicious or, indeed, a virtuous, cycle in our narratives that end up being detrimental not just to our field but to the lives of real children. Of particular note is the need to avoid the construction of critiques of dominant children's rights discourses that end up essentializing Southern or Northern childhoods or reinforcing binaries between the Global North and Global South.

The importance of considering positionality and being critical of the critical children's rights approach itself is well laid out in the chapters of Brando (see Chapter 1, this volume) and Mortensen (Chapter 18, this volume). With specific regards to subjecting the critical children's rights approach itself to critique, Twum-Danso Imoh's (Chapter 8, this volume) analysis seeks to illuminate the extent to which historical developments, most notably colonialism, and more recent social changes, have led to a situation whereby some children's lives hold some synergy with dominant discourses of rights in Ghana, thereby requiring careful discussion and implementation of any alternative conceptualization developed in this context.

The fact that not all of our themes were comprehensively addressed by the chapters in the volume forces us to ask ourselves questions about the initial themes we identified and explore how they can be refined based on other themes that have emerged from contributors' discussions of the way they approach critical children's rights. A review of the chapters in the volume indicates an abundance of other themes that emerged that require consideration. For example, while our framework factors in situatedness, the specific role of the nation-state and national-level dynamics emerged as an additional, and critical, part of the contextual approach to rights as evidenced by the chapters of Reynaert (Chapter 14, this volume), Vucic (Chapter 12, this volume), and Llobet and colleagues (Chapter 15, this volume). In Reynaert's chapter, for example, he outlines the construction of children's rights in Flanders (Belgium) as a social praxis, developed by social movements and in connection with injustice and inequalities. Related to this is the extent to which some of the chapters, notably those by Reynaert (Chapter 14, this volume), Llobet and colleagues (Chapter 15), and Mortensen (Chapter 18, this volume) deploy the concept of situatedness in such a way that it problematizes the relationship between the present and the past, as well as the interplay between various scales of analysis, including the global and local, and the 'Global South' versus the nation-state. Situatedness, in these narratives, transcends mere acknowledgment of diversity or lived experiences. It foregrounds the contested nature of how rights are defined and operationalized in practice, highlighting disputes involving a wide array of social actors. These disputes encompass not only vertical power dynamics, such as North-South relations, but also a complex web of horizontal interactions. This political understanding of context and situatedness inherently challenges the notion of critical knowledge that fails to account for the multiplicity of actors and the specific meanings that key concepts such as 'rights', 'emancipation', and 'equality' acquire in diverse contexts. Moreover, it underscores the point that the notion of 'context' itself is not a static backdrop, but is, rather, a construct shaped, at least in part, by the research process. An example is the role of history, a framing that underpinned the respective chapters of Balagopalan (Chapter 13), Sandin (Chapter 11, this volume), and Vucic (Chapter 12, this volume). Balagopalan, for instance, highlights the contribution that adopting an approach that allows for the historicizing of rights-subjectivities can make to children's rights. Specifically, she illuminates how this approach can help us to understand, and critically engage with, the varied ways the differential working out of citizenship informs the rights-oriented claims of marginalized children in particular. Sandin, in turn, employs the concept of 'children's rights regimes' to analyze how children's rights are historically constructed and changed. The construction process of children's rights is historically not a homogeneous process, but rather driven by complex interactions between national, regional, and international transformations. This lens of children's rights regimes, with a focus on the analysis of long- and medium-term structural changes, contributes to better understanding the role children's rights play in society. A final theme that emerges from the volume that can further strengthen our five-pronged framework is the nature of criticality itself which is well explored in Brando's chapter (see Chapter 1, this volume). Specifically, how can our framework be further strengthened by a deeper interrogation of what it means to be critical in children's rights research?

These emerging themes lead us to pose the following questions: what is the significance of these patterns for our initial five themes? What value do they hold? Do we need to refine our framework bearing in mind some of these emerging issues raised by contributors to the volume? While we do not think there is a need to redefine our framework based on these emerging themes, they are vital as they shed light on pathways that need to be considered in the elaboration of future directions of the Critical Children's Rights Studies field.

Drawing lines in the sand: a theme requiring more attention in critical children's rights scholarship

One area that we recognize as requiring more attention within our typology is the lines that we draw in the sand in relation to what is tolerable and intolerable in child welfare. In essence, the question here is: at what point, as critical children's rights scholars, do we say 'enough is enough; not anything goes' in relation to perceptions and treatment of children in the vast range of political, economic, cultural, and social contexts in which they live their lives?

As has already been stated in this volume, central to the critical children's rights field is the notion of situatedness, notably the importance of understanding how the role that local contexts, and all their attendant attributes such as relationships and cultural traditions, shape children's lifeworlds and meaning-making of the notion of rights (see Introduction, this volume; see also Reynaert et al., 2012; Hanson & Nieuwenhuys, 2013; Quennerstedt, 2014). The concept of situatedness is, in fact, in many ways a commonsense approach as it could be argued that many theories and frameworks are developed from the standpoint of a particular situation, including the very concept of human rights, which can be traced back to developments within a particular part of the world at a given moment in historical time, but yet is now touted as being universal (see Pannikar, 1982 cited in Dembour, 2001; Haraway, 1988). This recognition of how the local, or the particular, is key to explaining, and framing, social phenomena is central to the importance of situatedness within critical children's rights scholarship. As Hanson and Nieuwenhuys (2013) assert, it is in the local where we can see children's daily struggles for rights play out. Thus, the field seeks to understand, and explain, social problems by interrogating the local context in the hope of illuminating the complexities driving the issues facing many children and their families in diverse contexts. However, the critical children's rights field does not seek to achieve this in order to be able to proffer one-size-fits-all solutions to injustices targeting children. At the same time, in the adoption of situatedness by critical children's rights scholarship it has long been made clear that the use of this notion does not lend itself to cultural relativism. This is not an 'anything goes' position as Vandenhole et al. (2015) were keen to clarify in the earlier handbook on children's rights, also published by Routledge.

Unlike a relativist position, situatedness, as we understand it, draws a line in the sand at some point; it does not shy away from making moral judgments. Its position on this is clear; while local contexts need to be foregrounded to effectively understand, or make sense of, children's lifeworlds, they cannot be justifications for harms inflicted on children. This standpoint draws some of its influence from Dembour (2001) who situates herself in what she recognizes as an unstable position that exists between universalism and particularism. As she explains:

> Rather it is a position that makes sense of the fact that a moral agent is inevitably drawn into a pendulum motion. Thus, as one accepts being drawn towards relativism, there is a moment when getting as it were too close to it, one is compelled to revert to universalism and vice versa.
>
> (Dembour, 2001, p. 56)

For Dembour, there are occasions when particularism must be maintained; however, there also exist other times when it becomes necessary to revert to universalism. While acknowledging the between and betwixt position in which Dembour situates herself, and the unstable nature of the swinging pendulum concept that she develops, we similarly take the view that when critical children's rights scholars veer too close to a particularist position, they steer themselves away. However, the difference between our position and that of Dembour's is that we do not revert to abstract universals. Rather, we maintain our focus on the local, on the particular, if you will, to find pathways for social change or transformations, with the understanding that by centring our focus on the local we can identify better ways to care for children in the context in which they live their everyday lives (see Sanders, 2009).

The focus on the local, or the particular, for solutions can be attributed to the recognition that within the concept of situatedness is an understanding that culture is not static and bounded. Further, in relation to contexts in the Global South this perspective recognizes that such societies are neither homogenous nor detached from processes of historical change – a view that has previously been used to make the case for cultural relativism, and which, as a result, allowed the development of positions of moral neutrality and inaction in situations that others, some of whom lived in these very situations, clearly recognized as intolerable (Merry, 2003; Dembour, 2001). In fact, one could argue that the very notion of situatedness is key to counteracting the resulting outcome of the Northern-dominated gaze of the South which has tended to reinforce notions of 'otherness' and homogeneity, leading to binary ways of thinking centred around 'us' versus 'them' which overlooks the complexity of particularist negotiations of power and rule that underly the moralities of rights. This not only results in paternalistic portrayals of 'the South' as the archaic Other of 'the North' but also foregrounds the naivety of an imagery of a homogeneous anti-colonialist 'South'. Thus, the concept of situatedness is an important lens through which to challenge these tropes and, instead, illuminate the fact that heterogeneity and historical change are equally important when analyzing both the Global South and the Global North. What all this means for critical children's rights scholars is that the local, which includes 'the cultural', is seen as contested, constructed, dynamic, and very often intertwined with the global, leading to a blurring of distinctions between what exactly is purely local and what is truly global. As a concept that is dynamic and contested, then, the local is seen as a site which reflects power struggles and ongoing shifts and variability about values and norms due to historical processes and broader social changes. This fluidity and dynamism of the local lends itself to possibilities for introspection by groups sharing a particular culture which can lead to intra-cultural dialogue and, eventually, societal transformation. This is an argument made by Makau Mutua (2001, p. 245) as he makes the case for the recognition of a 'common universality' as a counter to the savages, victims, and saviour (SVS) tropes that he finds is prevalent in human rights literature:

> Stepping back from the SVS rhetoric creates a new basis for calculating human dignity and identifies ways and societal structures through which such dignity could be protected or enhanced. Such an approach would not assume, *ab initio*, that a particular cultural practice was offensive to human rights. It would respect cultural pluralism as a basis for finding common universality on some issues. With regard to FGM, for instance, such an approach would first excavate the social meaning and purposes of the practice, as well as its effects, and then investigate the conflicting positions over the practice in that society. Rather than demonizing and finger-pointing, under the tutelage of outsiders and their local supporters, the contending positions would be carefully examined and compared to find ways of either modifying or discarding the practice without making its practitioners feel shameful of their culture and of themselves. The zealotry of the SVS approach leaves no room for a deliberative intra-cultural dialogue and introspection.

This approach to the local within critical children's rights scholarships would, if they were ever to be asked, have the support of many contemporary anthropologists who must be seen as distinct from classical anthropologists. The latter, arguably, foregrounded the understanding of cultural relativism that exists in human rights discourses and the public imagination today due to its tendency to reify culture (Merry, 2003; Dembour, 2001; see also Hanson, this volume). However, in recent decades the discipline has evolved, resulting in understandings of culture as more fluid, contested and changing (Merry, 2003; see also Merry, 2001). This outlook that underpins the work of contemporary anthropologists has facilitated their ability to identify where to draw the line in their defence of culture. This emerges in much of Sally Engle Merry's work. For example, in her 2003 article about 'Human rights and the Demonization of Culture (and Anthropology Along the Way)', she talks about an instance when she refused to defend culture at all costs after the gang rape of a woman in Pakistan to the clear frustration of the journalist interviewing her:

> A few weeks ago, I received a phone call from a prominent radio show asking if I would be willing to talk about the recent incident in Pakistan that resulted in the gang rape of a young woman, an assault apparently authorized by a local tribal council. Since I am working on human rights and violence against women, I was happy to explain my position that this was an inexcusable act, that many Pakistani feminists condemned the rape, but that it was probably connected to local political struggles and should not be seen as an expression of Pakistani 'culture'. In fact, it was the local Islamic religious leader who first made the incident known to the world, according to news stories I had read. The interviewer was distressed. She wanted me to defend the value of respecting Pakistani culture at all costs, despite the sentence of rape. When I told her that I could not do that, she wanted to know if I knew of any other anthropologists who would. I could think of none, but I began to wonder what she thought about anthropologists. Anthropologists, apparently, made no moral judgments about 'cultures' and failed to recognize the contestation and changes taking place within contemporary local communities around the world. This also led me to wonder how she imagined anthropologists thought about culture. She seemed to assume that anthropologists viewed culture as a coherent, static, and unchanging set of values. Apparently cultures have no contact with the expansion of capitalism, the arming of various groups by transnational superpowers using them for proxy wars, or the cultural possibilities of human rights as an emancipatory discourse. I found this interviewer's view of culture wrong-headed and her opinion of anthropology discouraging.
>
> (Merry, 2003, p. 55)

This quote is significant for three reasons. First, it clearly shows the association between anthropology and cultural relativism within the public imagination to such an extent that anthropologists are seen as the go-to academics for those seeking to defend culture in the face of utterly heinous acts. Second and related, the journalist's response appears to equate the defence of the 'native' at all costs with a progressive and anti-imperialist position. Third, it highlights how this association is disconnected from the theorization and practice of contemporary anthropologists. Therefore, while making clear the extent to which critical children's rights scholarship does not adopt a relativist stance, it is also important to acknowledge that it may still hold some affinity with, and can learn from, the discipline of anthropology, especially in its contemporary form when seeking to identify how, and where, to draw its own line in the sand when it comes to determining the acceptable and unacceptable in child welfare and well-being.

In search of our red lines: exploring different value systems and frameworks

In recognizing the insufficient discussion about what 'not anything goes' means in concrete terms in the current framing of the critical children's rights field we have sought, in this section, to articulate our understanding of 'what does go' and 'what doesn't go' in relation to what is tolerable and intolerable in the treatment of children in the communities in which they live their everyday lives. Of course, we cannot be too prescriptive in this exercise. After all, in the same way that different scholars approach critical children's rights in diverse ways, resulting in substantial dynamism in our field, so also must there be understanding that researchers working in this domain will set limits between what is acceptable and unacceptable in different ways based on the context in which they are researching and on the subject that is the focus of their endeavours. Often too this will depend on exactly where they position themselves on the critical children's rights continuum.

What we, as editors, can offer are some ideas and possible frameworks upon which scholars can reflect as they determine where they set their own red lines between the tolerable and the intolerable on the issues they research. The first argument we advance for consideration takes the view that while centring our focus on the particularities of local situations or contexts in understanding children's lives, there is a need to not lose sight of the basic values put forward by the Enlightenment tradition, which, some would assert, sets out the basic values of many modern societies. The argument here is that although Critical Children's Rights Studies adopt a position of situatedness and contextual normativity, there still needs to be a recognition that this contextual normativity is not endless. The work of Mouffe (2011) may be instructive here as she argues, in relation to the discipline of politics, that while this disciplinary area is understood in different ways, these different meanings still have to accept the basic values in society. While valid in many respects, the problem with this approach is its continued unproblematic acceptance of Enlightenment values (individuals as autonomous instead of relational; the need for objectivity and rationality in making judgements), many of which underpin the stance of those adopting a universalist position in children's rights or human rights more generally. Adopting these standards, dare we say, uncritically may lead us, in our attempts to strive for some kind of rationality and objectivity, to buffer our critical stance, to revert to thinking in abstracts which can be made to appear 'universalizable' across contexts.

However, the basic stance of identifying certain core values that cut across many worldviews remains a valid point. The key, from our perspective, is to decentre our focus from Enlightenment traditions and cast our eyes further afield to identify norms about humanity drawn from other traditions. The aim of this exercise is not to discount Enlightenment traditions altogether, but to identify local forms of meaning-making and other traditions *in addition* to that of the Enlightenment, and place them all in a calabash of sorts to explore what they can, *together*, offer us in our search for core basic values. In relation to the possibilities that exist in other traditions, Dembour (2001, p. 70) refers to Spanish priest Raimon Panikkar (1982) who conceives of human rights as 'one window on the world' in a context whereby other windows or visions of humanity also exist. As a result, he argues that we should:

> Look for functional equivalents to human rights in non-Western societies, through 'good manners' or *li* in Confucian culture, for example or *Svadharma* in India. We must accept that there are a number of worthwhile visions of how to achieve human dignity.
>
> (Pannikar, 1982 cited in Dembour, 2001, p. 70)

One can add to the traditions Pannikkar specifies, others such as: the Bantu concept of *Ubuntu,* which can be translated as 'humanity to others' or as 'I am because we are'; and the Andean Indigenous cosmology of *buen vivir* which, in brief, foregrounds principles of living in harmony with nature and with other people if one is to achieve a fulfilling life. It is worth noting that in reviewing the precepts of other traditions, especially in relation to their understanding of humanity and human dignity, it is possible that many, like the Enlightenment, in their initial articulation, had a narrow understanding of what it meant to be human, resulting in the exclusion of certain groups. Therefore, what would be required is to place these traditions in dialogue with each other with the understanding that in the same way culture is fluid, so also are these articulations of worldviews. The significance of this is that such variability will have implications for how such views may be operationalized in the modern day. It is hoped that such a dialogue would pave the way for a broadening of their understanding of humanity, if narrow in its initial formulation, and that children are effectively considered as human beings worthy of the same dignity that should be afforded to others. Thus, if we analyze values taken from the Enlightenment, which have underpinned the development of human – and children's – rights discourses, in addition to those drawn from other traditions of thought such as *Svadharma*, *Ubuntu* and *buen vivir*, what common, or shared, values about humanity can we identify? How can critical children's rights scholars proceed to use these to determine what is acceptable or not acceptable in the treatment of children?

Highlighting the limitations of the abstract universalism that underlies Enlightenment values, and trying to find a corrective to it, as it were, is not a new exercise. Those adopting feminist theoretical frameworks have long problematized this worldview. As Cockburn (2005, p. 75) helpfully explains:

> Feminists have long argued against the universalism assumed in liberal rights-based approaches (Plumwood, 1993), instead advocating an ethic that is pluralist. What conventional universalist arguments have assumed is a particular perspective that is male, western, middle class and white, and applied this to all circumstances such conceptions seek to

> then create the world in its own image, irrespective of whether anybody actually agrees or disagrees with this image.

In relation to difference, while the Enlightenment tradition seeks to impose a uniformity on all individuals, overlooking or disapproving of differences, feminist traditions have sought to highlight difference as a positive and abstract universalism as exclusive (see, for example, Haraway, 1988; Young, 1990).

It is within the context of trying to challenge the values underpinning the Enlightenment and the dominant liberal rights model that the concept of the ethics of care emerged (see Freeman, 2020; Cockburn, 2005). This approach, initially developed by Carol Gilligan (1982), seeks to provide an alternative to the ethics of rights. It does so by beginning its articulations with the premise that the notion of care lies at the heart of ethics. As Allmark (1995, p. 19) explains, Gilligan's main argument is that 'the detached impartial observer ideal of morality, characteristic of ethics since the enlightenment, is flawed and inappropriate, particularly for women'. The alternative advanced is an approach that foregrounds involvement in the situation and a demonstration of care for others. While the concept of the ethics of care has significantly evolved from Gilligan's initial thinking over the years, it maintains its focus on relationships which foreground the recognition of interdependence, responsibility, responsiveness, mutuality, trust, vulnerability, and the importance of context (see, for example Tronto, 1993). It is worth noting that this framework has also been critiqued (see Cockburn, 2005; Allmark, 1995; Freeman, 2020). However, these critiques of the ethics of care approach are neither here nor there for our purposes as we, as critical children's rights scholars, are not seeking to adopt this framework in its entirety. Rather, what interests us is how this framework can offer a way to combine a critical stance with notions, and acts, of care while still illuminating the deficiencies associated with dominant children's rights discourses. To that end, our goal would be to borrow key elements of its approach, notably the concepts of responsibility and the responsiveness of researchers as moral agents as well as draw on its strong critique of the concept of the autonomous monadic individual. A consideration of these values may help critical children's rights researchers reflect on how they demonstrate such attributes in their research.

A final idea that we will take into account in this section is offered by Vandenhole (2020) who considers one particular approach to addressing the dilemma of determining 'what does not go' which centres around the concept of the local. He draws on the work of Dembour (2006) who, in her search to avoid the 'the tolerance of the intolerable', suggests two criteria to measure how societies determine what is intolerable. These criteria outlined by Dembour (2006, p. 163) are as follows:

> What does culture stand for? There is a risk of reification of culture and to obliterate the dissent around cultural issues which exist in society; Who holds the cultural values attributed to them? It is to be verified

> whether those who are subordinate or marginalized regard their situation as culturally appropriate.
>
> (cited in Vandenhole, 2020, pp. 197–198)

Drawing on a culture's own assessment, Dembour argues, provides the space needed for cross-cultural criticism to take place without the risk of being accused of neocolonialism. Bearing these criteria in mind, Vandenhole attempts to apply them to early marriage by asking the following questions: What does culture stand for in societies where early marriage is practiced? To what extent is culture reified? How do girl brides look at their situation? In trying to answer these questions he resorts to looking to regional human rights instruments for answers, notably the African Charter on the Rights of the Welfare of the Child (ACRWC), the first regional treaty on children's rights. In articulating the answer to his question, he highlights the rigid position of the ACRWC on the definition of childhood and notes that while the Charter recognizes the importance of children's responsibilities despite the pitfalls that such a concept may entail, it remains steadfast in its provision against early marriage. He proceeds to argue that 'in one reading, this may be seen as confirmation that early marriage is seen by many as an intolerable cultural practice', adding later that

> Whereas the ACRWC is generally culturally sensitive, it draws a red line for early marriage. To that extent the ACRWC can be seen as an authoritative voice on culture and cultural practices, which may show that early marriage is intolerable and should not be condoned.
>
> (Vandenhole, 2020, p. 198)

While Vandenhole, a legal scholar, reasonably foregrounds the ACRWC in his search for an authoritative voice on what is considered intolerable, this limits us to taking our direction from regional treaties, and by extension, regional and national elites who may be as Eurocentric in their positioning on such issues as those working in the head office of international agencies/organizations operating within frameworks seeking to implement universalizing agendas. It is possibly because of these limitations that ultimately, Vandenhole, in his analysis, discounts the focus on the ACRWC as a potential way forward and turns to Hanson and Nieuwenhuys' (2013) living rights framework for a more effective approach (see Vandenhole, 2020).

Therefore, an approach focusing on the local requires moving beyond the realm of regional or national laws as well as the perspectives of elites. This is important as laws may be disconnected from communities and elites may not only carry quite distinct views from the various local populations amongst whom they live, but they may also denigrate such groups due to feelings of superiority on account of their education and social status. We must make clear at this point that we are not saying that the views of elites in diverse contexts are not important. Of course they are, as they are part and parcel of determining the nature, structure, and dynamics of a given local context.

In fact, considering their views further reinforces the plural nature of these societies, especially in relation to childhood constructions and experiences and child-rearing practices (see Twum-Danso Imoh, 2019; Llobet & Vergara del Solar, 2022). What we are saying, rather, is that identifying what it means to be local cannot stop at the level of regional, or indeed, national laws and the elites who devise them. In addition to eliciting these, we need to access the views, standpoints, and experiences of those who hold meaning for the everyday lives of children living in the context of communities that are marginalized, deprived, or far removed from seats of governance such as traditional/community/religious leaders, parents or so-called 'caregivers', and professionals who shape, and influence, the daily lives of children. Most important for consideration are the perspectives and experiences of the children and young people most affected by the subject under discussion, as research has repeatedly shown that they have clear ideas and opinions about not just their own lives but about the broader societies in which they live and, for that matter, the state of the world itself. If we return to Vandenhole's (2020) attempt to see if the local can help us find an authoritative voice on early marriage, then these are the critical authoritative voices (note the use of the plural instead of the singular) that need to be foregrounded. Thus, it is by centring the local, the particular, that we will find answers to help us determine where we draw our red lines between what is acceptable and what is not. However, to do this effectively there is a need to take seriously the starting point of local communities, and be prepared to engage in open dialogue underpinned by the principles of mutual respect, reciprocity, empathy, compassion, and understanding (see Twum-Danso Imoh, 2016). Such a dialogue will need to create space for groups who are differentially positioned to be able to express their views and experiences due to the recognition that culture is not, and has never, been consensual or free of power struggles.

Therefore, what we suggest is needed is to move away from elites of societies and immerse ourselves in diverse local communities to better understand how different groups living side by side conceptualize the tolerable and intolerable, the distinctions they make between the two, how it contrasts with others in the same community and the reasons for this, and the actions that they would like to take, or are already taking, to address what they deem to be heinous. This latter point about communities already taking steps to address practices they understand to be intolerable reinforces a key tenet of critical children's rights scholarship which is the recognition of cultures and societies as fluid and, hence, subject to change. The resulting outcome of such changeability across generations is that, if ever there had been a time when such societies held uniform and consensual views on their practices, that historical moment no longer exists, as diverse views can be identified depending on the social positioning of different actors within communities. What this means, in effect, is that focusing on the local for solutions does not require us to take a laissez-faire approach to child maltreatment. Instead, the plurality of views, conceptualizations, and lifestyles that exists in a given context presents opportunities for researchers seeking to determine the tolerable versus the intolerable that recognize not only the local, but also the fluid and plural nature of what the state of being local means. Moreover, it suggests the need for more collaboration between critical children's rights scholars and a range of actors living in the communities in which we work, or around which we centre our theorizations. While this collaboration may be constructed in different ways due to the precepts of different disciplines, it is important that scholars find ways to collaborate with children themselves, even if it is through mediating groups, such as grassroots organizations, as young people are best placed to determine where we must draw the red line in relation to their well-being and welfare within their contexts. If we return to the concept of situatedness with which we started this section of the chapter, we can make the argument that in the same way we draw on the concept to interrogate the local in relation to the daily struggles over rights in which children are engaged, we must also look to this very local, in identifying solutions to mitigate the complexities identified. This focus on the local is not just about subject matter; it is also about the identification of partners within communities, including children themselves, who can collaborate with us, or better still, lead us in the process of taking action.

The state of criticality vs. the state of activism: mutually exclusive standpoints?

Having put forward various factors critical children's rights scholars can consider when thinking about drawing their red lines in relation to what represents the intolerable in the treatment of children, the question then becomes: so what? What do critical children's rights scholars do with these red lines once determined or set? This leads us to a key tension that persists within the field. Specifically, as already indicated in the introduction, the critical children's rights field underscores the importance of a redefinition of the connection between being a critical children's rights scholar and being a children's rights activist (see Introduction, this volume). The fundamental questions that underpin this viewpoint are as follows: can one be a critical children's rights researcher and also a children's rights activist? Are the two, in effect, mutually exclusive? The argument that a critical stance requires a detachment of some kind is a position unambiguously asserted by some critical children's rights scholars (see Reynaert et al., 2012; Quennerstedt, 2014). Quennerstedt (2014), for example, has argued that the distinction between detached critical children's rights scholars who are observers on one hand, and those who are advocates taking action after becoming moved by a situation on the other, has to be maintained. She goes on to suggest that 'a key to differentiating between the roles is to adopt a critical approach to the opponents and practices being studied as well as your own particular points of departure and "truths" held in the research field' (Quennerstedt, 2014, p. 110). Part of the reason for this insistence on the separation of these two sectors can be attributed to how scientific knowledge is utilized, and engaged with, by activists as opposed to critical scholars. In particular, in the case of the activist, scientific knowledge is drawn upon as a partisan tool in order to achieve a certain political goal resulting, sometimes, in these goals overriding certain 'truths' or creating a lack of nuance in the approach to a particular issue. In relation to children's rights specifically, Fonseca and Cardarello (2005) assert that while key tenets of the 'children's rights' discourse can result in forming alliances between academics and practitioners, these concepts can also lose their intended meaning in the process of becoming used as political tools. This dynamic is often compounded by the fact that many activists operate on a playing field upon which messages that are short with clear, straightforward, easily digestible points, are the key to achieving impact and influence. On the other hand, for critical children's rights scholars the field on which they operate is quite different; they seek to defend scientific evidence as worthy of merit in and of itself, without necessarily using it to achieve a particular political goal. This, thus, allows them a deeper and, dare we say, more critical engagement, with the contested nature of the concept of children's rights.

However, the different playing field on which they operate does not automatically infer that critical children's rights scholars remain aloof, or detached, from dire happenings occurring in the world around them. This is far from the case given that they are first, and foremost, human beings who are in the world, part of the world, and, importantly, affected by the world. Added to that for many, contributing to social change is a key strand of their research and impact activities. In fact, we would argue that such a contribution is critical to the deconstruction phase of the typology we have put forward in this volume. This notwithstanding, we argue that while critical scholars play a role in bringing about social change, their approach, or position, is distinct to that of activists as they draw, and deploy, different tools in making this contribution. Bearing this in mind, then, the question here becomes: how do critical children's rights scholars, whose goal is the defence of 'scientific evidence' and rigour, take action in relation to complex children's rights issues from their distinguished position as academics without falling into the epistemological Enlightenment trap outlined earlier in the chapter?

At the time of writing this chapter, conflicts, or political instability, were ongoing, or erupting, in diverse locales – Sudan, Ukraine, Haiti, Yemen, and Israel/Palestine. This latter crisis, which has involved repeated and brutal bombardments of ordinary citizens in Gaza by the Israeli government, has seen some academics reach their emotional breaking point and, thereby, explore ways to take action. By doing so, did these academics assume a more activist position? In other words, by taking action on a particular issue do scholars abandon a systematic approach and a critical perspective – one that acknowledges the complexity of power – in order to deliver an unequivocal condemnation of ongoing violence and oppression in various parts of the world? Does activism entail adopting opposition to any conflict, regardless of one's actual knowledge of the situation? Or does scholarly involvement require that one's voice gain relevance and legitimacy through expertise and rigorous scientific work? Furthermore, does remaining silent on a particular conflict constitute an ethical failure as well as suggest a form of selectivity that undermines the critical nature of the children's rights scholarship we are advocating for?

As we have already stated, the critical children's rights field is an area of research which is approached from various angles and disciplines with scholars operating at different points on the continuum of what it means to be critical as well as setting out their own lines in the sand to determine the tolerable and intolerable in terms of the treatment of children. Bearing that in mind, we do not seek to prescribe a particular standpoint that academics must adopt in determining how they set the boundary between activism and critical scholarship. However, what we do want to put forward for consideration and reflection is the need for a systematic approach in the actions of critical children's rights scholars on pressing global issues that affect children. While the call for a systematic approach does not prevent scholars from using their voices (or indeed, pens/keyboards) to speak out, or engage in action, on specific subjects or on parts of the world with which they are most familiar, it also encourages them to take a holistic approach and consider all situations whereby children's well-being is at stake. Given the state of the world today this would involve calling for an end to not just the Israeli bombardment of Gaza but also to the conflicts in Sudan and Ukraine, the crisis in Haiti, the suppression of girls' rights to education or to sexual and reproductive services, notably those that relate to abortions, in cases of pregnancy following rape in Afghanistan and the USA respectively, or even to the epidemic of child poverty, which remains the leading cause of death for children worldwide. Such an adoption of a systematic approach would prevent critical children's rights scholars from falling blindly into activism.

Thus, far from arguments calling for the detachment of critical children's rights scholars we take the position that those operating within the field of critical children's rights can remain socially engaged. For us, the key is to utilize the tools at the disposal of such academics to undertake socially engaged research, including that which is participatory in nature, fully consider the perspectives of the 'oppressed' in our research as well as seek to foreground the voices of such marginalized groups in debates that we engage in as researchers. This points to the moral responsibilities that we, as researchers in a relatively privileged position, have to those we research. This focus on the moral responsibilities of producing socially engaged research requires us to not only consider how our research serves to advance our careers, but how it can ultimately help those who are amongst the most vulnerable in our societies.

The important point to note about undertaking socially engaged research is the need for us to build bridges between scholarship and activism, as the achievement of such research cannot be achieved without collaboration with those working in the world of activism. Thus, while some critical children's rights scholars reasonably insist on redefining the relationship between scholarship and activism (see Introduction, this volume), this does not mean that opportunities and benefits of collaboration are not valued, or are disregarded, because both groups seek to achieve the same end goal at the end of the day even though they may use different tools in realizing the change they want to see. Therefore, while we acknowledge the need to redefine the relationship between activism and academic scholarship, we maintain that a relationship between the sectors which acknowledges that each has its distinct and complementary role in relation to children's rights remains absolutely central to strengthening the field of critical children's rights and, more importantly, is vital in contributing to improving the lives of children in diverse parts of the world.

Future directions of critical children's rights scholarship

After a consideration of how the various chapters align with our typology and a review of other emerging themes, including those around drawing lines in the sand between what is tolerable and intolerable in relation to child welfare, we now come to the task of tying all these different strands together to identify future directions for critical children's rights scholarship. In effect, what do all of the issues raised in this chapter, or, indeed, the book as a whole, mean for how we go about strengthening our field of critical children's rights? Next, we put forward six points for consideration when thinking about the future directions of the field.

First, the argument constructed in section 3 ('Drawing lines in the sand: a theme requiring more attention in critical children's rights scholarship') is based on ideas and conversations that we, as editors, have had during the latter stages of producing this research companion. Thus, that section outlines our vision and our own strategies for how we would forge a way through our research to set our own red lines in determining the tolerable and intolerable in the treatment of children in relation to the geographical contexts and subject areas that frame the bulk of our research activities. However, we are very conscious that we do not have all the answers to address the key questions of: 1) When do we say 'enough is enough' or 'not anything goes' in relation to children's lived experiences? 2) How do we determine the actions we take once we are clear about our red lines? Hence, what is now needed is a much more focused, and systematic, conversation about the determination or identification of red lines in the treatment of children within critical children's rights scholarship involving a range of academics working on diverse contexts in the North and South from a range of disciplines and grappling with different topics and theories within their research in this area. Such dialogue between scholars within the field has to be acknowledged as an essential part of strengthening the field and ensuring that it achieves, and maintains, broader relevance and impact within wider children's rights and childhood studies discourses.

Second, in the introduction, we address the issue of epistemic injustice, focusing not only on the silencing of children's own perspectives on rights but also on the marginalization of knowledge about children's rights produced in languages other than English (see Introduction, this volume; see also Penn, 2005;

Flint et al., 2022). While there is a substantial body of scholarship being developed in other languages on children's rights and childhoods more generally that runs parallel to English-language dominated discourses, much of the knowledge produced in these language traditions remains largely disconnected from the broader global knowledge production ecosystem. The dominance of English as the universal language of academia has resulted in scholars operating in other language traditions, whether it be Spanish, Swedish, Arabic, or Chinese, being acutely aware of debates that prevail within the English language, while the reverse is seldom true. Achieving greater epistemic justice will require not only fostering dialogue to include these perspectives, but also challenging the imposition of a singular, English-language-centric approach to scientific enquiry as 'the gold standard'. It is important to note that the problem here is not only about how the dominance of the English language in academia excludes all other languages, including many European ones. The epistemic injustice in the global knowledge production system also affects scholars from countries in the Global South where English is the (or one of the) official language(s) due to the fact that these contexts were formerly part of the British Empire which means that such academics have been educated in English and live in contexts where English is the language of not only educational institutions, but also politics, business, media, and civil society. The evidence suggests that despite the fact that this group produces scholarship in the English language, they are disadvantaged within academic scholarship due to significant barriers and processes within the global knowledge production ecosystem (and indeed, broader world order) that seeks to marginalize and exclude them from engaging in ongoing scientific scholarship and debates (see, for example, Collyer, 2018). Part of the problem resides in how the English language socialization of this group from an early age has resulted in a disassociation within individuals between the language of intellectual scholarship and the language they engage in every day in their homes, communities, and, possibly, in their very thinking process. Twum-Danso Imoh et al. (2022, p. 5) explain it well in a recent editorial for the journal *Third World Thematics*:

> As Nguigwa Thiong'O (1987) puts it, the adoption of English as the language of intellectual endeavours in territories previously colonised by Britain has led to 'a deliberate disassociation of the language of conceptualisation, of thinking, of formal education, of mental development from the language of daily interaction in the home and in the community' (in Murphy & Zhu, 2012, pp. 919–920). Hence, the fact that most high-impact journals are produced in English has exclusionary consequences for significant numbers of academics from the non-English-speaking parts of the world as well as from so-called 'Anglophone' contexts.

Third, to strengthen this field there is a need to talk more with others outside this area; this includes other academics who adopt a more mainstream approach to children's rights, but also practitioners and policy-makers who make decisions, and design programmes, that directly impact the lives of children and their families. Without doing so we risk remaining marginalized within the broader field of children's rights. In effect, we need to not only continue our conversations with like-minded scholars who, very often, concur with our ideas to some degree, but we also need to take steps to ensure a broader engagement with the ideas that we are developing by those outside of the critical children's rights field. Taking such a step may lead to feelings of discomfort and will require the holding of difficult conversations for both those working from a critical children's rights perspective and those adopting a more mainstream approach. However, such a dialogue is vital, especially if we want to ensure that the research conducted under the banner of critical children's rights achieves a wider impact, not just on academic debates, but also on the lives of 'real' children in the plurality of contexts in which they reside.

Fourth, children's rights are deeply intertwined with the structure of the nation-state and international bodies. The enforcement of regulations and legal provisions depends on the existence of a state capable of implementing them and being held accountable by the appropriate international bodies. However, the contemporary development of communication technologies poses a significant challenge to the tools and foundational nature of these institutions, as well as their ability to protect rights and prevent violations. Nation-states are often ill-equipped to safeguard children's rights against emerging forms of violence facilitated by the internet, including sexual exploitation and trafficking that occur on, or are mediated by, social media platforms. This includes the use of a child's virtual image in contexts of sexual exploitation. This highlights the urgent need for adaptive mechanisms and transnational collaboration to address these challenges.

Fifth, the conversation about emancipation, oppression, and the pursuit of equality as a fundamental human right has advanced more in some parts of the world than in others, yet it remains a critical topic of debate for, at least, the past decade. However, a consensus between rights and emancipation is still far from being achieved. In particular, it seems evident that we need a deeper understanding of how the necessary institutionalization of a rights framework such as the UNCRC may have consequences that perpetuate or exacerbate inequality. While some of these consequences are unintended, we have to acknowledge that others are inherent within global institutional rights frameworks and structures.

Finally, we are witnessing a historical shift in the perceived value of Western ideas and institutions of democracy. Many analysts have raised concerns about the rise of new forms of authoritarianism and, more alarmingly, the growing tendency to abandon democracy as an ideal, and human rights as foundational principles of a democratic society. In this context of existential threats, a pressing challenge emerges, notably, how do we illuminate the relevance of a critical approach to children's rights and ensure it remains both meaningful and capable of driving social transformation?

These directions of critical children's rights scholarship are far from exhaustive. However, what we have focused on here stems from a commitment to fostering international dialogue, promoting equality across ages, genders, classes, and races, and upholding the idea that children's rights, and human rights more generally, remain powerful tools for achieving these goals. They represent a collective effort to build on the five themes that we, as editors, identified as the foundation of this project. We believe these ideas, alongside our five themes, provide a strong starting point which will enable the critical children's rights field to address the pressing challenges that lie ahead in the coming decades.

References

Allmark, P. (1995). Can there be an ethics of care? *Journal of Medical Ethics, 21*(1), 19–24.

Cockburn, T. (2005). Children and the feminist ethic of care. *Childhood, 12*(1), 71–89.

Collyer, F. M. (2018). Global patterns in the publishing of academic knowledge: Global North, Global South. *Current Sociology, 66*(1): 56–73.

Dembour, M.-B. (2001). Following the movement of a pendulum: Between universalism and relativism. In J. Cowan, M. Dembour & R. A. Wilson (eds.) *Culture and rights: Anthropological perspectives* (pp. 56–79). Cambridge University Press.

Dembour, M.-B. (2006). *Who believes in human rights? Reflections on the European convention.* Cambridge University Press.

Flint, A., Howard, G., Baidya, M., Wondim, T., Poudel, M., Nijhawan, A., Mulugeta, Y., & Sharma, S. (2022). Equity in Global North–South research partnerships: Interrogating UK funding models. *Global Social Challenges Journal, 1*(1): 76–93.

Fonseca, C., & Cardarello, A. (2005). Derechos de los más y menos humanos. In S. Tiscornia & M. V. Pita (eds.) *Humanos, tribunales y policías en Argentina y Brasil. Estudios de antropología jurídica* (pp. 9–41). Antropofagia.

Freeman, M. (2020). *A magna carta for children? Rethinking children's rights.* Cambridge University Press.

Gilligan, C. (1982). *In a different voice: Psychological theory and women's development.* Harvard University Press.

Hanson, K., & Nieuwenhuys, O. (2013). Living rights, social justice, translations. In K. Hanson & O. Nieuwenhuys (eds.) *Reconceptualizing children's rights in international development: Living rights, social justice, translations* (pp. 3–28). Cambridge University Press.

Haraway, D. (1988). Situated knowledges: The science question in feminism and the privilege of partial perspective. *Feminist Studies, 14*(3), 575–599.

LLobet, V., & Vergara del Solar, A. (2022). Untangling the Latin American child: Heterogeneous temporalities of Latin American 'modern' childhoods. *Third World Thematics: A TWQ Journal, 7*(1–3), 110–125.

Merry, S. E. (2001). Changing rights, changing culture. In J. Cowan, M. Dembour & R. A. Wilson (eds.) *Culture and rights: Anthropological perspectives* (pp. 31–56). Cambridge University Press.

Merry, S. E. (2003). Human rights law and the demonisation of culture (and Anthropology along the way). *POLAR: Political and Legal Anthropology Review, 26*(1), 55–76.

Mouffe, C. (2011). *On the political.* Routledge.

Mutua, M. (2001). Savages, victims, and saviors: The metaphor of human rights. *Harvard International Law Journal, 42*(1), 201–245.

Penn, H. 2005. *Unequal childhoods: Young children's lives in poor countries*. Routledge.
Quennerstedt, A. (2014). Children's rights research moving into the future: Challenges on the way forward. In M. Freeman (ed.) *The future of children's rights* (pp. 106–120). BRILL Nijhoff.
Reynaert, D., Bouverne-De Bie, M., & Vandevelde, S. (2012). Between 'believers' and 'opponents': Critical discussions on children's rights. *The International Journal of Children's Rights*, *20*(1), 155–168.
Sanders, B. (2009). Childhood in different cultures. In T. Maynard & N. Thomas (eds.) *An introduction to early childhood studies* (2nd ed., pp. 9–20). SAGE.
Tronto, J. (1993). *Moral boundaries: A political argument for an ethic of care*. Psychology Press.
Twum-Danso Imoh, A. (2016). Tackling the physical punishment of children in resource poor contexts: The utility of a community starting point approach for action and intervention in children's rights programming. *The International Journal of Children's Rights*, *24*(2016), 469–487.
Twum-Danso Imoh, A. (2019). Terminating childhood: Dissonance and synergy between global children's rights norms and local discourses about the transition from childhood to adulthood in Ghana. *Human Rights Quarterly*, *41*(1), 160–182.
Twum-Danso Imoh, A., Rabello de Castro, L., & Naftali, O. (2022). Studies of childhoods in the Global South: Towards an epistemic turn in transnational childhood research? *Third World Thematics: A TWQ Journal*, https://doi.org/10.1080/23802014.2022.2161619
Vandenhole, W. (2020). Decolonising children's rights: Of vernacularisation and interdisciplinarity. In R. Budde & U. Markowska-Manista (eds.) *Childhood and children's rights between research and activism: Honouring the work of Manfred Liebel* (pp. 197–206). Springer.
Vandenhole, W., Desmet, E., Reynaert, D., & Lembrechts, S. (eds.). (2015). *Routledge international handbook of children's rights studies*. Routledge.
Young, I. M. (1990). *Justice and the politics of difference*. Princeton University Press.

Index

Note: Page numbers in *italic* indicate a figure on the corresponding page.

Kolibri 360 GmbH
Ferdinand-Jühlke-Straße 7
99095 Erfurt, Deutschland
produktsicherheit@kolibri360.de